THE MYSTICAL THOUGHT OF MEISTER ECKHART

THE EDWARD CADBURY LECTURES
2000–2001

The Mystical Thought of Meister Eckhart

The Man from Whom
God Hid Nothing

BERNARD McGINN

A Herder and Herder Book
The Crossroad Publishing Company
New York

The Crossroad Publishing Company
481 Eighth Avenue, New York, NY 10001

Printed in the United States of America

Library of Congress Cataloging-in-Publication Data

McGinn, Bernard, 1937–
    The mystical thought of Meister Eckhart : the man from whom
God hid nothing / Bernard McGinn.
        p.   cm.
    "A Herder and Herder book."
    Includes bibliographical references and index.
    ISBN 0-8245-1914-0; 0-8245-1996-5 (pbk.)
    1. Eckhart, Meister, d. 1327.   I. Title
BV5095.E3 M33 2001
230'.2'092—dc21
                                              2001001533

1   2   3   4   5   6   7   8   9   10   06   05   04   03   02

Dedicated
to dear friends
who have made me feel at home
in Chicago
for more than thirty years:
Bob and Peggy Grant
Michael Murrin
and
Kenneth Northcott

Contents

Preface

I BEGAN READING MEISTER ECKHART almost fifty years ago in the translation of Raymond Bernard Blakeney first published in 1941. For a young student still struggling to learn Latin and modern German (let alone Middle High German), Blakeney's version was an eye-opening introduction to a mystical teacher and preacher who has fascinated me ever since. Though the Blakeney translation has its problems and has been superseded by more accurate versions, it should be hailed for the role that it had in making Eckhart available to the Anglo-American audience. Eckhart has a way of getting through to readers, despite the difficulty and frequent obscurity of both his original Latin and Middle High German texts, and the translations that sometimes betray him.

Over four decades I have lived with Eckhart. Since the late 1970s I have also tried to make his mystical thought available to others, through two volumes of translations published by Paulist Press in the Classics of Western Spirituality series, as well as in a number of articles and studies devoted to the German Dominican. The present monograph is the result of an unforeseen accident, since I had not conceived that I would ever get the chance to write an independent volume on Eckhart.

During the academic year 1999–2000, a time I spent in the academic Elysian fields of the National Humanities Institute in North Carolina, I plunged into the research and writing of volume 4 of my ongoing history of Western Christian mysticism, *The Presence of God* (three volumes have been published between 1991 and 1998).[1] The fourth volume, to be called *The Harvest of Mysticism: 1300–1500,* was to begin with Eckhart and those who formed his world, both as teachers and as his students and followers. In the course of writing up the materials relating to Eckhart, I eventually realized that my account had grown far beyond the bounds of anything that could form even a substantial chapter or two in the larger volume. A full presentation of Eckhart's mysticism, however, seemed to me a real desideratum. Despite several fine studies available in English and the new wealth of excellent works in German, I felt that there was more to say—as, indeed, with Eckhart there always will be. Hence, after consultation with the publishers and editors at Crossroad, especially Gwendolin Herder and Michael Parker, I decided to publish *The Mystical Thought of Meister Eckhart: The Man from Whom God Hid Nothing* (a contemporary characterization of Eckhart) in its full form.[2] At a later date, suitably revised and shortened parts of this monograph will make up part of what I hope to say about the great Dominican in *The Harvest of Mysticism.*

In closing this brief explanation of how the present volume came to be, I wish to thank the National Humanities Center and its excellent staff for their unfailing kindness and helpfulness during the months when the manuscript was being prepared. My gratitude is also due to the Department of Theology of the University of Birmingham, where much of the book formed the basis for the Edward Cadbury Lectures of 2000–2001. My wife, Patricia, oversaw much of its gestation and has read and helped me edit many sections of the volume. My research assistant, Scott Johnson, also read the manuscript and helped catch a number of errors and typos. Over the years, I have had the opportunity to learn much from many Eckhart scholars—the list would be too long to give here. However, I do want to say a special word of thanks to my friends and colleagues Frank Tobin and Donald F. Duclow, who read the entire manuscript and made many helpful suggestions for clarification and enrichment.

It is my fervent hope that this volume will serve, at least in some way, to assist others to pursue the wisdom of unknowing that is the heart of Meister Eckhart's message.

BERNARD MCGINN
August 6, 2000
Feast of the Transfiguration

Abbreviations

EDITIONS

The critical edition of Meister Eckhart's works is:

> *Meister Eckhart: Die deutschen und lateinischen Werke herausgegeben im Auftrag der deutschen Forschungsgemeinschaft* (Stuttgart/Berlin: Kohlhammer, 1936–).

The Latin works (hereafter LW) will comprise six volumes, of which four are complete. The Middle High German (hereafter MHG) works (hereafter DW) will be in five volumes, of which four are complete. Texts will be cited by volume and page number, as well as line numbers for direct quotations. The numbering of subsections introduced by the editors of the LW will also be employed (e.g., n. and nn.). The following standard abbreviations for the various works will be used:

Latin Works

Acta	*Acta Echardiana* (LW 5:149–240 thus far)
In Eccli.	*Sermones et Lectiones super Ecclesiastici c. 24:23–31* (LW 2:29–300)
In Ex.	*Expositio Libri Exodi* (LW 2:1–227)
In Gen.I	*Expositio Libri Genesis* (LW 1:185–444)
In Gen.II	*Liber Parabolorum Genesis* (LW 1:447–702)
In Ioh.	*Expositio sancti Evangelii secundum Iohannem* (LW 3)
In Sap.	*Expositio Libri Sapientiae* (LW 2:301–643)
Proc.Col.I	*Processus Coloniensis I* (= Acta n.46: LW 5:197–226)

Proc.Col.II	*Processus Coloniensis II* (= Acta n.47: LW 5:227–)
Prol.gen.	*Prologus generalis in Opus tripartitum* (LW 1:148–65)
Prol.op.expos.	*Prologus in Opus expositionum* (LW 1:183–84)
Prol.op.prop.	*Prologus in Opus propositionum* (LW 1:166–82)
Qu.Par.	*Quaestiones Parisienses* (LW 1:27–83)
S. and SS.	*Sermo* and *Sermones* with Latin numeration (LW 4)
Théry	Gabriel Théry, "Edition critique des pièces relatives au procès d'Eckhart contenues dans le manuscrit 33b de la bibliothèque de Soest," *Archives d'histoire doctrinale et littéraire du moyen âge* 1 (1926–27): 129–268.

German Works

BgT	*Daz buoch der goetlîchen troestunge* (DW 5:1–105)
Par.an.	*Paradisus anime intelligentis (Paradis der fornunftigen sele),* ed. Philip Strauch, Deutsche Texte des Mittelalters 30 (Berlin: Weidmann, 1919).
Pfeiffer	Franz Pfeiffer, *Meister Eckhart* (Göttingen: Vandenhoeck & Ruprecht, 1924). Photomechanischer Neudruck der Ausgabe von 1857.
Pr. and Prr.	*Predigt* and *Predigten* (DW 1–4)
RdU	*Die rede der underscheidunge* (DW 5:137–376)
Vab	*Vom abegescheidenheit* (DW 5:400–434)
VeM	*Von dem edeln menschen* (DW 5:106–36)

TRANSLATIONS

Essential Eckhart	*Meister Eckhart: The Essential Sermons, Commentaries, Treatises, and Defense,* translation and introduction by Edmund Colledge, O.S.A., and Bernard McGinn (New York: Paulist Press, 1981).
Teacher and Preacher	*Meister Eckhart: Teacher and Preacher,* ed. Bernard McGinn with the collaboration of Frank Tobin and Elvira Borgstadt (New York: Paulist Press, 1986).
Largier	Niklaus Largier, *Meister Eckhart Werke,* 2 vols. (Frankfurt: Deutsche Klassiker Verlag, 1993).
Lectura Eckhardi	*LECTURA ECKHARDI: Predigten Meister Eckharts von Fachgelehrten gelesen und gedeutet,* ed. Georg Steer and Loris Sturlese (Stuttgart: Kohlhammer, 1998).
Walshe	M. O'C. Walshe, *Meister Eckhart: Sermons and Treatises.* 3 vols. (London/Dulverton: Watkins & Element Books, 1979–87).

N.B. All translations from Eckhart's Latin writings in this volume are my own. With regard to the more difficult task of rendering the Meister's MHG texts into English, I have compared the translations that have been produced in the past two decades and have been happy to cite from those versions in most cases. In a number of places, however, I found that no version quite captured what seems to me to be Eckhart's point, so I have elected to produce my own translation. All MHG translations note the version being used.

OTHER ABBREVIATIONS

DS   *Dictionnaire de spiritualité ascétique et mystique doctrine et histoire,* ed. Marcel Viller et al., 16 vols. (Paris: Beauchesne, 1937–94).

PG   *Patrologiae cursus completus: Series Graeca,* ed. J.-P. Migne, 161 vols. (Paris: J.-P. Migne, 1857–66).

PL   *Patrologiae cursus completus: Series Latina,* ed. J.-P. Migne, 221 vols. (Paris: J.-P. Migne, 1844–55).

SC   *Sources chrétiennes,* ed. Jean Daniélou et al. (Paris: Éditions du Cerf, 1940–).

STh   Thomas Aquinas, *Summa theologiae*

Vg   Vulgate Bible. See *Biblia Sacra iuxta Vulgatam Versionem,* ed. Robert Weber et al. (Stuttgart: Deutsche Bibelgesellschaft, 1983).

VL   *Die deutsche Literatur des Mittelalters Verfasserlexikon,* 2nd ed., ed. Kurt Ruh et al., 10 vols. (Berlin/New York: Walter de Gruyter, 1978–).

CHAPTER 1

Meister Eckhart
Lesemeister and Lebemeister

Ez sprichet meister Eckehart: wêger wêre ein lebemeister
    denne tûsent lesemeister;
aber lesen und leben ê got, dem mac nieman zuo komen.

Thus says Meister Eckhart: "Better one master of life
than a thousand masters of learning;
but no one learns and lives before God does."[1]

*P*ERHAPS NO MYSTIC IN THE HISTORY of Christianity has been
more influential and more controversial than the Dominican
Meister Eckhart. Few, if any, mystics have been as challenging
to modern readers and as resistant to agreed-upon interpretation. In
his own day Eckhart commanded respect as a famous Paris *magister*
(i.e., *lesemeister*), a high official in his order, and a popular preacher and
spiritual guide (*lebemeister*). But the shock of his trial for heresy (Eckhart
was the *only* medieval theologian tried before the Inquisition as a
heretic) and the subsequent (1329) condemnation of excerpts from his
works by Pope John XXII cast a shadow over his reputation that has
lasted to our own time.[2] Despite the papal censure, Eckhart, at least in
his vernacular works, was widely read in the later Middle Ages.[3] During
the sixteenth century, however, the split in Christendom and the struggle over orthodoxy led to Eckhart's gradual fading from the scene,
although mystics such as Angelus Silesius (1627–1677) still show the
impact of his thought. In the nineteenth century, interest in Eckhart
was revived by German Romantics and Idealist philosophers. The
appearance of Franz Pfeiffer's edition of the Meister's sermons and

treatises in 1857 marked the beginning of the modern study of Eckhart, a broad stream of research that has grown unabated for a century and a half.[4] The great critical edition of the Dominican's Latin and German works, begun in 1936 and now nearing completion, has provided a sound textual basis for scholarship without, of course, eliminating the conflict of interpretations. The growing host of new translations and studies of Eckhart over the past two decades indicates that the medieval Dominican, for all the controversy surrounding him and the difficulty of understanding his powerful message, continues to be a resource for all who seek deeper consciousness of God's presence.[5]

Who was Meister Eckhart? Why were his preaching and teaching so powerful and so controversial? What was the relation between Eckhart the *lesemeister* and Eckhart the *lebemeister,* and between the learned Latin writings that give us access to the former and the more than one hundred sermons and handful of treatises that allow us to overhear Eckhart the preacher and "soul friend"? This work will try to answer these questions in six chapters: (1) an introduction to the Meister's life and writings; (2) a consideration of some of the problems and issues involved in interpreting Eckhart; (3) an attempt at a general characterization of Eckhart's mysticism as the "mysticism of the ground"; and (4) a consideration of Eckhart the preacher through an analysis of a "sermon cycle" unique in his oeuvre; and (5) and (6) two chapters presenting the main themes of Eckhart's teaching on how all things flow out from and return to the divine *grunt* (ground).[6]

ECKHART'S LIFE AND WORKS[7]

Eckhart was born not long before 1260, probably at Tambach near Gotha in Saxony, from a family of the lower aristocracy.[8] (In some notices he is called "Eckhart of Hochheim," a designation used as a family name, not to indicate his birthplace.) We know little of his early life before April 18, 1294, when as a junior professor he preached the Easter Sermon at the Dominican convent of St. Jacques in Paris.[9] We can, however, surmise the following.

Eckhart probably entered the Dominican order about the age of eighteen, presumably in the mid to late 1270s. At one point in the Easter Sermon he says, "Albert often used to say: 'This I know, as we know things, for we all know very little.'"[10] This reference to a saying of Albert the Great, whom Eckhart frequently cited with respect, suggests that the young friar did part of his early studies of philosophy and theology at Cologne before Albert's death in 1280. At some time he was sent on to Paris for higher theological studies, and he was eventually promoted to *baccalaureus,* that is, lecturer on the *Sentences* of Peter Lombard, in the fall of 1293.[11]

Eckhart's period of study at Paris was a time of turmoil in the world of medieval philosophy and theology. The condemnation of 219 propositions by Stephen Tempier, archbishop of Paris, in 1277, had not only placed Thomas Aquinas's teaching under a cloud (about twenty of the condemned propositions could be found in Thomas),[12] but had also led to a great debate over the relation of philosophy to theology. Traditional disputes between Dominican and Franciscan theologians, such as the priority of intellect or will in final beatitude, were now exacerbated by a more fundamental disagreement over the legitimacy of using any natural philosophy at all (save for logic) in the work of theology. The opposition of many Franciscans to the thought of Aristotle and his Arab followers was encouraged by the growth among the philosophers in the arts faculty of a naturalistic theory of human nature and knowing. Throughout his life, Eckhart resolutely championed the Dominican position that philosophy and theology did not contradict each other and that philosophy was a necessary tool for Christian theology.[13] Both his historical situation and his own convictions, however, led Eckhart beyond Albert and Thomas Aquinas: not only was there no contradiction between philosophy and theology, but, as he wrote in his *Commentary on the Gospel of John:*

> What the philosophers have written about the natures and properties of things agree with it [the Bible], especially since everything that is true, whether in being or in knowing, in scripture or in nature, proceeds from one source and one root of truth. . . . Therefore, Moses, Christ, and the Philosopher [i.e., Aristotle] teach the same thing, differing only in the way they teach, namely as worthy of belief, as probable and likely, and as truth.[14]

This conviction is already evident in Eckhart's first works as a *baccalaureus theologiae.*

In the fall of 1294 Eckhart was called back to his Saxon homeland and made prior of his home convent at Erfurt and vicar of Thuringia (i.e., the local representative of the provincial). During the next few years he must have had considerable contact with Dietrich of Freiburg, who was the provincial of Teutonia between 1293 and 1296. Although claims for Dietrich's influence on Eckhart are often exaggerated, there is no question that, for all their differences, Eckhart learned much from his distinguished confrere.

Eckhart's earliest vernacular work, *The Talks of Instruction* (*Die rede der underscheidunge*) date from this time (c. 1295–1298).[15] This popular work (fifty-one manuscripts are known), modeled on Cassian's *Collations*, is a series of talks delivered to Dominican novices, but probably also intended for a wider audience, given its composition in the vernacular. It consists of twenty-three chapters that fall into three parts: chapters 1–8 deal primarily with denial of self through obedience; chapters 9–17 with various practices of the Christian life; and chapters 18–23 with a series of questions concluding with a long treatment of exterior and interior work. Against former views of the *Talks* as an uninteresting "youthful" work (Eckhart would have been close to forty at the time of its composition), recently scholars such as Kurt Ruh and Loris Sturlese have rightly seen the collection as important for understanding Eckhart's development.[16] In emphasizing the metaphysical basis of Christian ethical practice, Eckhart sounds a note that will be constant in his subsequent preaching and teaching. In eschewing all external practices of asceticism in favor of the internal self-denial of radical obedience understood as *abegescheidenheit* (detachment, or better, the "cutting away" of all things), the Dominican spiritual guide introduces one of his most characteristic themes. Finally, in identifying the intellect as the power in which the human being is informed by God,[17] he announces the centrality of *intelligere/vernünfticheit* in his later mystical thought. The emphasis on intellect, of course, had been important to the German Dominicans since the time of Albert. Eckhart's preoccupation with it was to bear mature fruit in the first decade of the new century.

In 1302 Eckhart was called to return to Paris to take up the external Dominican chair of theology as *magister actu regens:* the acme of academic success. As was customary, his time in this position was brief, but the short *Parisian Questions* that survive from this academic year (1302–1303) demonstrate that his thinking on divine and human *intelligere* had already led him to a position beyond those held by Albert, Thomas, or Dietrich of Freiburg.[18] When Eckhart says, "It does not now seem to me that God understands because he exists, but rather that he exists because he understands,"[19] he has stood Thomas on his head in the service of a different form of metaphysics.[20] Eckhart's criticism of "ontotheology," that is, a metaphysic centering on being, or *esse,* marks an important stage in his intellectual development.[21] His teaching is rooted, in part at least, in his distinctive doctrine of analogy, which appears here for the first time. "In the things that are said according to analogy, what is in one of the analogates is not formally in the other. . . .

Therefore, since all caused things are formally beings, God will not be a being in the formal sense."[22] Since *esse* here is being treated as "the first of created things," it cannot as such be in God. What is there is the *puritas essendi*, which Eckhart identifies with *intelligere*. In the scholastic *quaestiones*, however, Eckhart does not develop a central theme of his subsequent teaching and preaching, namely, that it is in the human intellect understood as the ground that we find a relation to God that surpasses analogy.

During this first Paris mastership Eckhart also presented his teaching on *intelligere* in a public disputation with the Franciscan Master Gonsalvo of Spain on the question of the priority of intellect or will in the beatitude of heaven.[23] Eckhart's side of the disputation does not survive, but in Gonsalvo's *quaestio* there is a summary of eleven arguments (*rationes*) of Eckhart "to show that the intellect, its act and habit are more excellent than the will, its act and habit."[24] Alain de Libera has shown how a careful analysis of these *rationes* sets out the main themes of the Dominican's understanding of the role of *intelligere* and its relation to the views of Thomas and Dietrich.[25]

The implications of this understanding of *intelligere* for the divine–human relation became evident in Eckhart's vernacular preaching after autumn 1303, when he was called back to Germany to take up the important position of provincial for the newly created province of Saxonia, consisting of forty-seven convents in eastern and northern Germany and the Low Countries. A number of sermons from the period of Eckhart's service as provincial (1303–1311) can be found in the collection known as the *Paradise of the Intelligent Soul* (*Paradisus anime intelligentis*), which was probably put together around 1340 at Erfurt, Eckhart's own convent and the base for his activities as provincial.[26] The main purpose of this collection of sixty-four sermons was to serve as a handbook for learned preachers in their defense of Dominican views, especially of the priority of intellect over will, against the Franciscans. In this collection, as Kurt Ruh puts it: "Latin and German meet each other in a vernacular work."[27]

The thirty-two Eckhart sermons found in the collection set the tone for a daring message about the relation between the human intellect and God. In the key piece, Eckhart's Pr. 9 (= Par.an. no. 33), the master once again insists that God is above being and goodness. He then goes on to exegete the "temple of God" referred to in Ecclesiasticus 50:7 as the intellect (*vernünfticheit*). "Nowhere does God dwell more properly," he says, "than in his temple, in intellect, . . . remaining in himself alone where nothing ever touches him; for he alone is there in his stillness."[28]

Although Pr. 9 does not consider the relation between the intellect and the ground of the soul, another sermon in the collection, Pr. 98 (= Par.an. no. 55), shows that Eckhart was already employing the language of the ground in his vernacular preaching. In speaking of the soul's birth within the Trinity, Eckhart says:

> There she is so purely one that she has no other being than the same being that is his—that is, the soul-being. This being is a beginning of all the work that God works in heaven and on earth. It is an origin and a ground of all his divine work. The soul loses her nature and her being and her life and is born in the Godhead. . . . She is so much one there that there is no distinction save that he remains God and she soul.[29]

Thus, the major themes of Eckhart's preaching had clearly emerged in the first years of the fourteenth century.

It is difficult to know how many of Eckhart's surviving vernacular sermons date from this time. Along with the pieces found in the *Paradise of the Intelligent Soul*, Georg Steer has argued that the important Christmas cycle of four "Sermons on the Eternal Birth," to be treated below in chapter 4, can be dated to between 1298 and 1305.[30] We do know that some of Eckhart's most important Latin works come from his years as provincial, notably the *Sermons and Readings on the Book of Ecclesiasticus* he delivered to the friars at chapter meetings.[31] This work, which Loris Sturlese has characterized as "a little *summa* of Eckhart's metaphysics,"[32] is important for showing how the Dominican's metaphysics was already being presented in a perspectival—or, better, dialectical—way.

The *Parisian Questions* had denied that *esse* understood as something creatable could be applied to God. In the *Sermons and Readings* Eckhart, using the same doctrine of "reversing" analogy (i.e., what is predicated of God cannot be formally in creatures, and vice versa), ascribes transcendental *esse* to God in order to explore the "loaned" character of created *esse*. As he puts it in commenting on Ecclesiasticus 24:29 ("They that eat me shall yet hunger"): "Every created being radically and positively possesses existence, truth, and goodness from and in God, not in itself as a created being. And thus it always 'eats' as something produced and created, but it always 'hungers' because it is always from another and not from itself."[33] Toward the end of this comment Eckhart moves into explicitly dialectical language. If hungering and eating are really the same, "He who eats gets hungry by eating, because he consumes hunger; the more he eats the more hungry he gets. . . . By eating he gets hungry and by getting hungry he eats, and he hungers to get hungry for hunger."[34] It is no accident that in this work we also find, perhaps for the first time in his writings, another keynote of Eckhart's thought, the identification of God as the "negation of negation" (n.60).

On the basis of the manuscript discoveries and research of Loris Sturlese,[35] scholars have now abandoned the older view that the surviving parts of Eckhart's great attempt at a new and original form of *summa*, what he called *The Three-Part Work* (*Opus tripartitum*), belonged to his second period as *magister* at Paris (1311–1313).[35] Large portions of what survives of the project must be dated to the first decade of the fourteenth century. Here is how Eckhart describes the work in the "General Prologue" he wrote to introduce it:

> The whole work itself is divided into three principal parts. The first is *The Work of General Propositions*, the second *The Work of Questions*, the third *The Work of Expositions*. The first work contains a thousand or more propositions divided into fourteen treatises corresponding to the number of terms of which the propositions are formed. . . . The second work, that of questions, is divided according to the content of the questions, treating them according to the order they have in the *Summa* of the noted doctor, the venerable friar Thomas of Aquino. . . . The third work, that of expositions, . . . is subdivided by the number and order of the books of the Old and New Testaments whose texts are expounded in it.[36]

Whether or not Eckhart had already conceived of the project during his first period as master at Paris, it seems likely that it was during his service as provincial that he wrote the following: the "Prologue" to *The Book of Propositions* treating the basic term "Existence is God" (*esse est deus*);[37] the first, or literal, *Commentary on Genesis;*[38] and the *Commentary on the Book of Wisdom,* whose dialectical interests reflect the *Sermons and Lectures on Ecclesiasticus.*[39] It is difficult to know when the other surviving parts of *The Work of Expositions* were written. These include the *Commentary on Exodus,* with its important discussion of God as *esse* (see Exod. 3:14) and on the names of God,[40] and the great *Commentary on the Gospel of John,* Eckhart's longest work.[41] At some stage the second part of *The Work of Expositions,* called *The Work of Sermons,* was also compiled.[42] This was meant to provide model sermons in Latin, showing young friars how to use scriptural texts for preaching. The fact that many of the pieces contained in it are no more than sermon sketches indicates that the work is unfinished.[43]

Eckhart says that he began the composition of *The Three-Part Work* "to satisfy as far as possible the desires of some of the diligent friars who already for a long time with pressing requests had often asked and compelled me to put in writing what they used to hear from me in lectures and other school activities, and also in preaching and daily conversations."[44] It is important to remember that Eckhart intended this work for these *fratres studiosi,* that is, only for those who were eager and able to absorb it.[45] He was well aware that "at first glance some of the following propositions, questions, and expositions will seem monstrous, doubtful, or false." But, as he went on to say, "it will be otherwise if they are considered cleverly and more diligently."[46] Eckhart also insisted that it was only on the basis of the philosophical truths demonstrated in *The Book of Propositions* that the subsequent solutions to disputed questions and the "rare new things" (*nova et rara*) found in his scriptural commentaries could be understood (n.11).[47] His conviction concerning the conformity between reason and revelation, and philosophy and theology, already noted, was the grounding insight of the project. At the beginning of the *Commentary on John* he put it this way: "In interpreting this Word [i.e., *In principio erat Verbum*] and everything else that follows my intention is the same as in all my works—to explain what the holy Christian faith and the two Testaments maintain through the help of the natural arguments of the philosophers."[48] Some would have it that texts such as this show that Eckhart was a philosopher, not really a theologian, and certainly not a mystic whose writings *must* run counter to rationality. Eckhart's life and thought, however, demonstrate that it is possible to be all three at one and the same time.

The way in which Eckhart's teaching and learned preaching in the vernacular came to maturity in the years between 1303 and 1311 may cast light on the MHG poem in the form of a liturgical sequence called the "Granum sinapis" ("The Mustard Seed") and the Latin commentary that exegetes it—a sign of the two-way conversation between Latin and the vernacular in the new mysticism of the later Middle Ages.[49] In recent years noted Eckhart scholars, such as Kurt Ruh and Alois M. Haas, have argued for the authenticity of this sequence—a profound poetic expression of the main themes of the Dominican's mysticism.[50] The linguistic virtuosity displayed in Eckhart's sermons here takes poetic wing. The Latin commentary, while deeply learned, displays some decidedly un-Eckhartian themes, especially in its emphasis on the superiority of the "height of affection" (*apex affectus*), a term taken from Thomas Gallus, an author rarely used by Eckhart himself.[51] It is likely to have been composed by a friar within his circle, but one whose mystical stance was rather different from Eckhart's own. We have no direct evidence for when the poem was written, but a likely time would have been during Eckhart's tenure as provincial. During this period he was making a special effort to instruct his confreres about the relation between the unknown God and the soul—a union to be realized through intellect (*vorstentlichkeit* in the poem). Furthermore, both the Latin and the German works from this period demonstrate a new level of synthesis in Eckhart's thought, and the "Granum sinapis" is one of the best summaries of Eckhartian mysticism.

Eckhart's career as provincial was a successful one. He founded three convents for women and was elected vicar of Bohemia in 1307, as well as provincial of the other German Dominican province, Teutonia, in 1310 (he was ordered to decline this second honor by the Dominican Master General). On May 14, 1311, the General Chapter held at Naples posted him back to Paris for a second stint as *magister*—a rare privilege, hitherto granted only to Thomas Aquinas. Eckhart spent two academic years at Paris (autumn 1311 to summer 1313). Here he lived in the same house as the Dominican inquisitor, William of Paris, who had been responsible for the execution of the beguine Marguerite Porete on June 1, 1310. Eckhart's use of Porete's mystical themes (sometimes even close to her actual words) show that he took a view of the daring beguine very different from that of his Dominican confrere.[52] The stimulus of reading Porete, and later the encounter with the beguines in Strasbourg and Cologne, were probably influential on Eckhart's turn toward more intensive vernacular preaching in the final decade and a half of his life.[53]

This is not to say that Eckhart's reaction to the mystical currents of his time, especially those pioneered by women, was uncritical.[54] His attitude toward many of the ideas put forth by beguines and others, especially their emphasis on visionary experience, was designed to serve as what might be called a critical correlation for some of the exaggerations he noted in contemporary mysticism. In addition, some of his later vernacular sermons can be viewed as critiques of the tendencies condemned by the Council of Vienne in 1311 as evidence of the *secta libertatis spiritus*.[55] But Eckhart learned much from the women mystics, especially from Porete and probably also from Mechthild of Magdeburg, the German beguine whose visionary collection *The Flowing Light of the Godhead* was composed with the assistance of her Dominican confessor, Henry of Halle.[56] Furthermore, even when he was in disagreement with these mystics, Eckhart was far from an inquisitor. The purpose of his preaching was not to recriminate and condemn but to invite believers, even those who might be in error, to come to a deeper and more authentic realization of their inner union with God. Just as Thomas Aquinas a generation before had tried to mediate (without success) between radical Aristotelians who affirmed that Aristotle was "rationally" correct (however much his views conflicted with faith) and traditionalist theologians who believed that Aristotelian philosophy was a danger to theology, so too Eckhart's attempt to harmonize the aspirations of those who sought indistinct union with God with the rigidifying doctrinal and moral positions of the fourteenth-century church was doomed to failure.

We do not know why Eckhart left Paris, probably in the summer of 1313. Well over fifty at this time, he did not return to Erfurt and his own province, but rather was called to Strasbourg in the Alsatian Rhineland to function as a special vicar for the Dominican Master General, first Berengar of Landora and then Hervaeus Natalis.[57] Strasbourg was an important center of female piety, not only because of its seven convents of Dominican nuns, but also because of the many beguine houses found in the city and its environs. It was also a flashpoint for the debates over mysticism that were growing in the aftermath of the condemnation of the beguines and the *secta spiritus libertatis* at the Council of Vienne and the subsequent publication of a modified version of this decree in the *Clementina* canonical collection of 1317.[58] The bishop of the city, John I of Zurich (1306–1328), was a fierce opponent of heresy and of all suspect religious groups.[59]

In Strasbourg Eckhart plunged into the life of a *lebemeister*, preaching and giving spiritual counsel more fully than he had been able to do during his tenure as university professor and official of his order. Although only a few of Eckhart's sermons can be explicitly tied to the *cura monialium*, there is no reason to doubt that the intense interest in mystical piety found among late medieval women was a significant inspiration for Eckhart during the last decade of his preaching and teaching. Evidence exists concerning his visits to the Dominican convents of Katharinental and Ötenbach in the upper Rhine area during the time of his stay in Strasbourg.[60] He also visited the nearby convent of Unterlinden in Colmar.

A considerable number of Eckhart's surviving MHG sermons (totalling 114 in the projected critical edition) appear to come from his time in Strasbourg and the last years in Cologne.[61] This fact reflects not only Eckhart's devotion to the care of souls but also a conscious effort to create a new vernacular theology that would, in the words of Thomas Aquinas, "hand on things understood through contemplation to others" (*contemplata aliis tradere*).[62] Marie-Anne Vannier has argued that the theme of the "nobleman," that is, the person who has attained divine sonship through the birth of the Word in the soul, emerges as central in the sermons that can be tied to Strasbourg.[63] She contends that such sermons as Pr. 71, a meditation on the "Nothingness" of God, in which the preacher ties the birth motif to a profound meditation on the divine *niht*, date from this time.[64]

In one of the sermons that appears to come from the last decade of his life, Eckhart summarized the message of his preaching under four themes:

> When I preach, I am accustomed to speak about detachment, and that a man should be free of himself and of all things; second, that a man should be formed again into that simple good which is God; third, that he should reflect on the great nobility with which God has endowed his soul, . . . ; fourth, about the purity of the divine nature, for the brightness of the divine nature is beyond words. God is a word, a word unspoken.[65]

In another sermon, Pr. 6 on the text "The just will live forever" (Wis. 5:16), he put his message even more succinctly: "Whoever understands the difference between Justice and the just person, understands everything I say."[66] In his earlier Pr. 9, discussed above, Eckhart was even more parsimonious about the essence of his preaching. Speaking about the nature of the word *quasi* as a *bîwort*, or ad-verb, he says: "I would now like to focus on the little word *quasi* which means 'as' . . . . This is what I focus on in all my sermons."[67] Thus (to take him at his word), the essence of all Eckhart's preaching can be reduced to understanding that the intellect is nothing but an *ad-verbum*, that is, something that has no existence apart from its inherence in the Word, in the same way that the "just person" (*iustus*) inheres in divine "Justice."

The emphasis in the Strasbourg sermons on the "noble man" (*edler mensch*), "Justice and the just person" (*gerechticheit und gerehte*), the one in whom the birth of the Word has been achieved, suggests that Vannier's contention that the *Commentary on John* was written during Eckhart's time in Alsace may well be correct.[68] At the beginning of his long treatment of the Prologue to the Gospel, Eckhart once again takes up the issue of analogy. Although "in analogical relations what is produced derives from the source . . . [and] is of another nature and thus not the principle itself; still, as it is in the principle, it is not other in nature or supposit."[69] On the basis of this metaphysical axiom, the Dominican engages in an extended exploration of the relationship between Unbegotten and Begotten Justice in the Trinity, as well as a further consideration of Divine Justice and the "just person." (These treatments are close to those seen in Pr. 6.) Speaking formally, that is, from the perspective of the just or noble man, *insofar as* he preexists in Divine Justice, Eckhart can say, "The just man in justice itself is not yet begotten nor Begotten Justice, but is Unbegotten Justice itself": that is, he is identical with God the Father.[70] Again and again, more than twenty-five times in the course of the commentary, Eckhart returns to the exploration of the relations between divine *Iustitia* and *iustus,* the just person.[71]

Loris Sturlese has suggested that Eckhart's move to Strasbourg marked a decisive "turn" in his Latin writing career. On the basis of the evidence of the new "Prologue" to *The Work of Expositions* in which Eckhart lays out his "parabolic" theory of exegesis, as well as the second Genesis commentary (*The Book of the Parables of Genesis,* probably composed during this time),[72] Sturlese claims that Eckhart abandoned the unfinished *Three-Part Work* to concentrate on a new project, *The Book of the Parables of Natural Things.*[73] Other students of Eckhart do not think the evidence supports any total abandonment of the *Three-Part Work.*[74] One can, nevertheless, agree with Niklaus Largier that there was a "hermeneutical turn" in Eckhart's Latin works during the second decade of the fourteenth century (whether it was begun in the second Paris period or at Strasbourg), one in which Eckhart's exegesis began to concentrate more and more on bringing out the parabolical riches of the biblical text to serve as the foundation for his intensified vernacular preaching.[75]

Eckhart's new vernacular theology also led to the composition of further treatises in German. The most noted of these is the so-called *Blessed Book* (*Liber Benedictus*), consisting of the *Book of Divine Consolation* (BgT) and a sermon "On the Nobleman" (VeM),[76] the only vernacular sermon for which we can say in secure fashion that Eckhart himself expressed full responsibility.[77] The *Book of Divine Consolation* tapped into a long tradition of consolatory literature in the Middle Ages, dating back to Boethius's sixth-century *Consolation of Philosophy.* A manuscript witness in Eckhart's subsequent investigation for heresy connects the book with Queen Agnes of Hungary (c. 1280–1364), and many scholars have seen it as a consolatory piece sent to the queen in a time of need. (Others have argued that it may have been part of a collection of suspect texts put together at the monarch's request and later forwarded to Eckhart's accusers.) In any case, there is nothing to tie the book specifically to Queen Agnes. As Kurt Ruh says, "Eckhart's consolation is the consolation meant for anyone who wants to leave the world behind."[78]

There is good reason to think that the book was written about 1318.

As a vernacular expression of some of the most daring aspects of the Dominican's teaching, it played a prominent role in the accusations soon to be brought against him. Like the *Talks of Instruction*, the *Book* is divided into three sections. The first deals with "various true sayings" designed to "find complete comfort for all sorrows." The long second part details "thirty topics or precepts" for gaining great consolation, while the third part provides examples of what "wise men" have done and said in the midst of suffering.[79]

This *Book of Divine Consolation* provides valuable evidence concerning Eckhart's teaching in the vernacular and the opposition it was beginning to elicit in an era rife with fears of heresy. At the conclusion of the *Book*, the Dominican addresses possible complaints against his putting forth such deep matters to a general audience. First of all, he defends himself (citing Augustine) against those who have already misunderstood him and attacked him. "It is enough for me," says Eckhart, "that what I say and write be true in me and in God."[80] Then he goes on to answer those who might argue that such lofty things should not be presented to a general audience. Eckhart's response encapsulates his claim for the importance of the new vernacular theology:

> And we shall be told that one ought not to talk about or write such teachings to the untaught. But to this I say that if we are not to teach people who have not been taught, no one will ever be taught, and no one will ever be able to teach and write. For that is why we teach the untaught, so that they may be changed from uninstructed into instructed.[81]

Eckhart was soon to have direct experience of those who misunderstood him—and who also had the power to act on it.

The *Blessed Book* raises the question about the other vernacular treatises ascribed to Meister Eckhart. In his 1857 edition Pfeiffer included no fewer than seventeen of these, but with the exceptions of the *Talks of Instruction* (= Pfeiffer treatise XVII) and the *Book of Divine Consolation* (= Pfeiffer treatise V), the rest have been judged inauthentic, however much they resonate with Eckhartian language and themes. Debate still continues about the short tractate *On Detachment* (*Von abegescheidenheit*) (= Pfeiffer treatise IX). Although Josef Quint, the major editor of Eckhart's MHG works, included this penetrating investigation of one of his major themes in the critical edition of the vernacular works,[82] recent scholarship, such as that of Kurt Ruh, has been generally negative toward the authenticity of the treatise.[83]

In late 1323 or early 1324 Eckhart left Strasbourg for the Dominican house at Cologne with its noted *studium generale*, the intellectual home of the order of preachers in Germany. It has often been said that Eckhart went there to head the *studium,* but, as Walter Senner has shown, the evidence for this is not strong.[84] We do not really know why Eckhart removed to Cologne. The city was a center of beguine piety, and therefore also of fears about dangerous and heretical mysticism; but it goes too far to suggest that Eckhart was specifically sent there to preach against heresy.[85] In any case, despite the Meister's advancing years (he was nearing seventy), his status as a great *lesemeister* must have brought renewed fame to the Cologne *studium,* and his reputation as a great preacher and *lebemeister* was doubtless of advantage to the whole population of this bustling Rhineland city.

Eckhart's time in Cologne was brief, but filled with activity and controversy. A number of his surviving sermons can be ascribed to the three years between his arrival (possibly early 1324) and the spring of 1327 when he left the city for the papal court at Avignon, the last way station of his life.[86] The drama of his trial for heresy, partly reconstructable through the documentation that remains to us, has always been a subject of interest and dispute. The critical edition of the *acta* relating to these events is still in process, but recent work has clarified a number of points.[87]

Older suppositions that Eckhart's trial was a result of tensions between the Dominicans and Franciscans have long been put to rest. The accusations against Eckhart make sense only within the context of fears concerning the "Heresy of the Free Spirit" that had been increasing since the turn of the century. Henry II of Virneburg, the powerful archbishop of Cologne (1304–1332), was a noted opponent of heresy and a strong ally of Pope John XXII in his struggle against Emperor Lewis of Bavaria.[88] Some of Eckhart's enemies within the Dominican order played a role in the accusations against him (two "renegades" are mentioned in the sources—Hermann of Summo and William of Nideggen), but Archbishop Henry would not have needed prompting to pursue heresy wherever he scented it.

It appears that some of the Dominican authorities already had suspicions about Eckhart's preaching. The Dominican General Chapter held in Venice in the spring of 1325 had spoken out against "friars in Teutonia who say things in their sermons that can easily lead simple and uneducated people into error."[89] In light of these growing clouds, it appears that the friars of the Teutonia province tried to forestall a move against Eckhart by conducting their own investigation. On August 1, 1325, John XXII appointed Nicholas of Strasbourg and Benedict of Como as visitors of the province (Acta n.44). Nicholas presented a list of suspect passages from the *Book of Consolation* to Eckhart, who responded sometime between August of 1325 and January of 1326 with a lost treatise "Requisitus," which satisfied his immediate superiors of his orthodoxy. During 1326, however, Archbishop Henry was preparing his case. A list drawn up by the two renegade Dominicans consisting of seventy-four excerpts from Eckhart's Latin and German works was presented to the archbishop sometime during that year.[90] A second list of passages taken from the vernacular sermons was also prepared sometime before September of 1326.[91] On September 26, 1326, Eckhart appeared before the diocesan inquisitorial commission consisting of Reiner Friso and Peter of Estate to defend himself against the charge of heresy. Theologians had often been investigated for censure of erroneous views in the Middle Ages, but Eckhart's trial *for heresy* before the inquisition was unprecedented.

Eckhart's "Defense" ("Verteidigungsschrift," or "Rechtfertigungsschrift" in German) gives us an important insight not only into late medieval heresy trials but also into the Meister's self-understanding.[92] Eckhart's September rebuttal did not—and probably could not—satisfy the inquisitors. Sometime later that fall a third list, now lost, of extracts from his *Commentary on John* was also compiled (references will be noted in the forthcoming Acta n.49). There may also have been other lists. Throughout the attack on his reputation and orthodoxy, Eckhart insisted on several essential premises underlying his case. The first is that he could not be a heretic: "I am able to be in error, but I cannot be a heretic, for the first belongs to the intellect, the second to the will."[93] Thus, he always proclaimed himself willing to renounce publicly anything found erroneous in his writing or preaching—he did, indeed, admit that some of the articles were *erronea et falsa,* but never *heretica.* Second, Eckhart said that the often "rare and subtle" passages (*rara et subtilia*) in his works had to be explained in light of his good intentions and within the context of the preaching genre. For instance, in responding to a series of extracts relating to the birth of the Word in the soul, he says: "The whole of what was said is false and absurd according to the imagination of opponents, but it is true according to true understanding. . . ."[94] Eckhart often appealed to his good intentions in presenting his hyperbolical preaching. For example, in defending a daring statement from Pr. 6 ("God's being is my life; since my life is God's being, God's essence is my essence"), he responds: "It must be said that this is false and an error, as it sounds. But it is true, devout, and moral of the just person, insofar as he is just, that his entire existence is from God's existence, though analogically."[95] The phrase "insofar as he is just" (*inquantum iustus*) used here is crucial, both for understanding Eckhart's defense, and for the proper interpretation of his preaching and teaching.

As a trained scholastic theologian, Eckhart was well aware of the distinction between speaking of the relation between two things on a material, or actual, level (i.e., insofar as they are different things), and on a formal level (i.e., insofar as they possess the same quality). The foundation of his many discussions of the relation of *iustitia* (Divine Justice, or "Rightfulness") and the *iustus* (the "rightly-directed person") rests on this language of "formal-speaking," as is evident in the *Commentary on John*. The just person precisely *insofar as he is just* (not in his total existential reality) must have everything that Divine Justice possesses. However, when Eckhart presented his teaching about the meaning of formal predication in the vernacular, the technical Latin qualifications of the *formaliter/actualiter* distinction were often less clear (though he does use the phrase "insofar as" in his German preaching from time to time). In his vernacular theology, Eckhart was not as concerned with such distinctions precisely because of his recognition of the difference between the role of the *lebemeister* and that of the *lesemeister*. Nevertheless, when taken to task, he tried to show his accusers that the message of his MHG preaching was not different from what could be found in his scholastic writings. (This was one thing upon which he and his inquisitors were in agreement, since they condemned passages from *both* Latin and vernacular texts.) Hence, it comes as no surprise that the first principle he invoked in introducing his Cologne defense was that of formal predication. As he put it: "To clarify the objections brought against me, three things must be kept in mind. The first is that the words 'insofar as,' that is, a reduplication, exclude from the term in question everything that is other or foreign to it, even according to reason."[96] This shows that not to understand the *inquantum* principle is not to understand Eckhart.

Apart from the intellectual resources Eckhart called upon to counter his critics, there were also institutional and canonical ones. He boldly announced at the beginning of the Cologne process, ". . . according to the exemption and privileges of my order, I am not held to appear before you or to answer charges."[97] The Dominicans, after all, were a canonically exempt order, that is, free of episcopal control and directly under the pope. Eckhart rightly claimed that only the pope, or the University of Paris as his delegate, had the power to investigate a *magister theologiae* for heresy.[98] To the pope he had appealed, and to the pope he would go.

Throughout the trying months of late 1326 Eckhart had the full support of the local Dominican authorities, as can be seen by Nicholas of Strasbourg's three official protests against the actions of the inquisitors in January of 1327 (Acta nn.50–52). However, the evidence of the warnings against dangerous preaching given by the General Chapters of 1325 and 1328 indicate that the international leaders of the order had distanced themselves from Eckhart without attacking him personally.[99] Both Nicholas and Eckhart asked for "dimissory" letters allowing the case to be forwarded to the papal court at Avignon. On February 13, 1327, Eckhart also preached a sermon in the Dominican church at Cologne. At the end, he had his secretary read out a public protestation in Latin of his innocence and willingness to retract any errors. Eckhart himself translated the text into German, so that his audience, the vernacular public whom he had served so well, could understand it.[100] This was an important act. By *publicly* proclaiming himself willing to retract any and all error, Eckhart had effectively forestalled any attempt to try him as a heretic. Sometime in the spring of that year, when the roads became passable, Eckhart, accompanied by other ranking members of the Teutonia province, began his journey to Avignon.

Our knowledge of the last year of Eckhart's life is fragmentary. We know that Pope John XXII appointed two commissions, one of theologians and the other of cardinals, to investigate the charges against the Dominican master. We have the names of the commissioners, including Cardinal William Peter de Godino, who was probably a former student of the Meister. We also know that the commissions reduced the unwieldy body of some 150 suspect articles down to a more modest twenty-eight. The important document known as the *Votum Avenionense* gives us, in scholastic fashion, these articles, the reasons why they are judged heretical, Eckhart's defense of each, and the rebuttal of the commissioners. Although it is a summary of his case, rather than his own production, this document (probably dating from late 1327) allows us a final opportunity to hear Eckhart still sounding the major themes of his preaching and teaching.

Eckhart's Avignon defense summarizes many themes that had been part of his preaching for more than three decades. For example, with regard to what became article 13 of the subsequent bull of condemnation ("Whatever is proper to the divine nature, all that is proper to the just and divine man"), the *Votum* says:

> He verifies this article, because Christ is the head and we the members; when we speak, he speaks in us. Also, in Christ there was so great a union of the Word with flesh that he communicated his own properties to it,

so that God may be said to suffer and a man is the creator of heaven. To Christ himself it properly belongs to be called "a just person insofar as he is just," for the term "insofar as" is a reduplication that excludes everything alien from the term [being employed]. In Christ there is no other hypostasis save that of the Word; but in other humans this is verified more or less.[101]

The *Votum* makes clear that in the case of each of the twenty-eight articles still under investigation, the commission was not convinced by the Dominican's explanations. However, it also confirms that a basic shift had taken place in Eckhart's case—he was no longer on trial as a heretic, but was being investigated for the possible censure of various articles he had once taught, which, *if judged heretical*, he had promised to renounce.

Even after the recommendations of the joint commissions, John XXII still sought further input in the delicate matter of condemning a Paris master. At some stage in the proceedings he asked Jacques Fournier, the future Pope Benedict XII, to look at the dossier and to give his opinion (Acta n.58 forthcoming). Fournier's response does not survive. The next secure date in the process comes on April 30, 1328, when the pope wrote to Bishop Henry of Cologne to assure him that the case against Eckhart was moving ahead, although the accused was dead. It was long thought that the actual date of Eckhart's death was lost. But Walter Senner discovered that a seventeenth-century Dominican source noted that Eckhart was remembered in German convents on January 28,[102] so we can surmise that he died on that day in 1328—the same day on which the Catholic calender now celebrates the feast of his illustrious predecessor Thomas Aquinas.

On March 27, 1329, Pope John issued the bull "In agro dominico," an unusual step, since Eckhart was already dead and he was not being personally condemned as a heretic.[103] Doubtless the pope's fear of growing mystical heresy and pressure from his ally Henry II had convinced him to bring the case to a definitive conclusion. It has often been said that John XXII tempered the condemnation of Eckhart's articles by restricting the circulation of the bull to the province of Cologne, but Robert E. Lerner has shown that this is not the case—a copy of the document was also sent to Mainz, and there is evidence of a vernacular version from Strasbourg.[104] Pope John obviously meant to quash Eckhart's influence decisively, as the personally defamatory language used in the preface to the text clearly shows.

The bull witnesses to papal fears of Eckhart's vernacular theology by expressly noting that his errors were "put forth especially before the uneducated crowd in his sermons." Strangely enough, although the Avignon *Votum* treated all twenty-eight articles as heretical, "In agro dominico" divides the list into three groups: the first fifteen containing "the error or stain of heresy as much from the tenor of their words as from the sequence of their thoughts"; a second group of eleven, which are judged "evil-sounding and very rash and suspect of heresy, though with many explanations and additions they might take on or possess a catholic meaning"; and two appended articles, which Eckhart had denied saying (though they certainly reflect passages in his works), which are also judged heretical. We do not know if this confusing distinction between the heretical and the merely dangerous articles was introduced by the pope himself, or at some other stage in the process. Finally, at the end of the bull the pope absolves Eckhart himself of heresy, noting that on the basis of a public document, "the aforesaid Eckhart . . . professed the catholic faith at the end of his life and revoked and also deplored the twenty-six articles, which he admitted that he had preached, . . . *insofar as* they could generate in the minds of the faithful a heretical opinion, or one erroneous and hostile to the faith." So Eckhart, even at the end of his life, maintained his integrity through the invocation of an *inquantum* that the pope either let pass or did not catch.

CHAPTER 2

Approaching Eckhart
Controversies and Perspectives

*T*HE CONDEMNATION OF ECKHART is the most powerful but by no means the only reason he has proven controversial down through the centuries. At the present time, when even Pope John Paul II has quoted the Dominican theologian with approval,[1] debates over how far Eckhart is to be seen as "heretical" are no longer a burning issue. His good intentions, as well as the spiritual profit so many have taken from his writings, clearly show that he was never a heretic, by either medieval or modern standards.

In the late nineteenth century Eckhart scholarship shifted the debate away from the question of heresy to the consistency and coherence of his philosophical and theological thought in relation to the triumphant Neoscholastic Thomism of post–Vatican I Catholicism. From this perspective, the Dominican scholar, Heinrich Seuse Denifle (1844–1905), who was the first to recover Eckhart's Latin works, judged him "an unclear thinker who was not conscious of the consequences of his teaching in relation to his mode of expression."[2] Other Catholics, such as Otto Karrer, sought to show Eckhart's essential conformity with orthodoxy as represented by Thomas Aquinas.[3] After 1950, however, the revived study of patristic theology connected with "la nouvelle théologie," and especially the theological revival encouraged by Vatican II, made possible greater appreciation of the variety of forms of theology, rendering these debates less relevant. In recent decades there has been increasing effort to try to understand Eckhart on his own terms— What was he trying to do and how successful was he in accomplishing his aims?

The attempt to grasp Eckhart from within has by no means led to agreement about the fundamental nature of his teaching and preaching. Serious controversies still divide Eckhart scholarship, especially the debate about whether the Dominican is to be thought of as a "mystic" or as a "philosopher-theologian."[4] Questioning whether the title "mystic" is appropriate for Eckhart seems to have begun in 1960 with Heribert Fischer, who assumed the editing of Eckhart's Latin works after the death of Josef Koch. Fischer noted that Eckhart did not write a treatise on mystical theology as such, nor even on the charismatic gifts; for Fischer, Eckhart was a theologian, not a mystic.[5] In 1977 C. F. Kelley in his insightful *Meister Eckhart on Divine Knowledge* claimed that Eckhart's notion of knowing from the perspective of God as "Principle" is a "pure metaphysics" that is not to be confused with either ontology or mysticism, which Kelley claimed is always rooted in the individual self and in ecstatic experience.[6] The most insistent denial of the title of mystic to Eckhart, however, has come from the Bochum philosopher Kurt Flasch, whose 1974 paper "Die Intention Meister Eckhart" argued that because Eckhart always sought to explain his teaching "through the natural arguments of the philosophers" (see In Ioh. n.2), the identification of Eckhart as a mystic hinders rather than helps us to understand him.[7] For Flasch, Eckhart is a philosopher, *not* a mystic. (He entitled another article, "Meister Eckhart: An Attempt to Rescue Him from the Mystical Torrent.")[8] Flasch's position has been echoed by a few other recent Eckhart scholars, such as Burkhard Mojsisch;[9] but it has been criticized by others, such as Kurt Ruh, Alois M. Haas, and Niklaus Largier.[10]

There are two fundamental problems with the position of Fischer, Flasch, Kelley, and others who deny that Eckhart is a mystic. The first is the "either-or" mentality that tries to divide what Eckhart sought to keep together; the second is an inadequate view of mysticism. Eckhart was both *lesemeister,* learned philosopher and theologian, and *lebemeister,* master of the spiritual life. To be sure, the term "mystic" is a modern creation,[11] but as used here I believe that its meaning is not far from what was intended by the MHG *lebemeister.* Furthermore, most contemporary scholars of mysticism, whatever their disagreements, scarcely think of mysticism in the manner Flasch and his colleagues conceive of it, that is, as something private, purely emotional, irrational, and always based on claims of personal ecstatic experience. If that is the true definition of mysticism, Eckhart is not a mystic, but neither is John of the Cross or a host of the other figures traditionally identified as mystics in the history of the church. Eckhart very rarely speaks *in the first person* about his own God-consciousness, but he everywhere speaks out of his conviction of the need to become one with Divine Truth: "For I say to you in everlasting Truth that if you are unlike this Truth of which we want to speak, you cannot understand me."[12]

Few thinkers have valued the unity of truth more than Meister Eckhart.[13] We do him a real disservice if we try to divide and separate what he sought to keep in living union. Hence, it is important to investigate how Eckhart conceived of the inner harmony of reason and faith, philosophy and theology, thought and practice, in order to be able to read him from the proper perspective and to show why he should be considered both mystic and philosopher-theologian.

Thomas Aquinas, and to a lesser extent Albert the Great, had distinguished between the natural truths about God that were explored by philosophers and strictly supernatural truths, such as the Trinity, which reason could not attain on its own and therefore have to be revealed in order to be known.[14] *Sacra doctrina,* as presented in Aquinas's *Summa,* considered both kinds of truths (see STh 1a, q.1, a.1), because revelation also taught natural truths that were necessary for salvation but that not all humans might be able to attain on their own (e.g., that God exists). Meister Eckhart, despite his respect for Thomas, rejected this distinction and created his own form of the view held by thinkers like John Scottus Eriugena that saw no essential difference between philosophy and theology.

All scholastic theologians believed that there could be no *conflict* between faith and reason, between nature and scripture, because each has its source in the one Divine Truth. Eckhart went further. In a passage dealing with the necessity of the Incarnation from the *Commentary on John* Eckhart says: "Moses, Christ, and the Philosopher teach the same thing, differing only in the way they teach, namely as worthy of belief [Moses], as probable or likely [Aristotle], and as truth [Christ]."[15] This suggests that there is no difference in the *content* of philosophy and theology, though there is a difference in the way in which philosophers and theologians grasp the truth of their respective disciplines. Thus, philosophy as a discipline is not limited to what Thomas Aquinas called natural truths about God, but includes teachings such as the Trinity and the Incarnation, which Eckhart saw as fully "rational" in the deepest sense because the philosopher could find evidence for them in the natural world. For Eckhart creation clearly reveals that God is Trinity and that the Second Person of the Trinity became flesh for our salvation.

Does Eckhart's statement about Aristotle and Christ teaching "the same thing" mean that the content of pagan philosophy and what the Christian philosopher teaches is *in all cases* identical? A number of texts seem to militate against this view. In these passages Eckhart contrasts the "pagan masters who knew only in a natural light" with "the words of the sacred masters who knew in a much higher light."[16] In Pr. 101 he says that those who considered the soul's nobility on the basis of their "natural intelligence" (*natiurliîche vernunft*) were never able to enter into or to know the ground of the soul which is attainable only by unknowing.[17] In all these passages Eckhart is talking about the naked intellect, which alone gives access to the ground where the soul is finally satisfied with "the Only One" (*dem ainigen ain*).[18] Hence, it seems that with regard to the deepest core of Eckhart's teaching—that concerning the ground of the soul—the natural light of reason needs the assistance of a higher illumination, which is really a form of not-knowing (*unwizzen*), or learned ignorance (*unbekante bekantnisse*). But Eckhart may not have thought that all pagan masters were excluded from this knowledge. In another sermon (Pr. 28) he has remarkable praise for "Plato, the great cleric" (*Plâtô, der grôze pfaffe*). In dialectical fashion, Eckhart ascribes to the ancient philosopher knowledge of "something pure that is not of this world," something out of which "the eternal Father derives the plenitude and the depth (*abgrunt*) of all his deity." The Father bears this here (i.e., in us), so that we are the very Son of God, "and his birth is his indwelling and his indwelling is his outward birth."[19] Although Eckhart does not employ the term *grunt* here, it is clear that he is speaking about Plato having an awareness of the unity of ground, something that in Pr. 101 he had denied to other "pagan masters."

These conflicting texts raise the question of whether Eckhart thought that there was a realm of theological truth distinct from natural philosophy. More precisely, does his teaching on the ground belong to Christian theology or to general philosophy? I believe that we should say it belongs to both. Although Eckhart may not explicitly say so, the evidence of the passage from Pr. 28, as well as his whole way of arguing in the scriptural commentaries, speaks against any essential difference. At the outset of the *Commentary on John*, for example, he says that the purpose of the work is "to explain what the holy Christian faith and the two testaments maintain through the help of the natural arguments of the philosophers."[20] The prologue of the *Book of the Para-*

bles of Genesis echoes this, saying that the second Genesis commentary seeks "to show that what the truth of holy scripture parabolically intimates in hidden fashion agrees with what we prove and declare [i.e., philosophically] about matters divine, ethical, and natural."[21] Eckhart believed that there was no gap or difference between what scripture teaches and what "unknowing philosophy" proves and declares. Nor does the divine light that enables thinkers to grasp *docta ignorantia* need to be restricted to Christians, as his praise for Plato shows. The highest form of philosophy investigates and shows the full harmony of all three categories of truths: *divina-naturalia-moralia* (i.e., divine matters, or theology, including the Trinity, natural philosophy, and ethics).[22] It also teaches natural reason's insufficiency to attain the ground unless it surrenders itself to the action of the divine light.[23] Some might call this "mystical irrationality." Eckhart thought of it as the higher form of suprarational knowing needed to bring reason to its goal.

Eckhart's notion of the perfect conformability of the Bible and philosophy did not make the Bible into a philosophical book (because its teaching is presented *parabolice* not *demonstrative*), but it did mean that commentary on scripture and preaching the word of God could be presented in philosophical form. For Eckhart philosophy is not the basis of belief, but its employment in exegesis is an important part of the preacher's calling. In the *Commentary on John* he says: "Just as it would be presumption and recklessness not to believe unless you have understood, so too it would be sloth and laziness not to investigate by natural arguments and examples what you believe by faith."[24] For Eckhart, then, scriptural commentary serves as the instrument for the creation of a philosophical-theological exposition of the deepest mysteries of God, nature, and ethics, an exposition that, in turn, provides the material for Eckhart's novel form of biblical preaching. Although the German Dominican had once planned a systematic presentation of his thought in *The Three-Part Work,* the bulk of his surviving writings indicates that he came to the conclusion that his audience was best served through his exegesis and preaching rather than system-building. As Niklaus Largier has argued, this shift suggests that Eckhart believed that the goal of attaining true "subjectivity," that is, mystical union, was best realized within a hermeneutical situation in which the exegete-preacher and the attentive hearer "break through" the surface of the biblical word to reach the hidden inner meaning that negates ordinary reason and the created self.[25] Like the great masters of the monastic mystical tradition, but in his own key, Eckhart believed that mystical consciousness was fundamentally hermeneutical; that is, it is achieved in the act of hearing, interpreting, and preaching the Bible.

The importance of Eckhart the preacher has long been recognized; deeper investigation of Eckhart the exegete has only recently begun.[26] Like the other great biblical interpreters of the patristic and medieval periods, Eckhart was less concerned with presenting a theory of exegesis than in actually doing the work of interpretation. Here, however, I will concentrate on abstracting his "theory" from programmatic statements and a few examples, leaving the demonstration of his hermeneutical practice to later chapters.

Eckhart's exegesis emerges as both traditional and innovative. The traditional aspect of the Dominican's mode of interpretation is best seen in his firm adherence to "spiritual" hermeneutics, that is, the conviction that the literal sense of the biblical text is only the starting point for grasping the inner meaning of what God wants to say to humans.[27] The original character of Eckhart's exegesis (most evident in his practice) resides in the creative way he went about forging an exegesis that was at once philosophical and mystical. For the philosophical aspect of his hermeneutic the Dominican was deeply indebted to Maimonides, whose *Guide to the Perplexed* in its Latin form (*Dux neutrorum*) provided him with both a model and a source for many individual readings.[28] The mystical aspect of the Dominican's interpretation was deeply influenced by the great exegetes of the Christian tradition, Augustine above all. Despite his debts to others, however, Eckhart's form of "mystical hermeneutics" is very much his own.[29]

In an aside in one of the sermons he preached at Cologne, Eckhart says that the day before he had interrupted a debate in the schools with the statement, "I am amazed that scripture is so rich that no one has ever penetrated to the ground of the least word of it."[30] For Eckhart, the profundity of the Bible, indeed, of every text in the Bible, means that it contains an inexhaustible fecundity of truths. To try to give his hearers some sense of this richness, Eckhart compares scripture to flowing waters in one sermon.[31] In another homily he uses a metaphor based on Gregory the Great's description of the Bible as a deep sea in which lambs (i.e., humble people) touch bottom, cows (the coarse-grained) swim, and elephants (clever people) plunge in over their heads.[32] Citing Augustine, he says that it is the person "who is bare of spirit and seeks the sense and truth of scripture in the same spirit in which it was written or spoken" who will best understand it.[33]

To seek for the truth of the Bible in the divine spirit is the first principle of Eckhart's hermeneutics. That "truth" is *the Truth*, that is, the

Divine Word himself, because for Eckhart the entire meaning of the Bible is christological. "No one can be thought to understand the scriptures," he says, "who does not know how to find its hidden marrow—Christ, the Truth."[34] It is only in and through Christ that the verities hidden under the scriptural *parabolae* (i.e., stories and figurative expressions) can be discerned. These truths, as Eckhart lists them in his "Prologue" to the *Book of the Parables of Genesis,* include the properties of the divine nature which "shine out in every natural, ethical, and artistic work." In other words, what is *intimated* in the parables is also what was to have been *demonstrated* in the other parts of the *Three-Part Work.*

Even those accustomed to the variety of meanings given to individual biblical texts by earlier exegetes will be surprised at the exuberant plethora of readings Eckhart draws out of many passages, such as the first verse of John's Gospel or Wisdom 8:1.[35] It is not just the number of the readings, but the seemingly arbitrary, bizarre character of so many of these interpretations that surprises the modern reader. Eckhart himself adverted to this in the "General Prologue" to *The Three-Part Work* in a text already cited: "Note that some of the following propositions, questions, and interpretations at first glance will appear monstrous, doubtful, or false; but it will be otherwise if they are considered cleverly and more diligently" (Prol.gen. n.7). The Dominican deliberately adopted a strategy designed to shock the reader. He obviously thought that his excessive mode of exegesis corresponded to the intention of the biblical text itself, which so often spoke "excessively." At the end of the *Commentary on John,* in commenting on the hyperbolic claim of John 21:25 that the whole world could not hold all the books that would give the full tale of Christ's signs, he says:

> Such a mode of speaking, that is, excessively, properly belongs to the divine scriptures. Everything divine, as such, is immense and not subject to measure. . . . The excellence of divine things does not allow them to be offered to us uncovered, but they are hidden beneath sensible figures.[36]

In the Latin commentaries, where Eckhart has to deal for the most part with the fixed text of the Vulgate, the various interpretations he gives are often the product of a philosophical-theological impulse to investigate every implication of a word or passage. The same impulse is found in many of the German sermons, but in the vernacular works Eckhart also often employs expansions, repunctuations, and interpretive translations or rewritings in order to bring out the inner meaning of a passage.[37] There is a sense in which the Meister, especially in the MHG sermons, plays with the biblical text.[38] The Dominican consciously adopted this fluid hermeneutic of multiplication and mischievousness for the good of his students and his lay audience. In the second prologue to the *Work of Expositions* he says: "The main authorities [i.e., passages] are often expounded in many ways so that the reader can take now this explanation, now another, one or many, as he judges useful."[39] The more, the more useful, is a key principle of Eckhart's exegesis.

Eckhart's readings are likely to seem especially perverse to modern readers concerned with the narrative context of the biblical story and its historical *Sitz im Leben*. His procedure is the reverse. Even by the standards of traditional spiritual exegesis, Eckhart shows little interest in the biblical story line.[40] Rather, he dehistoricizes and decontextualizes the text into sentences, fragments, or even individual words that he then recombines with other biblical passages in a dense web of intertextuality through a system of cross-referencing that is one of the main characteristics of his hermeneutics.[41] This too was a conscious choice. In one place he says: "In explaining a passage under discussion many other texts of the canon of scripture are often brought forward, and all these passages can be explained in their proper places from this one, just as it is now explained through them."[42] Intertextuality of this sort was not new, but Eckhart's dehistoricizing form of it fits his "principial" way of knowing: that is, seeing all things from the divine perspective, the "now" (*nû/nunc*) of eternity in which all words and expressions are one in the eternal Divine Word. Such multiplicity does not, for Eckhart at least, introduce confusion, because all these meanings come from one and the same source of Divine Truth.

In line with the traditions of spiritual exegesis, Eckhart insists that all biblical texts, but especially the words of Christ, have two levels, one according to "the plain meaning and surface of the letter" (*secundum planum et superficiem litterae*), the other which "is hidden beneath the shell" (*latet sub cortice*).[43] When it comes to investigating *sub cortice*, however, the Dominican shows no interest in the traditional enumeration of three spiritual senses (allegorical, tropological, anagogical), and, even though he cites with approval Maimonides' distinction of two kinds of biblical *parabolae*, he does not use it in practice.[44] In his exegesis, as everywhere in his thought, Eckhart is concerned with the basic opposition between inner and outer. Typically, however, the seemingly clear distinction between outer shell and inner kernel, letter and "mystical meaning" (*mystica significatio*),[45] soon becomes unstable and paradoxical in Eckhart. This is evident both in theory and in practice.

In his general comments on hermeneutics in the prologue to the *Book of the Parables of Genesis* Eckhart takes up the traditional problem of the relation between the literal and the hidden meaning of scripture. Citing Augustine's discussion of the variety of true meanings that an expositor can gather from scripture (even meanings that were not known to the human author), Eckhart advances the bold claim:

> Since the literal sense is that which the author of a writing intends, and God is the author of holy scripture, ... then every true sense is a literal sense. It is well known that every truth comes from the Truth itself; it is contained in it, derived from it, and is intended by it.[46]

The import of this remarkable statement is that the spiritual meaning has become a new form of infinitely malleable letter. The outer and the inner have traded places, or even merged. As Donald Duclow puts it, "when the letter thus fuses with its multiple meanings, the very boundary between text and interpretation becomes indistinct."[47] (Eckhart, as we shall see, loved indistinction.) By means of such a procedure we might say that the exegete has become the text in the sense that it is he/she who provides the meaning adjudged as truly divine. Even more radically, the mystical interpreter has become one with God, the author of the Bible.

Why did Eckhart reverse the polarities of traditional exegesis in this paradoxical way? If the main concern of Eckhart's exegesis, as we have seen, is to "break through the shell" of literalism to reach the infinite inner understandings that become a new "letter," exegesis of necessity explodes upon itself. It is the very nature of the Dominican's exegesis and his biblical preaching to encourage such a "breaking through," which "explodes" both the text and the self into divine indistinction.

In Sermon 51 Eckhart discusses another aspect of this self-negating hermeneutics by proclaiming that "all likenesses must be broken through" (*so muessent die gleychnuss alle zerbrechenn*), that is, that all images and discrete meanings must eventually be destroyed as the exegete pursues his task. This sermon contains one of the Dominican's most interesting discussions of the nature of scripture, its images, and their relation to the Father's "own image, abiding in himself in the ground." Nature, Eckhart says, teaches us that we must use images and likenesses, "this or that," to point to God. But since God is not a "this or that," in order to plunge back into the divine source and become the one Son, all images must go. Eckhart expresses the necessity for this exegetical iconoclasm in a way that subverts the traditional teaching about penetrating the external letter to reach an inner meaning, or "form" of discrete knowledge. As Susanne Köbele has shown, Eckhart is talking here about two stages of movement beyond the surface rather than the traditional single movement from letter to spirit:

> I have said before the shell must be broken through and what is inside must come out, for if you want to get at the kernel you must break the shell. And also, if you want to find nature unveiled, all likenesses must be broken through, and the further you penetrate, the nearer you will get to the essence. When the soul finds the One, where all is one, there she will remain in the Single One.[48]

"Breaking through" and "penetrating into indistinction in the Single One," fundamental motifs of all Eckhart's mystical teaching, are therefore also the essence of his hermeneutics. Eckhart is an apophatic exegete.[49]

Eckhart the exegete and Eckhart the preacher are inseparable in the sense that his preaching always took its departure from a biblical text found in the liturgy and therefore must be understood within this biblical-liturgical context. Eckhart's convents at Erfurt, Paris, Strasbourg, and Cologne were not isolated monastic communities but urban houses for preachers and teachers charged with the *cura animarum*. In their spacious Gothic churches, such as those that still survive in Erfurt and Cologne, Dominicans like Eckhart served the northern European townfolk in an age when the liturgy still played a role in society almost impossible to conceive of today.

Current interest in medieval preaching has cast new light on the importance of the sermon for understanding medieval culture. In recent years Eckhart scholarship has profited from several important investigations of the context, content, and literary dynamics of the Dominican's mode of preaching.[50] Just as Bernard of Clairvaux's mysticism reached its acme in the lush rhetoric of his *Sermons on the Song of Songs,* Meister Eckhart's place in the history of Western Christian mysticism is tied to the profound and often startling homilies he preached both to religious and to laity. As Kurt Ruh puts it: "Eckhart's German preaching without a doubt stands at the middle of his creativity. He understood himself more as preacher than as professor and scholar."[51] To be a preacher was not only the essential task of the order to which he belonged, but it was a vocation that Eckhart said called for a special relation to Christ: "Thus the preacher of the Word of God, which is 'God's Power and God's Wisdom' (1 Cor. 1:24), ought not exist and live for himself, but for the Christ he preaches."[52]

In approaching Eckhart the preacher, it is important to remember the liturgical context of the Dominican's preaching. Eckhart did not create his homilies in a vacuum, or as freestanding discourses to be read by an interested reader anywhere and anytime, though that is how most approach him today. Rather, Eckhart's sermons were liturgical acts delivered to worshiping communities mediated by the texts and the meaning of the particular feasts of the church's calendar, and, above all, by the fundamental purpose of the eucharistic action itself—uniting Christ and his body through the re-presentation of the Lord's saving death. Joachim Theisen, whose book *Predigt und Gottesdienst* shows how the liturgical readings and texts of the Dominican missal illuminate the Meister's surviving sermons, summarizes Eckhart's preaching program thus: "It is the fundamental intention of his preaching to point out the actuality of the mystery that is being celebrated and to draw the community into this actuality."[53] This is why Eckhart has so little interest in the historical reality of the events of Christ's life in his homilies. It is the presence of the Word made flesh *here and now* that is his concern.

Just as the hidden and silent divine mystery present in the Father expressed himself in speaking the eternal Word, so too the preacher takes as his task "re-speaking" the Word of Truth present in the biblical texts of the liturgy so that the community can hear the Word and follow it back into "the simple ground, into the quiet desert, into which distinction never gazed . . ." (Pr. 48). Reiner Schürmann spoke of the "ontological meaning" of Eckhart's preaching, that is, how the very act of preaching as creation of the word to be heard by others so that they too may find the source from whence the word is formed mirrors the "event character" of Eckhart's metaphysical view of the God–world relation.[54] But the preacher cannot really convey the message that lies hidden behind all words, and even beyond the Divine Word himself in the hidden depths of deity, unless he himself has participated in this inner speaking, that is, unless he speaks "out of the ground" of God.[55] In his *Sermons and Lectures on Ecclesiasticus* Eckhart makes this clear in giving his own etymology of Paul's command to Timothy: "Preach the word" (2 Tim. 4:2). "'Preach,' as it were, 'say beforehand,' that is, 'first say within.' Or 'preach,' that is, 'say outwardly,' or 'bring out from within' so that 'your light may shine before men' (Matt. 5:16)."[56] Eckhart invites his audience to hear what he has heard and to become one with him in the one ground—"If you could perceive things with my heart," he once said, "you would well understand what I say; for it is true and the Truth itself speaks it."[57] This is a bold claim for any preacher to make, but Eckhart does not advance it on the basis of his individual authority or his own learning, as an *esse hoc et hoc,* that is, a creature. He makes it out of the oneness of Divine Truth.[58] In one of the few places where he speaks of his own consciousness of God, Eckhart makes it clear that he thinks of his own union with God as a grace for all: "I will tell you how I think of people: I try to forget myself and everyone and to merge myself, for them, in Unity. May we abide in Unity, so help us God. Amen."[59]

Many insightful studies have been written about Eckhart's use of language and what it has to say about mystical language in general.[60] This is not the place to take up the broad issue of the nature of mystical language as such, but some reflections on Eckhart's particular form of mystical speech are important for framing the proper perspective for reading him. Older claims that Eckhart single-handedly created German mystical and/or philosophical-theological language must be abandoned. The Dominican was part of a broad effort in the thirteenth and fourteenth centuries to make MHG an apt instrument for speculation and mysticism. But there is also no doubt about Eckhart's genius in forging a distinctive mystical style of preaching, one that was famous and controversial in his day as in ours.

The variety of verbal strategies that Meister Eckhart makes use of in his vernacular preaching defy easy summary. His creativity in using speech to overcome speech and lead it back into the divine ground can be best appreciated by taking sermons as wholes and subjecting them to careful literary and theological analysis.[61] There have also been a number of attempts to summarize Eckhart's basic linguistic techniques. Alois M. Haas, for example, singled out paradox, oxymoron, and negation as the general *modi loquendi* of mystical speech and also studied the particular forms these topoi took in Eckhart's *Logos-mystik*.[62] More recently, on the basis of a treatment of three representative sermons, Burkhard Hasebrink analyzed Eckhart's "appellative speech" (*inzitative Rede*), that is, the way in which his sermons both invite the hearer to become one with the message and yet seek to destroy formal meaning through mystical *gelassenheit*.[63] Among the "macro-techniques" of appellative speech, according to Hasebrink, Eckhart gave particular importance to two forms of attaining thematic coherence. The first is a strategy of "paradigmatic substitution," by which the preacher constantly shifts back and forth from one or the other paradigm of his exploration of the union of God and human (e.g., birth of the Son, emanation, immanence, etc.) to create a "chain of substitutions" that invites the listener to make the message his/her own.[64] The second essential technique of Eckhart's appellative speech act, for Hasebrink, is the frequent use of "conditional relationships," that is, how Eckhart's address to his congregation puts the burden on them to realize the message by frequent use of conditional forms—"*If* you want this or that, you must do this or that." Eckhart is not interested in directing or in giving good advice, let alone orders, to his audience; he rather invites them to undertake what they know is for the best.[65]

The particular details, or "micro-techniques," of Eckhart's way with language have also been the subject of considerable study. In English Eckhart scholarship, Frank Tobin has cast light on many of the strategies that made Eckhart's preaching so fascinating to his original audience, and still today, even in translation, make reading him an arresting experience.[66] The Dominican's use of language is inseparable from his wider ontology (remember that in the *Parisian Questions* he held that "the Word" of understanding [*wort/verbum*] is prior to being [*wesen/esse*]).[67] What he does with words is meant to reveal the fundamental structures of reality, but also to subvert them and surpass them. As Tobin puts it: "In reading his works we sense the appropriateness of the adage that in recognizing the boundaries of language and human thought one can in some sense transcend them."[68]

Just a few of Eckhart's rhetorical strategies can be mentioned here by way of illustration. For example, he often gives the same word (e.g., *eigenschaft, berüeren*) shifting, or opposing, meanings. Some of these significations were already present in MHG vocabulary; at other times the Dominican was "stretching the envelope," creating new fields of meaning, as in the case of *grunt;* or forging neologisms, such as *isticheit,* to express mystical themes in the vernacular. Eckhart's relentlessly apophatic discourse is found not only in the larger semantic structures of his discourse, but in his very word formation with its frequent use of negative particles and prepositions (e.g., *un-/ab-/ent-/über-/-los/âne/sunder*). Tobin has studied such procedures as "accumulation, antithesis, parallelism, and hyperbole," which Eckhart employed to enrich his vernacular teaching.[69] A very frequently employed trope is chiasmus (i.e., using two or more words or phrases and then repeating them in reversed order). This was especially useful for expressing the Dominican's dialectical view of the God–world relationship.[70] The fact that chiastic passages are found throughout both Eckhart's Latin and German works raises a final issue that needs to be discussed in order to get the proper perspective on reading the Dominican mystic—How are we to relate the Latin and German sides of his mystical thought and expression?

The debate over the relationship between the Latin Eckhart and the German Eckhart shows no signs of going away, though it has become more nuanced in recent years.[71] Older presentations, pitting the Latin scholastic against the German mystic, or Eckhart's Latin "ontological" writings against his German "ethical-mystical" works, no longer hold water; but this has not meant an end to disagreements. On the one hand, there are those who minimize the difference between the German and the Latin. A Germanist of the stature of Walter Haug, for example, has claimed that "in principle one can conceive of his [Eckhart's] preaching just as well in Latin as in German."[72] Those who advance the argument that Eckhart is a philosopher, not a mystic (e.g., Flasch and Mojsisch) go even further in denying any real difference between the Dominican's two corpora.[73] On the other hand, many Germanists maintain a distinctive worth (*Eigenwert*) to Eckhart's German sermons. Thus, Kurt Ruh speaks of "the greater spiritual value [*der spirituelle Mehrwert*] of the vernacular";[74] and Susanne Köbele proclaims, "The new content of mystical expression [in the thirteenth century] is closely bound up with the medium of the vernacular."[75] Burkhard Hasebrink, however, has shown how the way in which the *Eigenwert* argument has been advanced often rests upon an understanding of "the vernacular as a worldly, lay, non-scientific, and experiential medium of speech," a position that cannot be demonstrated in Eckhart's case.[76] He advances the case for a more precise evaluation of the intimate relation between Latin and MHG in Eckhart's writings characterized as a "shifting of boundaries" (*Grenzverschiebung*).[77] We should also remember the sage comment of Alois Haas: "Eckhart has a theology of the Word, not a theology of the German language."[78]

In relating the Latin and German sides of Eckhart's production it is important to steer a safe course between Scylla and Charybdis. On the one hand, we have to avoid any simple opposition between the "creativity" of the MHG preacher and the more traditional and technical scholastic thinker, if only because Eckhart's mysticism was daring both in Latin and in German. On the other hand, one cannot deny that the possibility offered to the Dominican by what Kurt Ruh has called the *kairos*, or "decisive moment,"[79] of MHG at the turn of the fourteenth century was a significant factor for understanding the form and impact of his preaching and teaching. Above all, we must try to overhear the "conversation" between Latin and German within Eckhart himself in order to reconstruct the fullness of his thought. What is all too often overlooked is the striking fact that Meister Eckhart is the *only* major figure in the history of Christian mysticism in whom we can observe the full dynamics of the interplay between Latin mysticism (almost a millennium old by the time he wrote) and the new vernacular theology (still aborning, despite the achievements of the thirteenth century).

To appreciate this conversation means avoiding the kinds of universalizing contrasts still found in some studies. For example, it is not just the vernacular Eckhart who is daring, dangerous, and even possibly heretical.[80] The fact is that in the Cologne and Avignon proceedings Eckhart was taken to task for *both* his Latin and his vernacular works. Among the articles condemned in the papal bull, fifteen are taken from the German works and thirteen from the Latin—Eckhart was an equal-opportunity heretic when it comes to language! Furthermore, Eckhart could express his message of the union of indistinction in Latin as well as in German, though not, of course, in precisely the same way. Eckhart's dialectical mode of thought, which breaks through analogical understandings of the God–human relation to advance to indistinct union with God in the ground is, indeed, at its most creative in his MHG sermons, but it is also found throughout his Latin works, especially in his discussions of the transcendental predicates, such as *esse* and *unum*.[81] Eckhart's place in the history of Western mysticism is primarily rooted in the German preaching of the *lebemeister,* but his vernacular message cannot be understood apart from the Latin learning of the *lesemeister* who had absorbed and recast the spiritual wisdom of a millennium. Without the Latin Eckhart, the German Eckhart would remain even more difficult to understand than he was—an anomaly rather than a hinge between the old mysticism and the new.

CHAPTER 3

Eckhart and the
Mysticism of the Ground

*T*HE POWERFUL FLOOD of mystical literature that first became evident in the teaching and preaching of Meister Eckhart at the turn of the fourteenth century was to flourish for two hundred years and more in a multitude of sermons and treatises in the vernacular, both by noted mystics, like John Tauler and Henry Suso, and by lesser-known figures and anonymous "friends of God." But Eckhart and his followers were not the only mystics in late medieval Germany. During the thirteenth century important women, especially Mechthild of Magdeburg (died c. 1280), had enriched the story of German mysticism. Cistercian nuns of the convent of Helfta in Saxony, as well as cloistered Dominican sisters in the Rhineland and south Germany, also made important contributions.[1] Where does Eckhart's form of mysticism fit into this broad picture? What are its essential characteristics?

There are many descriptions and analyses of the mysticism produced in German-speaking lands in the late Middle Ages. The various attempts to provide accounts under some general rubric are useful in highlighting one or other aspect of an impressive body of literature (and art) that can be spoken of as mystical in the sense of teaching or witnessing to the transformation of consciousness through a direct encounter with God's presence. One often employed description is "German mysticism" (*die deutsche Mystik*)—a term that encompasses all the mystical literature produced in late medieval German-speaking territories while privileging vernacular mystical texts. This description was created in the heyday of nineteenth-century German Romanticism, though it has remained popular through the twentieth century.[2] Obviously, it is not incorrect to speak of "German mysticism," but the term has the disadvantage of putting Eckhart and his followers in such a broad category that what is distinctive of their mysticism is not clearly identifiable.

A number of other studies have used descriptions based on geographical location, religious affiliation, or ideational content. An example of the first approach is the use of the phrase "Rhineland mysticism" for Eckhart and his followers, as well as for the Dutch mystics of the fourteenth and fifteenth centuries.[3] But Meister Eckhart was born and did his earliest vernacular preaching in Saxony, far from the Rhine, and the mysticism he initiated spread throughout Germany, so there are limits to the adequacy of this geographical characterization.

Others have approached Eckhart from the perspective of the religious community to which he belonged. Eckhart was a Dominican, and much of the literature that was influenced by him was produced by fellow Dominicans. Hence, many scholars, from Carl Greith in the nineteenth century down to Kurt Ruh in our own, have used the "Mysticism of the German Dominicans" as an appropriate rubric.[4] But not all of Eckhart's followers were Dominicans, as texts like the *Theologia Deutsch* demonstrate, and the German Dominican order produced a variety of forms of mysticism, as can be seen in the case of the writings of the nuns of the order. Eckhart's mysticism is the mysticism *of* a Dominican, but it should by no means be identified as distinctive of the Order of Preachers.

Many attempts have been made to characterize Eckhart's mystical preaching and teaching by identifying its distinctive approach, mode of thought, or fundamental concepts and themes. For example, given the highly intellectual nature of Eckhart's presentations, it has been popular to speak of "speculative mysticism" in connection with Eckhart and his followers.[5] Josef Quint, the editor and interpreter of Eckhart's MHG works, adopted the term in an influential essay,[6] as have many other Eckhart scholars.[7] Eckhart and his followers are certainly "speculative" mystics in the sense that they emphasize the role of the intellect in the return to God; they also often set forth their teaching in complex philosophical language. Nevertheless, "speculative mysticism" is most often employed as a contrast to "affective mysticism," such as one finds, for example, in Bernard of Clairvaux. But all Christian mystics recognize the importance of love as well as knowledge; they all have a role for *both* affectivity and speculation. Typing Eckhart as a speculative mystic risks neglecting the important role that love plays in his teaching, as well as forgetting his declaration that ultimate union with God goes beyond love and knowledge. Even if one were to allow the term "speculative mysticism" as a way of talking about Eckhart's view of the importance of *intellectus/vernünftikeit*, the term is too general to be of help in setting off Eckhart from mystics of an equally philosophical temperament.

A similar critique can be made for a number of related attempts at characterization, such as the contrast between Eckhartian *Wesensmystik* (i.e., the mysticism of being) and the *Minnemystik* (love mysticism) of Bernard and most medieval women mystics. Once again, Eckhart and his followers have a place for both *minne* and *wesen*, though not in equal doses, just as love and knowledge play a part in all Christian mystics, though admittedly in different combinations and valuations.[8] Categorizations based on separating the two basic interrelated modes of human striving to find God (i.e., love and knowledge) ultimately cannot reveal much about how one mystical system differs from another.

Given the difficulty of attempts to find categories to describe the mysticism of Eckhart based on geography, religious order, and mode of thought, the wisest course might be to eschew general characterizations altogether. But the need for some kind of term to distinguish the form of mysticism initiated by Eckhart from other mystical traditions continues to impel scholars to put forward new descriptions to help illuminate the fundamental intent of the Dominican's teaching.[9]

It is my conviction that the search for more adequate terms to describe particular types of mysticism should begin with the texts of the mystics themselves, rather than with our modern vocabulary and methodological perspectives. Powerful new forms of mystical speech came to birth in Eckhart, his contemporaries, and his followers, and it is worth investigating the terms *of their own making* that shed light on what was distinctive, daring, even dangerous in their thinking. This is also the case in other periods in the history of mysticism. For example, much of the mysticism of the twelfth century can be understood as sharing a common interest in the theme of the "ordering of love" (*ordo amoris*, see Song of Songs 2:4), without suggesting that all twelfth-century mystics gave the notion equal attention or treated it in the same way.[10] Now I would like to propose that the description "mysticism of the ground" (MHG *grunt/grund*) can provide a helpful prism for understanding the special character of the mysticism of Eckhart and those influenced by him, Dominican and non-Dominican.[11]

Grunt is a deceptively simple word, but as used by Eckhart, its complexity, creativity, and power are truly remarkable. *Grunt* can be termed a "master metaphor," or what scholars of MHG, following the lead of Hans Blumenberg, have recently spoken of as a *Sprengmetapher* ("explosive metaphor").[12] *Grunt* can be described as an "explosive metaphor" in the sense that it breaks through previous categories of mystical speech to create new ways of presenting a direct encounter with God. When Eckhart says, as he frequently does, "God's ground and my ground is the same ground," he announces a new form of mysticism.

While explosive metaphors such as *grunt* are based on and embrace deep philosophical and theological speculation, their function is both theoretical and practical, or better, pragmatic: they are meant to transform, or overturn, ordinary limited forms of consciousness through the process of making the inner meaning of the metaphor one's own in everyday life. *Grunt* can also be described as a "master metaphor" because of the way it brings into focus the whole range of language strategies found in Eckhart to describe the relationship between God and the human person. Hans Blumenberg, for example, made use of the famous definition of God found in the Hermetic *Book of the Twenty-Four Philosophers,* "Deus est sphaera infinita cuius centrum est ubique, circumferentia nusquam" ("God is the infinite sphere whose center is everywhere, whose circumference nowhere") to illustrate the nature of the *Sprengmetapher.*[13] When applied to *grunt,* this Hermetic definition also suggests the organizing power of what I am calling a master metaphor. From this perspective, *grunt* is the protean term everywhere at the center of Eckhart's mysticism, which, paradoxically, vanishes from our grasp when we try contain it in a definable scheme, or circumference, of speculation.[14] The consciousness of the ground, a form of awareness different from all other forms of experience and knowing, is the foundation of Meister Eckhart's mysticism.[15]

SEMANTICS AND SOURCES

Grunt, its substantive relatives (*abgrunt/gruntlôsicheit*), and derived adjectives (e.g., *grundelôs/ungruntlich*) are widely present in the vernacular works of Eckhart, as well as of his followers Henry Suso and John Tauler.[16] The term is also important to the sermons and treatises ascribed to Eckhart,[17] and in many other vernacular mystical texts of the fourteenth century. Its role in Dutch mysticism, especially in John Ruusbroec, highlights the affinity, as well as the real differences, between the German Dominican and the Dutch canon.

The semantic basis in Germanic linguistics for *grunt* is evident from the fact that there is no *real* equivalent for it in the other vernacular mysticisms of the late Middle Ages or in Latin mystical literature, though naturally there are a variety of analogues. In the Spanish-language mysticism of Teresa of Avila and John of the Cross the "center of the soul" (*centro del alma*) plays a somewhat comparable role (one that may have been mediated through Latin translations of Eckhart and Tauler), but without the exuberant semantics so characteristic of *grunt* and its cognates.[18]

Almost everyone who has written on Eckhart has had something to say about his teaching on *grunt*.[19] Discussions of its use in Tauler, Suso, and other mystical texts also exist.[20] In 1929 Hermann Kunisch devoted a monograph, still often cited, to the use of *grunt* in German mysticism of the fourteenth and fifteenth centuries.[21] Despite these discussions, one can agree with Susanne Köbele when she says that with regard to much of the secondary literature on this central theme "one appears to be left in the lurch, when not led into error."[22] Recent research, however, has begun to reveal something of the complexity and depth of the term, as well as its centrality for understanding Eckhart.

According to scholars of Middle High German, the word *grunt* is used in four general ways, two concrete and two abstract.[23] *Grunt* can, first of all, be understood as physical ground, that is, the earth. *Grunt* can also mean the bottom or lowest side of a body, surface, or structure (Latin: *basis/profundum/fundamentum/fundus*). (This sense of *grunt* is etymologically related to *abgrunt* [*abyssus*], originally used to indicate hell conceived of as the bottom of the universe.) Abstractly, *grunt* is employed to indicate the origin (*origo*), cause (*causa*), beginning (*principium*), reason (*ratio*), or proof (*argumentum*) of something. Finally, *grunt* is employed as what is inmost, hidden, most proper to a being (*intimum/abditum/proprium*)—that is, its essence (*essentia*). The semantic richness of this simple German word, especially its spectrum of both concrete and abstract significations, made it a seed ripe for flowering in the age of linguistic creativity that has been spoken of as the *kairos* of German vernacular in the thirteenth and early fourteenth centuries.

In attempting to discover how Eckhart and his followers used the language of *grunt* it is important to cast a glance back, not only over the uses of the term in previous German mystics but also over the history of the Latin terminology related to it. In earlier mystical literature in German, Mechthild of Magdeburg, writing between c. 1250 and 1280, employed *grunt/gruntlos/abgrunt* a number of times, but without the richness of Eckhart's development and certainly not as a key term to explore the God–human relationship.[24] The beguine occasionally speaks of God as *grundelôs*,[25] and so too the soul;[26] but God is never identified with the *grunt*, though Wisdom and Truth are (only once each).[27] *Abgrunt* for Mechthild keeps its physical meaning, being used in the negative sense for hell.[28]

A more instructive parallel to Eckhart can be found in the Dutch beguine Hadewijch's use of the terms *gront* and *afgront* (abyss) to present the mutual interpenetration of God and human in the love union.[29] For Hadewijch, ground, abyss, and depth (*diepheit*) are terms that can be used both of the unknowable divine nature and of the human soul insofar as it can never be separated from its exemplary existence in God. In a passage from Letter 18 the beguine speaks of the mutual interpenetration of the "bottomlessness" of the soul "in which God suffices to himself" and God himself conceived of as "a way for the passage of the soul into its liberty, that is, into his ground that cannot be touched without contact with the soul's depth."[30] This remarkable text (there are others like it) is close to Eckhart, although there is no evidence to suggest that the Dominican could have known Hadewijch's writings which were not "published" until the middle of the fourteenth century.[31] They serve to remind us that the creation of *grunt/abgrunt* language was not a solitary effort but a response to a widespread yearning to express a new view of how God becomes one with the human person. While it is true that *grunt* was emerging as an important mystical term in several Germanic vernaculars, it is in the works of Meister Eckhart that the word first achieves centrality as a way of presenting mystical consciousness.

Because Eckhart was such a well-trained theologian, the hunt for the Latin sources for *grunt* has played an important role in Eckhart scholarship. *Grunt*, perhaps more than any other term in Middle High German, provides us with a perspective for observing the "conversation" between Latin and the emerging vernaculars that was part of the new mysticism of the later Middle Ages.[32] The search for the Latin background to *grunt*, however, has sometimes masked an essential point concerning the dialogue between scholastic Latin and vernacular preaching in the works of Eckhart—there are many equivalents for *aspects* of *grunt* in Latin, but there is no single Latin word that "means" *grunt*; that is, the vernacular word has a richer range of significations, offers more subtle possibilities for use, and presents us with a more adequate way to study Eckhart's new teaching about mystical union than any word in the learned but less flexible language of the schools.[33]

Above all, *grunt* was a term for the preacher, providing Eckhart, Tauler, and other *lebemeister* with a tool for inculcating mystical transformation that was as simple and direct as it was profound and polymorphic.[34] Nevertheless, unless we pay attention to the Latin words that refract aspects of the background and meaning of *grunt* we will not fully understand how Eckhart made use of his theological heritage at the same time that he "exploded" it.

Grunt was often applied to the "innermost of the soul" (*innigsten der sêle;* DW 2:259.7), what Eckhart, Tauler, and others spoke of metaphorically as "spark," "castle," "nobleman," "highest point," "seed," etc. Since a pioneering article of Martin Grabmann in 1900, much scholarly effort has been devoted to studying how *grunt* and its related terms are connected to Latin theological expressions for the depth of the soul conceived of as *imago dei*—expressions such as *fundus animae, scintilla animae, apex mentis, abditum animae/mentis/cordis, principale cordis/mentis, supremum animae, semen divinum, ratio superior, synderesis, abstrusior memoriae profunditas,* etc.[35] These terms all pertain to what has been called the mysticism of introversion, whose great source in the West is Augustine of Hippo.[36]

Eckhart knew these terms and made use of many of them in his Latin works. For example, S. XLIX says that the image of the invisible God resides *in supremo animae,*[37] while other Latin Sermons speak of the *abditum mentis* or *abditum animae* identified with the *essentia animae* as the place where God alone can come into the soul.[38] Eckhart's exegesis of Genesis 1:26 in his *Book of the Parables of Genesis* identifies the true image of God in which we are created with the Augustinian *ratio superior.*[39] The technical term *synderesis* (= *principale mentis*) is also used occasionally both in the Latin works and in German sermons.[40] (*Scintilla animae* itself occurs only in the Cologne defense.)[41] These inherited terms reveal aspects of what Eckhart meant by the "ground of the soul" (*grunt der sêle*), but in the Latin sermons they are not a central object of preaching in the same way that *grunt* is in the vernacular homilies. It is precisely because these Latin terms are one-sided, signifying only the anthropological aspect of the union of God with the soul, that they cannot function as the master metaphor for the praxis of attaining the dynamic identity that fuses God and the soul in one *grunt.*

Eckhart and his followers also employed *grunt* to indicate the hidden depths of God. The Latin background for this usage has a different semantic field from that of the terms used for the depths of the soul—another indication that *grunt* as a master metaphor is more than just a translation of any one Latin word. Here too, considerable research has been devoted to studying the terms used for the divine essence in the tradition and taken up by the Dominican in his Latin works. Certainly, words such as *deitas*,[42] *essentia*, and *principium* are helpful for grasping how Eckhart's preaching of the divine *grunt* flows from and is illuminated by the technical vocabulary of scholastic theology, but the Dominican's notion of the *grunt götlîches wesens* has a range of meanings and usages that surpasses any of these Latin terms.

First of all, it is important to note that Eckhart never used *grunt* of God in the sense of *causa*, because God as *grunt* lies at a deeper level than God as efficient cause of the universe.[43] *Grunt*, of course, can be rendered as *essentia* and *deitas/divinitas*, but these abstract terms lack the dynamic character so important to the Dominican's preaching on the ground. *Grunt* used of the divine ground could also be translated by *fundus divinitatis*, as we can see in the case of the Latin version of a text from Eckhart's vernacular Sermon 15 found in the first list of suspect articles from the Cologne trial.[44] But Eckhart himself did not utilize this vocabulary, and so it is difficult to think that Dionysian texts about the "almighty depth (or ground) of God" had any decisive influence on his understanding of *grunt*, as has been claimed.[45]

More important to our understanding of *grunt* is its link with *principium*, the term Eckhart uses to present the "formal emanation" of the Three Persons in the Trinity.[46] *Principium* is fundamentally a relational noun—"*Principium*, like the word *primum* [first], indicates a relation of order and of origin."[47] *Principium* is used to express the active nature of divine emanation, both the "inner boiling" (*bullitio*) within God and the "boiling over" (*ebullitio*) of creation. *Grunt*, however, points to the pure potentiality of the hidden divine mystery. Although the two terms differ, they imply each other, as Pr. 69 shows when it speaks of intellect bursting "into the ground from which goodness and truth come forth and perceiving [God's being] *in principio*, in the beginning. . . ."[48]

Reflection on God as *principium*, since it remains in the realm of formal causality, that is, the emanation of the same from the same, can also be a springboard for investigating the inner presence of God in the "just person as such" (*justus in quantum justus*), as the lengthy reflections on divine *justitia* and *justus* in the commentary on the Johannine Prologue demonstrate.[49] This is one of the places in the Latin works where Eckhart comes close to the kind of formulations found in his vernacular preaching about the mutuality of the divine-human ground. But we must note that *principium* is not really a correlative term for Eckhart—it is predicated of the divine side, but not the human, in the union of identity.

The term in the Latin works that comes closest to *grunt* as an explosive metaphor for indicating the identity of God and human has not been sufficiently emphasized in most previous discussions. Eckhart's reflections on God as *unum*, or "Absolute Unity," often took on a dialectical character that allowed him to explore the identity of *unum* as distinct-indistinction, the *negatio negationis* at the heart of all reality. Although this form of dialectic is set forth primarily in an abstract way and from the divine perspective in the most important text on *unum*, the commentary on Wisdom 7:27 ("And since it is one, it can do all things"),[50] in some of the Latin Sermons on *unum* we find expressions of a praxis for attaining identity with God that is similar to the vernacular language of the ground.[51] This can be seen, for example, in S. XXIX, which deals with the relationship between *intelligere* and *unum*.[52] It is also evident in S. IV on the Trinity, where Eckhart says:

> Just as *God* is totally indistinct in himself according to his nature in that he is truly and most properly one and completely distinct from all things, so too man in God is indistinct from everything which is in God . . . , and at the same time completely distinct from everything (my italics).[53]

In such passages, *unum*, like *grunt*, is employed to express *both* the divine and the human poles of fused identity.

The link between Eckhart's teaching about *unum* and his use of the language of *grunt* is also clearly demonstrated by an important passage in Pr. 13 where the Dominican contrasts the "oneness in the Godhead" with all forms of "likeness" (*glîcheit*). We are, indeed, "like" God insofar as God bears his "like" in me (i.e., the Son) and "from the likeness arises love which is the Holy Spirit."[54] But God as the motionless source moving all things from within and "returning" them to himself is beyond likeness. Eckhart says: "The more noble anything is, the more steadily it moves. The ground 'hunts' (*jaget*) all things. Wisdom and goodness and truth add something; oneness adds nothing other than the ground of being."[55] Within the One as ground motion and rest are paradoxically identical.[56]

Finally, when we look at the relation between Eckhart's use of the term *abgrunt* (employed six times) and the Latin *abyssus*, we again note considerable differences between the Latin background and the German word, at least in its mystical deployment.[57] The biblical *abyssus* only gradually came to be applied to God.[58] Augustine and early medieval mystics did not speak of God himself as an *abyssus*, using the term positively to refer to divine judgment, or more often negatively of hell and the perverse depth of the human heart. It is among the twelfth-century Cistercians that we begin to get the first mystical appropriations of the word,[59] but it is only with the thirteenth-century mystics, especially the Dutch Beatrice of Nazareth and Hadewijch, as well as the Italians Angela of Foligno and Jacopone da Todi, that *abyssus/abisso/ afgront* takes its place as a key term in mystical vocabulary.[60] Eckhart is not likely to have been familiar with any of these texts, but a mystical work he almost certainly knew, the *Mirror of Simple Souls* of Marguerite Porete, also made much of the language of the abyss (Old French *abysme*) to understand the mystery of the divine-human identity.[61] Eckhart's use of *abgrunt* must be seen in this context, but in his case it is clear that *grunt* is the central metaphor. *Abgrunt* is a secondary and derivative term.

From the perspective of semantics, then, we can conclude that the relation of the MHG *grunt* to traditional Latin terms for the depth of the soul and the inmost nature of God casts light on aspects of the vernacular term, but cannot explain its function as a master metaphor "exploding" previous forms of mystical discourse. *Grunt* is more than a translation. It is a new creation whose significance can only be appreciated by exploring its contexts and meanings within the vernacular sermons and treatises of Eckhart himself.

CONTEXTS AND MEANINGS

At the conclusion of Pr. 42, Eckhart addresses his hearers with the following words:

> Now know, all our perfection and our holiness rests in this: that a person must penetrate and transcend everything created and temporal and all being and go into the ground that has no ground. We pray our dear Lord God that we may become one and indwelling, and may God help us into the same ground. Amen.[62]

In this passage note that Eckhart does not qualify the *gruntlôs grunt* as either God's or the soul's. It is both. This is why elsewhere he insists, "If anyone wishes to come into God's ground and his innermost, he must first come into his own ground and his innermost, for no one can know God who does not first know himself."[63]

This helps us to see why it is better to speak of the "mysticism of the ground" than the "mysticism of the ground of the soul."[64] The essential point, as Eckhart often put it, is that "God's ground and the soul's ground is *one* ground."[65] It is not because *either* the soul is grounded in its essential reality, *or* God in his, but because they are *both grounded in the same ground* in a fused identity that Eckhart and his followers found the language of the ground so rich in meaning.[66] As he put it in Sermon 5b: "Here God's ground is my ground and my ground is God's ground. Here I live out of what is mine, just as God lives out of what is his."[67] It is true that Eckhart often speaks of God "penetrating" and "being in" the soul's ground, thus indicating an analogical relationship between two realities.[68] But, as Otto Langer has pointed out, texts such as those cited above indicate that on the deepest level, that of fused identity, there is only one univocal *grunt*.[69]

The univocal and dialectical understanding of *grunt* explains the advantages of the "mysticism of the ground" over other descriptions of what is distinctive of Eckhart in the world of late medieval mysticism. Within the contours of Eckhart's thought, the ground is nothing other that the "uncreated something *in* the soul" (not *of* the soul), a term often linked with metaphors such as the "little spark" (*vunkelîn*), or the "little castle" (*burgelîn*).[70] Central as these metaphors are for understanding the Dominican's teaching about the soul, they are *not* used of the divine nature, and thus they lack the power of *grunt* to express the fused identity of both God and human.

It is also important to consider the relation between *grunt* and *geburt,* the birth motif. This is one of the most common themes in Eckhart's vernacular preaching.[71] The mysticism of birthing was not new with Eckhart, but had deep roots in Christian history, having been first formulated by Origen.[72] But Eckhart brought the birth of the Word in the soul to remarkable new heights of subtlety and daring. Since the Son's birth can only take place in the *grunt,* these two aspects of Eckhart's mysticism are inseparable. Nevertheless, they are not the same. Eckhart says that the birth of the Son does not exhaust what takes place in the ground. In Pr. 48, for example, he speaks of the "uncreated light," which comprehends God without a medium, a comprehension that "is to be understood as happening when the birth takes place." But this "spark of the soul" is not only not content with creatures, but also "is not content with the Father or the Son or the Holy Spirit . . . so far as each of them persists in his properties." It is not even satisfied with "the simple divine essence in its repose." No,

> It wants to go into the simple ground, into the quiet desert, into which distinction never gazed, not the Father, nor the Son, nor the Holy Spirit.

... For this ground is a simple silence, in itself immovable, and by this immovability all things are moved, all life is received by those who in themselves have rational being.[73]

Although there are places in Eckhart's sermons that identify the *grunt* with the divine Fatherhood,[74] radical texts that speak of going into the *grunt* that lies deeper than the Trinity, beyond the birth of the Word,[75] point to one of the most difficult and dangerous aspects of his preaching, but also to what is distinctively Eckhart's own.

One of the most striking of these passages occurs in a sermon originally edited by Franz Pfeiffer (No. LVI), which, after some doubts, seems now accepted as genuinely Eckhartian.[76] In this homily the Meister uses the unusual language of "God becoming and unbecoming" (*got wirt und entwirt*). On the basis of the distinction often employed in the MHG sermons between "God" and "Godhead," Eckhart says that as long as he was "in the ground, the depths, the flood and source of the Godhead," no one asked him anything, because while God acts, the Godhead does not. The Godhead *becomes* "God" in the flowing of creation.[77] God *unbecomes* when the mystic is not content to return to the "God" who acts, but effects a "breaking through" (*durchbrechen*) to the silent unmoving Godhead, one that brings all creatures back into the hidden source through their union in the deconstructed "intellect." Eckhart says: "But when I enter the ground, the bottom, the flood and source of the Godhead, no one asks me where I come from or where I have been. There no one misses me, and there God 'unbecomes.'"[78] On the basis of texts such as these, we can say that *grunt* includes the mysticism of the divine birth, but also, at least in some sense, goes beyond it.[79]

The language found in these texts shows how the mysticism of the ground challenged traditional Christian understandings of union with God.[80] Augustine of Hippo, the father of Western mysticism, had deliberately avoided using "union" language in speaking of the modes of achieving direct consciousness of God's presence, probably because he was aware of Plotinian notions of union (*hênosis*) with God that he thought did not preserve the proper distinctions between created and uncreated being.[81] (Other ancient Christian thinkers, notably Pseudo-Dionysius, were more open to Neoplatonic union language.) The monastic tradition of Western mysticism, as set forth especially in the twelfth century by the Cistercians and Victorines, understood union with God as *unitas spiritus:* a loving union of two spirits—one created and one uncreated—in which absolute loving harmony coexisted with distinction of substances. A favorite biblical text for this was 1 Corinthians 6:17: "Qui adhaeret Domino, unus spiritus est" ("The one who cleaves to God is one spirit [with him])." Bernard of Clairvaux, the supreme mystic of the monastic tradition, was no metaphysician, but he insisted "manet quidem substantia" ("The substance [of the person] remains").[82] To the Cistercian and his contemporaries, the mysticism of the ground would have appeared dangerous, perhaps even heretical. Eckhart knew Bernard well, but he clearly had a new conception of union. For the Dominican, as well as some of the anonymous sermons and treatises written under his influence, the goal of the Christian life was union of identity or of indistinction (*unitas indistinctionis*) in which there was no difference at all between God and human: "God's ground and the soul's ground is one ground."

Eckhart was not the first mystic of the thirteenth century to say that the human person is capable of attaining indistinction with God. Language suggesting this can be found in a number of the female mystics who antedate the Dominican, such as Mechthild of Magdeburg and Hadewijch (if we think of her as writing c. 1250–60). Above all, indistinct union had been richly developed in Marguerite Porete's *Mirror of Simple Souls*.[83] Eckhart knew Porete's book,[84] but one should not think that the Dominican developed his form of *unitas indistinctionis* from the beguine. Similarly, although Eckhart and his followers made use of Neoplatonic concepts of union drawn from Christians such as Dionysius, and even from pagans such as Proclus, what was happening in Germany around 1300 was not merely a case of reviving something from the past. Neoplatonism provided helpful philosophical categories for exploring and presenting a novel understanding of union that was too widespread and popular to think of it as only a learned literary phenomenon. In the same way, new emphasis was given to biblical texts (e.g., John 17:21) as expressing a union beyond that of the distinction between Creator and creature. What emerges in Eckhart's mysticism of the ground is something new, a creation designed to express the spiritual needs of a specifically late medieval audience avid for total transformation into God.

If the "mysticism of the ground" provides a helpful way to understand the distinctiveness of Eckhart's teaching, it is also important to note that it is only within the context of observing how the preacher actually used *grunt* language that we can get some sense of its power as an explosive metaphor. *Grunt* is employed by Eckhart in a rich variety of ways, but the basic intention of the semantic field of ground-language is always geared to one goal: achieving indistinct identity of God and human in what Eckhart calls the "simple One" (*einvaltigez ein*).[85]

As Susanne Köbele reminds us, "*grunt* has . . . no other 'meaning' than the identity of the divine ground with the ground of the soul. This identity is a dynamic identity."[86] *Grunt,* therefore, should be understood not as a state or condition, but as the *activity* of grounding—the event or action of being in a fused relation.[87]

Although the mysticism of the ground centers on fused identity, the ways in which *grunt* is employed relate to many other aspects of Eckhart's mystical teaching. For example, two of the most potent symbols for expressing indistinct identity found in the Christian tradition were those of ocean and desert—the vast and empty terrains of human experience that suggest the infinity of the divine nature in which the soul may sink and vanish.[88] Eckhart was particularly drawn to the language of the desert (*einoede/wüeste/wüestunge*), using it a dozen times or more.[89] The power of the "desert" to express experiences of disorientation and terror in the face the unknown was also found in contemporary MHG secular literature.[90] Eckhart may have had such motifs in mind in employing the desert to refer to both the limitlessness of the soul and to the unfathomable expanse of the hidden divinity. Thus, the desert motif can be said to form a corollary to *grunt* as a metaphor for fused identity.[91] Although Eckhart did not make as much use of the ocean metaphor, a passage from Pr.7 ("Intellect takes God as he is known in it, but it can never encompass him in the sea of his groundlessness"),[92] shows how the two images of infinity are interchangeable.

The fused identity, or union of indistinction, that is the essential meaning of *grunt* implies so broad a range of other corollaries and themes in Eckhart that only a few can be mentioned here. For instance, many Christian mystics have insisted that God is ultimately unknowable and therefore unnameable. Hence, if the soul in its ground is absolutely one with God, it too must be as nameless and unknowable as God. As Pr. 17, one of the more detailed treatments of the soul's ground, puts it: "Whoever writes of things in motion does not deal with the nature or ground of the soul. Whoever would name the soul according to her simplicity, purity and nakedness, as she is in herself, he can find no name for her."[93] Eckhart, like John Scottus Eriugena, taught a form of negative mystical anthropology in which God and soul are ultimately one because both are radically unknowable.[94]

Identity without distinction is a paradoxical notion, and Eckhart delights in creating seeming contradictions, oxymora, and other forms of wordplay in speaking of the ground. These are present even in his earliest vernacular work, the *Talks of Instruction,* which employs ground language ten times.[95] The "groundless ground" (*gruntlôs grunt*), "groundless Godhead" (*gruntlôsen gotheit*), as well as the various uses of *abgrunt,* all provide the Dominican with the opportunity for word games that are meant to be both playful and serious insofar as they "play" a role in the practice of deconstructing the self and freeing it from all that pertains to the created world. Identity in the ground is a "wandering and "playful" identity in the sense that we are often unsure whether the language used is meant to refer to God, or to the soul, or to both—or maybe even to neither, at least insofar as we understand them. This is exactly what Eckhart had in mind. Therefore, the commentator and translator should not try to add qualifying terms like "divine" or "human" to *grunt* when Eckhart's text does not contain them. The language of the ground is meant to confuse in order to enlighten.

Although nothing "happens" in the ground, since it is beyond all movement and distinction as we know it, even the dynamic procession (*bullitio/uzbruch*) that gives rise to the Persons of the Trinity, the ground is transcendentally real as "pure possibility," to use Niklaus Largier's formulation.[96] As the unmoved source of all movement, *grunt* is the "place" from which the mystic must learn to live, act, and know. In the ground there can be no distinction between knowing and acting, or theory and practice. Nevertheless, as one's actions come forth from the ground into the world of distinction, they have to be expressed in the language proper to that world. Therefore, as Eckhart puts it in speaking of knowledge, "The more someone knows the root and the kernel and the ground of the Godhead as one, the more he knows all things."[97] In the same way, when discussing life and activity, Pr. 39 advises: "Go into your own ground and there act, and the works that you do there will all be living."[98] So too, Pr. 16b, a homily on soul as *imago dei,* concludes by telling the hearer: "You should pass through and pass over all virtues and should only take hold of virtue in the ground where it is one with the divine nature."[99] Thus, acting out of a "well-exercised ground" (*wol geübte grunt*), as Pr. 86 says of Martha in Luke 10,[100] is to live and act "without a why" (*sunder/âne warumbe*)— the core of Eckhartian ethics.

Finally, one other central aspect of *grunt* must be considered in order to grasp why the mysticism of the ground provides a good characterization of the Dominican's mysticism. This is its relationship to Christ. Eckhart insisted that the only way to the realization of our indistinct identity with God is through the action of the Word becoming man.[101] In the Incarnation the Second Person of the Trinity took (or rather is always "taking" on) human nature—not a human person—so that now all who possess human nature are absolutely one in Christ. Indeed, we are identical with Christ *insofar* as we are sons. Eckhart's functional Christology implies that the one ground in which we attain fused identity with God is rooted in the oneness of Christ's ground. This teaching is explored in Pr. 67, one of Eckhart's most difficult sermons, and one in which the word *grunt* occurs no fewer than ten times.[102]

Eckhart's theme in Sermon 67 is how God lives in the soul: first, by charity; then, by his image, through which we come to share in the life of the Trinity. The preacher says that the place of this contact "is the essential understanding of God, of which the pure and naked power is *intellectus,* which the masters term receptive" (i.e., the possible intellect). But he then turns to a higher form of union:

> Above this [the soul] grasps the pure "absolution" of free being that is there without being there, that does not give or receive. It is pure "isness" that is there divested of all being and "isness." There it takes God bare as he is in the ground, there where he is above all being. If there were still being there, the soul would take being in being; there is nothing there save one ground.[103]

Eckhart says that this state is the highest spiritual perfection that can be attained in this life, but he then goes on to speak of a higher perfection to come in heaven, one that is attainable in and through Christ as he exists in the ground. In what follows it seems as if Eckhart is talking about a union already somehow present in our oneness with Christ, but one that cannot be perfectly realized because of the unavoidable tension in this life between the "outer man" (*der ûzerster mensche*) and the "inner man" (*der inner mensche*). Considered from the point of view of the ground, however, just as humanity and divinity form "one personal being" (*éin persônlich wesen*) in Christ, losing our self-awareness allows us some access to this inner unity. "I have the same substrate (*understantnisse*) of personal being—which personal being I myself am—anytime I completely deny my self-awareness, so that in a spiritual way I am one according to the ground, as the ground itself is one ground."[104] Giving up self-awareness, of course, is nothing else than Eckhartian detachment, true poverty of spirit, and the "deconstruction" (*entbilden*) of all images and quotidian consciousness.[105]

Eckhart follows this discussion of the highest form of perfection with a dense section devoted to the relation of inner and outer man. Basically, he advises the outer man not to become enamored of what we would call "mystical experiences"—"the flowing in of grace from the personal being in many modes of sweetness, comfort, and inwardness." These are good, but they are not "the best thing," because they may cause the inner man "to be drawn out of the ground where he is one" (*herûzbiegen ûzer dem grunde in dem er ein ist*). Just as the inner man "loses his own being through his ground becoming one ground" (*entvellet sînes eigens wesens dâ er in dem grunde éin grunt ist*), the outer man must lose his own substrate and come to rely on the "Eternal Personal Being," that is, Christ. Thus, as the preacher concludes, "there are two forms of being" in Christ: the "bare substantial being" of the Godhead, and the "personal being" of the Word. But both are one "supposit" (*understôz*), that is, one subsisting individual. However—and this is Eckhart's decisive point—the same unity is realized in us insofar as we are sons and demonstrate our sonship by "following him in his works." Since we possess human nature, the same nature that the Word united to himself, by grace we are now Christ's "personal being." That means that the *grunt* as identity or fusion of God and human is nothing other than Christ's ground. Eckhart expresses this in the following convoluted way:

> So since God-Christ eternally dwells within the Father's ground and I in him, one ground and the same Christ [is] a substrate of my humanity. It is as much mine as his in the one substrate of Eternal Being, so that the double being of body and soul will be perfected in the one Christ—one God, one Son.[106]

Although this perfection may not be fully attained until after the resurrection of the body, Eckhart's closing prayer leads one to think that he believed the transformation must be begun in this life. If "God became man so that man might become God," the ancient Christian adage at the center of Eckhart's view of redemption,[107] then his teaching on the *grunt* must be seen as Christological at its core.

Grunt is a simple term, filled with spatial and tactile immediacy. Yet it is also an extraordinarily complex word that creates what Josef Quint called "a mystical word-field" (*mystiche Wortfeld*), that is, a new way of using metaphors to express in concrete fashion what cannot ultimately be said in concepts.[108] To put it another way, *grunt* is a master metaphor that is also an explosive metaphor in the sense that it breaks through old categories, inviting the hearer to perform the same breakthrough in life.

The extraordinary complexity and subtlety of Eckhart's thought continue to resist any simple summary. The constant themes of his preaching, especially the role of intellect in the birth of the Son in the soul, have long been seen as crucial for understanding the Meister's message. In recent decades new attention to such underlying metaphysical motifs as the doctrine of analogy, the dialectics of *unum* as distinct-indistinction, and the role of formal predication (e.g., the just man *insofar as* he is just), have helped us to a better grasp of the characteristics of the Dominican's teaching. Even more recently, attention to the linguistic strategies of Eckhart the preacher, such as his use of metaphor, "appellative" speech, and deconstructive techniques, have allowed us deeper insight into how in Eckhart's case the medium is indeed the message. The argument of this chapter is that the term *grunt*, at once simple and profound, provides a fulcrum or focus that allows us to relate these important aspects of Eckhart's mysticism, and many more, not into any rigid system, but into the process of passing from something into nothing, which was the goal of his preaching and teaching.

The Preacher in Action: Eckhart on the Eternal Birth

*M*EISTER ECKHART* was a noted *magister theologiae,* a profound metaphysician, and an original scriptural exegete. All these aspects of his achievement as *lesemeister,* however, were harnessed to his Dominican vocation as a *lebemeister,* that is, preacher and spiritual guide. Eckhart was no less a theologian, philosopher, and exegete in his sermons than in his Latin works, though in a different register. Hence, although students of philosophy and theology rightly investigate Eckhart's technical scholastic works, a larger public continues to read and ponder his vernacular sermons and treatises for inspiration and insight into how to live. Neither side of the Dominican's heritage can be neglected if we wish to grasp the depth of his message about the one ground of God and human. Nevertheless, it is within the very act of preaching and the ascesis of attentive listening that awareness of the divine birth taking place in the ground is attained. In order to convey how Eckhart actually presented his mystical teaching, it will be helpful to present a detailed analysis of a group of four sermons the Dominican constructed as a preaching cycle unique in his oeuvre. This will give us a sense of what linguists call the "pragmatics," or situational context, of the Meister's message.

FOUR SERMONS ON THE *ÊWIGE GEBURT*

Four sermons originally edited by Pfeiffer in 1857 (Pfeiffer I–IV) have been shown by Georg Steer to constitute a single cycle on the eternal

53

birth of the Word in the ground of the soul.[1] Eckhart planned these sermons as a systematic presentation of the essence of his mystical preaching to be given at a specially appropriate liturgical time of the year, the
Christmas season. The audience, Steer argues, was his fellow Dominicans. (Three times in the sermons he notes that they are being given "to
learned and illumined people, who have been taught and illumined by
God and scripture," contrasting them to simple laity.)[2] This interpretation seems correct, not only because the cycle takes on something of the
structure of a *collatio* for the brethren, at times utilizing a question-and-
answer format similar to that found in the *Talks of Instruction*,[3] but also
because of the proximity of some of the central motifs of the sermons
to the *Talks* and to the *Sermons and Lectures on Ecclesiasticus,* which
were given to Dominicans as *collationes* in the first years of the fourteenth century. Furthermore, the first sermon in the cycle is based on a
text from the book of Wisdom that shows affinities with Eckhart's relatively early *Commentary on Wisdom.*[4] Given these connections, it is
likely that the cycle can be dated to c. 1303–1305, that is, in the early
years of Eckhart's provincialate.

The four sermons form an extended meditation on the meaning of
Christ's birth based on key texts from the liturgy of the Christmas season. Though the birth of the Son in the soul is found almost everywhere in the Dominican's preaching, nowhere else does he make it the
subject of a sermon cycle.[5] Because the eternal birth takes place in the
fused identity of the *grunt,* these sermons also contain one of the
Dominican's most extensive explorations of the language of the ground
(the term and its derivatives appear no fewer than thirty-three times).[6]
In addition, so many other of the major themes of Eckhart's preaching
appear in this Christmas cycle that it can be described as a vernacular
summa of his mysticism.

Many of Eckhart's surviving sermons have an improvisational character, appearing as a series of virtuoso variations on oft-repeated
themes. Others are more carefully constructed around the development of one or more key images or motifs based on scriptural texts
(e.g., Pr. 71 on the four meanings of Acts 9:8, or Pr. 52 on the three
meanings of being "poor in spirit" from Matt. 5:3).[7] The cycle on the
eternal birth is more symphonic in character. It begins with a citation
of the Old Latin version of Wisdom 18:14, setting forth the three major
themes or leitmotifs of what will follow—*medium-silentium-verbum
absconditum.* Eckhart then develops and orchestrates these themes
through a series of deeper explorations and quasi-scholastic questions
and answers, finally concluding where mystical discourse so often ends,

in "peace and inward silence" (*dirre ruowe und disem inwendigen swî-genne*: Pr. 104A.579–80)—a return to the silence of the text from the liturgy that was his starting point. Throughout this mystical symphony Eckhart deliberately engages his audience in a dialogue designed to bring them to a new level of awareness (five questions and answers in Pr. 102, and six each in Prr. 103 and 104). Speaking to a restricted group of learned God-seekers, he also feels free to indulge as much as anywhere else in his surviving works in paradox, oxymoron, and hyperbole—the *rara et subtilia* that comprise the "shock-treatment" of a mystical discourse designed to awaken by challenging traditional modes of speaking and understanding. But these sermons, like many others, also make use of arresting metaphors and examples drawn from everyday life to concretize the message. As usual, Eckhart does not speak of himself or his own experience; but anyone who reads these homilies carefully cannot doubt that he speaks out of the ground.

Sermon 101 starts by citing Wisdom 18:14-15, the Introit, or opening chant, for the mass of the Sunday within the octave of Christmas. Rather than taking up the traditional motif of the three births of Christ (from the Father in eternity, from Mary in time, and in the hearts of the faithful today), a characteristic theme of Christmas preaching before and after him, Eckhart explodes the distinction of births by claiming that the eternal birth of the Word from the Father is actually "now born in time, in human nature." He argues this case, in typical fashion, on the basis of a distinctive reading of the Introit achieved by adding to it a text from Job 4:12 not found in the liturgy, and then by translating the whole in a way that sets up the three themes of his message about the birth: "When all things were in the *medium*, in *silence*, then there descended down into me from on high, from the royal throne, *a hidden Word*" (my italics).[8] To paraphrase: the silencing of the "medium," that is, anything between God and the soul, makes possible the birth of the hidden Word in the ground. Eckhart's interpretive reading of the Wisdom text already makes clear an essential characteristic of his preaching as pointed out by Joachim Theisen—salvation history (the text from Wisdom first referred to the coming down of God at the Exodus, and then typologically to Christ's birth) becomes immanentized in the eternal now through liturgical reenactment.[9]

As an aid for following the intricate architecture of the rest of the cycle, in his introduction to Pr. 101 Eckhart briefly sets forth the three issues he will discuss in his first homily before developing them in more depth in those to come. The first theme concerns "where in the soul God the Father speaks his Word, where this birth takes place, and where she is receptive of this work."[10] The second has to do with a person's conduct with regard to the birth, especially whether it is better to co-operate with God's action, or "whether one should shun and free one-self from all thoughts, words, and deeds . . . , maintaining a God-receptive attitude. . . ."[11] Finally, the third issue concerns the profit that comes to us from the birth.[12] At the end of the introduction, Eck-hart makes the same point that he does in some of the Latin works written for his Dominican students: "I shall make use of natural proofs, so that you yourselves can grasp that it is so, for though I put more faith in the scriptures than in myself, yet it is easier and better for you to learn by means of arguments that can be verified."[13] This does not mean that he will not use the Bible and theological authorities, but rather, as he later said at the beginning of the Commentary on John, he wants "[t]o explain what the holy Christian faith and the two testa-ments maintain through the help of the natural arguments of the philosophers" [In Ioh. n.2]). Indeed, as the sermon proceeds, natural reason, at least as represented by philosophers, seems to be more and more undercut, until Eckhart claims that "those who have written of the soul's nobility have gone no further than their natural intelligence could carry them; they had never entered her ground, so that much remained obscure and unknown to them."[14]

Eckhart's desire to do what is "better" for his audience is evident from the dialogical form he adopts as he begins the treatment of the first question. An imagined interlocutor asks, "But sir, where is the silence and where is the place where the Word is spoken?" The answer is given in terms of the doctrine of the ground. The birth takes place "in the purest thing that the soul is capable of, in the noblest part, the ground, indeed, in the very essence of the soul which is the soul's most secret part," its "silent middle" into which no image or form of activity from outside can enter. According to the Dominican, "This [ground] is by nature receptive to nothing save only the divine essence, without mediation. Here God enters the soul with his all, not merely with a part. Here God enters the ground of the soul." Such teaching, of course, is found in many of Eckhart's sermons, but rarely is it expressed so insistently.[15] Also customary is the discussion that follows in which Eckhart contrasts the activity of the soul's powers (memory, intellect, will), which function by means of images of things taken in from the outside through the senses, with the action of God coming into "the ground where no image ever got in, but only he himself with his own being."[16] God's "perfect insight into himself" (volkomen însehen in sich selber), effected without any image,[17] is the source of the birth of the

Son in eternity and also in the ground and essence of the soul. "In this true union lies the soul's entire beatitude."[18] Only in the silence and stillness of the ground is God free to touch the soul with his own essence and without images.

The motif of pure interiority and utter stillness provides the key for the second theme to be explored—the relation between our actions and the consummation of the divine birth.[19] Eckhart is uncompromising in insisting on the importance of utter passivity as the only possible preparation, though he does warn that this message is only for "good and perfected people" who have absorbed the essence of the virtues and follow the life and teachings of "our Lord Jesus Christ."[20]

Eckhart's extended treatment of the question of preparation in the second part of Pr. 101 raises a significant issue: what was the Dominican's attitude toward special states of consciousness, what are often called "mystical experiences" today? Here and elsewhere Eckhart sometimes uses German terms such as *geziehen* and its equivalents ("to be drawn up or out of")[21] to describe the inward withdrawal that he contends is a necessary, if not sufficient, precondition for realizing the birth of the Word in the soul's ground. He also cites two of the most noted biblical examples of such total self-forgetfulness (being "unaware of all things," *aller dinge . . . unwizzende*): Paul's ascent to the third heaven (2 Cor. 12:2),[22] and Moses' forty-day fast on Sinai (Exod. 24:18). Robert Forman has argued that Eckhart's use of *geziehen/gezücket* to indicate a state of withdrawal from all sense experience (i.e., a form of contentless pure consciousness) shows that he was not totally averse to seeing a relation between such states and the path to awareness of the *êwigen geburt.*[23] These passages from the Christmas cycle confirm that the Dominican not only recognized the existence of states of ecstatic withdrawal (he could scarcely not have, given their scriptural warrant), but he also felt that they could be useful, *if* properly understood. Indeed, he expends some effort in analyzing them in this second part of the sermon, citing authorities, both Christian (Anselm, Dionysius, Augustine) and pagan (Avicenna), on the necessity for inward emptying of the mind to achieve mystical consciousness.

Four points deserve to be mentioned to put this discussion of states of withdrawal into context. The first is that it is not at all clear that Eckhart thought that the withdrawal and passivity required for the birth always had to involve what could be technically called "rapture" (*raptus*) or "ecstasy" (*exstasis/excessus mentis*). The second is that he insists that all forms of withdrawal are God's work, not ours, however much we may strive to make ourselves ready for them. The third, as Forman himself admits, is Eckhart's unrelenting opposition to seizing on "ways" to God, even the way of rapture: there is no single "way" to God.[24] Finally, Eckhart, at least in Pr. 101, seems to be counseling some kind of permanent state of withdrawal, as evidenced by his references to Paul's three days of totally forgetting the body and Moses' forty days of absorption, which left him as strong at the end as he was at the beginning. These comments suggest that Eckhart may well be using the examples hyperbolically—that is, true rapture ought to be long-lasting, even permanent. The basic thrust of Eckhart's argument, however, is clear: the birth takes place only in an inner condition of total passivity.

In the course of investigating our conduct with regard to the birth, Eckhart finally turns to the third key term embedded in his scriptural-liturgical base text, the "hidden Word" (*verborgen wort*). The "hiddenness" of the Word introduces some characteristic reflections on negative theology. Eckhart first paraphrases texts from Dionysius about God's lack of all images and the divine "hidden silent darkness,"[25] and then frames another rhetorical question from the audience: "What does God do without images in the ground and the essence?"[26] His answer is that he has no answer, because everything we know by ordinary consciousness comes through images (*bilde*), but this is not how God is attained. Knowing God—or more precisely, *striving* to know God—is a constant pursuit of what is by definition unattainable. As he puts it:

> This not-knowing draws her into amazement and keeps her on the hunt, for she clearly recognizes "that he is," but she does not know "what" or "how" he is. When someone knows the causes of things, he tires of them and seeks something else to uncover and to know, complaining and always protesting, because knowing has no resting point. Therefore, the unknown-knowing [i.e., *docta ignorantia*] keeps the soul constant and still on the hunt.[27]

This appeal to the mystical topos of *epektasis,* that is, that the only way to gain God is by constant unfulfilled pursuit, is a close parallel to the way Eckhart develops the theme of simultaneous eating and hungering after God in the *Sermons and Lectures on Ecclesiasticus*—another argument for dating these sermons to the first years of the fourteenth century.

The reflection on *epektasis* prompts the investigation of another mystical paradox—how the Word can be both expressed and hidden. This too is a theme Eckhart touches on in other sermons.[28] His treatment here, as elsewhere, is dialectical; that is, he shows how it is of the very nature of the Divine Word to be hidden in its revelation and revealed in its hiddenness: the two sides of the coin are inseparable. In an original reading of 2 Corinthians 12, Eckhart invokes Paul as a witness to this paradox and a confirmation of the new mode of consciousness to be found in the ground. Paul was caught up into the third heaven, came to know God, and "beheld all things." Eckhart goes on, "When he returned he had forgotten nothing, but it was so deep in his ground that his intellect could not reach it; it was veiled from him. He therefore had to pursue and search for it in himself and not outside."[29] We might interpret this by saying that to come to awareness of God in the ground is a question of performance, not communication; that is, this incommunicable knowledge keeps the mystic ever on the inward path, not turned outside. Eckhart enforces the point by citing a number of corroborating authorities, pagan and Christian.[30]

As he moves toward the third and final part of the introductory sermon, Eckhart once again marks the transition by introducing an objection, this one expressing a naturalistic view of the soul: "Now, sir, you want to upset the natural course of the soul and go against her nature. Her nature is to take things in from the senses and in images. Would you upset this order?" Eckhart's response is sharp, even dismissive: "No! What do you know of the nobility God has given to the soul, which is not yet fully described; even more, still hidden!"[31] The Dominican rounds against those who have written on the soul on the basis of only "natural intelligence," citing two of his favorite Johannine texts (John 1:5 and 11–12) about the Divine Light shining in the darkness and being received only by its own. This critique of anthropological naturalism returns Eckhart once again to the main theme of the cycle, the *êwige geburt.* "The use and fruit of this secret word and darkness," as he puts it, are our being born in the same divine darkness as Christ is—"a child of the same heavenly Father." The absolute priority of the dark way to God, taught by the Bible and tradition (especially Dionysius), receives a ringing confirmation: "Though it may be called an unknowing, an uncomprehending, it still has more within it than in all knowing and comprehending outside it, for this unknowing lures and draws you from all that is known, and also from yourself."[32] Eckhart concludes the sermon by invoking Christ's teaching about abandoning all things (Matt. 10:37) as confirmation of the need for giving up all externals to retreat into the inner ground where God enters without image in absolute stillness.[33]

Eckhart was not content with laying out the essential parameters of the eternal birth, as the following sermons show. While the teaching about the birth of the Word in the hearts of the faithful had deep roots in Christian mysticism,[34] Eckhart must have realized that his form of "birthing mysticism," and especially its connection with his new teaching on the *grunt,* were unprecedented and controversial. The following three sermons of the Christmas cycle investigate the implications of this radical teaching, largely through a technique of question and answer that invites the hearer to full participation in the task of coming into the ground.

Pr. 102, delivered on the feast of the Epiphany, takes as its theme a text from the Gospel that explicitly mentions birth: "Where is he who is born King of the Jews" (*Ubi est qui natus est Rex Judaeorum?* [Matt. 2:2]). In this homily the preacher teases out some of the deeper implications of the eternal birth through a series of five questions and responses reminiscent of a scholastic *sic et non,* though transposed into a lively vernacular expression.

Once again, Eckhart begins by underlining his claim that various forms of divine birth should not be distinguished—"The eternal birth occurs in the soul precisely as it does in eternity, no more and no less, for it is one birth, and this birth occurs in the essence and ground of the soul."[35] The first question posed for a deeper understanding of this identity of births concerns how the soul is better suited for the birth than other "rational creatures" (*vernünftigen crêatûren*).[36] Eckhart's answer is that the soul, insofar as it alone is made to the natural image of God (cf. Gen. 1:26), is the only being that can be born and give birth in God. This reflects the Dominican's constant teaching about the fundamental difference between beings that possess intellect and therefore are in some sense begotten from God (*inquantum intellectus*) and other beings that are merely created. The second question asks what purpose grace or goodness have if the "work of the birth" *must* take place in the ground of the soul that is possessed by all humans.[37]

Eckhart's answer is constructed in terms of an analysis of the relation between the ground or essence of the soul and its powers. Although the birth can take place only in the ground, not in the powers, during our earthly existence the powers, when mired in sin, are capable of blocking the reception of what he calls the "light" because of "guile and darkness." The light experience that Eckhart speaks of here is not the visible light of the Eastern Christian Hesychast tradition, but is the enlightened impulse to turn away from the world that makes us "weary of all things that are not God or God's." If we possess this luminescent desire, we will continue to seek the ground within; if we do not, it is a sign that "this birth cannot coexist with the darkness of sin, even though it takes place not in the powers but in the essence and ground of the soul."[38]

The third question (Pr. 102.69–96), one that Eckhart describes as a "good one," asks why the powers of the soul should be concerned at all, since the birth takes place only in the ground. Eckhart's answer is that God intends to bring the whole soul and all her powers to himself, the "most blessed end." In the present life, however, the powers are divided, distracted, and enfeebled and must therefore be concentrated and drawn within, just as Archimedes, the mathematician, drew his attention within in so powerful a way that it cost him his life when he could not respond to the soldier who asked his name. The fourth question is also a "good one" (Pr. 102.97–125): "Wouldn't it be better that the powers not hinder God's work? Yet, says the questioner, "There is in me no manner of creaturely knowing that is not a hindrance, in the way God knows all things without hindrance, and so too the blessed in heaven."[39] Eckhart says that God and the blessed do indeed see all things in the one divine image (*bild*), but here below we have to turn from one type of knowledge to another, thus weakening and dissipating the soul. To gain the birth, the soul must be "empty, unencumbered, free" (*ledige unbekümberte vrîe* [Pr. 102.111]), containing nothing but God alone. Once again he insists on the priority of silence and unknowing: "Here he must come to a forgetting and not-knowing. There must be a stillness and a silence for the Word to make itself heard."[40] It is interesting to note at this point how "hearing" the Word has become equivalent to "bearing" the Word. In Pr. 57 Eckhart put the same insight in a more lapidary form: "The Father's speaking is his giving birth; the Son's hearing is his being born."[41]

The final question of the second sermon of the Christmas cycle explores the nature of the *unwizzen* that is needed for the birth (Pr. 102.126–65). Ignorance is a lack; how can it make humans blessed, asks the interlocutor? Eckhart answers by distinguishing mere ignorance from *learned* ignorance:

> One must here come to a transformed knowing, and this unknowing [*unwizzen*] must not come from ignorance [*unwizzenne*]; rather, from knowing one must come into an unknowing. Then, we will become knowing with divine knowing and then our unknowing will be ennobled and clothed with supernatural knowing. And here, in that we are in a [state of] receiving, we are more perfect than if we were active.[42]

By this claim Eckhart decisively distances himself from his confrere Dietrich of Freiburg, who had placed beatitude in the active intellect.[43] This leads him to an even more daring statement. Most Christian theologians (e.g., Thomas Aquinas), citing Matthew 5:8 ("Blessed are the pure of heart, for they shall *see* God"), and building on the Greek ideal of *theōria,* had placed the essence of heavenly bliss in the vision of God. Eckhart, however, says, "In eternal life we shall rejoice more in our power of hearing than in that of sight."[44] Hearing is passive, drawing the Word within, while seeing is active and therefore less perfect. Reception, passivity, suffering, or "undergoing" is the essential characteristic of the beatified soul, both here and hereafter. It is the way in which the soul comes to equal God in infinity. In a text that echoes language found in Marguerite Porete (whom Eckhart is unlikely to have known at this time) the Dominican concludes:

> For just as God is almighty in working, so too is the soul without ground [*abgründic*] in receiving, and therefore she is transformed with God and in God. God must act and the soul must receive. He must know and love himself in her. She must know with [his] knowledge and must love with his love, so that she is therefore more blessed with what is his than with what is hers; and also her blessedness is more dependent on his working than on her own.[45]

In her Letter 18 the Dutch beguine Hadewijch had also spoken of the mutual infinite abyss(es) of God and the soul, as noted in the previous chapter; but she had stressed the active character of the two participants. Eckhart, at least in this text, combines infinite divine action with infinite human passivity and reception.[46]

At the end of this sermon, which contains some of the Dominican's most powerful language about *unio mystica,* Eckhart returns to the christological text from the Gospel reading, praying to the "newborn King" to help us become children of God. As analyzed in our treatment of Pr. 67 in the previous chapter, realizing the birth of the Word in the ground is inseparable from the Incarnation of the Divine Word: the ground that we seek to attain is nothing other than the ground of Christ. For Eckhart, this is the essential message of the Christmas season and its liturgy.

The final two sermons of the cycle on the *êwige geburt* are based on texts from the Gospel for the Sunday within the Octave of the Epiphany, the account of the twelve-year-old Jesus teaching the doctors of the law in the Jerusalem temple. (Pr. 103 treats the verse, "When Jesus was twelve years old" from Luke 2:42, while Pr. 104 considers Luke 2:49: "I must be concerned with the things that belong to my Father.") As Georg Steer has noted, it is scarcely an accident that each sermon is structured around six questions, thus making a total of twelve.[47] Eckhart is suggesting that perfect wisdom is being conveyed by these twelve questions, no matter how "juvenile," or "new," they seem.

The six questions in Pr. 103 expatiate on the second and third issues governing the whole cycle: What kind of preparation is needed for the eternal birth? And what is its profit? The Gospel story begins with an image to drive home Eckhart's teaching about how to attain the birth. Just as Joseph and Mary had to leave the crowd and return to their point of origin (*ursprunc*), that is, the temple, in order to find Jesus, "if you would find this noble birth, you must leave the crowd [i.e., the external powers of the soul] and return to the origin and ground whence you came."[48] The first question in the homily (Pr. 103.15-38) asks whether a person can find the birth through divine things brought in from outside, that is, conceptions of God as good, wise, and so on. Eckhart's answer is no—everything must well up from within, from God's own activity, while we remain totally passive and receptive. The "natural light" of the intellect avails nothing; it must become "pure nothing" (*lûtern niht*) and go out of itself so that God can bring in a "new form" (*niuwe forme*) that will contain all that has been left behind "and a thousand times more."

The paradoxicality of this "pure unknowing and forgetting of self and all creatures" is taken up in the second question (Pf. 103.39–75), which is in the form of a dialogue between Eckhart and an insistent questioner who finds such "unknowing knowledge" (*unbekantez bekantnisse*) and "darkness" (*dünsternisse*) hard to fathom. Eckhart strives to help him by giving it a name—"Its name is nothing else but potential receptivity (*mügelich enpfenclicheit*), which certainly does not lack being nor is it deficient; rather, it is only in potential receptivity in which you will be perfected."[49] This odd term is Eckhart's invention to describe the nature of the ground of the soul in the language of the schools taken over into the vernacular. Again, he emphasizes the necessity for the constant pursuit of inward receptive stillness, which, paradoxically, is also described as a form of intellect (*vernunft*) that never rests in its swift motion until it has reached "the supreme height" (*daz aller hoehste*) of God.

In order to follow this potentiality to its goal and gain "Him who is all things," one must become empty and bare as the desert.[50] "The true Word of eternity is spoken only in oneness, where a man is a desert and alien to himself and multiplicity."[51] (As pointed out in chapter 3, Eckhart often uses desert language as a way of expressing the ground.) More rare, though akin to language found in Mechthild of Magdeburg, is the description here of this inner self-naughting as "rejection, desolation, and estrangement from all creatures."[52] Although Eckhart made detachment, or the cutting-free from all creatures and oneself, a central part of preaching, he seldom sounds the note of tortured estrangement and utter desolation found in many of the women mystics and in his disciple John Tauler.[53] In answering this second question the Dominican brings together a range of motifs, images, and scriptural texts of great richness for understanding his thought.

The third question (Pr. 103.76–106) takes off from the estrangement of the desert, wondering whether, if the "exile is prolonged" (Ps. 120:5) by God giving no light or help, it would not be better to pray, or read, or listen to sermons, or perform some virtuous work in order to drive away the darkness and alienation. Again, Eckhart responds with an emphatic verbal marker: "No, this you should know in the truth . . . This is true" (Pr. 103.83–85). Complete stillness and emptiness is always the best state for receiving God's action. We must not think of preparation for the birth as something wherein we cooperate with God. We do not "operate" in any way. Picking up on a theme that occurs often in his preaching, Eckhart notes that God must act and pour himself into us *when we are ready,* that is, when we are totally empty of self and creatures. God does not work like a human carpenter, now and then, or when he wants to. No, God's very nature compels him to "pour great goodness into you whenever he finds you so empty and so bare."[54]

The fourth and fifth questions are relatively brief considerations of the nature of mystical consciousness. The first query asks whether one can become aware of God's presence in some sensible way (Pr. 103.107–20); the second whether it is at least possible to have some sign to recognize that it has taken place, even if we don't feel it (Pr. 103.121–40). Eckhart's answer to the first question is that it is all up to God: "Your being aware of him is not in your power but in his. When it suits him he shows himself, and he can hide when he wishes."[55] So Eckhart does not deny the possibility of some form of consciousness of the birth of the Word in the soul, but he clearly does not think that it is necessary or all that important. It is more vital to consider the *signs* of the birth. The Dominican says that there are three of these, but he will mention only one here, a motif that he repeats a number of times in his sermons. In ordinary life we are hindered or held back by the three conditions of our estrangement from God—time, multiplicity, and matter.[56] But, Eckhart says:

> Once the birth has really occurred, no creatures can hinder you; instead, they will all direct you to God and this birth. . . . Yes, all things become simply God to you, for in all things you notice and love only God, just as a man who stares long at the sun in heaven sees the sun in whatever he afterward looks at.[57]

Finally, the sixth question (Pr. 103.141–77) returns to issues of practical spirituality, in this case penitential exercises (*pênitencienleben*). Do we lose anything by dropping these? Eckhart is on dangerous ground here, as we know from his trial some quarter-century later. His answer is framed with care. Penitential exercises were created because of the opposition between spirit and flesh in a fallen world. The spirit is a "foreigner" (*ellende*) here, and so the body needs to be curbed by penance so that the spirit can learn to resist it. But the "bridle of love" (*zoum der minne*) is a thousand times stronger. "With love you overcome [the body] most surely, with love you load it down most heavily. Therefore, God lies in wait for us with nothing so much as with love."[58] Eckhart closes the sermon with an extended analogy on love as the fishhook that binds us most securely and yet most freely to God—"Therefore, just watch for this hook, so as to be blessedly caught: for the more you are caught the more you are free"—another of the Dominican's dialectical paradoxes.[59]

In the final sermon of the Christmas cycle on the *êwige geburt* Meister Eckhart further probes both the theoretical and the practical aspects of the Word's birth in the ground of the soul. Josef Quint expressed doubts about the authenticity of this long sermon, but Georg Steer, on the basis of new manuscript evidence, convincingly argues that it is really by Eckhart.[60] Indeed, the homily's teaching can be seen as forming a corroboration and completion of a number of the themes treated in the previous three homilies. Jesus' answer to his worried parents from Luke 2:49, "I must be concerned with the things that belong to my Father," is immediately referred to "the eternal birth that now [i.e., in the infancy narrative] happened in time, and yet is daily born in the soul's innermost, and in her ground, apart from every accident [of time]."[61]

Throughout the six quasi-scholastic *quaestiones* that constitute Pr. 104, Eckhart is concerned with helping his questioner (obviously a theologically well-informed Dominican student) to grasp the import of the paradoxes implied in the eternal birth. His answers are both solutions to problems and deepenings of the essential mystery through the mystical therapy of *docta ignorantia*. He sets up the strategy of paradox with a brief introduction identifying "power" (*gewalt*) as the Father's attribute or "concern." Eckhart says that although the birth can only take place by a withdrawing of the senses to a state of inner passivity, this "requires a mighty effort to drive back the powers of the soul and inhibit their functioning."[62] How is this combining of total passivity and mighty effort to be understood?

The first question (Pr. 104A.31–130) has to do with whether or not the birth happens continuously or only at intervals when great effort is being made. Eckhart's answer comes in the form of a consideration of the relation of the soul's power of intellect to the eternal birth.[63] Eckhart begins by distinguishing three modes of intellect—active intellect (*würkende vernunft*), passive intellect (*lîdende vernunft*), and what he calls potential intellect (*mügelîche vernunft*).[64] The active intellect exerts itself rationally in creatures, striving to bring them back to God. But when God acts the spirit must be passive, that is, as Pr. 102 already said, the passive intellect comes into play. Now Eckhart introduces potential intellect as a preparatory power, readying the soul for its encounter with God:

> But the potential intellect pays regards to both, to the activity of God and the passivity of the soul, so that this may be achieved as far as possible. . . . Now before this is begun by the spirit and completed by God [that is, the divine action on the passive intellect], the spirit has prevision of it, a potential knowledge that it can come to be thus, this is the meaning of the potential intellect, though often it misses the goal and never comes to fruition.[65]

What Eckhart seems to be trying to describe here is a form of what scholastics would call an "obediential potency" to the divine activity, one that is also the place or power where ecstatic experiences are found, as a kind of "spillover" from the divine birth in the ground. Rather cryptically, he continues: "When the spirit strives with all its might and with real sincerity [presumably in the *vermügende vernunft*], then God's Spirit takes charge of the spirit and its work, and then the spirit sees and experiences [*lîdet*] God."[66] In conformity with traditional teaching on ecstasy or rapture, Eckhart says that such seeing and "undergoing" cannot be lengthy because of the strain it puts on the body. He illustrates this by discussing two noted biblical examples of such experiences—that of the three apostles at Christ's transfiguration (Matt. 17:1–8 and parallels) and Paul's vision of God on the road to Damascus (Acts 9:1–9). Echoing language he used in Pr. 103, Eckhart says that God alone decides when to reveal or conceal himself according to what best suits us—"For God is not a destroyer of nature; rather, he perfects it."[67]

This first question of Pr. 104 contains one of Eckhart's most sustained, if not always clear, discussions of ecstatic consciousness. Three points may be helpful for understanding this teaching. The first is that Eckhart recognizes the divine pedagogy of making use of these experiences for the profit of souls intent on true inwardness. The second is that the Dominican does not consider them essential, and he insists that they take place in the powers of the soul, not in the ground where the birth is realized. Finally, if the Christmas sermon cycle is as early as I surmise, then the fact that Eckhart later dropped the triple distinction of intellect used here to explain ecstasy may suggest a growing suspicion of the usefulness of such states.

The second question addressed to Eckhart (Pr. 104A.131-209) concerns the seeming contradiction between the Dominican's insistence on keeping "the mind (*gemüete*) free of all the images and works" that are found in the powers of the soul and the Christian obligation to perform outward works of charity. Eckhart's answer is that the contradiction is only apparent. He cites "Master Thomas," who, although he upheld the traditional superiority of the contemplative life over the active, also said that "the active life is better than the contemplative *insofar as* in action one pours out for love that which one has gained in contemplation."[68] Here Eckhart is arguing for a living union between action and contemplation, an issue he was to return to in his later Pr. 86 on Mary and Martha.[69] If loving action comes from "the ground of contemplation" (*grunde der schouwunge*), it is all one. "Thus too, in this activity," says Eckhart, "we remain in a state of contemplation in God. The one rests in the other, and perfects the other."[70] Eckhart affirms that this is the meaning of the whole life of Christ and his saints, citing a variety of scriptural texts on the necessity for fruitful activity and on outward preaching of the Word hidden within the soul (e.g., 2 Tim. 4:2).[71]

The following three questions addressed to Eckhart take up various contradictions that seem to flow from his teaching about the birth. The first (Pr. 104A.210–85) involves the conflict between the images necessary for performing any good action, internal or external, and the silence and quiet Eckhart counsels as necessary for the birth. His answer once again returns to the relation between the active and the passive intellect. The active intellect is directed to understanding the images of natural things and imprinting them in the passive intellect. In the birth, God replaces the active intellect: "What the active intellect does for the natural man, that and far more God does for one in detachment: He takes away the active intellect from him and, installing himself in its stead, he himself undertakes all that the active intellect ought to be doing."[72] This new mode of supernatural operation removes all conflict between images and quiet silence. When God acts in the place of the agent intellect, "he engenders many images together in one point" (*sô gebirt er manigiu bilde miteinander in einem puncten*).

Although Eckhart does not say it expressly, we may surmise that this is another of the signs that the birth is being realized in the essence of the soul. Citing Paul ("I can do all things in him who strengthens me" [Phil. 4:13]), he argues that the concentration of all possible good works in "a flash concentrated in a single point" (*in einem blicke und in einem puncten*) is evidence that the images are not ours but God's. Born in the eternal now, they do not conflict with the silence and rest of the birth.

The fourth question (Pr. 104A.285-354) raises another problem concerning the intellect and the birth of the Word in the ground. In ordinary knowing the powers of memory, intellect, and will always seek support by fastening on their object. So when natural activity is taken away, where is their support? Eckhart's response concentrates on the nature of intellect's activity. He begins by admitting that intellect always wants to penetrate into the ground, or essence, of what it seeks to know before it can "rest" by declaring the truth of what is. But even in natural knowing, the intellect often spends a long time, "a year or more," pursuing some natural truth. This is *a fortiori* true in relation to God. "Therefore," he says, "the intellect never rests in this life. . . . However much God may reveal himself in this life, yet it is still as nothing to what he really is. Though truth is there, in the ground, it is yet veiled and concealed from the intellect."[73] So, the questioner has mistaken the true nature of intellect: it is more itself in what it seeks than in what it finds. The constant pursuit, or *epektasis,* of the "God who withdraws himself step by step" (*ziuhet ir got vürbaz und vürbaz*) in order to lure the soul on "to grasp the true groundless Good" (*ze begrîfenne daz gewâre gruntlôse guot*) is an essential concomitant of the birthing process.

The last of these three queries about the role of the faculties notes the seeming contradiction between the "great clamor of yearning" implied in this constant pursuit of the hidden God and the "perfect peace and absolute stillness" of the birth (*dum medium silentium*). Eckhart's answer is to direct his interlocutor's attention to God rather than to self. If *you* (Eckhart insists on the personal address throughout) have truly emptied yourself of all things in total abandonment, then "whatever is born in or touches you . . . is no longer yours, it is altogether your God's."[74] Here the Dominican appeals to an example he frequently uses elsewhere—that of the light which is essentially in the sun and only formally in the air that it passes through. "It is the same with the soul," he continues. "God bears his Son and his Word in the soul and the soul conceives it and passes it on to the powers in many ways—as desire, as good intention, as work of love, as thanksgiving, or however it concerns you. It is all his and not at all yours."[75] He closes this question by invoking another of the major themes of the Christmas cycle: total self-abnegation and becoming a desert. We should be the "voice crying in the desert" (Matt. 3:3)—"a desert of yourself and of all things" (*habe dû dich dir selber und aller dinge wüeste*).

Finally, in the sixth question (Pr. 104A.426–585), Eckhart once again returns to the nagging issue of what role pious practices play in preparing for the eternal birth. Given how often he has to explain this, we can imagine that it reflects real problems that his charges had in understanding his teaching. Becoming a desert seems to mean that one should not perform any external work of piety, but Eckhart once again tries to clarify in what sense this is true on the basis of distinguishing, as he often did, between the outer and the inner person.[76] "All outer works" (*alliu ûzwendigiu werk*) were created to curb the outer man's inclination to distraction and sin and leave him ready for divine action. So, Eckhart counsels, whenever anyone realizes that "God's spirit is not working in him" (*daz der geist gotes in im niht enwürket*), he or she should take up these practices, though "not from selfish attachment" (*und niht in keiner eigenschaft im selber*), that is, without any sense that these practices give us a claim upon God.

In what follows, though, Eckhart once again shows the daring that was eventually to prove his undoing—his appeal to radical inwardness and personal conviction: "If someone knows himself to be well trained in true inwardness, then let him drop all outward disciplines, even those he is bound to and from which neither pope nor bishop can release him." This bold statement is followed by a somewhat niggling discussion about the different kinds of vows (though perhaps one of importance for his audience vowed to the religious life). It is significant, given the Meister's later involvement with the *cura monialium*, to note that he deliberately says that his consoling message about the force of vows is intended for nuns as well as for monks (Pr. 104A.500–506).

Finally, as Eckhart approaches the end of this sermon treatise on the *êwige geburt*, he once more notes the significance of the audience he has in mind, repeating that what he has had to say was meant for clerics, that is, "learned and illuminated folk." This audience, as well as the at times scholastic character of the question-and-answer format used in these sermons, gives the cycle a somewhat more elitist flavor than much of Eckhart's later preaching. But even at this early stage he does not forget the "simple laity" (*lûtern eien*) who understand only corporal discipline. Eckhart extends to them the same privilege about freedom from vows made before a priest (as contrasted with vows made to God)—Do whatever work brings you nearer to God's love, he tells them.

This discussion of vows leads into a concluding paragraph that does not distinguish between clergy and laity in relation to the birth of the Word. Citing Paul once again ("The letter [outward practices] kills, but the spirit gives life" [2 Cor. 3:6]), Eckhart summarizes his sermon-treatise with a universal appeal: "Your spirit should be elevated, not downcast, but rather ardent, and yet in a detached, quiet stillness."[77] With this recommendation for what to ordinary logic can only seem like yet another mystical paradox (ardent detachment?), Eckhart closes this unique example of a sermon-cycle, as he often later did, with a prayer to the Trinity:

> That we may here so seek this peace and inward silence, that the eternal Word may be spoken within us and understood, and that we may become one therewith, may the Father help us, and that Word, and the Spirit of both. Amen.[78]

CHAPTER 5

The Metaphysics of Flow

*T*RYING TO FORCE A MYSTIC as creative as Eckhart into a rigid system of thought is a self-defeating project that can only blunt the depth and challenge of his message. Nevertheless, Eckhart was trained in the thought patterns of high scholasticism and, at least in his projected *Work of Propositions,* had once intended to create a form of systematics. Even though both his surviving Latin works (primarily exegetical) and his vernacular sermons and treatises eschew system in favor of a moving (and often seemingly circular) presentation of the search for the fused *grunt* of God and human, Eckhart created these experiments in the hermeneutics of conversion on the basis of a distinctive metaphysical-theological perspective. So, while there is no substitute for following the Meister's ever-shifting mystical teaching across the range of his teaching and preaching, the discipline of reading Eckhart as *lebemeister* is much enriched by trying to grasp Eckhart the *lesemeister,* that is, by coming to grips with the overall perspective, the theological skeleton, so to speak, on which he hung the fabric of his mystical teaching.

A good way to understand Eckhart's implied systematics is through the dynamic reciprocity of the "flowing-forth" (*exitus-emanatio/ûzganc-uzfliessen*) of all things from the hidden ground of God, and the "flowing-back," or "breaking-through" (*reditus-restoratio/inganc-durchbrechen*), of the universe into essential identity with this divine source. From this perspective, Eckhart's metaphysics is aptly described as a "metaphysics of flow" (i.e., *fluxus*).[1] Gerard Manley Hopkins expressed this vision of reality in brief poetic form:

> Thee God, I come from, to thee go;
> All day long I like fountain flow
> From thy hand out, swayed about,
> Mote-like in thy mighty glow.[2]

Eckhart put it even more briefly: "I have often said, God's going-out is his going-in" (*Ich han ez ouch mê gesprochen: gotes ûzganc ist sîn inganc*).[3]

The process of *exitus-reditus* is often identified with the influence of Neoplatonism in Western thought.[4] To be sure, Neoplatonic thinkers, pagan and Christian, were among its most articulate and penetrating investigators. Nevertheless, Eckhart conceived of *exitus-reditus* as the fundamental law of reality taught by the Bible, both *in toto*, as found in the scriptural presentation of creation and consummation, and in individual verses (e.g., Eccli. 1:7: . . . *ad locum unde exeunt flumina, revertuntur, ut iterum fluant*—"The rivers return to the place from whence they flowed, so that they may flow again").[5] The Dominican employed a wide variety of Latin and German terms, as suggested above, to express this "bursting-forth" and "breaking-through." He even at times used emanation and return to structure summaries of his message, such as that found in the vernacular sequence known as the "Granum sinapis."[6] Beyond these explicit appearances, however, the pulse of this universal circle of activity provides a key for presenting the systematic perspective behind Eckhart's disparate works.

BULLITIO-EBULLITIO

A passage from one of Eckhart's Latin sermons discussing the nature of "image" (*imago/bilde*) provides a helpful entry into how the Dominican conceived of *exitus*. Here Eckhart says:

> . . . an image properly speaking is a simple formal emanation that transmits the whole pure naked essence, . . . an emanation from the depths of silence, excluding everything that comes from without. It is a form of life, as if you were to imagine something swelling up from itself and in itself and then inwardly boiling without any boiling over yet understood.

On this basis, he distinguishes three stages of productive *exitus*. The first is "inner boiling" (*bullitio*), the formal emanation that produces a "pure nature" within, one that is equal to its source, "in the way the Good diffuses itself." "The second stage," Eckhart says, "is like the boiling over (*ebullitio*) in the manner of an efficient cause and with a view toward an end [i.e., a final cause], by which something produces something else that is from itself, but not out of itself."[7] Eckhart notes that *ebullitio* is accomplished in two ways: "This production is either out of some other thing (and then it is called 'making' [*factio*]), or it is out of nothing (and then it is the third stage of production which is called 'creating' [*creatio*])."[8]

A number of other texts in the Latin works show how central emanation understood as comprising both *bullitio* and *ebullitio* is to Eckhart.[9] In his exegesis of the divine self-designation, "I am who am," of Exodus 3:14, Eckhart notes that the repetition found in this phrase,

> . . . indicates the purity of affirmation excluding all negation from God. It also indicates the reflexive turning back of his existence into itself and upon itself and its dwelling and remaining fixed in itself.[10] It further indicates a "boiling" or giving birth to itself—glowing into itself, and melting and boiling in and into itself, light that totally forces its whole being in light and into light and that is everywhere turned back and reflected upon itself.[11]

Eckhart goes on to identify this inner emanation not only with light (a favorite metaphor) but also with the "life" of "In him was life" (John 1:4). Thus, God's inner *bullitio/vita* is the source and exemplar of the "boiling over" that is creation—the emanation of divine Persons in the Trinity is the "prior ground" (*ratio est et praevia*) of everything that exists.

Eckhart also refers to boiling and boiling over in S. XXV, a discussion of grace understood as every gift from God. Putting forth his own understanding of the traditional scholastic distinction between "grace freely given" (*gratia gratis data*) and "saving grace" (*gratia gratum faciens*), he identifies the first with the gift of created being that all creatures receive from the overflowing goodness of the divine essence. "The second grace," he says, "comes from God as he is understood according to the property of 'personal notion,' and can be received only by intellective creatures." The two forms are rooted in the difference between *bullitio* and *ebullitio*: "God as good is the principle of the 'boiling over' on the outside; as personal notion he is the principle of the 'boiling within himself,' which is the cause and exemplar of the boiling over." Eckhart then underlines the implication of the *bullitio-ebullitio* dynamic for our return to God. "The first grace," he says, "consists in a type of flowing out, a departure from God; the second consists in a type of flowing back, a return to God himself."[12] In other words, although our *exitus* comes about through God's creative "boiling over" *outside* the divine nature, our *reditus,* or deification, takes place through the action of a grace that is rooted in the trinitarian "boiling" itself. Only by sharing in the inner activity of the three divine Persons can we attain our goal.

The form that this teaching takes in the German sermons is closer to an alternative Latin presentation of the same dynamic found in the *Commentary on John,* one that uses the language of two *fontes* in relation to the transcendental predicates of *unum* and *bonum:* "The One is the primal fountain of the first emanation, namely of the Son and the Holy Spirit from the Father by way of eternal procession. The Good is the source of the second, as we may say, the temporal production of creatures."[13] Eckhart appears to be referring to this "fontal" mode of presenting *bullitio* and *ebullitio* in Pr. 38: "I have spoken at times of two fountains. . . . The one fountain, from which grace wells up, is where the Father bears forth (*ûzgebirt*) his only-begotten Son. . . . The other fountain is where creatures flow out from God."[14] The Dominican at times uses the expressive word "break-out" (*ûzbruch*) for *bullitio:* "The first break-out and the first melting-forth is where God liquifies and where he melts into his Son and where the Son melts back into the Father."[15] Wherever in the German works we find the language of "breaking out," or its equivalents, we should bear in mind Eckhart's teaching on *bullitio* and the two forms of *ebullitio* (i.e., creating and making).[16]

Eckhart's *bullitio-ebullitio* dynamic reflects previous Dominican thought, but expands upon it.[17] The "metaphysics of flow" originated with Albert the Great, who used the term *ebullitio* to express how the Simple First Mover flows forth into all things.[18] Dietrich of Freiberg used *ebullitio* for the causative action of the separated intelligences and employed *ebullitio/combullitio* to describe the outward-inward exchange of energy (*transfusio*) in material bodies.[19] *Ebullitio* is also found in the fourteenth-century Dominican Berthold of Moosburg's *Commentary on Proclus's Theological Elements.*[20] Non-German thirteenth-century authors also used "boiling" and "boiling over." Thomas Aquinas, paraphrasing a passage in Dionysius's *Celestial Hierarchy* book 7, spoke of how love creates ecstasy, "because it burns, it boils over, and exhales outside itself."[21] Marguerite Porete, in her *Mirror of Simple Souls,* described the "boiling of love" by which the souls who have died the "death of the spirit" are perfectly united to God and receive "the flower of the love of the Godhead."[22] But none of these authors developed the all-important relation between trinitarian divine *bullitio* and creative *ebullitio. Bullitio-ebullitio* can be described as Eckhart's new "explosive metaphor" for presenting the metaphysics of flow.

PRINCIPIUM/TRINITAS

The potentiality for the "formal emanation" in the Trinity is, of course, nothing else than what the MHG sermons call the *grunt;* but the active source, or origin, of emanative "boiling" is what in the Latin writings is mostly referred to as *principium.*[23] The relation between *principium* and *bullitio* is made clear in an important passage from the *Commentary on John,* where Eckhart says:

> The One acts as a principle (*principiat*) through itself and gives existence and is an internal principle (*principium*). For this reason, properly speaking, it does not produce something like itself, but what is one and the same as itself.... This is why the formal emanation in the divine Persons is a type of "boiling," and thus the three Persons are simply and absolutely one.[24]

Eckhart was doubtless drawn to *principium* as an essential term for understanding emanation because of its role in two of the most important texts in the Bible—Genesis 1:1: *In principio creavit Deus caelum et terram;* and John 1:1: *In principio erat Verbum. Principium* is particularly helpful because it implies both "beginning" in the sense of duration and "origin" and "order" in the context of the metaphysics of flow.[25]

Principium first of all refers to the Father as the origin and source of the Son and Holy Spirit, the other two divine Persons. In a passage discussing seven reasons for the sending of the Holy Spirit (John 16:7), Eckhart summarizes his teaching on the two processions in trinitarian emanation, the act of generating (*generare*) by which the Father produces the Son and the "breathing" (*spirare*) by which Father and Son give rise to the Holy Spirit. The Son is able to act as a *principium* only through his dependence on the Father:

> The Son is the "Principle from the Principle," the Father is the "Principle without Principle." Therefore, it is necessary that the Son draw near the Father who is the source of the entire deity so that he can receive the power to flow, according to Ecclesiastes 1: "The rivers return to whence they flow, so that they may flow forth again" (Eccl. 1:7).[26]

The Father's fontality in the Trinity is one of the dominant themes of Eckhart's trinitarianism, discussed at length in his commentary on John 14:8—"Lord, show us the Father and it is enough for us."[27]

Principium also names the triune God as the source of *ebullitio*. Eckhart's two commentaries on Genesis are rich sources for investigating this aspect of his understanding of the metaphysics of flow. The first, or literal, *Commentary on Genesis* presents three understandings of *in principio*.[28] "Principle" first of all means "ideal reason," that is, the *Logos*, Reason, or Son, as "the Image or Ideal Reason" within God in which the essences of all things are precontained in a higher, or virtual way (according to Eckhart, this is also the meaning of John 1:1). Second, "principle" means intellect, indicating that God creates not from necessity of nature, as Avicenna and others held, but from his own act of understanding and free will.[29] Eckhart's third interpretation of the *principium* of Genesis highlights the duration aspect, one of the foremost points of criticism of his doctrine of *exitus*. Because *bullitio* and *ebullitio* have only one source, their duration must be one of simultaneity. *Principium*, says the Dominican, "is the very same now in which God exists from eternity, in which also the emanation of the divine Persons eternally is, was, and will be." Thus, "In the one and the same time in which he was God and in which he begot his coeternal Son as God equal to himself in all things, he also created the world."[30] Eckhart finds a scriptural warrant for this in a favorite psalm text: "God has spoken once and for all and I have heard two things" (Ps. 61:12). The two things are the two forms of *exitus*—"the emanation of the Persons and the creation of the world."[31] Although Thomas Aquinas, for example, was willing to say that the processions of Persons in the Trinity are the ideal reasons (*rationes*) for the production of creatures,[32] he did not claim that the universe, in its deepest reality, is eternal, nor did he think that all production has a trinitarian structure, as Eckhart did. This linking of *bullitio* and *ebullitio* led to the condemnation in the bull "In agro dominico" of three passages concerning the eternity of creation, two of them taken from this comment on the *in principio* of Genesis 1:1.[33]

Augustine, Aquinas, and others had found a "vestige" of the Trinity in all created things.[34] Eckhart's view of the single source and coeternity of both forms of "flowing forth" from the Principle meant that for him all activity is essentially trinitarian in its dynamism. If *ebullitio* has its root in the *bullitio* by which the Father gives birth to the Son and the two Persons emanate the Love that is the Holy Spirit, then *creatio* and even all *factio*, or making, express the same trinitarian mode of action. This is the foundation for Eckhart's a priori view of the Trinity, that is, that God as Trinity is a truth known not only by faith but also accessible through metaphysical analysis of the forms of *productio*.[35] This is also evident in Eckhart's understanding of Romans 11:36 ("All things are from him, and through him, and in him"). Traditionally, this verse had been understood to refer to the one God as the source of all things; but Eckhart, especially in S. IV, took these three forms of relationship as not only appropriated, but as proper to the three Persons—"from him" referring to the Father, "through him" to the Son, and "in him" to the Holy Spirit.[36]

Given Eckhart's conviction that the Trinity is a "rational" truth that can be demonstrated by a priori arguments, his trinitarianism is a fascinating example of what Werner Beierwaltes has termed the "serious game" of the dialogue between philosophy and theology that formed classical Christian speculation on God as three-in-one.[37] In his *Commentary on Wisdom* Eckhart summarizes his position as follows: "Every action of nature, morality, and art in its wholeness possesses three things—something generating, something generated, and the love of what generates for what is generated and vice versa."[38] Every natural activity, therefore, has some kind of image of the Trinity. What is distinctive of human nature is precisely the human ability to think and to make (*factio*), and to know that it thinks and makes. This conscious appropriation of the inner divine processions of Word and of Love makes human nature *imago dei* (Gen. 1:26) in the full and proper sense of image understood as formal emanation (more on this below).

Eckhart spells out his understanding of *principium* in even more detail in the *Book of the Parables of Genesis*,[39] and especially in his lengthy remarks on the second biblical *in principio* text, John 1:1.[40] The Dominican begins his treatment of the Prologue text by emphasizing how *In principio erat Verbum* reveals the necessary precontainment, or virtual existence, of all production in a prior reality: ". . . what is produced or proceeds from anything is precontained in it. This is universally and naturally true, both in the Godhead (the topic here) and in natural and artificial things" (n.4). Insofar as a carpenter, for example, makes a material chest or other piece of furniture, we have an example of efficient causality in which there is an analogical relation of superiority and inferiority between maker and made. But, insofar as "a chest in the maker's mind [i.e., *in principio*] is not a chest, but is the life and understanding of the maker, his living conception," we are dealing with univocal formal causality, that is, the inner production of something fully equal to the source. Eckhart concludes, "On this account I would say that what it says here about the procession of the divine Persons holds true and is found in the procession of every being of nature and art."[41] (Although Eckhart does not use the Bonaventurean term *reduc-*

tio, his position is similar to that of the Seraphic Doctor in "leading back" [*reduci*] all activity to its transcendental ground in the Trinity.)[42]

In analyzing the nature of principial activity within God, Eckhart says that God's Word is in the Father as "seed," as disclosing word or "expression," and as "idea and likeness." He then proceeds to explore the implications of these forms of preexistence in eleven more points (nn.5–12), before turning to how "the ideas and properties of natural beings," specifically an extended treatment of "the just person insofar as he is just," can be used to illustrate the inner relation of Unbegotten Justice (i.e., the Father), Begotten Justice (i.e., the Son), and the just human person (nn.13–22). The relationship is analyzed as involving that of an image to its exemplar (nn.23–27), and of an idea or *logos* as the formal principle to what depends on it (nn.28–37).[43] Finally, Eckhart summarizes the four "natural conditions of any essential principle," whether *in divinis* or *in naturalibus:* (1) it precontains its effect; (2) in a higher way; (3) it is always pure intellect; and (4) "in and with the principle and by its power the effect is equal in duration to the principle" (n.38 [LW 3:32]). Thus, "what the effect has in a formal way, . . . the Idea [i.e., principle] has . . . virtually" [i.e., in its power to produce]. This brings Eckhart back to his insistence on the eternal existence of all things in the divine Principle: "It is noteworthy that 'before the foundation of the world' [John 17:24] everything in the universe was not mere nothing, but was in possession of virtual existence."[44]

Eckhart returns again and again to the exploration of *principium* and the other key terms of his metaphysics of flow, especially *imago, idea, ratio.*[45] These treatments, however, do not really add anything new to what the commentary on John's Prologue explores in such detail. In the German sermons and treatises Eckhart is more concerned with discussing the nature of "image" (*bild*) as a way to understand formal emanation. Nevertheless, there are a number of passages dealing with the MHG term *begin* (which, like *principium,* can be translated either as "beginning" or "principle"), showing that Eckhart's principial perspective is no less present in the German than in the Latin works. For example, Pr. 22 contains a mini-exegesis of John 1:1 in which Eckhart first applies the verse to the Son's birth from the Father and then to all those who are born of God: "*In principio.* Here we are given to understand that we are an only son whom the Father has borne out of the concealed darkness of the eternal concealment, remaining within in the first beginning of the first purity, which is the plenitude of all purity."[46] An important discussion of the Trinity in the *Book of Divine Consola-*

tion also shows how Eckhart was able to employ the language of *principium/begin* as powerfully, if less frequently, in the vernacular as he did in his technical Latin writings.[47]

The theme of inner "boiling" from the ground understood as *principium* is at the core of Eckhart's doctrine of the Trinity, which is one of the most controversial of the later Middle Ages.[48] Like the teaching of William of St. Thierry in the twelfth century and that of Bonaventure in the mid-thirteenth, Eckhart's mystical teaching is nothing if not trinitarian, but precisely how he understands the Trinity and how the triune God functions in the wider context of his message about attaining indistinct union with God are issues that defy simple answers. As noted above in our discussion of the mysticism of the *grunt*, Eckhart's view of union challenged traditional understandings of the limits of uniting with God, and his discussions of how we become one with Father, Son, and Holy Spirit are also controversial. Specifically, Eckhart's mysticism seems to be both trinitarian and supratrinitarian in the way in which some of his sermons, at least, challenge the ultimacy of the Christian Trinity by inviting the believer into the "God beyond God," that is, "into the simple ground, into the silent desert, into which distinction never gazed, not the Father, nor the Son, nor the Holy Spirit" (Pr. 48).[49] One may wonder if Eckhart's teaching on the unity of *bullitio* and *ebullitio*, by making God's trinitarian life the inner reality of every mode of production, led to a reaction that heightened the need for an independent realm for God, beyond even that of traditional apophatic theology, in which "God could be nothing but God." Pondering the implications of this question introduces us to some of the most difficult areas in Eckhart's thought. In order to see how hard it is to find an easy answer, we must analyze in further detail what Eckhart has to say about God as Trinity.

Meister Eckhart's teaching on the Trinity is found throughout his works, but a few Latin discussions, such as the three mini-treatises on the Trinity in the John commentary, and S. IV,[50] provide helpful summaries of the doctrine employed throughout the German sermons and vernacular treatises.[51] These texts demonstrate the Dominican's mastery of the technical language of scholastic discourse on the Trinity regarding such terms as procession,[52] person, relation (*esse ad*), property or attribute,[53] mission, and the like. They also show that in its outward expression Eckhart's view of the Trinity is based primarily on Western sources, notably the Pseudo-Athanasian creed "Quicumque," Augustine's *The Trinity*, Peter Lombard, and Thomas Aquinas. But in its fundamentals Eckhart's view is distinctive and often bears comparison with rather different forms of trinitarianism, such as those of Dionysius and Bonaventure.[54]

A short and difficult passage from one of the Dominican's vernacular sermons is helpful in framing how he speaks about God as Trinity. In Pr. 10, Eckhart announces:

> Once I preached in Latin on Trinity Sunday and said: "Distinction comes from Absolute Unity, that is, the distinction in the Trinity." Absolute Unity is the distinction and the distinction is the unity. The greater the distinction, the greater the unity, for it is the distinction without distinction.[55]

What does Eckhart mean by this cryptic statement? The implications seem to run something like this. (a) In our realm of experience, distinction (this *is not* that) always involves numeration, while indistinction (this *is* that) implies the possibility of numeration by its very speaking of "this" and "that" (*hoc et hoc* in Eckhart's language). (b) But in God there is no possibility of numeration whatsoever—according to S. XI: "In the proper sense God is exempt from all number. He is one without Unity, three without Trinity, just as he is good without quality."[56] God's distinction (what sets him off from all other things) is to be utterly without numeration or any kind of distinction—that is, he alone is absolutely indistinct. (c) Hence, whatever is in God (i.e., the Trinity of Persons) must, by that very fact, be absolutely identical with the divine indistinction—"it is the distinction without distinction." Elsewhere Eckhart says this would be true of God even if there were a hundred, or a thousand divine Persons in God (!)—though we know by faith (and reason) that there are only three.[57]

The formulation from Pr. 10 shows that Eckhart believed that the dialectical relationship of God and creation, so central to his mysticism, was rooted in the deeper dialectic of indistinction in essence and distinction of Persons in the Trinity. This perspective must be kept in mind if we are to try to put together such contrasting assertions in Eckhart's works as: (1) God is so absolutely one that "*no distinction* can exist or be understood in God";[58] and (2) "God and Godhead are as *different* as heaven and earth."[59] How can there be both absolute oneness in God (i.e., *no* distinction) and yet so pronounced a distinction between God (the triune God of Christian belief) and the hidden Godhead?[60] The best way to approach this conundrum is from the point of view of the dialectical character of Eckhart's thought. That is, the truth of both opposed propositions begins to make sense only on the basis of the claim that the more distinct, or different, the Trinity of Persons is, the more indistinct, or absolutely one, the three Persons are in their pure potentiality, namely, in the divine ground. This indistinct-distinction is true both of the Trinity in itself and of the soul in union with the Trinity. As Eckhart puts it in Pr. 24, speaking of the soul, ". . . in the ground of divine being, where the three Persons are one being, there she is one according to the ground."[61]

The solution, then, rests in Eckhart's view of the *grunt gotes,* that is, the indistinct nonrelative "aspect" of God which is *absolutely* One (beyond all other forms of oneness) precisely in being three and vice versa. In most of the radical MHG texts in which Eckhart speaks of abandoning "God," or "going beyond" the Trinity of Persons, he also employs the language of penetration to the *grunt.*[62] The fact that *grunt,* as master metaphor, was not available for Eckhart in his Latin writings, and that he therefore needed to call upon a series of technical terms that could only refract elements of it (e.g., *essentia-deitas-divinitas*), helps explain why the scholastic works give us a different tone, though not, I believe, a different teaching.

From the viewpoint of ordinary Aristotelian logic, such dialectical predication does not resolve the contradictions present in the various forms of speaking about God, as Eckhart well knew. Its purpose is to jolt the hearer/reader into the recognition of the limits of all language when dealing with God and to remind her of the need to appropriate the explosive content of dialectic to deconstruct all forms of "knowing" into the "unknowing" that alone gives access to the *grunt.* Eckhart was quite open about this unknowing. In S. IV he says: "Note that everything that is said or written about the Holy Trinity is in no way really so or true." But if what we say is not really true, it at least points us in the right direction. In the same homily he goes on to say, "It is true, of course, that there is something in God corresponding to the Trinity we speak of. . . ."[63]

The Godhead insofar as it is a "simple ground" (*einvaltige grunt* and "silent desert" (*stille wüeste*) does not act—"God acts, while the Godhead does not act," as Pfeiffer's Sermon LVI puts it. In the Godhead God "un-becomes" (*entwirt*), so that this ground must be described as pure possibility, the unmoving precondition of all activity, even that of the divine *bullitio.*[64] It is only when we come to the "inner boiling" by which the three Persons flow forth in the processions characterized by mutual relations that we arrive at the level where "God becomes" (*got wirt*).[65]

The distinction between *grunt* as precondition (i.e., pure possibility) for emanation and the Father as actual source for the God who becomes is reflected in Eckhart's frequent appeal to what to many may seem a rather obscure axiom of scholastic trinitarian theology. In his *Commentary on Exodus* Eckhart says: "The better authorities say the potentiality of begetting in the Father is in the essence rather than the Paternity, and this is why the Father begets God the Son, but does not beget himself the Father."[66] This means that the root of all the Son's divine existence, wisdom, and power is from the ground or essence; but the ground itself does not beget, only the Father as Father does.[67]

The complexities and ambiguities of the relationship between the God who becomes and the God who un-becomes are evident in the ways in which Eckhart applies the transcendental predicates of existence (*esse-wesen*), oneness (*unum/unitas-ein/einicheit*), truth (*verum/intellectus-wârheit/bekantnisse*), and goodness (*bonum-güete*) to the Trinity. Following tradition, Eckhart describes these terms as "appropriated" to the various Persons, and hence really common to the divine essence as such. Nevertheless, his dialectical and apophatic trinitarianism effectively does away with any real difference between appropriated and proper properties. All terms are essentially appropriated, and these transcendental predicates can be used both of the Persons of the Trinity and of the divine nature itself, as we shall see below.

Eckhart employs two distinct patterns in applying the transcendentals to the Trinity, and, typically, it is not at all clear how they are to be related. The standard presentation is the more traditional one. Two of the three mini-treatises in the *Commentary on John* identify indistinct being or existence (*esse*) with the divine essence, and the One or unity with the Father, the True with the Son, and the Good with the Holy Spirit.

The longest of these treatments is Eckhart's commentary on John 14:8. The Dominican first provides sixteen reasons why, if we take "Father" for the "One,"[68] it was appropriate for the disciples to beg Christ to see the Father (nn.546–60); he then closes with eighteen more reasons why the same is fitting if the word "Father" is taken properly (nn.566–74). In between, Eckhart introduces a summary of his standard teaching regarding the transcendentals and the Trinity. "These four terms," he says, "are the same, and in relation to a subject or supposit are convertible in reality, but are distinguished from each other by their own idea or the property of each."[69] The idea of being "is indistinct and distinguished from other things by its very indistinction" (i.e., the proper characteristic, or distinguishing mark, of being, is that all things *are* being). So too, "God is distinguished by his indistinction from any other distinct things," and therefore "the essence itself or existence in the Godhead is unbegotten not begetting." On the other hand, Eckhart continues, "The One itself points to distinction," presumably because it is here seen as "personal and belonging to a supposit which is capable of action." It is "the first principle of all emanation, adding nothing to being except the negation of negation." Following the Augustinian lead in identifying *aequalitas* with the second Person, Eckhart continues: "The True from its property as a kind of equivalence of things and intellect and the offspring that is begotten of the known and the knower pertains to the Son. . . ."[70] The Good pertains to the Holy Spirit insofar as God is the principle of the good that formally resides in creatures. Eckhart summarizes:

1. "Existence is unbegotten and neither begetting or begotten; without a principle and not from anything."
2. "The One is without a principle, unbegotten but begetting" (i.e., the Father as "Principle without Principle").
3. "The True is begotten not begetting, having its principle from another" (i.e., Son as "Principle from the Principle").
4. "The Good is from another, having a principle, not begotten and not begetting, but creating and producing external created things" (i.e., the Holy Spirit).

Thus, the Father as the One "is the primal source of the first emanation [*bullitio*], namely, of the Son and the Holy Spirit from the Father by way of eternal procession." The Good [which is appropriated to the Holy Spirit, but is actually a common attribute] "is the source of the second, . . . the temporal production of the creature" (*ebullitio*).[71] This pattern of employing *esse-unum-verum-bonum* is used elsewhere by Eckhart.[72]

The first of the short treatises on the Trinity in the *Commentary on John*, however, sets forth the relation of the transcendentals to the Persons of the Trinity in a different way. Here Eckhart says:

> The works of the three Persons are undivided in the creatures of which they are one principle. Therefore, in creatures the being [*ens*] that corresponds to the Father,[73] the truth that corresponds to the Son, and the good that corresponds in appropriated fashion to the Holy Spirit are interchangeable and are one, being distinct by reason alone, just as the Father, the Son, and the Holy Spirit are one and distinct by relation alone.[74]

The "term One" (*li unum*), therefore, is not connected with any particular Person in the Trinity, but denotes the divine substance or essence.

Eckhart recognizes that this does not square with Augustine's ascription of *unitas* to the Father, but he defends his position by saying that Augustine does so "by reason of priority, or fontal diffusion and origin." "The term One," in this context at least, does not signify these positive notions of priority and the like and therefore can be ascribed to the divine essence.[75] In other words, Eckhart seems to be distinguishing two aspects or kinds of oneness: (a) *li unum*, or "the absolute, and totally indeterminate term One," which has no relation to anything positive or to any mode of production and therefore signifies the essence; and (b) the kind of prior, productive, and implicitly determinate Oneness that Augustine had in mind when he ascribed *unitas* to the Father in *On Christian Doctrine*.

It would be convenient if this distinction between two different views of Oneness in the Trinity were consistently observed across Eckhart's writings, but this is not the case. We might presume, on the basis of a number of texts in the first two trinitarian treatises, that there is a real distinction between Unity I (*li unum* as absolutely indistinct and the "negation of negation"),[76] and Unity II (unity as priority, implicitly determined by its place of origin in the emanative scheme). However, a passage in the third Trinity treatment in the *Commentary on John* explicitly goes against this. Here Eckhart says that the unity appropriated to the Father is nothing other than "the negation of negation which is the core, the purity, the repetition of the affirmation of existence."[77] So, the *negatio negationis* can be applied both to *li unum* when identified with the divine essence, or ground, and also to the Father as *unum*. Eckhart's two patterns of using the transcendental terms in relation to the *bullitio* in the Trinity do not seem to be fully consistent. Given the apophatic horizon within which the Dominican created his trinitarian theology, this is perhaps not unexpected.

From the perspective of Eckhart's mysticism, these discussions of the properties, or attributes, of the three Persons, are of importance especially because the return to God as ground is always by and in the Trinity. Just as the Father is the source of the *ûzganc* of all things, within and without the Trinity, so too he is the goal that "suffices" ("Show us the Father and it is enough for us" [John 14:8]).

Eckhart recognized that God as source of *bullitio* lies beyond all gender: our human term "Father" needs to be complemented by thinking of God as "Mother." Thus, in Pr. 75 he speaks of God as "eternally pregnant in his foreknowledge" of creation. The same homily also says that in begetting both his Only-Begotten Son and every indwelling soul, the Father "lies in childbed like a woman who has given birth."[78] Pr. 40

reverses this by speaking of Wisdom, traditionally ascribed to the Son, as "a motherly name" (*ein müeterlich name*), and claiming that both activity (the Father bearing) and passivity (the Son being born) must be thought of in God.[79] Another sermon (if it is indeed by Eckhart) goes even further in invoking the need for thinking of God maternally. Pfeiffer Sermon CIII analyzes the mode of the eternal birth of the Word from the Father on the basis of four questions. The third of these asks "Where does the Fatherhood (*vaterlicheit*) have a maternal name?" The answer given by Eckhart (or possibly a disciple) seems to be based on the distinction noted above between the essence, or "natural power" (*nâtiurlîchen kraft*), as the potentiality for generation, and the "personal power" (*persônlichen kraft*) as the active source of the bearing. Eckhart concludes:

> Where the personal nature keeps to the unity of its nature and combines with it, there Fatherhood has a maternal name and is doing a mother's work, for it is proper to a mother to conceive [i.e., to provide the ground which is the prior possibility]. But there, where the eternal Word arises in the essential Mind [= the Father], there Motherhood has a paternal name and performs paternal work.[80]

This suggests that the *grunt* is better spoken of in maternal rather than paternal language. A confirmation can be found in a passage in Pr. 71, where Eckhart's doctrine of the fused ground moves him to invoke God's pregnancy in recounting the story of a person (probably himself) who had the experience of bearing God in a "waking dream." Eckhart says: "It seemed to a person that he had a dream, a waking dream, that he was great with Nothingness as a woman with a child. In this Nothingness God was born."[81]

The Father as primordial fullness—the ultimate active source and therefore also in one respect the goal of the return—is so significant for Eckhart that he sometimes seems to fuse the Father with the suprapersonal and purely potential *grunt*. Breaking-through (*durchbrechen*) is usually employed in relation to the ground, but in Pr. 26 it refers to how the "soul's highest point" cannot be satisfied with the Persons of the Son or Holy Spirit, or even "God as he is God" with a thousand names, but rather, "would have him as he is Father" (citing John 14:8 again)."[82] Even more striking is a passage from Pr. 51, where Eckhart asserts the primordiality of the Father with regard to both emanation and return. In order to beget the Son, Eckhart says, the Father must remain "in himself the ground," where the image is eternally precontained.[83] Perhaps recalling John 14:8 again, Eckhart claims that the "Father is not *satisfied* till he has withdrawn into the first source, to the innermost, to the ground and core of Fatherhood, where he rejoices in himself there, the Father of himself in the Unique One." In this text there seems to be no difference at all between the Person of the Father and the *grunt*, so the preacher can go on to describe not only his own "captivation" (*ich han mich darinn vertoeret*) with the Father-ground, but also to remark on how all nature desires "to plunge into the Fatherhood, so that it can be one, and one Son, and grow beyond everything else and be all one in the Fatherhood."[84] Passages like this help explain what Eckhart meant when he cryptically interpreted Paul's promise that "we shall know God as we are known" (1 Cor. 13:12), as referring to the knowledge that God as Father has of himself "in that reflection [i.e., the Son] that alone is the image of God *and* the Godhead (*to the extent* that the Godhead is the Father)" (my italics).[85] Once again, Eckhart's trinitarianism deliberately seems to escape our attempts to reduce it to consistent and definable categories.

The Person of the Only-Begotten Son, perfect Image and Idea of the Father, whose eternal birth is also ours, has been emphasized as essential to Eckhart's mysticism by all his interpreters. I have already examined a major presentation of the Dominican's teaching on the eternal birth of the Word in chapter 4, and I will return to this theme in speaking of the *reditus* in chapter 6. Here a few remarks on how the Word proceeds from the Father will help deepen our grasp of the Son's role in the metaphysics of flow—both *bullitio* and *ebullitio.*

Eckhart adhered to the standard Augustinian and Thomistic view of the procession of the Word from the Father as a generation understood according to the model of an "intellectual procession" within God himself.[86] Hence, the whole of the Dominican's teaching on the nature of intellect is ultimately to be "reduced" (i.e., drawn back) into its source in the procession of the Word from the Father.[87] One central aspect of this procession, essential for understanding the dynamism of "inner boiling" as the paradigm and source for creative "boiling over," is how Eckhart conceives of the Father's "speaking of the Word" as the total and final expression of his hidden divine silence. As we have already observed in commenting on the sermon treatise on the eternal birth of the Son, the relation between silence and speaking was one of the central mysteries for Eckhart.[88] It is now time to consider this relationship from the wider perspective of both his German and Latin works.

In commenting on John 8:47 ("He who is of God hears God's words") Eckhart provides a summary of *when, where, what,* and *how* God speaks. While traditional teaching emphasized the beatific *vision* as the ultimate fulfillment of all human longing, Eckhart insists that in heaven "seeing and hearing are one" (In Ioh. n.487). Hence, in order to *see* the God who *speaks,* we must know *when* he speaks, that is (citing one of his favorite texts, Wis. 18:14), "While all things held quiet silence and night was in the midst of its course, your Almighty Word, Lord, came down from heaven."[89] We must also know *where* God speaks, which, Eckhart says, is in the desert, citing another favorite text, Hosea 2:14, "I will lead you into the desert and speak to your heart." *What* God speaks is "peace in his people and upon his saints and those converted in their hearts" (Ps. 84:9). Finally, *how* God speaks is answered with another oft-cited text from Job: "God speaks once and for all and will not say the same thing a second time" (Job 33:14).[90] Thus, it is only by coming into the silent darkness of the desert, where the Father speaks the Word once and for all, that we can attain perfect peace.

This ultimate form of speaking, of course, is not a word like the words we hear—"The Word which is in the silence of the fatherly Intellect is a Word without word, or rather a Word above every word," Eckhart says.[91] Nevertheless, it is only in and by this all-encompassing Word that all things are spoken—that is, that the universe itself comes to be.[92] "An effect [i.e., the world] is concealed in its analogous cause, hidden, silent, neither speaking nor being heard, unless it is said and brought forth in the word conceived and generated within or brought forth on the outside."[93]

These Latin discussions of the *Verbum* as the Father's sole communication form the basis for Eckhart's preaching about the mediation between silence and speaking as necessary for the breakthrough into the ground.[94] A well-known passage in Pr. 9 distinguishes three kinds of *wort:*

> There is one kind of word which is brought forth, like an angel and a human being and all creatures. There is a second kind of word, thought out and not brought forth, as happens when I form a thought. There is yet another kind of word that is not brought forth and not thought out, that never comes forth. Rather, it remains eternally in him who speaks it. It is continually being conceived in the Father who speaks it, and it remains within.[95]

The Word that "remains eternally in him who speaks it" is, of course, the silent Word.[96] Though silent, this Word is not totally inaccessible. Indeed, the purpose of the distinction is to emphasize the basic message of this sermon, that is, the soul must recognize its nature as "an adverb" (*biwort*) so that it can "work one work with God in order to receive its happiness in the same inwardly hovering knowledge where God is happy."[97] In Pr. 53, citing Augustine's observation on the contradiction of speaking about the ineffable God (*On Christian Doctrine* 1.6), Eckhart discusses how the divine nature is simultaneously unspeakable and yet spoken. "God is a Word that utters itself," he says. "God is spoken and unspoken. The Father is a speaking work, and the Son is a speech working" (*spruch wirkende*).[98] Therefore, the birth of the Son in the soul comes down to speaking the Word simultaneously within, that is, in the eternal silence, and without, that is, in creating and sustaining all things.[99] Robert Forman has correctly spoken of the "dynamization of silence" as a crucial aspect of Eckhart's mysticism,[100] but we should remember that this dynamization is not ours—it is essentially God's own.

The frequency with which Eckhart refers to the birth of the Word in the soul and his subtle discussion about the Word unspoken and spoken have attracted much attention. Less has been given to the Dominican's teaching on the Holy Spirit as procession from Father and Son, as source of the *ebullitio* of creation, and as the love which restores all things to God.[101] Nevertheless, although he speaks of it somewhat less often, it is fair to say that Pneumatology is no less important than Christology in understanding Eckhart. When the Meister discusses the procession of the Holy Spirit in the Trinity he adopts the standard Latin understanding of this as an emanation according to love; but, as in much else, he gives this doctrine his own distinctive twist.

S. IV is a good summary of Eckhart's trinitarian teaching, as well as an exposition exploring how existence *in* the Holy Spirit as *nexus*, or bond, of Father and Son, is the ground for our return to the source.[102] "All things are from him [the Father], through him [the Son], and in him [the Holy Spirit]," according to Eckhart's reading of Romans 11:36. The Meister takes the Spirit's "being in" all things as a proper attribute, and one that should be understood in reversible, or dialectical, fashion. "All things are in the Holy Spirit in such a way that what is not in him is nothing," just as "'All things are in him' in such a way that if there is anything not in the Holy Spirit, the Holy Spirit is not God."[103] Thus, the Holy Spirit can be seen as the Person of the Trinity who is the root of God's indistinct-distinction in relation to creation. "When we say that all things are in God [that means that] just as he is indistinct in his nature and nevertheless most distinct from all things, so in him all things in a most distinct way are also indistinct."[104] The root of this indistinct presence of all things in the Holy Spirit is his personal property as the "bond" between the Father and the Son: "'All things are in him' in such a way that the Father would not be in the Son nor the Son in the Father, if the Father were not one and the same as the Holy Spirit, or the Son [also] the same as the Holy Spirit."[105] In a passage in the *Commentary on John,* Eckhart explains the traditional denotation of the Holy Spirit as the *nexus* between Father and Son by invoking his special language of *in quantum,* the principle of formal reduplication. He says:

> The term "insofar as" is a reduplication. Reduplication, as the word testifies, speaks of the bond or ordering of two things. Reduplication expresses the folding together of two things, a fold or bond of two. Thus the Spirit, the third Person in the Trinity, is the bond of the two, the Father and the Son.[106]

This bond is understood as the mutual love of Father and Son, what Eckhart called the unitive "love of contentment" (*amor complacentiae/ amor concomitans*), which is conceptually different from, but really identical with, the "love breathed forth" (*amor notionalis/amor spiratus*), that is, the Holy Spirit understood as proceeding from Father and Son.[107]

For this reason, the very same love with which the Father loves the Son and the Son loves the Father must be the love by which we love God.[108] Eckhart took this doctrine literally and he expounds it in both his scholastic writings and his vernacular preaching, insisting that the love which draws us to God is not a form of created love, but is the very uncreated Love that is the Holy Spirit. This had been the teaching of Peter Lombard, but it was rejected by many authorities, including Thomas Aquinas. Here Eckhart, for once, was open about his difference from the Angelic Doctor. In Pr. 27, for example, he says: "The greatest masters say that the love with which we love is the Holy Spirit. There were some who would dispute this. That is eternally true: in all the motion with which we are moved to love, we are moved by nothing but the Holy Spirit."[109] Hence, Eckhart's mysticism has an important Spirit-centered dimension. This is evident in a passage from the John commentary that adapts the fusion language often employed in the MHG sermons—the "eye with which I see God is the same eye by which he sees me"—to the role of the Uncreated Love that is the Spirit. "In the sense that there is one face and image in which God sees us and we him, according to the Psalm text, 'In your light we shall see light,' so too the same Love is the Holy Spirit by which the Father loves the Son and the Son the Father [and] by which God loves us and we him."[110] We are fully united to God because we *are* the Holy Spirit, the very bond of the triune God.

Eckhart's treatment of the Trinity is among the most complex aspects of his thought. Like all Christian theologians, he held that the Trinity is a mystery unknowable to humans. Many concluded from this that the best way to present the mystery was through faithful adherence to enshrined formulas from creeds and councils and reverent exposition of the "dogmatic logic" of the terms found therein. Eckhart's trinitarianism was certainly reverent, but also experimental. He strove to find more adequate ways to express the inner dynamism of the divine *bullitio,* and also to show how God's inner life as a communion of three Persons is both the source of all that is and the way by which we find our way home. The experimental nature of Eckhart's trinitarianism leaves us with many questions, loose ends, and even inconsistencies— but this may be exactly what he had in mind.

Speaking about God: *De Nominibus Dei*

In his extended treatment of the divine names found in the *Commentary on Exodus* Eckhart notes that he had "often remarked on the names of God in different places," both those names found in scripture and the Catholic tradition, as well as "what some philosophers and Jewish authors think on this question."[111] Although Dionysius was the first to compose an explicit work *On the Divine Names* (c. 500 C.E.), the tradition of analyzing the divine names goes far back into the history of Christian theology and even more deeply into Greek philosophical speculation on the proper way to speak of the First Principle. We have already examined how Eckhart used the transcendental predicates (*esse/unum/verum/bonum*) to present his understanding of the dynamism of the trinitarian "boiling." It is now necessary to investigate two further questions: (1) how human language in general is used of God; and (2) what light this sheds on the application of the transcendental terms to the divine nature as such, not just to the Trinity of Persons.

Eckhart was obviously fascinated by the question of what we think we are doing when we attempt to speak about God. In one sense, his whole surviving corpus is an exploration of this issue. Why is speech necessary when silence is more fitting? What kinds of speech about God are there? What are their appropriate functions and limitations? The Dominican's experiments and reflections on these experiments are scattered throughout his writings.

The best way to begin investigating the modes of using words in relation to God is by distinguishing (1) predication, (2) analogy, and (3) dialectic. Eckhart explicitly differentiates the first two, and in practice he created a coherent exposition of the third mode of language without ever thematizing it.[112] Like all good scholastics, Eckhart had been well trained in logic, so we must begin at the level of predication.[113] In his prologues to *The Three-Part Work* and elsewhere, Eckhart adapts the traditional logical distinction between "two-term propositions" (*secundum adiacens*) and "three-term propositions" (*tertium adiacens*). A two-term proposition (e.g., Socrates is) is one in which the verb stands as the second term and denotes that the action is really taking place (the existential *est*), while in a three-term proposition (e.g., Socrates is a man) the verb stands as the copula between two terms indicating their logical compatibility without directly affirming actuality (the copulative *est*, i.e., *if* Socrates exists, he is a man).[114] Thomas Aquinas and many other scholastics had used the distinction,[115] but Eckhart adopted it in his own fashion. For Eckhart two-term propositions indicate substantial predication, while three-term propositions signify accidental predication. Two-term propositions imply the unlimited possession of the predicate: its absolute fullness. Hence, with regard to the transcendentals, two-term propositions (X is) are properly used only of God—"God alone properly speaking exists and is called being, one, true, and good" (i.e., formally speaking, God is-being, God is-good, etc.). Three-term propositions, indicating particular being (X is this), pertain to creatures, because "everything that is being, one, true or good, does not possess this from itself, but from God and from him alone."[116]

This divisive understanding of predication forms the foundation for Eckhart's better-known doctrine of analogy, which, since the time of Vladimir Lossky forty years ago, has been recognized as central to grasping the peculiar form of the Dominican's teaching about language and the God–world relation.[117] Here, again, although Eckhart at times appealed to Thomas Aquinas in setting forth his teaching, analogy for Eckhart is really different from what we find in the Angelic Doctor. A key text from the *Sermons and Lectures on Ecclesiasticus*, already cited, explains why:

> Analogates have nothing of the form according to which they are analogically ordered rooted in positive fashion in themselves, but every created being is analogically ordered to God in being, truth, and goodness. Therefore, every created being radically and positively possesses existence, life, and wisdom from and in God and not in itself. . . . [118]

Therefore, analogy does not indicate some kind of sharing of God and creature in a predicate (e.g., *esse*), but rather denotes the fact that God alone really possesses the attribute. As Dietmar Mieth puts it: "Analogy is not, as with Thomas, a connective relationship, but a relationship of dependence; analogy does not explain what something is, but where it comes from."[119] The reality of creatures in Eckhart's doctrine of analogy is the reality of a sign pointing to God.[120]

There is another characteristic of Eckhart's use of analogy that points beyond analogy itself in the direction of the third and most important level of language about God—dialectic.[121] As a number of investigators have noticed, Eckhart's use of analogy is reversible. If something is affirmed about God, it must be denied of creatures, at least in any real sense. On the other hand, anything that is affirmed of creatures must be denied of God. This is the root of the kind of extreme formulations about God and creatures that so upset the Dominican's inquisitors. In the bull "In agro dominico" examples of both kinds of statements based on reversed analogy come in for attack. Article 26, for example, condemns as "evil sounding, rash, and suspect of heresy" the statement: "All creatures are one pure nothing. I do not say that they are a little something or anything, but that they are pure nothing."[122] This is based on the predication of *esse* to God and therefore its entailed denial to creatures. The second appended article to the bull (denounced as "heretical") cites a passage from Pr. 9 that begins from implied "three-term predications" of goodness to creatures, and therefore boldly proclaims, "God is neither good, nor better, nor best; hence I speak as incorrectly when I call God good as if I were to call white black."[123] Eckhart's doctrine of analogy, then, is one of formal opposition, not the normal scholastic understanding of attribution (i.e., one being possesses a quality which can be rightly attributed to another), or proportionality (i.e., the way in which one being has a quality has some proportion to the way in which another has it).

The peculiarity of Eckhart's self-reversing analogy leads directly to the many passages in his teaching and preaching where the German Dominican employs the language of dialectical Neoplatonism, first created by pagan mystical theorists such as Plotinus and Proclus, and transformed for Christian use by Dionysius among the Greeks and John Scottus Eriugena in the Latin West.[124] By dialectical language I mean: (a) predicating determinations (e.g., God is distinct); (b) simultaneously predicating opposed determinations (e.g., God is distinct and God is indistinct); and (c) predicating a necessary mutual relationship between the opposed determinations (e.g., God is the more distinct the more indistinct he is). Dialectical language of this sort was the special linguistic strategy that allowed Eckhart to bring out the higher unity, or deeper "non-insight" (*unwizzen*), of the mutually opposed forms of analogical predications.[125] How far Eckhart was original here is difficult to determine. The Dominican was well acquainted with Dionysius and also with some texts of Proclus. The extent of his direct knowledge of Eriugena is unclear.[126] His form of dialectical Christian Neoplatonism, however, is not really reducible to its sources—it is a new rendition of an old theme designed to fit a changed situation.

Eckhart's use of dialectical language about God as three-and-one, as well as the God–world relation, is found throughout his Latin and MHG works, but in different registers. The Dominican's favorite way to formulate dialectical language is in terms of distinction and indistinction, but other forms of dialectic can also be found (e.g., similarity/dissimilarity,[127] eating/hungering,[128] height/depth,[129] within/without,[130] mobile/immobile,[131] mine/not-mine,[132] etc.). The scholastic writings contain a number of detailed explorations of dialectic;[133] the German sermons and treatises more briefly invoke dialectic when useful for the preacher's purposes.[134] In relation to both the Latin and the MHG works, however, not to appreciate how crucial a tool dialectic is for interpreting Eckhart would be a serious oversight.[135]

The most detailed of Eckhart's formal treatments on the dialectical character of divine predication comes in his commentary on the transcendental term *unum* found in Wisdom 7:27 ("And since Wisdom is one, it can do all things").[136] Eckhart begins his analysis by discussing the negative aspect of the meaning of *unum*, that is, indistinction— "The term 'one' is the same as indistinct, for all distinct things are two or more, but all indistinct things are one" (n.144).[137] As usual, he links the indistinction of *unum* with *esse*: God's indistinction from all things is the property of the first and highest *esse*.[138] On this basis, he moves on to advance three arguments why God must be one (n.146). Eckhart then introduces the positive pole of *unum*—"It should be recognized now that the term 'one' is a negative word [= indistinct], but is in reality affirmative. . . . It is the negation of negation which is the purest form of affirmation and the fullness of the term affirmed" (n.147).

The negation of negation is Eckhart's dialectical way of subverting the standard Aristotelian divide (both a logical and an ontological one) between "what is" and "what is not." God "negates" everything that we know "is"; but the negation of *all* that is (not just some particular form of existence) opens up vistas into a new world in which our distinctions between what is and what is not no longer pertain. God as *negatio negationis* is simultaneously total emptiness and supreme fullness. The extent to which Eckhart's dialectical reflections on the *negatio negationis* may or may not be a resource for current debates on surpassing "onto-theology" are not without interest, but the Dominican's reasons for questioning traditional ways of speaking about God were different from those of modern philosophers and thinkers.

Eckhart then proceeds to investigate the relation of the One to the many on the basis of the understanding of *unum* as the negation of negation:

> It [*unum*] signifies the purity and core and height of existence itself, something which even the term *esse* does not do. The term "one" signifies Existence Itself (*ipsum esse*) in itself along with the negation and exclusion of all nonbeing, which [nonbeing], I say, every negation entails. . . . The negation of negation (which the term "one" signifies) denotes that everything which belongs to the term is present in the signified and everything which is opposed to it is absent. (n.148)

Eckhart cites key Neoplatonic sources (Macrobius, Boethius, Proclus) to show that if God is the Absolute One in the sense given, he must be beyond all number and numeration—the characteristics of created things (nn.149–51). He is not a number, but the source of all numbers. "Every multitude participates in the One," as Proclus said.[139]

At this stage Eckhart is ready to draw together the two poles of understanding *unum*, positive and negative, to show that they are indissolubly linked in a dialectical coincidence of opposites. He begins with distinction. If we conceive of all creatures as numerable, then God must be utterly distinct from all things (n.154—first two arguments). However, this negation or distinction is founded on and implies the affirmation of God's indistinction. What makes God utterly distinct or different from everything else is that he alone is totally one or indistinct from everything. That is, in the fused mutuality of dialectical predication:

> Everything which is distinguished by indistinction is the more distinct the more indistinct it is, because it is distinguished by its own indistinction. Conversely, it is the more indistinct the more distinct it is, because it is indistinguished by its own distinction from what is indistinct.[140] Therefore, it will be the more indistinct insofar as it is distinct, and vice versa, as was said. But God is something indistinct which is distinguished by his indistinction, as Thomas says in 1a, q.7., a.1. (n.154).

The same kind of argument is then repeated beginning from the side of indistinction. Again, after two reasons showing why God must be indistinct from all things a third argument is advanced that is explicitly dialectical:

> Nothing is as indistinct from anything as from that from which it is indistinguished by its own distinction. But everything that is numbered or created is indistinguished from God by its own distinction, as said above. Therefore, nothing is so indistinct and consequently one, for the indistinct and the One are the same. Therefore, God and any creature whatever are indistinct (n.155).

To those unaccustomed to dialectical thinking this analysis may seem perverse—a mere word-game. Eckhart probably delighted in the game-like quality of the dialectic of *unum*, but his message was a serious one: the transcendental terms, especially *unum* and *esse,* in their very character as words, reveal that God is inconceivably transcendent in his immanence and immanent in his transcendence. This distinct-indistinction is, of course, nothing else but the "negation of negation" already referred to.[141] Eckhart employs this technical term often in his Latin works, but very rarely in the German sermons.[142] Although formalized discussions of distinction and indistinction and its expression as "negation of negation" are not featured in the vernacular works, I would suggest that another mode of presenting dialectic is widespread there—what else is *grunt* but a master metaphor for exploring the distinct-indistinction, or fused-identity, of God and the soul?

Eckhart's *Sermon for the Feast of St. Augustine* shows that he was aware of the traditional enumeration, elaborated by Thomas Aquinas, of the various ways in which the "names" of scripture and the "terms" of philosophical discourse could be predicated of God.[143] In STh 1a, q.13, a.1, Aquinas said that God could be known from creatures "according to [1] the condition of a cause, and through [2] the way of eminence, and [3] that of negation." In the language of the schools these ways of speaking—the *via causalitatis,* the *via eminentiae,* and the *via negationis*—became commonplace. (Aquinas leaves out of account here knowing God by way of univocal terms in which the same words are used in the same sense of God and creatures; see STh 1a, q.13, a.5.) Thomas obviously meant his treatment of the analogical use of terms such as *esse/unum/verum* of both God and creatures (e.g., q.13, aa.2-3, and 5) as an example of the eminent predication [2] that he contends is more adequate than merely using terms such as "good" of God because he is the *cause* of the goodness of creatures [1], or, as Moses Maimonides would have it, because saying "God is good" allows us to exclude what we know as evil from him without saying anything about his real nature [3]. How does Eckhart's dialectical language about God relate to Aquinas's teaching, as well as the forceful arguments of Maimonides for the ultimacy of the *via negationis?*

At first glance, Eckhart's treatise on naming God in the *Commentary on Exodus* seems to indicate that Maimonides wins out over Aquinas, perhaps not a surprising victory given that the Jewish sage is cited more often than both Thomas Aquinas and Augustine in this work.[144] But things are more complex than they seem, because the treatise on the divine names, as well as the wider consideration of this issue in the Meister's thought, indicates that Eckhart was engaged in a delicate three-way conversation with these two great thinkers to help work out his own position. The preeminence of negative predication is evident throughout the treatise, and Maimonides is often cited in this regard (see, e.g., In Ex. nn.37–44 and 177–84, which use Maimonides' *Guide* 1.50–63). However, from time to time, Eckhart appeals to Aquinas's language of analogy and thus seems to want to preserve something of the Thomistic *via eminentiae.*[145] This may seem like mere confusion, but I would argue that Eckhart is drawing on both Maimonides and Aquinas as resources for the creation of his own dialectical God-language.

The key to understanding how this language works within the framework of the treatise on naming God in the *Commentary on Exodus* is to see it in light of the dialectical texts already examined, such as that from the *Commentary on Wisdom.* For the sake of simplicity, the way in which Eckhart sought to utilize both Maimonides and Aquinas without ever really fully siding with either can be summarized as follows: (1) Maimonides is right to deny all predicates, perfections, or "dispositions" of God, because they are always based on our knowledge of perfections in created things (see In Ex. n.44). (2) Thomas Aquinas is right in claiming that *esse indistinctum* can be correctly predicated of God, because it is not a name or "disposition," i.e., something based on our knowledge of creatures.[146] (3) Both Maimonides and Aquinas are wrong because they fail to recognize that terms like *unum* and *esse indistinctum* are neither purely negative, nor analogical, but dialectic, that is, they fuse, or implode on themselves, when one tries to explore their logic.

In this final point, there may well be an important analogy between Eckhart and Aquinas. David Burrell has argued that "divine simpleness" (*simplicitas*) as explored in qq. 1–13 of the First Part of Thomas's *Summa theologiae* should not be seen as just another divine attribute, but as the foundation, or "formal feature," underlying everything we can say about God.[147] Perhaps "distinct-indistinction" plays a similar role in the German Dominican, that is, it is not an *example* of speaking about God; it is the underlying law of all such speech. As the Meister put it in his sermon "The Nobleman":

> In distinction you cannot find unity, nor being, nor God, nor rest, nor blessedness, nor enjoyment. Be one, so that you can find God. Truly, if you were really one, you would remain one even in distinction and distinction would be one for you, and nothing at all would be in your way.[148]

Dialectical thinking provides a helpful way to approach the controverted question of Eckhart's diverse treatments of the transcendental terms—*esse, unum, verum/intelligere,* and *bonum.*[149] The problem is well known. Unlike Thomas Aquinas, who always gave *esse,* or *ipsum esse subsistens,* priority in speaking about God, Eckhart says different things in different places. In his prologues to the unfinished *Three-Part Work* he studies *esse* as the fundamental transcendental term in a way that brings him close to Thomas Aquinas (though it is important to note that Eckhart reverses Thomas by his formulation *esse est deus*).[150] But, as we have seen, in the *Commentary on Wisdom* and elsewhere, he seems to give priority to *unum*—"It [*unum*] signifies the purity and core and height of existence itself, something which even the term *esse* does not do." A wide variety of texts, both in Eckhart's scholastic works[151] and in his vernacular preaching,[152] make it clear that *unum,* that is, Absolute Unity, has a special role in the way in which Eckhart speaks of God.

The question of the relation between *esse* and *unum* is further complicated when we note that in the *Parisian Questions,* as well as in S. XXIX, Eckhart explicitly denies that *esse* is the fundamental transcendental predicate. "It is not my current view," he says, "that God understands because he exists, but rather that he exists because he understands. God is an intellect and an act of understanding, and his understanding is the ground of his existence."[153] How then is God as *intelligere* related to God as *esse* and *unum?*

Eckhart begins to provide some help in the course of the *Parisian Questions* themselves, particularly when he cites the fourth proposition of the *Book of Causes* (*prima rerum creaturarum est esse:* "Existence is the first of created things"). This indicates that he is using *esse* here not as *esse indistinctum,* but as the particular being of creatures. Furthermore, as he develops his discussion, he is willing to admit that although "existence" is not in God, Exodus 3:14 shows us that "purity of existence" (*puritas essendi:* q.1 n.9) can be ascribed to him. Later, in the second of the *Parisian Questions*, he gives an important reason why *intellectus/puritas essendi* can be used as a primary name of God—"Intellect insofar as it is intellect, is nothing of the things that it knows. . . . If therefore intellect insofar as it is intellect is nothing, then neither is understanding some kind of existence."[154] (This is another example of Eckhart's reversing analogy.)[155] The second key text, S. XXIX, also elevates *intelligere* above *esse* and draws it close to *unum*—What is understanding except becoming completely one with what is understood? "Unity, or the One, seems to be proper to and a property of intellect alone." Therefore, "the one God is intellect and intellect is the one God."[156] Hence, when the proper distinctions and qualifications are made, Eckhart is saying that *esse, unum,* and *intelligere* can all be used in some way as appropriate language about God.

This helps explain why, despite these passages denying *esse* to God, even in his late vernacular preaching Eckhart often used "pure being" (*lûter wesen*), what the Latin works refer to as *esse indistinctum*,[157] as a legitimate form of God-language. As Pr. 91 puts it: "God is nothing but one pure Being, and the creature is from nothing and also has one being from the same Being."[158] The numerous places where the Dominican says that God must be thought of as "beyond being," or as a "being without being,"[159] can be squared with the *esse/wesen* formulations *if* we take the former set of texts as referring to the *puritas essendi*, and the latter to signal the *esse* that is the first of created things spoken of in the *Book of Causes*. Although this may be making Eckhart neater than he would want to be, he too tried to regularize his verbal "flow" when taken to task by the inquisitors.

Finally, even though Eckhart usually treats the transcendental term *bonum* as logically subsequent to and dependent upon *esse* and *unum*,[160] there are passages where he seems to give Goodness some degree of equality with the other transcendentals. For example, he several times cites a passage from Augustine's *The Trinity* in which the saint used an early version of the Dominican's favorite expression for created being (*hoc et hoc*). "This and that good [exist]," said Augustine; "take away this and that and see the Good Itself, if you can, and thus you will see God."[161] The Good that is not "this and that" is the very divine nature itself. Since transcendental Goodness reveals itself as absolute Love, Eckhart can also predicate this name of God. In Pr. 71, for example, Eckhart says that the soul thinks God has no other name save Love, so that "In saying 'love' it names him with all names."[162]

Thus, although Eckhart has been accused of confusion in his doctrine of God, at least by some critics, this does not seem to be the case.

Alternatively, other scholars have looked for a progression in his views from an early, more Thomist position to a subsequent overturning of this in favor of a radical "henology," or metaphysics of the One. But, as several recent interpreters have argued, there is really no opposition between "ontology" and "henology" in Eckhart.[163] From one perspective *esse* and *unum*, as well as *intelligere*, are terms that can be appropriately used in speaking about God, at least to the extent that they are employed dialectically. From another perspective, all are equally wanting. Within the context of his radical apophaticism, that is, the recognition that no human word is *really* adequate for speaking about God, Eckhart's position is that it is in the play of language explored through the therapy of preaching and second-order reflection on naming God that we can begin to understand both what language can do and what its limits are.[164]

In reading Eckhart, especially his Latin and German sermons, one is continually brought up short by the apophatic horizon that limits all forms of knowing and speaking about God. In the *Commentary on Genesis* Eckhart noted, following Aristotle, that there are two ways in which things are difficult to know for us, "either because they exceed the proportion of our intellect due to the eminence of their existence, . . . or because they fall away from the existence or being that is the intellect's object."[165] God so surpasses the measure of our intellect that there can be no real "knowledge" of him. Our intellect works by comparing one thing with another (*esse hoc et hoc*), but nothing can be compared to God because nothing is distinct from him.[166] We also have to make use of genus and species in speaking of things, but God has no genus and species, so these categories are only used "according to our mode of understanding," not according the reality of his indistinct Oneness.[167] God, as Eckhart never tired of saying, is strictly speaking "unnameable to us because of the infinity of all existence in him," though, paradoxically, we also can assert that he is "omninameable."[168] Hence, Eckhart qualifies the predicating of any names, even *esse indistinctum*, *intelligere*, and *unum*, of God with frequent proclamations that God is really "No-thing"—"God is nothing at all"; "God is a nothing and God is a something"; "God is uncreated 'Isness' and unnamed Nothingness."[169]

In the Meister's MHG preaching the overwhelming force of his desire to "speak" God to his audience (see, e.g., Pr. 60) collides with the immovable and impenetrable "unknownness of the hidden Godhead" (Pr. 15 [DW 1:253.1]) to produce many of his most striking and memorable passages. Whole sermons, such as Prr. 22, 52, 71, 80, and 83, are devoted to stripping away concepts and language in a form of intellectual ascesis designed to prepare for the "unknowing" that alone makes God present to us. Eckhart often uses a form of homiletic "shock therapy" in which he makes outrageous statements that taken at face value are almost blasphemous in character, as in the important treatise on speaking about God in the recently edited Pr. 95b, where he says: "The more a person denies God, the more he praises him. The more one ascribes unlike things to him, the closer one comes to knowing him than if one tried to express a likeness." The goal of this practice is the deconstruction that leads to silent union. "As the soul comes to knowledge that God is unlike every nature, it also comes to a state of amazement and is driven further and comes into a state of silence. With the silence God sinks down into the soul and she is bedewed with grace."[170] The unknowing found in such a state is total. "What is the last end?" Eckhart asks in Pr. 22. "It is the hidden darkness of the eternal divinity, and it is unknown, and it was never known, and it will never be known. God remains there within himself, unknown."[171] The mystery is even hidden from God.

CREATION AS *EBULLITIO*

Exitus/ûzganc is not limited to the God who "boils" within as Trinity, but it also "boils over" (*ebulliat*), pouring forth into the created universe. ("All things are God over-boiled," as I once read in a student paper.) A look at Meister Eckhart's doctrine of creation is necessary both for understanding how controversial his teaching was and also for grasping how in Eckhart's mysticism absolute detachment from all created things is the only way to really be able to enjoy them. We will investigate Eckhart's view of creation briefly under two headings: (1) the notion of creation itself, especially creation as continuous (*creatio continua*); and (2) the *esse*, or mode of existence, of created being.[172]

Like any good medieval theologian, Eckhart proposes a number of definitions of creation, all of which boil down to (or over into) the same thing. Most simply, creation is the "giving of existence" (*collatio esse*), or in an expanded formula based on Avicenna, "creation is the giving of existence after non-existence."[173] Following Maimonides and Aquinas, Eckhart also used the formula, "Creation is the production of things from nothing."[174] Since Eckhart uses *productio* and *emanatio* interchangeably, however, we can say that whenever he talks of God as "flowing into all creatures" he is speaking of creation: creation is the eternal constant activity of God's flow into creatures.[175]

Eckhart's understanding of creation centers on *esse*, which is both the "ground of creatability" (In Sap. n.24), and the purpose, or final cause, for God's creative action—"He created all things *so that they might be*" (Wis. 1:14).[176] But the function of *esse* in the production, or flowing, of all things from God, needs to be understood in light of Eckhart's teaching about the relation of *esse* and *unum*, and of God as the *principium*. An important text from the *Commentary on John* says: "Existence (*esse*) is a principle under the idea or property of the One, and from it proceeds the universe and the entirety of all created being."[177] What this means is that God as creator is to be understood in terms of God as the one formal cause, that is, the "ideal reason" of all things. "You must recognize," as Eckhart says in his *Commentary on Genesis*, "that the 'principle' in which 'God created heaven and earth' is the ideal reason. This is what the first chapter in John says, 'In the principle was the Word (the Greek has 'Logos,' that is, 'reason')."[178] According to Eckhart, the metaphysician does not seek proof through efficient and final causes, because they are external, but only through internal, that is, formal causality.[179] In contrast to Thomas Aquinas, whose view of creation was centered on God as efficient cause, Eckhart emphasized God's formal causality.

Eckhart's perspective on God as formal cause of the universe is evident in his use of the Neoplatonic notion of *causa essentialis*, a term that had its roots in Proclus and Dionysius and that had been developed by Albert the Great and Dietrich of Freiburg.[180] An "essential cause," as Eckhart defines it, is an agent "that is a principle in which there is Logos and Idea, . . . an essential agent that precontains its effect in a higher way and exercises causality over the whole species of its effect."[181] An essential cause must be intellectual in nature—"Every true essential agent is spirit and life."[182] It is also a universal agent—not a member of the genus it causes, nor the cause of a particular effect. In S. II the Dominican distinguishes between two kinds of essential causes. First there are the primordial, or original, "primal-prime causes" (*causae primo-primae*), "where the name of Principle is more proper than cause," and in which "the Principle totally brings itself with all its properties down into what is principled." The example cited for this is the way in which the Father generates the Son. There are also what Eckhart calls "second-prime essential causes" (*causae essentiales secundo-primae*), where "the cause brings itself totally down into what is caused so that each thing may be in the other in whatever way possible, as it says in the *Book of Causes*."[183] Eckhart's doctrine of *bullitio* and *ebullitio* suggests that both kinds of essential causality can be predicated of God—the former indicating his univocal production of the Son and Spirit (as well as intellect in the soul); the latter his role as essential but analogous cause of the universe. Eckhart never denied that God was the efficient cause of the universe, but because he defined efficient causality as extrinsic,[184] and nothing can be really extrinsic to God, the notion of *causa essentialis* is more congenial to him than the Aristotelian doctrine of efficient causality. Hence in S. IV, when he asks whether the "from which" of Romans 11:36 indicates God's efficient making of the universe, he answers that "'from' is properly not the efficient cause, but rather the idea of the efficient cause" (*ratio causae efficientis*).[185] Eckhart's metaphysics of flow, with its language of *principium* and *causa essentialis,* has a different emphasis from the doctrine of creation in Thomas Aquinas.

The ramifications of this view of God's causality in creation are far-reaching. Two of these are evident in the errors concerning creation that Eckhart singles out in his discussion of the production of the universe in S. XXIII. The first is that God creates outside himself, or alongside himself, in nothing. No, says Eckhart, "Everything that happens in nothing, is surely nothing. . . . By creating, God calls all things out of nothing and from nothing to existence."[186] Since he does this "in the Principle," he does it in himself. As the *Commentary on Wisdom* puts it, "He creates all things from himself and in himself."[187] Nothing can be outside of, or distinct from, the *esse* that is God. The second false view mentioned in the sermon and taken up in greater detail elsewhere is that "God created and rested from creating in the manner of other workers, according to the superficial sense of the text, 'God rested from all his work on the seventh day.'"[188] Eckhart combats this mistake by insisting that "God created in such a way that he is always creating." If there is no before and after for God in the simultaneous presence of his eternity to all other forms of successive duration, then creation must be a continuous activity—*creatio continua.* As he says in Pr. 30:

> That all creatures should pour forth and still remain within is very wonderful. . . . The more He is in things, the more He is out of things: the more in, the more out, and the more out, the more in. I have often said, God is creating the whole world now this instant. Everything God made six thousand years ago and more when he made this world, God is creating now all at once.[189]

God's continuous act of creation means that in its deepest reality creation is eternal, as Eckhart taught in his *Commentary on Genesis* and throughout his works. To think of a time *before* creation is as much of a category mistake as to think of God "resting" *after* he finished his work.[190] Despite the attacks on his views (as we have seen, the bull "In agro dominico" eventually condemned as heretical three propositions concerning the eternity of creation), Eckhart never wavered, during life and at his trial, in his conviction that the eternity of creation was a necessary implication of Christian faith, one that had been taught by Augustine and other authorities.[191] This did not mean, however, that Eckhart denied that the universe was also temporal, that is, something made in time. As he once put it, "Exterior creation is subject to the time that makes things old."[192]

How did the German Dominican put together these two seemingly contradictory assertions—the universe is eternal, and the universe is temporal? In order to understand this we need to call to mind his teaching concerning the two levels or aspects of created being—virtual existence (*esse virtuale*) and formal existence (*esse formale*).[193] In the *Commentary on Wisdom* the Meister says, "All things are in God as in the First Cause in an intellectual way and in the mind of the Maker. Therefore, they do not have any of their formal existence until they are causally produced and extracted *on the outside* in order to exist" [my italics].[194] Every creature, therefore, has both "virtual existence" in its essential cause and "formal existence" in the natural world;[195] or, to put it in another way, the *esse* of creatures is both "from another" insofar as it is virtually hidden in its cause, and yet "proper" to itself insofar as it exists in the world.[196] Eckhart, however, does not give very great value to the *esse formale* of creatures. Unlike Thomas Aquinas, for whom such formal existence was essential for giving creatures a reality of their own, the German Dominican's attention is always focused on the virtual, true, that is, the "principial" existence of things in God. This can be seen in the way in which in Pr. 57 he uses the Neoplatonic symbol of the mirror to describe the nature of *esse formale*.[197] A face is always a face, whether or not a mirror is present. The image of a face in a mirror is dependent on the real face, having no existence apart from it and not effecting any change in the face itself. Take away the mirror, and you have an analogy to how the *esse formale* of creatures relates to the *esse virtuale* of created things in God's mind.

At this point we may well ask how these two levels of the existence of things, the *esse formale* and the *esse virtuale*, are related. Once again,

Eckhart's approach is dialectical. In an important text on God as similar and dissimilar in the *Commentary on Exodus* he invokes the relationship of virtual and formal existence. The distinction between virtual and formal existence expresses the dissimilarity of God and creature. "The forms of things are not in God formally, but the ideas of things and of forms are in God causally and virtually. . . . Thus, the created thing and the form through which it has its name exists in itself but in no way in God." Therefore, Eckhart concludes, "the unlikeness remains, and the foundation of the likeness is lacking in each term, that is, in God and the creature."[198] But this dissimilarity is only half the story, because "the forms of things would not be produced by God unless they were in him. Everything that comes to be comes to be from something similar. . . . And so every creature is similar to God."[199] The root of this dissimilar-similarity is to be found in the dialectical principle Eckhart uses to set up the four examples he gives in this passage (the virtual/formal example is number 4). He expresses the principle as follows: "The third proposition is that nothing is both as dissimilar and as similar to anything else as God and the creature. What is as dissimilar and similar to something as that whose very 'dissimilitude' is its very 'similitude,' whose indistinction is its very distinction?"[200] To paraphrase: God and creatures are *unlike* (i.e., distinct, or different) in that God possesses the "*idea* of likeness" while creatures are *formally* like one another. But, since God's distinction resides in the "idea of *likeness*" (i.e., indistinction), then the more like he is, the more unlike, and vice versa.

When Eckhart defended his assertions regarding the eternity of creation in his trials at Cologne and Avignon, it is puzzling to note that he did not appeal to the distinction between the virtual (i.e., eternal) and the formal (i.e., temporal) aspects of creation, but rather to the Aristotelian categories of *actio* and *passio*—from an eternal action (*actio*), Eckhart contended, it does not necessarily follow that the created reception (*passio*) also be eternal. In his Avignon Defense, for example, he said:

> It is the same now of eternity in which God creates the world, in which God exists, and in which God generates his eternal Son. But it does not follow that because God's action is eternal that the world is eternal, because God produces the world from the start and out of time and in the now of time in such a way that the world and its creation is a reception (*passio*) in time, and the now of time and creation as reception are not in God but in the creature.[201]

The problem with this, as the Avignon inquisitors observed, is that, in the Aristotelian language of *actio/passio* drawn from the analysis of motion these two moments are *simultaneous* aspects of the same production, movement, or change. This is why Thomas Aquinas had denied that creation should be conceived of in terms of a motion, or change, but rather as the beginning of a relation of dependence (see STh 1a, q.44, aa.1-2). In his "Defense" Eckhart would have been better served by invoking the notion of *causa essentialis* and the distinction between *esse virtuale* and *esse formale*—categories more basic to his metaphysics of flow.[202]

Understanding creatures from the perspective of their *esse formale* also helps explain Eckhart's oft-repeated assertion that creatures *taken in themselves* are nothing.[203] "Every created thing of itself is nothing," as Eckhart often repeated both in his scholastic writings and in his preaching. One passage to this effect from Pr. 4, as we have noted, was condemned as heretical. In defending himself at Cologne and Avignon, Eckhart grew indignant: "To say that the world is not nothing in itself and from itself, but is some slight bit of existence, is open blasphemy."[204] He might even have appealed to Thomas Aquinas, who once said, "Each created thing, in that it does not have existence save from another, taken in itself is nothing."[205] To say that creatures are nothing for Eckhart is to say that the existence they possess is a pure receiving.[206] Poised between two forms of nothingness, the *nihil* by way of eminence that is God, and the *nihil* that marks the defect of creatures, Eckhart's mystical way will be an invitation to the soul to give up the nothingness of its created self in order to become the divine Nothing that is also all things.[207]

Finally, the nothingness of creation also helps us understand another peculiarity of Eckhart's teaching—his conception of creation as a "fall" away from Oneness, a form of "metaphysical sin" that is the ground for the evil that we find in the world. Creation *insofar as* it is the manifestation of divine goodness ("Goodness of its nature gives of itself," as a Neoplatonic axiom says)[208] is, of course, a single good and beautiful theophany. In accordance with another Neoplatonic axiom that "only one thing proceeds immediately from a single thing that is uniform in relation to itself," Eckhart taught that God's creative intention is directed to the entire universe, looking to "the whole universe itself, which proceeds from God as one whole thing, though in many parts. . . ."[209] (Eckhart playfully etymologized the Latin *universum* as meaning "uni-versum," that is, "directed toward the One.")[210] On the other hand, *insofar as* the one universe is composed of divergent creatures, it involves numeration, which is a "fall" (*casus*), a descent, and an imperfection. In the *Book of the Parables of Genesis,* Eckhart says: "Number and division always belong to imperfect things and come from imperfection. In itself number is an imperfection because it is a falling away or lapse outside the One that is convertible with being."[211] This metaphysical fall is the root of the possibility for *malum,* the mystery of evil.

Like all Western theologians since Augustine, Eckhart held that evil was not just a negation, but was a privation, the lack of a good that should be present.[212] Since created being already is a lack or falling away, *malum* has its ground in the deficient being of creatures. Eckhart, however, went further. Because everything is hidden in its opposite, just as the multitude is hidden in the One, and good in evil, the privation that constitutes evil is rooted in God's decision to create anything outside himself. A remarkable statement from S. VIII says, "Nothing itself, the root of evils, privation, and the many, is hidden in true and full existence itself. The reason is because it [nothing] is in it according to its mode, or rather it is in it and is it, as is said, 'What was made in him was life'" (John1:3–4).[213] For Eckhart, evil is ultimately no more than an illusion to be seen through in order to reach the God in whom all affirmation and negation are rooted. This led him to some extreme, even shocking, statements, such as: "In every work, even in an evil one, an evil I say both of punishment and of fault, God's glory is revealed and shines forth and gleams in equal measure." This passage, and two adjoining sentences from the same place in the *Commentary on John,* were condemned as heretical.[214] Although Eckhart analyzed the harmful effects of the fall of humanity on the order of the universe and in daily life,[215] his fundamentally optimistic view of creation had little appreciation for the demonic power of evil.

THE CREATION OF HUMANITY
AS *IMAGO/INTELLECTUS*

Humanity as *imago/bild* occupies a special place in Eckhart's doctrine of the outflowing of all things from the divine source. Although the universe is one and directed to the One, it is also multiple, hierarchically organized according to the three levels of existence, life, and intelligence. Each of these modalities exists principially in the next, so that mere being is life in living being, and living being is intellect in intellectual being.[216] The special status of intellectual being (comprising both men and angels)[217] is that in its Principle it is divine—*imago dei* in the fullest sense. Human destiny is to hear and respond to God's speech in creation and thus, as the *principium* in the created universe, to draw all things back to their ultimate source. In the *Book of the Parables of Genesis* Eckhart says:

> Thus God speaks in the same way through everything to all that is. He speaks, I say, all things to all. But some hear him and respond under the property of existence by which God is existence and the existence of all things is from him. Others hear him and receive God's Word as it is the first and true Life. These are all living things. The highest beings hear God not only through and in existence, or through and in life, but through and in understanding itself. In that realm understanding and speaking are the same.[218]

We will consider the role of humanity in the return in more detail below. Here it is enough to note one explicit treatment emphasizing the universal aspect of human *reditus,* that in Pr. 90, where Eckhart discusses how we come to share in Christ's four ways of knowing in order to draw all things back to God.[219]

The German Dominican sets forth his teaching about humanity as intellectual being throughout his Latin and German works.[220] Much of this is the standard medieval anthropology largely dependent on Augustine.[221] For Eckhart the account of the Fall in Genesis 3 is a message about human nature and moral decision. Adam, or the man, is parabolically interpreted as the higher reason (*ratio superior*) directed to God; Eve is the lower reason directed to the external world, while the serpent is the sensitive faculty.[222] Sin is the disordering of the hierarchical relation of the faculties so that the higher reason can no longer have direct contact with God (In Gen.II nn.139–44). In Pr. 83 Eckhart expands on this triple analysis, distinguishing three inferior powers of the soul (the power of discretion in the senses, and the irascible and appetitive powers), and three superior powers, the Augustinian triad of memory, understanding, and will.

Eckhart and the main tradition of Christian anthropology found the key to understanding the nature of humanity in Genesis 1:26, where God says, "Let us make man in our image and likeness." "This was said of the human race," according to the Meister, "in relation to the intellect that pertains to the superior reason—that by which it is the 'head' of the soul and 'God's image.'"[223] "Note that humanity is what it is through the intellect," as he put it in another place.[224] Though it was customary in Latin theology to identify the *imago dei* with the human intellect (i.e., superior reason), Eckhart's understanding of *imago/bild* and *intellectus/vernünfticheit* is distinctive. Image and intellect are essential themes of his preaching.[225]

Eckhart's remarks on Genesis 1:26 in his *Commentary on Genesis* are the obvious place to begin an analysis of how he understands humanity's character as *imago dei*.[226] Here he says:

> Now recognize that the rational or intellectual creature differs from every creature below it because those below are produced according to a likeness of the thing as it is in God and they have the ideas that are proper to them in God. . . . The intellectual nature as such has God himself as a likeness rather than something that is in God as an idea. This is because "The intellect as such is the power to be all things"; it is not restricted to this or that as to a species.[227]

The point is that, as we have seen in speaking of Eckhart's analysis of *imago* in S. XLIX above, "it is of the nature of an image that it fully expresses the entirety of what it images, not that it expresses some determined aspect of it."[228] Therefore, from the perspective of its relation to God, intellect is the image of the *whole* of divinity, while from the perspective of its relation to creatures, intellect, like God, images nothing because it has no determination. As Eckhart says in the *Parisian Questions:* "Intellect, insofar as it is intellect, is nothing of the things that it understands. . . . Therefore, if intellect, insofar as it is intellect, is nothing, then the act of understanding is not any kind of existence."[229]

Because the intellect is capable of being one with all things in coming to know them, it is more than just the formal existence of some divine idea in the world—it is the very presence of God as indistinct One in his creation. The *Commentary on John* takes this perspective even further when it says, "Man is created to the image of the entire divine substance, and thus not to what is similar, but to what is one; . . . [hence] a return to what is similar is not enough, but it must return to the One from which it came forth and this alone satisfies it."[230] The human intellect is essential to both the *exitus* and the *reditus* that form the dynamic of Eckhart's metaphysics of flow.

The text of Genesis 1:26 speaks of humanity as made *ad imaginem*. Other passages in scripture, especially Pauline ones like 2 Corinthians 4:4 and Colossians 1:15, identify the Only-Begotten Son as the real *imago dei*. The distinction between the Word as the true *imago* and humanity as made *ad imaginem* had already been developed in Latin theology, especially by Augustine. Eckhart used it, but in his own way. His detailed analysis of the nine characteristics of *imago* comes in an exegesis of the Colossians text in the midst of his commentary on John

1:1, speaking of the relation of Word to the Father.[231] But Eckhart was willing to apply the language of both *imago* and that of *ad imaginem* to the human intellect, using *imago* to emphasize the indistinction of the divine and human intellect, and *ad imaginem* to express the distinction of the human intellect from its divine source insofar as it possesses *esse formale*. Because God's ground and the soul's ground are one ground, the human intellect is not other than the Only-Begotten perfect Image in the Trinity; but it still remains a created, or as Eckhart sometimes says, "concreated" (*concreatus*), reality as well. In Pr. 40 the preacher deliberately emphasizes the two perspectives he employs: "In saying that man is one with God and is God according to that unity, one considers him according to [i.e., *inquantum*] that part of the image by which he is like God, and not according to his being created. In considering him as God, one does not consider him according to his being a creature."[232]

Eckhart returned to this challenging message about intellect as true *bild/imago* over and over again in his vernacular homilies. A look at Pr. 16b, given on the Feast of St. Augustine, provides a good example of how he presented it to a lay audience.[233] The Epistle text comparing Augustine to a "golden vessel" (Eccli. 50:10) provides the point of departure for an analysis of the difference between physical vessels and spiritual vessels like the soul, which literally become what they take in. "Thus," says Eckhart, "the soul wears the divine image and is like God."[234] Image implies similarity but also goes beyond it in expressing ontological dependence on what it images. Hence, there are two characteristics of every image. "The first is that it takes its being immediately and of necessity from that of which it is an image" (DW 1:265.9–10). Eckhart gives two examples: a branch growing out of a tree and a face reflected in a mirror. In nature, when an image is seen in a mirror, the image is merely a reflection in the already-existing mirror; when God forms an image of himself, however, he gives the very reality of the image and presents it with "everything that he has and can do." This is why the Son is properly called the "Image of God" as "the first bursting-forth from nature" (*êrsten ûzbruch ûz der natûre* [DW 1:266.9]).

What is true of the Son in the Trinity is also realized by the soul *insofar as* it is *imago dei*. "You should know that the simple divine image which is pressed onto the soul in its innermost nature acts without a medium, and the innermost and the noblest that is in [the divine] nature takes form in a most proper sense in the image of the soul."[235] Since there is no medium between God and the soul, their relation is one of formal emanation, not creation. "Here the image does not take God insofar as he is Creator; it takes him, rather, insofar as he is a being endowed with intellect, and what is noblest in [the divine] nature takes its most proper image in this image."[236] The second characteristic of image so conceived is its total dependence on the exemplar—"an image is not from itself, nor is it for itself." Eckhart lists four implications of this: (1) an image is completely from its exemplar and belongs to it totally; (2) it does not belong to anything else; (3) it takes its being immediately from the exemplar; and (4) "it has one being with it and is the same being" (*und hât éin wesen mit im und ist daz selbe wesen* [270.6]). This affirmation of the identity of the soul as image with God—which Eckhart here explicitly defends as something not just for the university classroom, but for the pulpit "for instruction" (*ze einer lêre*)—was later singled out for attack by the Cologne inquisitors.

In the latter part of the sermon Eckhart moves on to draw the practical application of his teaching on the image of God. Basically, he invites his audience to live according to the inner image—that is: be God's, not yours! Loving God for devotion or interior consolation is to make God into something to be used for something else (like a cow for its milk, he says). Loving God should be its own reward. Calling upon his often-employed language of Justice and the just person, he says:

> Only that person is just who has annihilated all created things and stands without distraction looking toward the Eternal Word directly and who is imaged (*gebildet*) and re-imaged (*widerbildet*) in Justice. Such a person takes where the Son takes and is the Son himself. The scripture says: "No one knows the Father but the Son" (Matt. 11:27);[237] and so, if you want to know God, you should not just be like the Son, rather you should be the Son himself.[238]

This sermon on the image of God, as mentioned, came in for attack at Cologne. The excerpted article is actually taken from an alternate version of the section dealing with the two characteristics of the image mentioned above (this text is edited as Pr. 16a). Following the mirror example it says: "Thus too I say of the image in the soul: what comes out is what stays within, and what stays within is what comes out. This image is the Son of the Father, and I myself am this image, and this image is wisdom."[239] As Loris Sturlese has observed, Eckhart's defense of this passage is crucial.[240] The Meister admits that what is said at the end—"that 'I am that image'—is an error and false." The reason, he avers, is that an image is not something created, and "angels and humans were created *after the image of God*" [my italics].[241] Once again, Eckhart is here invoking the principle of formal, or *inquantum*, speaking. Insofar as we are speaking about humans and angels as created *ad imaginem* (i.e., the existential "I" of our subjectivity), it is wrong to say that "I am that image"; but for those who can grasp that the intellect in the ground is beyond the existential created "I" as the true *imago* which is the Only-Begotten Son, the statement is a saving truth.

In three closely related sermons (Prr. 69, 70, and 72) Eckhart discusses the various kinds of images (*bilde*) in order to clarify the difference between knowing things through their created images and knowing God beyond all images in the true *Imago dei* that is the Son. Prr. 70 and 72 explore how three ways of knowing make use of images. Following Augustine (*Literal Commentary on Genesis* 12.34), in Pr. 72 Eckhart discriminates: (1) bodily knowing by means of the corporeal images the eye sees; (2) mental knowing by means of the images of bodily things; and (3) "the third [knowing which] is interior in the spirit, which knows without image or likeness, and this knowledge is like to that of the angels."[242] Pr. 70 helps explain this by noting that this third form of knowing is the knowledge that the angels and the soul have of themselves, not of other things—it is a knowing without image, likeness, or medium of any kind (Pr. 70 [DW 3:194]). This is the self-presence of intellectual being to itself, something which for Eckhart is not mediated by any image. Such self-presence provides the hint for how we come to know God without image or medium. "If I am to know God without medium," says Eckhart in Pr. 70, "without image, and without likeness, God actually has to become me and I have to become God."[243] In that union of indistinction we come to know God as he knows himself. Eckhart continues:

> It is a property of God that he knows himself without a "little bit" (John 16:16) and without this or that. Thus does an angel know God—as it knows itself.... But I say: We shall know him just as he knows himself—in that reflection (*widerbilde*) that alone is the Image of God and the Godhead (that is, to the extent that the Godhead is the Father). To the degree that we are like the Image into which all images have flowed forth and have left, and to the degree that we are re-imaged in this Image and are directly carried into the Image of the Father—to the degree that he recognizes this in us, to that degree we know him as he knows himself.[244]

Sermon 69 was also preached on John 16:16 ("A *little bit*," as Eckhart reads it, "and you will not see me").[245] Here the Dominican enriches his teaching on the image by relating it to the nature of the intellect as intellect. The "little bit" that gets in the way of seeing God is every kind of created being—any and all intermediaries. In physical seeing, says Eckhart, we do not see a stone itself, but an image of the stone. However, there is no infinite regress—that is, we do not need an image to see the image; the image itself is the medium. Extending the analogy, Eckhart says that in knowing spiritual things the eternal Word acts as the image without image that enables the soul to know God in that very Word itself (DW 3:168). Only the intellectual creature, however, has this relation to the Word. Eckhart explains it as follows:

> There is a power in the soul, namely intellect. From the moment it becomes aware of and tastes God, it has within itself five properties. The first is that it separates from here and now. The second, that it is like nothing. The third, that it is pure and unmixed. The fourth, that it is operating or seeking within itself. The fifth, that it is an image.[246]

The analysis of the meaning of these five properties makes it clear that there is no difference at all "insofar as intellect is concerned" between the divine Intellect (see S. XXIX and questions 1–2 of the *Parisian Questions*) and this power in the soul. This is because intellect *inquantum intellectus* is a true image in the sense of a pure formal emanation—"In this you have the whole sermon in a nutshell," says Eckhart. "Image [i.e., the Word] and image [i.e., human intellect] are so completely one and joined together that one cannot comprehend any distinction between them. . . . I say further: God in his omnipotence cannot understand any distinction between them, for they are born together and die together."[247] Furthermore, it is intellect that alone provides access to the ground. Eckhart ends the sermon in dramatic fashion:

> The intellect looks within and breaks through into every hidden cranny of the Godhead. It takes hold of the Son in the Father's heart and in the ground and places him in its own ground. Intellect penetrates within. It is not satisfied with goodness, or wisdom, or truth, or with God himself. . . . It never rests, it bursts into the ground from which goodness and truth come forth, and takes hold of it [i.e., the ground] *in principio,* in the beginning where goodness and truth are coming forth, before it has a name, before it breaks out. . . .[248]

Although in these three sermons on image and intellect Eckhart does not go on to draw out all the daring implications of the fused identity of the divine and human intellect in the one ground, these are certainly present by implication. Perhaps most disturbing was the recognition that from the point of view of intellect as intellect the human shares responsibility with God for creation itself. As Pr. 52 puts it: "For in the same being of God where God is above being and above distinction, there I myself was, there I willed myself and committed myself to create this man."[249]

This view of pure intellect was at the heart of one of the most controversial aspects of Eckhart's teaching and preaching, his claims about the "uncreated something" in the soul. One of the two appended articles in the bull "In agro dominico," dealt with this uncreated something—"There is something in the soul that is uncreated and not capable of creation; if the whole soul were such, it would be uncreated and not capable of creation, and this is the intellect." In his Defense Eckhart denied saying precisely this (*praeterea, hoc non dixi* [Proc.Col.I n.137]), though the article is quite close to a passage in Pr. 13.[250] In explaining what he meant, Eckhart once again appealed to the difference between the pure Intellect of God, that is, the Word which is "uncreated and has nothing in common with anything," and "the created human being which God made to his image and not [as] the image itself; and he clothed it not with himself, but [only] according to himself."[251]

This uncreated something in the soul is *intellect insofar as it is intellect.* Eckhart metaphorically characterized it in many ways, as we have seen—spark, castle, nobleman, seed, divine light, height, guardian, etc.[252] Pr. 2 describes it as a "simple one" (*einic ein* [DW 1:43]), and in S. XXXVI Eckhart used the Latin form of this, taken over from Proclus, the *unum animae*—"Jesus comes to this [city of the soul] to seek the whole, the one of the soul."[253] In understanding what Eckhart meant by these expressions, we need, as always, to be attentive to the formal character of *inquantum* language. The "uncreated something" is *intellect as intellect,* as virtual being, not as formal being in the world. It is something *in* the soul (or perhaps better, the soul is really *in* it); it is not *of* the soul; that is, it does not belong to the soul's created nature *ad imaginem.*[254] Though Eckhart does use the language of "part" and "power" of this uncreated something at times, these terms are misleading. The "uncreated something" is not and cannot be a part of any-*thing.* It is as mysterious and as unnameable in us as it is in God.

CHAPTER 6

Going without a Way: The Return to the Ground

WE HAVE FOLLOWED ECKHART'S PATH of the outflowing of all things within and without God. But Eckhart the teacher and preacher did not wish his audience merely to be content with whatever intellectual grasp of *bullitio* and *ebullitio* was possible for them—the purpose of his message was to rouse his hearers to a new state of awareness that would lead them back to the divine ground within. It is interesting to note that in the "Granum sinapis" sequence Eckhart spends the first three strophes describing the emanation of the Persons in the Trinity and the unknown nature of "the Principle [whose] point never moves" (*ist ein gesprink/gâr unbewegit stêt sîn punt*), and no fewer than five strophes exploring the path that is no-path back to God:

lâ stat, lâ zit,	Leave place, leave time,
ouch bilde mît!	Avoid even image!
genk âne wek	Go forth without a way
den smalen stek,	On the narrow path,
sô kums du an der wûste spôr.	Then you will find the desert track.[1]

It is, of course, impossible to make any separation between *exitus* and *reditus* in Eckhart's works—"God's going out is his going-in" (Pr. 53). But, just as the preacher can only present one aspect of the divine mystery at a time, so too, for the sake of clarification it is useful to sketch out the major themes of Eckhart's understanding of the return to God, as long as we realize that these do not constitute any itinerary of stages in the manner of some other mystics. For Eckhart one must

"Go forth without a way," because "[w]hoever is seeking God by ways is finding ways and losing God, who in ways is hidden" (Pr. 5b).

My consideration of Eckhart's doctrine of the return to God will begin with a treatment of the Dominican's understanding of Christ, the Godman. Just as creation, for Eckhart, is a continuous and eternal process (*creatio continua*), so too the Word taking on flesh is not a past event we look back to in order to attain salvation, but rather is an ever-present hominification of God and deification of humanity and the universe—an *incarnatio continua*.

ECKHART'S CHRISTOLOGY[2]

Eckhart's Christology was out of step with his times. He shares little of the new christological currents, both in theology and in devotion, that shaped the later Middle Ages. The importance of innovative forms of devotion to Christ's humanity that developed in the twelfth and thirteenth centuries, while sometimes exaggerated and misunderstood, is undeniable, as names such as Anselm of Canterbury, Bernard of Clairvaux, and Francis of Assisi, demonstrate.[3] Bernard's "fleshly love of Christ" (*amor carnalis Christi*), and Francis's stigmata seen as a literal sharing in Christ's passion (a new form of *imitatio Christi*) effected a revolution in piety.[4] The new forms of piety centering on Christ's life were accompanied by a search for better understanding of the person and work of Christ in the theology of the schools. On the basis of the Chalcedonian dogma that a full divine and full human nature were united in the Person of the Word (i.e., a hypostatic union), "faith seeking understanding" pursued more adequate expressions of how God and human are one in Christ. Since the early twelfth century, theologians had also begun to formulate new ways of understanding redemption. How had Christ redeemed us? How did the effects of his death and resurrection reach the believer? Anselm's concentration on the motif of *satisfactio* marked a key moment in the evolution of Western redemption theology. Most thirteenth-century scholastics devoted considerable effort to exploring the nature of the hypostatic union, as well as to analysis of the meaning of redemptive satisfaction.

When we look at Meister Eckhart's writings, both his technical scholastic works and his MHG sermons and treatises, we find almost nothing of this. There are no pictures of the infant Jesus in the crib or meditations on the bloody Christ on the cross. There is little consideration of the historical events of Christ's life. At times, Eckhart seems to go out of his way to avoid an obvious christological reading of a text.[5] On the more technical side, Eckhart spends no time discussing the various theories of the hypostatic union or of satisfaction. Only a single sermon gives any real attention to one of the hotly debated areas of speculative Christology, the question of the modes of knowledge, divine and human, enjoyed by Christ.[6] It is clear, then, that Eckhart's preaching and teaching are exceptions to much of late medieval Christology.

But does this mean that Christology is unimportant to Eckhart's message? Does his emphasis on the birth of the Divine Word in the soul reduce the historical events of Christ's life, especially the passion, to secondary or even unimportant status? If we think that the new spirituality of the *amor carnalis Christi* and the literal *imitatio Christi* is the only form of late medieval devotion to Christ, then we must answer yes. Likewise, if subtle analysis of the union of God and man in Christ is essential to Christology, then Eckhart has little to offer in this area. Nevertheless, Eckhart's view of the God-man and his theology of redemption are both original and essential for understanding his theology and mysticism. Numerous christological discussions in Eckhart's works show that without attention to the role of Christ it is impossible to understand his message or to attempt to put it into practice.[7]

Eckhart's Christology was fundamentally practical, or perhaps better, as some have called it, a "functional Christology."[8] Thinking about the mystery of the God-man was not meant to be an exercise in making scholastic distinctions, but in learning how to live the meaning of the life of the Incarnate Word. This emphasis on the practical payoff of his message also indicates that the *imitatio Christi* plays a role in Eckhart's thought, though one different from what we usually meet with in the late Middle Ages.

The best place to begin to grasp Eckhart's Christology is in his commentary on John's Prologue.[9] The lengthy remarks on vv. 1–10 ring the changes on the relation between the just person and Justice, the theological foundation of Eckhart's frequent preaching about the birth of the Eternal Word in the soul. However, when Eckhart reaches v. 11 ("He came into his own"), he reads the text both as expressing the universal reception of the Divine Word in all reality (especially in the intellect), and also as indicating the Word's assumption of human nature with its passibility and mortality. This leads him to an interpretation of v. 12b ("He gave them the power of becoming sons of God"), which emphasizes the core of his Christology, namely, his constant insistence on the *purpose* of the Incarnation. God's intention in sending his Son was that "man may become by the grace of adoption what the Son is by nature" (n.106). This version of the ancient patristic motto ("God became man that man might become God") was repeated often by Eckhart in his Latin works and especially in his vernacular preaching.[10] "Why did God become man?" he rhetorically asks in Pr. 29—"So that I might be born God himself" is the answer.[11]

The distinction between "Son by nature" and "sons by adoption" that Eckhart appealed to in interpreting John 1:12 was a motif rooted in Scripture, especially the Pauline letters, and can be found as early as Augustine.[12] He uses the distinction in numerous places in his Latin and German works.[13] When his Christology was taken to task in the trials at Cologne and Avignon, it is not surprising that he appealed to it to explain how his statements could be squared with traditional theology.[14] For example, his defense of the final article from the second list of extracts culled from his German sermons says: "Don't think that there is one Son by which Christ is God's Son and another by which we are named and are sons; but it is the same and is he himself, who is Christ, born as Son in a natural way, and we, who are sons of God analogically—by being joined to him as heir, we are coheirs."[15]

In commenting on John 1:12, Eckhart explains the divine intention in taking on human nature by calling on one of his favorite christological texts, 2 Corinthians 3:18 ("With faces unveiled reflecting as in a mirror the glory of the Lord, we are being transformed *in the same image* from glory to glory"). If the distinction of sonships emphasizes the traditional side of Eckhart's theology of the Incarnation, the stress on transformation into the *same*, that is, identical, image suggests its more daring aspects.[16] In concluding his reading of John 1:12, Eckhart returns to the first part of the verse and asks who are "the many who received him" and thus gained sonship? Here the Dominican introduces a third essential motif of his Christology, when he says that they are "as many as were empty of every form begotten and impressed by creatures" (n.110). Total purity, emptiness, detachment—abandoning the *esse hoc et hoc* of created being—is the condition for the possibility of receiving the "same image" which is Christ as God and man.

These three central motifs are fleshed out in Eckhart's comments on v. 14a ("The Word became flesh and dwelt among us"). Here Eckhart says, "It would be of little value for me that 'the Word was made flesh' for man in Christ as a person (*supposito*) distinct from me, unless he was also made flesh for me personally so that I too might be God's son."[17] Does this mean that we ourselves become the Second Person of the Trinity? Yes and no, according to Eckhart. Yes, in the sense that there is only one Sonship, which is not other than the Person of the Word; no, in the sense that "we are born God's sons *through adoption.*" In his defense at Cologne and Avignon, Eckhart would appeal to the *inquantum* principle to explain this kind of expression. *Insofar as* there is only one real Son of God, if we are sons (as scripture expressly says), we are indeed identically the same Son *insofar as* we are sons, univocally speaking. From the perspective of our existence as created beings, however, we are sons by adoption and participation, analogically speaking.[18]

Eckhart interprets the two parts of v. 14 as expressing the indissoluble link between the hominification of God and the divinization of man—"The Word was made flesh" in the Incarnation, "'and dwelt among us' when in any one of us the Son of God becomes man and a son of man becomes God."[19] When he turns to v. 14b ("We saw his glory, . . .), the wider cosmological implications of sonship, typical of his fusing of all truth, theological and philosophical, into a single system, emerge. Eckhart notes that in *Confessions* 7.9.13 Augustine said that he had found everything John wrote about the eternal generation of the Word in the "books of the Platonists," but he did not find there any reference to the Incarnation. Eckhart politely disagrees with the bishop, claiming that seeing the glory of the Incarnate Word, notwithstanding the truth of the historical birth of Christ, ". . . is contained in and taught by the properties of the things of nature, morality, and art. The Word universally and naturally becomes flesh in every work of nature and art and it dwells in things that are made or in which the Word becomes flesh."[20] Every time a form is generated and comes to perfection in the natural world, and even in the artificial world of human creativity, we can catch a glimpse of the glory of the Only-Begotten of the Father taking on flesh.

The full explanation for this claim is not given until the comment on v. 17 ("The law was given through Moses, grace and truth were made through Jesus Christ"). In contrasting Moses and the Old Testament with Christ and the New Testament, Eckhart once again speaks ontologically, comparing the Old Law to the imperfection of all forms of change, becoming, and multitude, while the grace and truth of Christ indicate "existence, generation, immutability, eternity, spirit, simplicity, incorruption, infinity, the one or unity" (n.186). This is so because it is the Incarnation that is the necessary link between the eternal emanation within the Trinity and the whole of created reality. As he puts it:

Again, note that because "The Word was made flesh," that he might dwell among us, as expounded above, . . . it seems fittingly added that the

Wisdom of God deigned to become flesh in such a way that the Incarnation itself, like a medium between the procession of the divine Persons and the production of creatures, tastes the nature of each. This
happens in such a way that the Incarnation itself exemplifies the eternal
emanation and is the exemplar of the entire lower nature.[21]

Here Eckhart goes beyond his usual formulations found in the exegesis
of the early verses of the Prologue and elsewhere, in which he roots all
making (factio) in the eternal emanation of the Word from the Father
without reference to the Incarnation. This passage expresses something
like the pan-Christic ontology of Maximus the Confessor and others,
who saw the Incarnation, the hominification of God, as the very purpose and inner reality of creation itself.[22] Eckhart makes the same point
with classic economy in S. XXV: "'I came forth from the Father and
came into the world' [John 16:28] through creation, and not only
through Incarnation."[23]

A look at another text in the Latin writings that provides an exposition of Eckhart's Christology helps fill out the picture presented in the
Commentary on John. In the Dominican's response to the second list of
articles presented to him at Cologne, he spends considerable time
defending article 27: "God gives nothing outside himself; he always
gives in eternity, not in time."[24] Eckhart's response to this objection
constitutes a mini-treatise in the form of a scholastic *quaestio* in which
he both defends the principle from an ontological perspective and also
shows how it is crucial for understanding Incarnation and redemption.

Eckhart begins by presenting four premises necessary for grasping
how God chooses us from all eternity, "although it is true that we
receive in time." Two of these echo the text from the commentary on
John 1:17 quoted above and emphasize the teleological connection
between creation and redemption. "This," he says, "is because the work
of creation, of nature, is ordered to the work of re-creation and grace,
as the material to the formal, matter to form, the passive to the active,
woman to man."[25] The fourth principle notes that while particular
agents intend and produce particular effects, the nature of a species
intends something similar to itself in species and nature. As applied
"principially to God," this helps us understand the identity of the one
Sonship in which our salvation rests. The conclusions that Eckhart
draws from these general principles are largely christological in nature,
another sign that for him creation and recreation are two sides of one
and the same coin. The core of his position is put as follows:

Everything that is declared in these four preliminary articles is manifest,
namely, that the Word assumed human nature from his first intention—

this human nature, that is, in Christ—for the sake of the whole human species. Therefore, by assuming that nature, in himself and through himself he confers the grace of sonship and adoption on all humans, me, you, and anyone at all who shares univocally and equally that nature, according to the text, "The Word was made flesh," namely in Christ, "and dwelt among us."[26]

Eckhart then draws out some necessary corollaries from this argument. Many of these are Christological and echo what can be found in the *Commentary on John,* such as the insistence that Christ assumes the human nature that is common to all, the necessity for loving all humans equally in Christ, and the need to put off everything that is ours or that is particular in order to love in this way.[27] Eckhart's defense of his teaching about Christ in article 27, as well as the numerous other appearances of Christology in the trial documents, provides ample proof of how important this aspect of his teaching was for him and for his critics.

On the basis of these two Latin treatments, it is clear that Eckhart's functional Christology was not concerned with exploring the mode of the union of God and human in the Incarnation. He concentrated, instead, on the redemptive significance of the Word made flesh. The same message is conveyed in his vernacular preaching. An analysis of two christological sermons, as well as some passages in the *Book of Divine Consolation,* will show how the Meister presented the meaning of the Incarnation to a lay audience.

Pr. 46 is relatively short, but typically Eckhartian in its depth and complexity.[28] In explaining John 17:3 ("This is eternal life"), the preacher underlines three key points with interjections like *Nû merket!* "Now note well!" The first is that in order to know God and reach blessedness we must become "one Son, not many sons; rather, one Son," since in God there is only "a single flowing out with the eternal Word" (*niht wan éin natiurlîcher ursprunc*). The second point explains how this is possible. Just as Eckhart's ontology distinguished between the *esse hoc et hoc,* the *diz und daz* of created reality, and the pure *esse indistinctum* of God, so too the economy of redemption demands that the Word did not assume *this or that* human person, but pure, unformed humanity in itself. It is this humanity, without image or particularity, that the Son takes to himself. Because we too possess this humanity, his Form or Image (i.e., the very Image he eternally receives from the Father) becomes the image of humanity. "Hence," Eckhart says, "it is just as true that man became God as it is that God became man. This is how human nature was transformed (*überbildet*); by becoming the divine image, that is, the image of the Father."[29]

In order to attain this transformation we must free ourselves from all the "nothing," that is, everything accidental, in us. What is accidental causes distinction, and distinction separates us from God. We leave behind every "accident of nature" (*zuoval der natûre*) by reaching into the power in the soul that is "separated from nothing" (i.e., indistinct). When we arrive at this power, where God "shines naked" (what Eckhart elsewhere calls "the spark of the soul"), we realize the status of being the one Son. Having attained this, we will have "movement, activity, and everything," no longer from our individual selves, but from the inner being and nature that the Son takes from the Father. We are now one in the unity of the Father and the Son so that "our" works (which are really now "his") come from within, not from outside, and are thus filled with divine life.[30]

How are we to go about freeing ourselves from the nothing that causes distinction, from our human personality considered as an "accident of nature"? Does the historical life of Jesus Christ play any role in this, or is the process one based only on insight into the transcendental meaning of the Incarnation? A brief look at a long and difficult sermon, Pr. 49 on the text "Blessed is the womb that bore you and the breasts that nourished you" (Luke 11:27), will help address these questions.[31] This sermon, as well as a number of other texts in Eckhart's writings, show that there is definite place for an *imitatio Christi*, even an *imitatio passionis*, in his teaching.

The homily begins with a treatment of the relation between the Virgin Mary's bearing the Savior and the birth of the Word in the soul of each Christian.[32] The Meister always insisted that it was because Mary was first completely attentive and obedient to God's word (Luke 11:28) that she merited to become the physical Mother of God and our exemplar. In the first part of the sermon Eckhart makes use of Gregory the Great's description of four things needful for hearing and keeping God's word as a way of beginning the journey toward attaining the one Sonship.[33] This can be described as a general imitation of Christ as "free and poor in all the gifts he gave." But giving is external, and Eckhart always wants to push into the inner meaning of reality. In the second part of the sermon (in which Eckhart says he will *really* begin to preach), he explores the interior understanding of hearing and keeping God's word. "Now, play close attention to the meaning of this," as he prefaces his remarks (433.7-8).

Here the preacher reverses his consideration of the mutuality of Father and Son considered in Pr. 46, this time beginning not from how the Son has everything *from* the Father, but rather from how the Father *needs* the Son as his perfect expression—"Whether he would or not he must speak this Word and beget it unceasingly.... So you see the Father speaks the Word willingly but not by will, naturally but not by nature."[34] Echoing what we have seen in the earlier sermon, Eckhart claims that in that same necessary speaking God speaks "my spirit and your spirit and every individual human's spirit equally in the same Word."[35] He develops this theme in terms of his customary teaching on how the soul in its ground possesses the divine power of begetting both the Word and itself in the eternal now. In what follows, however, Eckhart gives this theme a christological thrust by introducing John 12:24, a text that speaks of the grain of wheat falling into the earth in order to bear hundred-fold fruit. The grain is the soul of Jesus which falls into the "most glorious humanity of Jesus Christ" (*hôchgelobete menschheit Jêsû Kristi* [439.1]). Eckhart's rather obscure explanation of how this process takes place is not as important as why he invokes the motif of the death of the seed in the first place. Because Christ's fruitfulness comes from his suffering and death, if we too wish to be fruitful, we must follow his example.

In his consideration of the role of Christ's suffering and death here,[36] Eckhart insists that Christ's pain affected only his outer person: "So it is in truth, for when his body died in agony on the cross, his noble spirit lived in this [divine] presence."[37] In affirming a distinction between Jesus' outer suffering and his inner stability in God, Eckhart was giving his own version of a standard medieval perspective that modern Christologies have often found problematic—the insistence that even in his suffering Christ somehow never lost the enjoyment of the beatific vision. He was to return to this theme a number of times in his vernacular works.[38] In this sermon, however, what is more important is how Eckhart presents the relation between Christ's exterior suffering and the central theme of his Christology—God became man so that man can become God.

The grain of wheat that is Christ's human soul perished in the body of the God-man in two senses. First, Christ's human soul possessed an intellectual vision of the divine nature that it continued to enjoy in its ontological ground, but not in the consciousness of its lower powers during his lifetime. (This is the first, or spiritual, death.) Second, Christ's soul gave life to his human body with all that it suffered of "travail and pain and discomfort" throughout his life, until he surrendered it in dying on the cross (the second, physical, death). Both modes of dying are important. The spiritual death involved not turning away from God no matter what the body had to suffer, while the physical death of offering up all his sufferings to the glory of his heavenly Father "became fruitful . . . to the sanctification of human nature" (444.5–6). Following Christ's example, then, anyone who wishes to cast his soul/grain of wheat into the field of the sacred humanity of Jesus must also die in *both* physical and spiritual fashion.[39] Physical death is accepting willingly whatever suffering God may send us, regarding all our "suffering as trifling, as a mere drop of water compared to the raging sea, . . . compared to the great suffering of Jesus Christ."[40] The more significant spiritual suffering and death, however, is inward—nothing less than absolute abandonment to God's will, even if this should involve annihilation or consignment to hell: "You should let God do what he will with you, what he will—just as if you did not exist. God's power should be as absolute in all that you are as it is within his own uncreated nature."[41] According to Eckhart, Christ is the only model for such inner emptying: "Christ our Lord alone is the end to which we must strive and our goal under which we must stay, with whom we shall be united, equal to him in all his glory. . . ."[42]

It is evident from this sermon that Eckhart's mysticism did not neglect an *imitatio passionis*, though, as we might expect, he had little interest in exterior practices such as meditation on the blood-drenched Jesus on the cross, let alone physical attempts to inflict such suffering on oneself, such as his disciple Henry Suso portrayed in his *Life of the Servant*. Eckhart's reading of the *imitatio passionis* is that enough suffering will come in the course of any life to allow us to imitate the example of Jesus as a way to get beyond our individual wills. We do not need to seek out suffering; we need to transform the way we view suffering. Suffering is not a special way to God, but a way to discover that God is not found in ways.[43]

The role of suffering in imitation of Jesus received its most profound analysis in the *Book of Divine Consolation*, possibly written for the pious Queen Agnes of Hungary, who had undergone much suffering, including losing her father to assassination. Here Eckhart takes suffering into the heart of his dialectical understanding of God and God's relationship to us.[44] Just as Pr. 52 plumbs the depths of Eckhart's thought through a meditation on the first of the beatitudes ("Blessed are the poor in spirit," Matt. 5:3), the *Book of Divine Consolation* performs a similar analysis by focusing on the last beatitude, "Blessed are they who suffer persecution for justice' sake" (Matt. 5:10). Beginning

from commonplace observations found in standard consolation literature, Eckhart moves on through two deeper levels. The first identifies
suffering as consolation when we recognize it as God's will. The second,
typically Eckhartian and based on the identity between the soul's
ground and God's ground, asserts that when we accept suffering in this
way, God too must be said to suffer—"My suffering is in God and my
suffering is God."[45] This is not the place to lay out Eckhart's complete
analysis of this claim, but it is important to emphasize that he regards
the suffering of God not as a projection from our world (i.e., from
below, so to speak) but rather from above: God's desire to suffer is an
integral aspect of his eternal will for the Word to become man, and
therefore, central to the meaning of creation itself. As Eckhart ironically
put it in another passage in the treatise: "But God's Son by nature
wished by his grace to become man so that he might suffer for you, and
you want to become God's son and not man, so that you cannot and
need not suffer for God's sake or your own!"[46] This is an admirable
summary of Eckhart's view of the *imitatio passionis*.

It may be helpful at this point to summarize some key headings of
Eckhart's functional Christology. The Dominican's understanding of
the purpose of the Incarnation—God became man so that man can
become God—was scarcely new. Eckhart stands out among his contemporaries, however, in the emphasis he gave to this ancient theological truth, as well as in the variety of ways he presented it.[47] The
exemplum that Eckhart used in Pr. 22 to illustrate the divine love that
brought the Word down to take on human nature for our divinization
is among his most striking presentations of the theme. The story is that
of a "rich man" and his wife, who had the misfortune to lose an eye. In
order to prove the constancy of his love for her, he gouged out one of
his own eyes. Eckhart summarizes the purpose of God/the "rich man"
as follows: "'Madam, to make you believe that I love you, I have made
myself like you; now I too have only one eye.' This stands for man, who
could scarcely believe that God loved him so much, until God gouged
out one of his own eyes and took upon himself human nature."[48]

A second major theme concerns the Word's assumption of common
or universal human nature. It was, to be sure, standard teaching, at least
since the condemnation of Nestorius, that Christ did not assume a
human person, but human nature as such. Eckhart, however, gave this
teaching his own distinctive spin.[49] Because the Word assumed undif-
ferentiated human nature, not only is divine Sonship open to us only
in and through Christ, but we must be sons in *exactly* the same way that
he was.[50] This, of course, was the source of the many daring expressions

of the one Sonship for which Eckhart was taken to task in his trials. Several of these excerpts eventually featured in the bull of condemnation, notably articles 11 and 12. Article 11, from Pr. 5a, reads: "Whatever God the Father gave to his Only-Begotten Son in human nature, he gave all this to me. I except nothing, neither union, nor sanctity; but he gave the whole to me, just as he did to him."[51]

A third issue concerns how Eckhart's Christology relates to some of the more customary themes of medieval teaching about Christ. We have already remarked on his appeal to the traditional distinction between Son by nature and sons by adoption. It is also useful to note that the Meister's teaching on our union with Christ reflects the thirteenth-century development of the doctrine of the Mystical Body of Christ. The Dominican refers to Christ's Mystical Body in several places in his *Commentary on John*;[52] he also appealed to this teaching in the trial documents to explain some of his more problematic statements.[53] Nevertheless, Eckhart's theology of the Mystical Body departs from tradition in the emphasis it places on the physical and ontological *identity* between Christ and the believer.[54] The Meister certainly thought that his teaching was in conformity with what Paul had to say about the church as Christ's body (e.g., 1 Cor. 12), but he wished to go further than the usual understandings of oneness in Christ.

Another christological innovation in Eckhart concerns the relation of time and eternity, an area of some of the Dominican's more controversial speculations, as we have seen. In Galatians 4:4 Paul had said, "In the fullness of time (*plenitudo temporis*) God sent his Son." Eckhart does not read this passage, as was customary, in relation to the course of history, but rather as a reference to the "Now" of eternity breaking into human time. Paul's *plenitudo temporis* is comparable to when the day is "full" (i.e., at an end), because "if it were possible for the soul to be touched by time, then God could never be born in her, and she could never be born in God." Alternatively, the fullness of time is the gathering up the whole six thousand years of history into the "now of eternity, in which the soul knows all things in God new and fresh and present and joyous as I have them now present."[55] The total presentiality of Eckhart's functional Christology is well brought out in this reading of Paul—a new way of presenting the Incarnation as the meeting place of time and eternity.

If Eckhart's Christology is fundamentally functional, it is important in closing to highlight two of the practical conclusions of his view of the God-man. The first, already touched on above, concerns his view of the *imitatio Christi*. Eckhart's advice for living the life of Jesus is con-

cerned not with details of moral observance but with moral intentions—and only the most essential. As noted in the analysis of Pr. 49,
the imitation of Christ's passion was significant for Eckhart, but his dis-
interest in the outward aspect of the passion is evident in the *Commentary on John*.[56] When Eckhart considered the passion, he did not
treat the narratives of the death of Jesus, nor did he generally invite his
readers to picture Christ on the cross. He preferred to cite Matthew
16:24 and parallels: "If anyone wishes to come after me, let him take up
his cross and follow me." For Eckhart, imitation of Christ on the cross
was nothing more or less than total self-denial.[57] In his early vernacular treatise, the *Talks of Instruction*, he already insisted that to imitate
Christ means to be like him in totally surrendering to the Father, and
not in trying to follow the particulars of his life, such as his forty-day
fast in the desert.[58] Eckhart's view of self-denial, like his interpretation
of poverty in Pr. 52, was radical in the etymological sense of going to
the roots. What was essential was to appropriate the inner attitude that
Jesus had revealed in his suffering and death by becoming totally fixed
on God, no matter what the external situations in which we find ourselves.[59] Suffering, as pointed out above, is not a *way* to God, but is
actually identical with the goal—*if* we understand it as our surrender to
the God who totally surrenders himself to us—"In order to give himself totally, God assumed me totally."[60]

This approach to suffering as detachment and emptying is high-
lighted in a number of passages scattered through Eckhart's writings.
The treatise *On Detachment*, while it may not actually be Eckhart's, follows his spirit when it says: "The fastest beast that will carry you to perfection is suffering, for no one will enjoy more eternal sweetness than
those who endure with Christ in the greatest bitterness."[61] Taken out of
context, this sentence might seem to encourage physical forms of
passion-piety, but Eckhart (or whoever wrote the passage) proposed
these words in light of the declaration already noted from the *Book of
Divine Consolation*, "My suffering is God"—and therefore not really
me. As long as we consider anything, even suffering, under the rubric
of what is "mine," we will always be caught in distinction and be far
from God. If, in the midst of suffering, we learn that the pain is his—
as he made it in the passion—we are on the way to realizing the one
divine Sonship.

It is worth noting one final practical conclusion that Eckhart drew
from his functional Christology, though it may strike us as strange (and
certainly did so to his accusers). This is his claim that if Christ took on
universal human nature, we must love all humans universally and in

exactly the same way. One formulation of this, a rather obscure remark on John 21:15, made it into the bull of condemnation, although as one of the evil and rash-sounding, not heretical, statements.[62] Eckhart's view of loving all without distinction is more than the traditional claim that proper love of God is always measured by love of neighbor.[63] It is rather a necessary condition for truly detached loving, one that, in true *inquantum* fashion, is often extravagantly put. For example, Pr. 12 says: "If you love yourself, you love all men as yourself. As long as you love a single man less than yourself, you have never truly learned to love yourself—unless you love all men as yourself, all men in one man, that man being God and man."[64] Eckhart's texts on the necessity for this identical love of all for all may strike us as forced, but for him they were a necessary corollary to his belief that Sonship is one and the same in all the sons of God. Jesus provides the model for this paradoxical notion of universal and equal love for all, just as Jesus, the Incarnate Word, is the ontological bond of the entire process of emanation and return. In S. LVI Eckhart expresses the heart of his Christology in the following words: "Hence, all things must be dipped in the blood of Christ and brought back into the Father by the mediation of the Son himself; just as the Father does everything through the Son, so too must the flowing back match the flowing out."[65]

THEOLOGY OF GRACE

Eckhart's functional Christology is linked to his teaching on grace. In the *Commentary on John,* as we have seen, he defines the purpose of the Incarnation to be "that man may become *by the grace of adoption* what the Son is by nature" (n.106). In S. LII he expands on this: "God took on our vesture so that he might truly, properly, and substantially be man and man might be God in Christ. The nature taken up is common to all humans, neither more nor less. Therefore, every person can be God's Son, substantially in him, adoptively in self through grace."[66] These texts underline the necessary connection between the Incarnation and the role of grace in the return process.[67]

If grace is central for understanding Eckhart, however, it is not always easy to say exactly what he means by grace. His language often tends to be general, and, as we have found in other contexts, traditional formulations appear side by side with distinctive, and sometimes unusual and extreme expressions.[68] As in so much else, Eckhart can quote Thomas Aquinas in expounding grace, but his doctrine of grace in its fundamentals is rather different from that of Thomas.[69] What, then, was grace for Meister Eckhart?

On the most general level, Eckhart, like other theologians, holds that grace is every gift we receive from God, from the first grace of our created being (what he in some places calls *gratia gratis data*) to the gift of our return to God through intellect (*gratia gratum faciens*).[70] Eckhart takes up this distinction of graces in a small treatise in the *Commentary on Wisdom* that provides a good entry into his teaching.[71] Quoting his favorite axiom from the *Book of Causes,* he says that all things are a free gift (*gratia gratis data*) from the First who is "rich in itself." More important for his teaching and preaching, however, is the *gratia gratum faciens,* which is a "divine mode of existence" (*esse divinum*) given to the essence of the soul so that it can work divinely and spiritually. This grace, "which is called supernatural, is in the intellective power alone, but it is not in it as a natural thing, but is there as intellect so that it can taste the divine nature."[72] This is true of intellect "insofar as it is the image or [made to] the image of God" (n.274). So, truly "supernatural" grace is essential to the return process and is intimately connected to the intellect. But in what way?

This is where Eckhart's teaching on grace becomes somewhat unusual, at least from a Thomistic point of view. Eckhart agrees with Augustine and Thomas that grace is absolutely essential for the soul's return to God. He also stands with tradition in insisting that saving grace is nothing other than the grace made available to us in Christ. Indeed, the christological character of grace is evident both in the creative grace of *exitus* and the grace of recreation, or return: "And so *every* grace is in God alone, the Wisdom of God, the Son, because all his gifts are unmerited and are of him alone."[73] But Eckhart's teaching on grace departs from Aquinas in at least two ways. First of all, grace has a far more intellective cast for Eckhart than it does for Aquinas—for Eckhart, grace saves primarily insofar as it activates the intellect to become aware of itself as *imago dei*.[74] For Aquinas, on the other hand, "saving grace" (*gratia gratum faciens*) primarily elevates the fallen will, supernaturally enabling it to love God for God's sake alone.[75] Second, the relationship between grace and union is clear in Aquinas, but ambiguous in Eckhart. For Thomas Aquinas all union with God in this life takes place only in and through the action of supernatural grace. Eckhart, on the other hand, sometimes affirms that grace unites us to God, but at other times speaks of grace more as a means than an end— something necessary to attain indistinct union with God, but not that union itself. These seemingly contradictory statements parallel the clash between passages that speak about the "work of grace" and those that declare, "Grace performs no works, it is too delicate for this; work is as far from grace as heaven is from earth. An indwelling, and attachment and a union with God—that is grace. . . ."[76]

Grace is said to be the necessary means for attaining God in both the Latin and MHG works. For example, Pr. 96 says that every action or work (*ieglich werk*) flows from a particular form of being (*wesen*), as warmth does from fire. Without the grace that makes the soul like God and "God-colored" (*gotvar*) it could do no saving work.[77] Here Eckhart compares grace to an axe that enables the task of cutting to be done, concluding with the statement: "Grace brings the soul into God and brings it above itself, and it robs it of itself, and of everything that is creaturely, and it unites the soul with God."[78] In this sermon grace seems both active and unitive. S. XXV says the same, describing grace as a "boiling over" of the birth of the Son: "To the person who receives it grace is a confirmation, a configuration, or better, a transfiguration of the soul into and with God. Second, it makes one have one existence with God, something that is more than assimilation."[79] But elsewhere grace is clearly not unitive. "I say: grace does not unite the soul with God. It is a bringing to [the point of] fullness; that is its function, that it bring the soul back again to God."[80] In other places, such as in Pr. 82, Eckhart clearly distinguishes between two levels of union with God: one in which the soul is raised up by grace and united in a preliminary way; and a second in which grace, because it is a creature, must slip away, so that the soul no longer works by grace, but divinely in God as the "mode without mode."[81]

A key for understanding both how grace works and does not work and unites and does not unite can be found in Eckhart's teaching about the difference between the virtual and the formal modes of existence. In S. IX, preached on the text "the God of all grace" (1 Pet. 5:10), the Dominican says that if the grace of any single person is great,

> . . . how great [is the grace] of every human, and of all the different kinds of angels; how great it is to live there, that is, in the very "God of all grace," where already grace is not grace formally, but virtually (just as heat is in the sky)—there where there is neither goodness, nor delight, nor existence, but [only what is] above "in the region and realm of infinite unlikeness."[82]

From this perspective, we can also understand how, as Pr. 43 puts it, grace in its virtual state "has never done any work at all," but formally considered, "it flows forth in the doing of good works."[83]

The uniting with God that formal grace effects is not a real union from the perspective of the *ratio gratiae,* that is, the "grace beyond grace" which, in its virtual reality, is identical with the divine nature. This can be seen in Pr. 70, where the Dominican speaks about three forms of progressive illumination that lead the soul back to God. The natural light of the intellect, much higher than the sun's light, can, as we have seen, attain God in some way, but "intellect is little compared to the light of grace" that transcends all created things. "Yet the light of grace, great as it is, is little indeed compared with the divine light." As long as grace is growing in us, it is still grace in a formal sense and is thus distant from God. "But when grace is perfected in the highest, it is not grace: it is a divine light in which one sees God. . . . [At that point] there is no access, there is only an attainment."[84] In Pr. 75 a comparable pattern emerges in which Eckhart contrasts the light of the intellect with the stronger light of grace that draws a person into himself. Higher still is the light that is the divine Son being born in the Father's heart. "If we are to enter there," says Eckhart, "we must climb from the natural light into the light of grace, and grow therein into the light that is the Son himself. There we shall be loved by the Father in the Son with the love that is the Holy Spirit. . . ."[85] Despite a certain characteristic ambiguity, then, there does seem to be an inner coherence to the Dominican's theology of grace behind his at-times opposing formulations.[86]

In many late medieval mystics an investigation of their doctrine of grace would naturally lead into their views on how Christ's grace is mediated to the Christian community through the sacramental life of the church. Once again, however, Eckhart's theology of mysticism appears as anomalous, if not exactly subversive. On the surface at least, there is little ecclesiology or sacramentology in Eckhart. His earliest vernacular work, the *Talks of Instruction,* does offer some reflections on the role of the Eucharist and of confession to his audience of Dominican confreres,[87] but even in this work, Eckhart insists that outward practice means nothing without inward reception. This message was to become more pronounced in his later vernacular preaching to a largely lay, or at best semi-religious, audience. Although the Dominican's homilies were solidly anchored in the liturgical life of the worshipping community, as we have seen, Eckhart's uncompromising insistence on the inner appropriation of the saving mysteries had little room for preaching on the sacraments and other forms of devout practice.[88]

One exercise of the Christian life that Eckhart does discuss with some frequency is prayer.[89] Here too, as we might expect, his teaching is rather different from what we find in tradition and in most of his contemporaries. Eckhart's remarks about prayer were unconventional enough that two of them were included in "In agro dominico" as heretical. The first of these, drawn from the *Commentary on John*, expresses the heart of Eckhartian prayer: "He who prays for anything particular prays badly and for something that is bad, because he is praying for the negation of good and the negation of God, and he begs that God be denied to him."[90] Prayer, for Eckhart, should not be a petition for any-*thing* from God—that is the work of those he refers to as "asses" or spiritual "merchants."[91] Rather, it is the continuing dialogue (*confabulatio*) of the detached soul with God alone: a prayer without *eigenschaften* (i.e., personal attachments and concerns); a prayer to and for the Divine Nothing.[92] Both the prayers with which Eckhart the preacher concludes his sermons and the four prayers ascribed to him in manuscript sources amply illustrate his view of the prayer of detachment.[93]

It is important to get Eckhart's stance about practices of piety correct. In spite of his typical challenging statements about the uselessness of trying to find God in ways, the German Dominican never denied the efficacy of the church as the mediator of Christ's saving grace, nor did he attack the sacraments and the other ordinary means by which saving grace is communicated to the faithful. Even his condemned critical remarks about petitionary prayer need to be seen within the context of his hyperbolical style of preaching *rara et subtilia* in order to wake his audience from their moral and intellectual torpor. Eckhart was no rebel. But he was fixated on ends not on means, and one cannot escape the conviction that he was implicitly criticizing much of the preaching and religious practice he saw around him in the early fourteenth century by paying so little attention to such standard themes of medieval homiletics as faithful reception of the sacraments, practical moral advice, and fear of damnation.

DETACHING/BIRTHING/BREAKING-THROUGH

All of Eckhart's teaching and preaching in one way or another is geared to the overarching theme of helping Christians to return to their ground in the hidden God. We have already studied some of the major motifs and metaphors of the return, especially in investigating the *grunt* and in the analysis of Prr. 101–4 on the eternal birth. The purpose of this section is to give a summary account of the process of return by analyzing the three central activities that Eckhart uses to describe how the soul attains its goal: detaching; birthing; breaking-through.

Eckhart's notion of return is not a mystical itinerary in the usual sense; it is the attainment of a new form of consciousness, or awareness, as mentioned above. A central claim of my approach to the history of Western mysticism in the series entitled *The Presence of God* has been that consciousness of God's immediate presence provides the best general category for understanding the complex history of Christian mysticism. Although many mystics, Meister Eckhart among them, have given us detailed considerations of the notion of *unio mystica* (though few before the modern era used that term), I have argued that the permutations of presence provide a more helpful framework than the concept of union itself for subsuming the varied teachings of the mystics about their encounter with God. Consciousness of God's presence, even the awareness that comes in the midst of the sense of God's absence, is the formal feature of the various types of mystical language—union, contemplative vision, endless pursuit, divine birth, deification, and so on. Eckhart was especially attentive to the language of presence in the course of his preaching. His mysticism could be characterized as a mysticism of awareness of God's presence, as long as we realize that for Eckhart, as for so many apophatic mystics, the God who becomes paradoxically present is the "non-God, non-spirit, non-person, non-image" (Pr. 83) found in silence and darkness.

In his Latin works Eckhart notes scholastic discussions of the various ways in which God is present to all things, especially his immediate presence as *esse indistinctum*.[94] The same teaching is found in the MHG sermons, for instance, when the Dominican says, "All creatures have no being, because their being is suspended (*swebet*) in God's presence (*gegenwerticheit*)."[95] But what the Dominican wants his hearers to grasp is not the abstract truth that God is present in all things, but the reality of what it means to live in this awareness.[96] This message is found early and late in his teaching and preaching. For example, the sixth of the *Talks of Instruction* speaks of finding God's presence in everything. "He who has God essentially, takes him divinely. . . . God flashes forth in him always, in him there is detachment and turning away, and he bears the imprint of his beloved, present God."[97] The call to be "penetrated with divine presence" (*mit götlîcher gegenwerticheit durchgangen sîn* [208.11]) occurs often in this early work, which roots this insistence in the fact that "God is a God of the present," not of the past.[98] The absolute presentiality of the divine *nû*, in which "God is a pure instanding in himself, an instanding that supports all creatures,"[99] is found throughout the later German sermons. An especially important treatment is found in Pr. 9, one of Eckhart's most forceful statements of negative mysticism. In this homily Eckhart uses the planet Venus, which always stands near the sun, as an adverb to the divine Word, to figure "a person who wants to be always near to and present to God in such a way that nothing can separate him from God."[100] Constant awareness of the *gegenwerticheit gotes* is an essential part of the Meister's message.

How is one to attain this awareness of God's presence in the ground of the soul? Eckhart's attempts to lead his audience to this consciousness defy easy characterization, but we can gain a good sense of his many strategies by exploring three essential processes in attaining such awareness: detaching, or cutting off (*abescheiden*); birthing (*gebern*); and breaking-through (*durchbrechen*).[101] Although Eckhart used nouns developed from some of these verbs, it is important to emphasize that what he is speaking about are activities, not static states of being.

Meister's Eckhart's mysticism has often been described as one of "detachment," or, more literally (in his terms), of "cutting off, or away."[102] There are few motifs to which the Dominican appealed more often in his vernacular preaching.[103] The ways in which the preacher spoke of the need for separation from all earthly attachments in order to attain the freedom to find God are too varied to be expressed by any single term. Eckhart employed a range of verbs to try to convey his strategy for ending possessiveness: "detaching, cutting off" (*abescheiden/abgescheiden*); "leaving, letting go, resigning" (*lâzen/gelâzen*); "unforming" (*entbilden*);[104] "un-becoming" (*entwerden*). From these action words a series of nouns was formed to express various aspects of the deconstruction process, such as *abegescheidenheit*, and the rarely used (at least by Eckhart) *gelâzenheit*.[105] A set of adjectives expressing the freedom, emptiness, and nakedness of the dispossessed soul—*ledic, vri, lûter, blôz*—created another semantic range for proclaiming the same message.[106]

Eckhartian detachment, like so much in the Dominican's thought, is a process that is at once metaphysical, ethical, and mystical. It is rooted in the metaphysics laid out in detail in the Latin works, but is also present in more personal and direct registers throughout the vernacular treatises and sermons. Time and again the Dominican appeals to the principle that a receptive power cannot receive a form unless it is empty and free of other forms—the eye can only see color because it has no color of its own. On a higher level, the intellect can understand all things because it is no-thing in itself, but the capacity to know all. Intellect, then, must be empty and free of all created forms and all attachment to forms in order to receive God. As the treatise *On Detachment* puts it with concision: "You must know that to be empty of all created things is to be full of God, and to be full of created things is to be empty of God."[107] That is the law of the return. Total letting go, following the paradox of the Christian message ("He who would save his soul must lose it" [Matt. 16:25]), is the way to gain all things in the God who is the real being of all. "The more a person has left behind and the more poor he is," according to *Commentary on John*, "so much the more he finds; and what he has left behind, he finds in a higher and purer way."[108]

It will not be possible to try to survey all the ways in which Eckhart sought to preach this message of deconstruction,[109] but careful study of a few texts will suffice to show how radical Eckhart's mystical surgery was. Detachment was a central part of Eckhart's message from the beginning, as we can see from the *Talks of Instruction*, where three chapters introduce many of the aspects of the detaching process that Eckhart would preach on for the next quarter century. Chapter 3 deals with "unresigned people (*ungelâzenen liuten*) who are full of self will."[110] Spiritual restlessness, says Eckhart, comes not from things or situations, but from our own self-will: "You have to start first with yourself and leave yourself."[111] If we can learn to let ourselves go, we are in effect letting everything go. Here Eckhart cites two of his favorite biblical prooftexts for the necessity of giving up all things by first giving up self (Matt. 5:3 and 16:24). Such self-abandonment is to be understood as the truest form of self-knowledge: "Take a good look at yourself, and wherever you find yourself, let yourself go—that is the very best."[112] As Alois Haas has shown in his study of self-knowledge in Eckhart, it is only through the grace of Christ who has taken on the whole of human nature that humans can come to know themselves directly and essentially.[113] In perfect self-surrender, God's self-knowing becomes our self-knowing; or better, since there is no distinction in the one ground, there is only a single essential self-knowing. The metaphysics behind this daring claim was to be spelled out later on in the Dominican's teaching on intellect and the ground, but the ethical-mystical imperative is already present here in his first vernacular work.

The sixth of the talks ("Detachment and Possessing God" [DW 5:200–209) links letting go with awareness of the divine presence, as noted above. In this section, Eckhart once again says that only the internal state of being "God-mindful" allows us to have God ever present to us everywhere. "This true possessing of God depends on the mind (*gemüete*), and on an inner intellectual turning toward and striving for God, not in a continuous thinking [of him] in the same manner, for that would be impossible for nature. . . ."[114] God is beyond images and concepts, so it is only by "learning to break through things" (*Er muoz lernen diu dinc durchbrechen* [207.8]) and reaching the "inner desert" that we will find him. The teacher compares this mode of essential awareness of God to a continuous thirst and to a skill such as learning to write—at first it takes effort, but with practice it becomes second nature.

The longest consideration of detachment in the *Talks of Instruction* occurs in chapter 21 (DW 5:274–84), which treats of "Diligence." Learning to be "free in [doing] works" so that God can be always present to us demands "vigorous diligence" (*behender vlîz*) to keep free of both outward and inward images. Eckhart's treatment of this "inwardness" (*inwendicheit*) is reminiscent of the teaching found in the Sermon Cycle on the Eternal Birth treated above in chapter 4. Reaching such a condition involves careful and constant training of the intellect and the will—"There is no standing still for us in this life, and never has been for any man, however advanced he might be."[115] When what Eckhart calls the decisive and essential will has attained a constant "well-practiced detachment" (*wolgeüebete abegescheidenheit*), a person can begin to receive gifts from God. Just as individual consciousness vanishes in the true self-awareness that is God, so too the created will itself must be annihilated. "God never gave himself and never will give himself in another's will: he only gives himself in his own will. Where God finds his own will, there he gives himself and bestows himself in it with all that he is."[116] Hence, continues Eckhart, "We must learn to let ourselves go until we retain nothing at all that is ours. . . . We should put ourselves with all that is ours in a pure un-becoming of will and desire into the good and beloved will of God, along with everything we could will or desire in all things."[117] Here the un-forming and un-becoming of the created will, later to be powerfully proclaimed in the Eckhart's preaching, is already present in germ.

The most famous sermon on the need for annihilating the created will is Pr. 52, Eckhart's exploration of the three forms of poverty suggested by the beatitude "Blessed are the poor of spirit for theirs is the kingdom of heaven" (Matt. 5:3). Although this homily does not use the terms "detaching" or "detachment," its fifteen references to the adjective "free" (*vri*) and three uses of "empty" (*ledic*)—both of God and the soul—show that it must be ranked among the premier Eckhartian texts on the need for radical deconstruction of the created self. Edmund

Colledge and others have shown how this sermon contains echoes of the doctrine of annihilation of the created will found in Marguerite Porete.[118] Although this is an important witness to the Dominican's respect for the most profound woman mystic of his time, it is clear that Eckhart had already recognized that without such negation of both intellect and will no real consciousness of God could be attained.

The poverty sermon has been often analyzed and studied.[119] Here I wish only to highlight how Eckhart's carefully orchestrated three realizations of poverty of spirit—wanting nothing, knowing nothing, and having nothing—are nothing more or less than the absolute freedom that is the prerequisite for becoming truly aware of the God beyond all conceptions of "God." Any form of attachment, even to our good works, or to our own will to follow God, must be relinquished, according to Eckhart. One must strive to become as free of one's created will as one was before creation—an "empty existence" (*ledic sîn*) in which God as creator no longer is of concern.[120] Becoming free of will, for Eckhart, involves letting go of the will to be free of will. It means the rejection of all human works. As Michael Sells has shown, this is not a form of quietism or a lack of productivity—"The rejection of 'human' work is not a rejection of activity, but of the identification of the agent with the ego-self. . . . The true actor is the divine who works in the soul."[121] The return process frees us from God as creator and returns us to a blessedness beyond loving and knowing where "God is free of all things and therefore is all things." It is interesting to note, however, that in this radical expression of the meaning of freedom and detachment to a lay audience, Eckhart recognizes that the message may well be lost on many of his hearers: "Whoever does not understand what I have said, let him not burden his heart with it; . . . for this is a truth beyond speculation that has come immediately from the heart of God."[122]

One of the questions that emerges concerning Eckhart's view of detaching from all created things and desires is how this process relates to the other virtues of the Christian life.[123] It is clear that for Eckhart detachment is not just another virtue, just as it is not just another form of experience. As Denys Turner puts it, "Detachment and interiority are, for Eckhart, not so much the names of experiences as *practices for the transformation of experience;* . . . 'Detachment', in short, is the ascetic practice of the apophatic."[124] We must beware, then, of any easy importation of modern psychological categories back into Eckhartian detachment.

The MHG treatise *On Detachment,* even if it may not be from Eckhart's own hand, is helpful for understanding how detachment, as the

relinquishing of all possessiveness, is to be understood as a formal feature of all true virtue, rather than just another example of the genus.
The treatise begins with typical Eckhartian boldness, proclaiming
detachment as superior to humility, traditionally the foundation of all
the virtues, and even more important than love, the summit of the
Christian life, as well as mercy. The reason for this superiority is that
detachment, defined here as the spirit's standing "immovable against
whatever may chance to it of joy or sorrow, shame, and disgrace," is
actually a fundamental characteristic of the divine nature—"God has it
from his immovable detachment that he is God, and it is from his
detachment that he has his purity and his simplicity and his unchange-
ability."[125] However, it is clear from the treatise that there can be no
detachment without perfect humility and that the love to which
detachment is superior is the "interested" love by which we love God as
our final good. The higher, purer form of detached love is explored in
Pr. 27 preached on the text, "This is my commandment, that you love
one another as I have loved you" (John 15:12). In this homily Eckhart
says that Christ is enjoining on us "a love so pure, so bare, so detached
that it is not inclined toward myself nor towards my friend nor anywhere apart from itself."[126] This love is nothing else than the Holy
Spirit. Such detached divine love has no goal apart from God and
goodness. Because it is one with divine love, it possesses all virtues and
virtuous deeds. "If your love is really so pure, so detached, and so bare
in itself that you love nought but goodness and God, then it is certain
truth that all the virtuous deeds performed by all men are yours as per-
fectly as if you had performed them yourself."[127] Loving detachment is
the heart of all true virtue.

Many aspects of Eckhart's view of detachment are paradoxical
enough to have attracted the attention of his opponents, though there
is no explicit condemnation of the term in the bull "In agro dominico."[128] It is surprising that one of the most radical corollaries of the
apophasis of possessiveness did not arouse more controversy—this is
the notion, found in the treatise *On Detachment* and in many places in
his sermons and other writings, that true detachment "compels"
(*twinget*) God to work in us.[129] In the treatise, Eckhart says that
detachment surpasses love because love compels me to love God but
detachment compels God to love me. Pr. 48 has a particularly strong
form of this notion of how absolute self-emptying "forces" God to fill
the vacuum in the soul because it is really nothing else but his own
emptiness. Speaking of the person "who has annihilated himself in
himself and in God and in all things," Eckhart says that "God must

pour the whole of himself into this man, or else he is not God."[130] In order to understand this kind of language we must be mindful of the absolute identity in the one ground that annihilating detachment creates, or perhaps better, borrowing a word from Simone Weil, "decreates." In this ground God *must* be God, and therefore must flood into what is grounded.

The process of detaching the soul from all things, especially from the created self, raises the question of the status of the "I" and subjectivity in general in the Dominican's mysticism. This issue has produced considerable discussion in recent years and some disagreement between those who would see Eckhart's thought as the beginning of a trajectory that leads to modern theories of transcendental subjectivity, and those who argue that his notion of the destruction of the created self should be viewed primarily within the context of medieval theology, asceticism, and mysticism.[131] In both his Latin and his German works, Eckhart contended that the pronoun "I" rightly belongs only to God. In Pr. 28, for example, he says, "'Ego,' the word 'I,' belongs to no one save God alone in his oneness."[132] God's absolute self-presence allows him to announce his name as "I am who am" (Exod. 3:14). But in places in his sermons Eckhart himself speaks this "I." A good example can be found in the poverty sermon, where, toward the end, we find the remarkable sentences: "In my birth all things were born and I was the cause of myself and of all things; and if I would have wished it, I would not be nor would all other things be. And if I did not exist, God would also not exist. That God is God, of that I am a cause. . . ."[133] Here, of course, Eckhart is speaking in the voice of the eternal unborn self, not the created corruptible self. The created *ego* of our formal being is a false self, a "pseudo-I." It is only by deconstructing this self—a process Eckhart often describes using the verbs *entbilden* and *entwerden*—that we can find the true self, the "transcendent-I" who exists virtually in the ground of God. "You must un-form (*entbildet*) yourself in such a way," as the *Book of Divine Consolation* says, "that you may be transformed (*überbildet*) in God alone, and be born in God and from God. . . ."[134] *Entbilden,* the process of un-forming the created form of the soul, is nothing other than what Eckhart elsewhere speaks of as *entwerden,* or un-becoming. God himself "becomes and unbecomes," as Pfeiffer LVI says. In the twenty-first chapter of the *Talks of Instruction,* following a passage cited above about negating the created will, Eckhart says, "The more we un-become in what is ours, the more truly we become in that [i.e., the divine will]."[135] This process of deconstructing created subjectivity and ordinary forms of consciousness, especially as expressed in the verbs *entbilden* and *entwerden,* as Wolfgang Wackernagel has shown, is one of the dominant metaphors in Eckhart's teaching and preaching, occurring in the *Book of Divine Consolation,* as well as in some of Eckhart's most radical sermons (e.g., Prr. 28, 52, 77). Wackernagel characterizes it as "a vision devoid of reflexive consciousness, and it opens out into a sort of unknowing of the soul itself in the ground of divinity."[136]

As the passage from the *Book of Divine Consolation* cited above shows, it is in and through the deconstruction of self in detaching, letting go, relinquishing, unbecoming, that the birth of the Word in the soul takes place. Detaching and birthing should be seen not as successive stages in a mystical path but as two sides of the same coin. Although we have already investigated Eckhart's characteristic theme of the birth of the Word in analyzing Prr. 101–4 above, it will be useful to explore the relationship between detaching and birthing more closely through a look at Pr. 2, Eckhart's homily on the soul as virgin wife.

Meister Eckhart's apophatic deconstruction of intellect, will, and the subject itself has important ramifications for the understanding of gender, both in his day and in ours. Considerable attention has been given to the Dominican's connections with the female mystics of his time, both the Dominican nuns that he visited, preached to, and counseled and the many anonymous beguines he must have known in Strasbourg and Cologne. His links to mystical texts written by women, especially Marguerite Porete's *Mirror* and Mechthild of Magdeburg's *Flowing Light,* have been the subject of important studies in recent years. Mystical discourse often subverts ordinary understandings of the self and the gender identity that is part of self-awareness. Eckhart's radical explorations of language about God and self provide many examples of this—Pr. 2 is one of the prime cases.[137]

It was customary in earlier Western mysticism, given the feminine gender of nouns referring to the soul (e.g., *anima/sêle*), for male mystics to adopt, at least in part, a female self-understanding in their encounters with God. The combination of physical virginity with spiritual erotics is a powerful motif through much of the history of Christian mysticism.[138] Though Eckhart cited the Song of Songs for its emphasis on singled-minded devotion to love of God, he rarely makes use of the erotic imagery of the Song, let alone the new forms of erotic language favored by contemporary women mystics.[139] But the Dominican was fascinated with images of bearing and giving birth, and especially by the paradox explored in Pr. 2 of the virgin who is also a wife.[140] He wishes his audience to identify with fruitful femininity, but a fruitfulness that can be achieved only by radical detachment.

According to Luke 10:38, "Jesus went into a village and a woman named Martha received him into her house." Eckhart's rendering of this into MHG already reinterprets the Latin to highlight a new message: "Our Lord Jesus Christ *went up into* a *little castle* and *was received/conceived* by *a virgin who was a wife*" (the italicized words indicate the alterations important for Eckhart's teaching).[141] The first part of the homily deals with the paradox of the virgin wife. "Virgin," Eckhart says, "is as much to say as a person who is empty of all foreign images, as empty as he was when he did not exist."[142] Thus, the virgin signifies the utterly detached person. To an imaginary questioner who asks how it can be possible to be without any images at all, Eckhart responds that it is all a matter of attachment or possessiveness (*eigenschaft*)—if we are not attached to any of the countless images in the mind, and also not attached to any of our works, we can be as "empty and free and maidenly" (*ledic und vrî . . . und megetlich*) as Jesus himself and therefore be united to him. But being a virgin is not enough. Eckhart goes on:

> Now mark what I say and pay careful attention. If a person were to be a virgin forever, no fruit would come from him. If he is to become fruitful, he must necessarily be a wife. "Wife" is the noblest word that can be spoken of the soul and is much nobler than "virgin." That a person receive God in him is good, and in the reception he is a virgin. But that God becomes fruitful in him is better, for the only gratitude for the gift is fruitfulness with the gift. The spirit is a wife in the gratitude that gives birth in return, bearing Jesus back again into the Fatherly heart.[143]

In this passage Eckhart artfully fuses the paradox of virgin purity and wifely fruitfulness, especially through the linguistic ambiguity of *enphâhen* (meaning both "receive" and "conceive") and the reciprocity of thankfulness and fruitfulness, which mirrors the fused identity of God and human in the eternal birth of the Word. Since this fruitfulness is nothing else than the divine fruitfulness itself, the virgin wife, unlike ordinary spouses (i.e., those who are attached to their works and practices), can bear fruit a hundred or a thousand times a day "out of the most noble ground, or better said, yes, from that same ground from which the Father begets his eternal Word she is fruitfully bearing along with him."[144]

In the second part of the sermon Eckhart turns to an issue that has often come up in our discussion: "the little castle" (*bürgelîn*), that is, the power in the soul in which the divine birth takes place. Eckhart's consideration here is of the utmost significance for the proper evaluation of his thought on the return to God. First of all, he analyzes the power in the soul that is untouched by time because of its contact with the eternal now. Although Eckhart does not name it here, this is obviously the intellect. "For in this power," he goes on to say, "the eternal Father is giving birth to his eternal Son without cease in such a way that the same power is bearing the Son along with the Father and also bearing itself, the same Son, in the one power of the Father."[145] Here we see the identity of Sonship that so troubled Eckhart's judges and that was eventually condemned in the bull "In agro dominico." Eckhart then briefly discusses the second spiritual power of the soul, the will.

After an interlude on the nature of suffering, the Dominican concludes with an important treatment of the "little castle" itself. The preacher notes that he has often spoken of "the one power in the soul that alone is free," calling it many names. Now he refuses to name it. "It is neither this nor that; rather, it is a 'something' higher above this and that than the heaven is above the earth. . . . It is free of all names, and stripped of all forms, completely empty and free as God is empty and free in himself."[146] It is as one and simple (ein und einvaltic) as God is. Eckhart then briefly returns to "the same power of which I have spoken" (i.e., the intellect) in which the birth takes place in order to set up the most radical part of his message, namely, that the unnamed power lies beyond all powers and even beyond the Persons in the Trinity.[147] Neither intellect nor will can see into this bürgelîn. Even God cannot look into it for an instant "insofar as he possesses himself according to modes and personal properties." When it comes to the grunt (which is what Eckhart is speaking of here without using the word) God can penetrate only insofar as "He is a simple One, without mode or property: there in the sense that he is not Father, or Son, or Holy Spirit, and yet is a something that is neither this nor that."[148] God's ground and the soul's ground is one and the same ground, which in some way resides deeper even than the birth of the Son in the soul.

Before turning to the third essential motif of the dynamism of the return, breaking-through into the ground, we need to consider the wider historical context of Eckhart's teaching about the birth of the Word in the soul. The Dominican preached the geburt in season and out, and it is worth pondering why he made it so central to his message.[149] As Hugo Rahner showed in a seminal article, the motif of God's birth in us, sacramentally and mystically, is among the most ancient themes in Christian tradition, rooted in scripture and explicitly set forth as early as Origen.[150] Despite the fact that the divine birth was taken up by some earlier Latin mystical authors, notably John Scottus Eriugena and Cistercians such as Guerric of Igny, there was little precedent for the way in which Eckhart made *geburt* the focus of his preaching. As Hans Urs von Balthasar put it: "He [Eckhart] melted down the philosophy of every thinker and recast it into the central mystery of the divine birth."[151] The motivation for this general smelting process is elusive, though some evidence exists regarding its reception. For example, the Augustinian friar Henry of Friemar produced three brief Latin treatises probably in 1309 concerning the birth of the Word in the soul in which he cautioned against the dangerous conclusions to which some were taking this ancient motif of Christian theology.[152] If Eckhart had already been preaching on this topic in the Sermon Cycle on the Eternal Word, as suggested above, Henry may well have had him in mind. It is obvious from the Cologne proceedings that Eckhart's preaching on the birth was one of the issues that the opponents seized on with special vehemence. But all this does not help us understand why the Dominican preacher made *geburt* so central to his preaching. One might hazard the supposition that the birthing motif shows us Eckhart both as a man of his times and as a critic of some aspects of late medieval piety. The concentration on the Person of Jesus in late medieval piety is evident in art and literature, as well as in theology and devotional literature. Eckhart too is centered on Jesus, but in a special way. His Jesus is not the infant in the crib, the suffering Christ, or the erotic lover, but the God-man whose taking on of general human nature makes possible our becoming aware of what is always happening in the now of eternity—the birth of the Word from the Father and in the depths of the soul.

Meister Eckhart's third dynamic metaphor for understanding the return to God is that of "breaking-through" (*durchbrechen*) beyond all conceptions of God known by philosophy or revealed in scripture, "into the silent desert where distinction never gazed" (Pr. 48).[153] No aspect of Eckhart's mysticism has rightly been seen as more radical; yet, looking at this language in light of what we have already seen about the Dominican's teaching on the Trinity and on the *grunt* itself, we can see that it is integral to his thought and its application to the lives of his hearers.

The relationship of breaking-through and birthing has elicited attention from many students of Eckhart. In one sense, many of the Dominican's formulations give breaking-through an ultimacy that even the birth of the Word in the soul does not have, as suggested in the passage from the end of Pr. 2 on the *bürgelîn*. But it is important to think of the three basic activities of the return process as having a reciprocal and dialectical relationship—all are simultaneous in the *nû* of eternity and simultaneously interdependent.[154] On the one hand, there is no break-through without loss of all possessiveness and realization of the birth; and on the other, the birth of the Word in the soul and leading a per-fectly detached life express the identity in the ground achieved in the breakthrough. The relation between birthing and breaking through is the same as the fused identity of hidden ground and "boiling" Trinity.

As we have already noted in looking at some of the texts speaking of the breaking-through, Eckhart most often uses *durchbrechen* and its equivalents (e.g., *zerbrechen*: Pr. 51 [DW 2:473.5-9]) to express the need of going beyond God conceived of as creator and as possessed of any attributes, even those of the three Persons of the Trinity. "In the break-ing-through," as Pr. 52 says, "when I come to be free of will of myself and of God's will and of all his works and of God himself, then I am above all created things, and I am neither God nor creature, but I am what I was and what I shall remain, now and eternally."[155] The power in the soul that effects this breakthrough is the intellect, which is never satisfied with goodness, wisdom, truth, or even God himself; but "forces its way in," "bursts into the ground," and "breaks through to the roots."[156] Other texts speak of the mutual breaking-through of God and human, implying the language of the fused ground. Pr. 26, for example, says that the spirit must transcend all number and multiplicity in order to have God break through it. "And just as he breaks through into me, so I break through in turn into him. God leads this spirit into the desert and into the unity of himself, where he is simply one and welling up into himself."[157] The mention of the desert (*einöde/wüestunge*) intro-duces another of the Dominican's favored metaphors for expressing the pure emptiness of the fused ground.

Moses' encounter with God in the wilderness of Sinai provided a scriptural basis for the rich evolution of the desert motif in Christian mysticism.[158] Although Dionysius never explicitly identified God with the desert, the way in which the Dionysian *Mystical Theology* links Moses' desert journey to Sinai with apophatic mysticism laid the basis for such identification, which appears first in John Scottus Eriugena.[159] In the twelfth century, the Cistercian "myth of the desert" led to con-siderable use of the desert motif among the White monks, both to sig-nify the inner solitude of the heart stripped and ready to receive God, and also (at least in Isaac of Stella) to point to the hidden God. In the thirteenth century, Thomas Gallus, the Victorine commentator on Dionysius and the Song of Songs, identified the desert of Song 3:6 and Exodus 5:3 with "the inaccessible and singular supersubstantial soli-tude of the eternal Trinity" described by Dionysius in the *Divine Names* and *Mystical Theology*.[160] As a profound student of Dionysius, Eckhart need not have known Gallus to make the identification on his own. The Dominican uses the desert motif more than a dozen times to refer both to the uncreated something in the soul and to the inner ground of God.[161] Eckhart often employs a text from Hosea 2:14 in which God announces that he will lead rebellious Israel out into the desert to woo her anew. At the end of the sermon entitled "Of the Nobleman," for example, Eckhart summarizes how the breakthrough of the desert journey leads to indistinct union:

> Who then is nobler than he who on one side is born of the highest and the best among created things, and on the other side from the inmost ground of the divine nature and its desert: "I," says the Lord through the prophet Hosea, "will lead the noble soul out into the desert, and there I will speak to her heart," one with One, one from One, one in One, and in One, one everlastingly. Amen.[162]

One of Eckhart's most powerful uses of breakthrough language is found in a MHG sermon on three forms of the soul's death, first edited by Franz Jostes over a century ago, and sometimes referred to under the title "How the Soul Went Her Own Way and Lost Herself."[163] Eckhart scholars such as Friedrich Schulze-Maizier, Alain de Libera, and Oliver Davies have accepted the sermon as probably authentic, and it relates to other passages in Eckhart that pick up on the theme of *mors mystica,* a recurrent motif in the history of Christian mysticism.[164] This homily also shows how breaking-through into the God beyond God is a passage into a form of transcendent subjectivity.

After a lengthy discussion of trinitarian theology in the first part of this long sermon, the preacher turns to the relation between the nobility of the soul's image of God and its divine source in part 2. This section, like Pr. 52, is carefully constructed according to a threefold model: three forms of going out from the soul's being (*wesen*)—as created being; as being in the Word; and as being possessed "in the overflowing nature that is active in the Father."

Going out from created being is achieved through inward self-abandonment, following Christ's command to take up the cross, deny oneself, and follow him (Matt. 16:24 again). This stage begins with the practice of virtues, seen as modalities of the love that transforms us into God. Eckhart, however, like Marguerite Porete, advances the claim that the perfection of virtue is "to be free of virtue" (*Daz ist volkumenheit der tugent, daz der mensche ledik ste der tugent* [92.31–32]). This should not be taken to mean that the virtues are destroyed or abandoned; rather, they are possessed in a higher way. The spiritual death to our created being is the total abandonment of self and all things, and even of God (John 12:24 is cited)—"Here the soul forsakes all things, God and all creatures."[165] Eckhart says that such forsaking of God is not an exaggeration but a necessity: "As long as the soul has God, knows God and is aware of God, she is far from God . . . ," so, "the greatest honor the soul can pay to God [is] to leave God to himself and to be free of him."[166] However, such "mystical atheism" is only the beginning.

Eckhart (or his follower) next turns to the necessity for the soul to go out from the being that it has in the eternal Image in God, that is, "the light of the Uncreated Image, in which the soul finds her own uncreatedness."[167] This "divine death" (gotlich tot) is needed because even though the soul has returned to her uncreated state in the Word as Image of the Father, she still finds herself in the multiplicity and distinction of the Persons of the Trinity. It is at this juncture that the preacher invokes the language of breaking-through:

> And so the soul breaks through her eternal Image in order to penetrate to where God is rich in unicity. That is why one master says that the breakthrough of the soul is nobler than her flowing out. . . . This breaking-through is the second death, which is far greater than the first.[168]

This "wonder beyond wonders" means the death of God, at least God as the Son. When the Son turns back to the divine unity, he loses himself, and hence when the soul "breaks through and loses herself in her eternal Image, then this is the death of the soul that the soul dies in God."[169] Here the soul goes beyond the identity she has with God in the eternal Image. There is no longer any kind of imaging, and even the identity that implies two distinct things becoming one is lost. There is only nothingness.

It is hard to see at this stage what kind of death might be left, but the preacher manages a further dying, one that involves a death to all works and activity, even in God. This is the attainment of what might be called a unity beyond identity, which is also a kind of transcendent self-discovery. This final non-stage, if I read it rightly, takes off from the Father's "pre-ebullitional" sense of himself as the potential source of the Son and Holy Spirit, something that also implies the subsequent ebullitio of creation.[170] Hence, if the soul is to reach "divine union at the highest level" (gotlich einung . . . in der hohst [95.14]), it must give up all the "divine activity" (gotlicher wirkung) that is associated with the Father as Father. The preacher describes what happens next in terms that go beyond anything found explicitly elsewhere in Eckhart's authentic sermons, but that are extensions of the most radical aspects of his preaching. Basically, the third death involves getting rid of all the potentiality for activity, within and without God, that is found in the Father. The puzzling thing is that the sermon identifies this highest state with the "kingdom of God" (*daz reich gots*) preached so often in the Gospels and mentioned twenty times in this sermon. (One might have thought that the final death is so far beyond anything like the "God" of thought or revelation that only negative expressions could be used.) The exposition of the final death is verbose, though these lines (ed. 95.5–98.8) so often pick up on themes present elsewhere in Eckhart that they form an argument for the authenticity of the piece. (Is it Eckhart repeating himself, or a student striving to show that he too is "Eckhart"?) What is new in this conclusion of the sermon is the notion that this final death is a transcendent self-realization.

The sermon describes the third death as the necessary corollary of the second. After the second death, when the soul recognizes that she cannot enter the "kingdom of God" on her own, she must be ready to give up even more. But what is there left to give? In a dark saying, the homily continues,

> Then the soul perceives herself, goes her own way and never seeks God; and thus she dies her highest death. In this death the soul loses all her desires, all images, all understanding and all form and is stripped of all her being. . . . This spirit is dead and is buried in the Godhead, for the Godhead lives as no other than itself.[171]

This new "place" where the soul finds herself is identified as "the fathomless ocean of the Godhead" (*in disem grûndlosen mere der gotheit* [95.38–39]). Here, as "soul loses herself in all ways, . . . she finds that she is herself the same thing which she has always sought without success."[172] Paradoxically (as ever), Eckhart says that this is a *new* kind of image, the "highest image in which God is essentially present with all his divinity since he is in his own kingdom" (96.6–7). The fusion of subjectivity, however, remains christological—"God became another I so that I might become another he. As Augustine says, God became man so that man might become God."[173] In this vein, the sermon concludes by insisting that the three deaths can only be attained by the action of grace, and that works based on living in God's kingdom are a single living work performed without distraction or self-interest, the kind of acting "without a why" that will be explored below in relation to Pr. 86. Indeed, this sermon on "How the Soul Lost Herself" is very reminiscent of the well-known "Martha and Mary" homily. Both go beyond the limits of sermons generally accepted as authentic works of Eckhart, at least in particulars. But if they are not by Eckhart, who preached them? Was there a mystical preacher more Eckhartian than Eckhart himself?

UNION WITH GOD AND LIVING WITHOUT A WHY

On the basis of this survey of the three essential interrelated metaphors for *reditus*, we can now summarize what Eckhart taught about union with God as the goal of all existence: "Every desire and its fulfillment is to be united to God."[174] In a sense, of course, everything Eckhart says both about creation (especially the divine immanence in all things) and about the return speaks of union. God's presence to all things as *esse indistinctum* indicates that there are really two aspects to union for Eckhart: the preexisting essential union that is God's abiding indistinction from all things as their true reality; and the union to be achieved by our becoming "aware" through "unknowing" of that presence by the process of detaching, birthing, and breaking-through.[175]

"You should completely sink away from your you-ness and flow into his his-ness and your you and his his shall become one 'our' so totally that with him you eternally comprehend his unbecoming Isness and his unnamed Nothingness."[176] In formulations like this from Pr. 83 Eckhart tortures language and syntax in his attempts to express the inexpressible union of indistinction. In other places he speaks more directly: "Between man and God there is not only no distinction, there is no multiplicity either—there is nothing but one."[177] Eckhart was uncompromising in his insistence that union with God was absolute and total identity, without medium of any kind.[178]

In the history of Christian mysticism it is possible to distinguish two broad models of understanding union with God—union as the perfect uniting of the wills of the divine and human lovers, the *unitas spiritus* suggested by the oft-cited text of 1 Corinthians 6:17 (*Qui autem adhaeret domino unus spiritus est*); and union as indistinct identity between God and human in what Eckhart called the *grunt,* or *ein einic ein,* "A Single One."[179] The Dominican thought that union of wills was not enough. As we have seen in Pr. 52, the created will must be annihilated so that there is nothing but the divine will working in itself in order for true unity to be attained. As Pr. 25 puts it:

When the will is so unified that it forms a Single One, then the heavenly Father bears his only-begotten Son in-himself-in-me. Why in-himself-in-me? Because then I am one with him; he cannot shut me out. And in that act the Holy Spirit receives his being and his becoming from me as from God. Why? Because I am in God.[180]

Eckhart did not invent indistinct union. It had deep roots in Neo-platonism, both pagan and Christian (e.g., Proclus and Dionysius are Eckhart's primary authorities), and similar views had already been advanced by some of the female mystics of the thirteenth century, notably Marguerite Porete. But no mystic in the history of Christianity was more daring and more detailed than Eckhart in the way in which he explored how true union with God must go beyond the mere unit-ing of two substances that remain potentially separable in order to attain total indistinction and substantial, or essential, identity.[181] "God is indistinct," as he once said, "and the soul loves to be indistinguished, that is, to be and to become one with God."[182]

Such an understanding of mystical union was and is controversial, and one still occasionally hears Eckhart accused of pantheism. The Dominican's response to such accusations was to show how his teach-ing was rooted in scripture and tradition and to insist on the necessary distinctions that need to be kept in mind to understand his "rare and subtle" teaching about mystical union. First of all, Eckhart appealed to scriptural texts, such as John 17:21, Christ's prayer to his Father for all who will believe in him, "that all might be one, as you, Father, in me, and I in you, that they may be one in us."[183] Eckhart took this passage literally, as he says in S. XXX: "All the saints are one thing in God, not [just] one."[184] Second, we must remember that Eckhart's notion of indistinct union, like all his thought, is fundamentally dialectical, that is to say, union with God is indistinct in the ground, but we always maintain a distinction from God in our formal being as *ens hoc et hoc*. Even in the ultimate union of heaven, Eckhart insists, this distinction will remain.[185]

The implications of Eckhart's view of indistinct union are many, and some of them have already been discussed. It is worthwhile now trying to summarize how Eckhart understood union. Indistinct union, for Eckhart, is a mutual and continuous state of nonabsorptive "aware-ness" of identity in the *grunt*. Ecstatic states play at best a preparatory and nonessential role. Union is also a form of deification, which, in the ultimate analysis, goes beyond knowing and loving, at least as we expe-rience them in ordinary conscious states.

The language of the dual breaking-through found in Pr. 26 discussed above shows that Eckhart, like the beguine mystic Hadewijch, stressed the mutuality of indistinct union. Of course, from the perspective of the soul's created being there is no mutuality at all—pure existence has nothing in common with nothing. But from the perspective of the *grunt der sêle,* there is a meeting of equals. According to Pr. 5b: "Go out of yourself completely through God, and God will go completely out of himself through you. When the two have gone out, what remains is a Simple One. In this One the Father bears his Son in the inmost source; out of it the Holy Spirit blossoms forth. . . ."[186] One of the ways that Eckhart spoke of this mutuality of God and human in the one ground was through the metaphor of the gaze of a single eye upon itself in a form of specular identity—"The eye in which I see God is the same eye in which God sees me. My eye and God's eye is one eye and one seeing, one knowing, and one loving."[187] Or, as another sermon puts it, "You must know in reality that this is one and the same thing—to know God and to be known by God, to see God and to be seen by God."[188] A lengthy treatment of the identity of knower and known in the act of knowing found in the *Commentary on John* lays out the metaphysical foundations for this teaching that "one is the face and image in which God sees us and we him."[189]

It is obvious that, according to Eckhart, our union with God is a continuous state, at least in some way. This is certainly true for the metaphysical indistinction that undergirds the union of awareness, but it should be clear from all that has been said about detachment, birthing, and breaking-through that these are meant to be realized in an uninterrupted fashion—at least on one level. Eckhart explicitly says this in many places, such as Pr. 86 to be treated below, as well as in the passage from the sixth of the *Talks of Instruction* cited above: "True possessing of God depends on the mind, and on an inner intellectual turning toward and striving for God, not in a continuous thinking [of him] in the same manner, for that would be impossible for nature. . . ."

For Eckhart, this continuous union with God is not an "experience" in any ordinary sense of the term—it is coming to realize and live out of the ground of experience, or better, of consciousness. It is a new *way* of knowing and acting, not any *particular* experience or act of knowing *something.*[190] Indeed, as we have seen, it is actually achieved by not-knowing (*unwizzen*). While this not-knowing is reached through the practice of states of interiority, as we have seen in analyzing Prr. 101–4, it is not dependent on them; it depends on God's gift, as Eckhart made abundantly clear over and over.

Most of Eckhart's late preaching emphasizes that the capacity to become "unknowingly" aware of the *grunt* is open to all believers and is fully compatible with a life of activity and service. The universalizing of the call to mystical union that was such an important aspect of the new mysticism of the thirteenth century was, if anything, heightened in Meister Eckhart's preaching.[191] Pr. 66 is one of the most powerful statements of this point. Preaching on the text from Matthew 25:23, "Well done, good and faithful servant, enter into the joy of your Lord," the Meister invites all in his audience to become "good and faithful servants" by becoming wholly free of self and giving themselves totally to God. The good and faithful servant is someone who has been faithful over "small things"—the littleness that is the whole of creation. To someone who is faithful in this way God is compelled to give his own inner joy. Eckhart becomes almost rhapsodic:

> But I say yet more (do not be afraid, for this joy is close to you and is in you): there is not one of you who is so coarse-grained, so feeble of understanding, or so far off but that he can find this joy within himself, in truth, as it is, with joy and understanding, before you leave this church today, indeed before I have finished preaching. He can find this as truly within him, live it and possess it, as that God is God and I am a man.[192]

The universality and presentiality of the possibility of union helps explain the Dominican's attitude toward states of mystical absorption, rapture, ecstasy, as well as visions and the like. Eckhart recognized that these forms of special mystical consciousness did exist, and that they might even be useful if understood in the proper way. But they did not pertain to the essence of union, and they might be harmful if they came to be seen as either a necessary "way" to the goal, or confused with the goal itself. Eckhart often refers to Paul's famous ascent to paradise described in 2 Corinthians 12 as an example of the kind of "raptured" realization (*raptus/exstasis mentis*) of the unknown God that is not incompatible with true mystical union.[193] In MHG, as we have seen, he makes use of the verbs *gezücket/enzücket* with some frequency to describe absorptive states of consciousness.[194] He also recognized that experiences of "enjoyment of God," which he spoke of as *gebrûchenne,* had their place.[195] The danger with such states, however, is the temptation to become attached to them and therefore to fail in the only necessary practice, complete dying to self in "cutting off" all earthly things and our desires in order to concentrate on God alone. In Pr. 41 Eckhart forcefully rebukes those who want to "taste God's will" as if they were already in heaven. "They love God for the sake of something that is not God," he says. "And if they get something they love, they do not bother about God, whether it is contemplation, or pleasure, or whatever you will—whatever is created is not God."[196] It would be easy to parallel this passage with many others, but the point is made.

If the highest form of union is meant to be in some way constant, Eckhart also holds that it is realized in activity, at least the kind of transcendent activity that is the welling-up, or *bullitio,* of life within the Trinity. This is especially evident in Pr. 6, a sermon on the text "The just will live forever" (Wis. 5:16), and one of Eckhart's most detailed expositions of the relation between Justice and the just person in his vernacular works.[197] In it the Meister put forward some of his most dangerous formulations on the birth of the Word in the soul and on the union of indistinction.[198] Toward the end of sermon, in discussing the ceaseless activity of the Father in giving birth to the Son, he emphasizes how the union found in the birth in the soul is a mutual fused "working" (*würken*) and "becoming" (*werden*) in which God and I are one—"I take God into me in knowing; I go into God in loving. . . . In this working God and I are one; he is working and I am becoming."[199]

The mention of both knowing and loving in this passage from Pr. 6 raises another important issue for the proper understanding of Eckhartian union—what are the respective roles of intellect and will? Nothing could be more evident than Eckhart's conviction that union with God takes place in the soul insofar as it is intellective, a position he was happy to share with Maimonides—"In the essence [of the soul], as intellective, it is joined to what is higher than it, God, as Rabbi Moses has it: And thus it is 'offspring of God.'"[200] As the famous Latin sermon on God as intellect puts it: "The one God is intellect and intellect is the one God. . . . Therefore, to rise up to intellect, and to be subordinated to it, is to be united to God."[201] The treatment of intellect given above, especially as found in Latin texts like *Parisian Questions* qq. 1–2, and S. XXIX, let alone the numerous MHG treatments of the way in which *vernünfticheit* is necessary for attaining union,[202] make the "intellectualism" of Eckhart's view of union unmistakable. And yet nothing is ever that simple in Eckhart.

First of all, we must remember that Eckhart's view of the nature of the intellectual act that makes us one with God is of an unusual kind—it is an unmediated and direct intellectual grasp of God and the soul as one with God. It is not the kind of reflexive act of understanding that we are accustomed to in knowing something and being able to reflect on what we know. The most detailed discussion of this comes at the end of the Sermon "On the Nobleman," which is appended to the *Book of Divine Consolation.* Here Eckhart disagrees with those who place the ultimate blessedness of heaven (and by extension our direct knowing of

God in this life) in the reflex act of knowing that we know God.[203] He holds that a reflex act does indeed *follow* from the direct, unmediated knowing, but "the first thing in which blessedness consists is that the soul beholds God nakedly." He continues:

> From there she takes all her being and her life, and she draws all that she is from God's ground, and she knows nothing of knowledge, of love, or of anything at all. She is totally still and alone in God's being, knowing nothing there but being and God.[204]

God himself, not my knowledge of God, is true beatitude, though, like the "nobleman" in the sermon text (Luke 19:12), Eckhart admits that the soul must not only "go out to a distant country to gain a kingdom" (i.e., see God alone in true felicity), but also "return," that is, "be aware and know that one knows God and is aware of it."[205] The return to awareness, however, is an effect of *beatitudo*, not constitutive of it.

A second problem that confronts a purely intellectualist interpretation of the blessedness of union, both here and hereafter, is the fact that there are passages in Eckhart that, contrary to his usual practice, insist that it is love that brings us to final union with God. For example, Pr. 60, a homily on the cosmic eros theme that has many affinities with Dionysius without actually quoting him, accepts the traditional identification of the cherubim with the "understanding (*bekantnisse*) that brings God into the soul and guides the soul to God, but cannot bring her into God." The highest power, the love identified with the seraphim, "breaks into God leading the soul with understanding and all her powers into God and unites her to God. Here God is acting above the power of the soul, not as in the soul, but divinely as in God."[206] One may treat this passage as an anomaly, or even a contradiction. Nevertheless, it suggests that the Dominican's views on union are more complex than often thought. Both knowing and loving unite in one way (with the usual preference being given to intellect), but from another perspective *neither* unites in the ultimate sense *insofar as* they are powers of the soul.[207]

A number of Eckhart's sermons make it clear that both love and knowledge need to be surpassed to attain the union of indistinction. Even within the analysis of intellect itself, it is important to remember Eckhart's teaching from the Sermon Cycle on the Eternal Birth that it is the passive, not the active, intellect that provides final access to the ground. In Pr. 71 he says that beyond the intellect that seeks, "there is another intellect that does not seek but rather remains in its simple pure being which is enveloped by this [divine] light."[208] A number of sermons, however, go further in stressing the limitations of all forms of intellect. There are well-known passages in such sermons as Prr. 39, 43, 52, and 83,[209] but perhaps the most informative text occurs in Pr. 7, where Eckhart initially follows his usual line, claiming intellect is higher than love because it penetrates beyond truth and goodness to take God as bare being. Then he switches ground: "But I maintain that neither knowledge nor love unites. . . . Love takes God with a coat on [i.e., as goodness]. . . . The intellect does not do this. The intellect takes God as he is known in it, but it can never encompass him in the sea of his groundlessness."[210] Here Eckhart, surprisingly, identifies the unifying force above knowledge and love as "mercy" (*barmherzicheit*), but throughout the sermon, because he equates mercy with what God works "in the groundless ocean" (121.12), and also with "the completely mysterious something [in the soul] that is above the first outbreak where intellect and will break out" (123.6-8), it is clear that what he is talking about is nothing else but the *grunt*. Mercy here is "the soul in its ground" (*diu sêle in ir grunde* [124.102]), the ultimate "place" of indistinction beyond all knowing and loving. As Pr. 42 puts it: "Where understanding and desire end, there is darkness, and there God shines."[211]

Eckhart's understanding of union, finally, is divinizing: God became man that man might become God. He does not use the terms *divinizatio/deificatio*, preferring *transformatio* (see 1 Cor. 13:12), *transfiguratio*, and other words taken from scripture, both in his Latin writings and his vernacular preaching.[212] A passage from one of his Latin sermons summarizes the process of divinization, weaving together a rich range of terms to describe the work of the soul leading to vision and union, including the transformation process by which we become identical with the inner eye in which God sees us in the same way we see him:

> The soul, in order that it may see God, must
> first, be configured to God through transfiguration;
> second, be exalted and purified;
> third, be purified from every imperfection;
> then, be drawn out and transcend itself insofar as it is a [created] nature;
> then, be drawn out from the body and matter, so that it can return upon itself and discover God within, in itself.[213]

How does the person live who has attained this constant, non-absorptive, indistinct union in the one ground? How does she conduct herself in the world, or, as some of Eckhart's expressions about leaving behind the body and matter might suggest, out of the world? The

answer that Eckhart gives to these questions revolves around his teaching concerning "living without a why" (*âne warumbe/sunder
warumbe/sine cur aut quare*). In the *Commentary on Exodus*, to begin
with an example from the Latin, Eckhart says:

> It is proper to God that he has no "why" outside or beyond himself.
> Therefore, every work that has a "why" as such is not a divine work or
> done for God. . . . There will be no divine work if a person does some-
> thing that is not for God's sake, because it will have a "why," something
> that is foreign to God and far from God; it is not God or something
> divine.[214]

As might be expected, Eckhart preached his practical message of living
without a why more often than he commented on it in his scholastic
writings. He linked it to the most common themes of his preaching,
such as the birth of the Word in the soul: "And so the Son is born in us
in that we are without a why and are born again into the Son."[215]

What does it mean to live "without a why," and where did the expression come from? As far as I have been able to determine, however much
the notion of pure spontaneous living may reflect Gospel injunctions
to become like a child (e.g., Matt. 18:1–5), the expression "to live without a why" was a creation of thirteenth-century mystics. The earliest
use I have found is in the Cistercian mystic Beatrice of Nazareth, whose
Seven Manners of Loving was originally written down sometime
between 1215 and 1235.[216] In discussing the second "manner," Beatrice
describes a form of disinterested love (not unlike Bernard's view of
amor as its own reward), noting that in this state the soul acts "only
with love, without any why (*sonder enich waerome*), without any reward
of grace or of glory. . . ."[217] The expression "without a why" (*sans nul
pourquoy/sine propter quid*) also occurs a number of times in Marguerite Porete's *Mirror*, a text known to Eckhart.[218] This does not mean
that Eckhart merely adopted this motif from Porete and others. Living
"without a why" was a necessary implication of the new mysticism of
the later Middle Ages, especially in its dialectically apophatic forms. A
mysticism based upon a "wayless way" to an unknown God of absolute
freedom can only bear fruit in a "whylessness" that will probably seem
either empty of meaning or potentially dangerous to those who know
nothing of it.

Nothing could simpler than living *âne warumbe* to those who have
reached detachment; nothing seems stranger to those who are still
caught in the toils of attachment and who act for any purpose other
than God. Eckhart does nothing to lessen the paradox; rather, a survey

of the different places where he speaks about "living without a why" is often an exercise in creative tautologies.[219] As the word-master he was, Eckhart can arrest us with concrete analogies, as when he compares God and by extension the person who lives without a why to a frisky horse, gamboling about in a field.[220] A good way to understand Eckhart's "without a why" is to see it as his new version of a theme that had a long history in Christian mysticism, the insistence on pure disinterested love. "He who lives in the goodness of his nature lives in God's love, and love has no why," as he put it in Pr. 28.[221] In a passage that might have been written by Bernard of Clairvaux himself, he says: "The lover as such does not seek to be loved. Everything that is not loving is foreign to him. This is all he knows; this is free, and for its own sake. . . . He loves in order to love, he loves love."[222] Indeed, the Dominican read and quoted Bernard often, and no other text more frequently than the abbot's famous statement that "the reason for loving God is God, and the measure of loving him is without measure" (*sine modo*).[223] All humans have some notion of what it means to love spontaneously. What makes Eckhart's insistence on living *âne warumbe* unusual is how he heightens the ante by inviting the hearer to aim for *total* spontaneity and freedom at every moment in the *nû* that is all moments simultaneously. This is the achievement of perfect detachment.

Freedom and pure spontaneity do not rule out all intention, at least the pure interior intention to give up attachment and to direct the self totally to God. Eckhart was unwavering in his insistence that "Goodness stands in the interior act," not in anything exterior.[224] Other theologians would have agreed that interior intention should be the primary motivation of the action of what Eckhart called "a God-loving soul" (*ein gotminnendiu sêle* [Pr. 20b; DW 1:345.9]). But Eckhart took this further into dangerous waters by so emphasizing interiority that exterior work of any kind is characterized as "not properly commanded by God," "not properly good or divine," "heavy and oppressive," and "not speaking to God and praising him" as does the interior act.[225] When taken to task for this teaching in the trials at Cologne and Avignon, he defended himself by citing Thomas Aquinas; but Thomas's doctrine was actually not what Eckhart said it was.[226] This emphasis on interior motivation is part and parcel of Eckhart's teaching that it is only God's working within that counts. This perspective allows him to hold that *all* activities, not just pious practices, give equal access to God—what is important is the divine intention behind every action. As the *Talks of Instruction* say, "In your works you should have a constant mind and constant trust and constant love for your God, and constant seriousness. Surely, if you were constant in this way, then no one could keep you from having God present."[227]

In order to see how Eckhart conceived of life lived without a why and to understand how, despite his emphasis on inwardness and even on fleeing materiality and the body, his mysticism is a mysticism of everyday life, it will be helpful to look at two sermons in which the Dominican spoke about the practice of true living. These homilies, one a short and relatively pastoral *collatio* (Pr. 62), the other a long and difficult sermon preached for the feast of Mary Magdalene (Pr. 86), will demonstrate how Eckhart broke through the traditional distinction between the active life and contemplative life, traditionally represented by Martha and Mary, creating a new model of sanctity—"living out of a well-exercised ground." In this light, it is worth recalling that Eckhart had already spoken of this integration in the last of his sermons on the Eternal Birth (Pr. 104), also using Martha and Mary. "It is all the same thing," he said there, "for we have only to be rooted in the same ground of contemplation and make it fruitful in works, and thus the purpose of contemplation is achieved. . . . Thus, in this work we possess nothing but a state of contemplation in God. The one rests in the other and brings it to fulfillment."[228]

Pr. 62 is a short treatment of what it means to live the life of detachment from self and pure attachment to God alone.[229] Eckhart begins by reflecting on the need for believing "in God" (*an got*), rather than merely "believing God"—a distinction based on Thomas Aquinas's notion of the difference between the final object and material object of faith, which would probably have been familiar to an audience of friars.[230] He employs the distinction to underline once again the point that directing our every effort to God as God, not for what God might give us, is the only proper moral intention. We should not even desire the spiritual gifts that were so much a part of the forms of late medieval piety and mysticism—"A person should seek nothing at all, neither knowledge nor understanding nor inwardness nor piety nor repose, but only God's will."[231] Total conformity to God's *one* will, and to nothing else, is what God demands; all forms of special exercise are useless. The "ordinary Christian life" (*ein gemeine kristlichen leben* [62.2]) is more than enough, *if* it is lived out of the sense that we have the love of God within us.

In the second part of the sermon Eckhart develops this total surrender in practical directions. The first is the acceptance of suffering, should it be our lot, as God's will for us, and therefore something we should receive with "quiet trust" (*senftmüetiger getriuwunge* [65.5]). The second point is the need to create what Eckhart calls "a properly ordered conscience" (*eine geordente conciencie* [66.1]) that accepts all things equally from God. Finally, the preacher closes with a mixture of radical and pastoral statements. The righteous man has no need of God (!), but only because he already has him. Outward works are not a sign of progress, but rather "a waxing love for the eternal and a waning interest in temporal things" is what we should seek to possess. Eckhart ends the sermon with an effective concrete *exemplum*. Although he often preached his message of total abandonment as if it were a once-and-forever moment, here he counsels that the most important thing is to get started from where we are, like a painter beginning a painting one stroke at a time, or a man setting off on a long journey with the first step (something the peripatetic friar knew all too well). "In all a person does he should turn his will Godward, and, keeping God alone in his mind, forge ahead without qualms about its being the right thing, or whether he is making a mistake."[232] This sense of the necessity of making progress wherever we find ourselves conforms to Eckhart's observation at the end of Pr. 39 that always, both here and in heaven, we are both "being born," or at a distance from God, and truly "born," that is, living in "oneness and nakedness of Being" (DW 2:265-66). In other words, the coexistence of *esse formale* and *esse virtuale* will remain forever.

The down-to-earth practicality of Pr. 62 is in sharp contrast to the bravura pyrotechnics and unresolved complexities of Pr. 86, but the message is not essentially different, although we recognize Eckhart the lover of "rare and subtle things" more in the latter sermon. Lengthy analyses have been devoted to this homily, especially the insightful volume of Dietmar Mieth.[233] Here, I wish to provide only some reflections on how the homily enables us to see that Eckhart's mysticism taught that true contemplation of God is realized in fruitful action, that the only way to proper engagement with the temporal world is through total detachment from it.

The contrast between the active and contemplative lives in the history of Christian mysticism is part of its inheritance from classical antiquity as mediated through the patristic period and taken up by medieval mystics.[234] From the time of Origen, the father of Christian mysticism, a number of biblical pairs, notably the sisters Mary and Martha of Luke 11, but also Rachel and Leah (Gen. 29–30), and Peter and John (John 20:1–10), had been employed as allegorical illustrations of the difference between the contemplative life devoted solely to love of God and the active life of charitable service to neighbor. Both were seen as necessary to Christian perfection; but the mystical tradition, beginning with Augustine and carried on especially by Gregory the Great and Bernard of Clairvaux, had insisted on the preeminence of the *vita contemplativa*. Various theories about how to relate the two had been put forward, but in general the mystics taught that in this fallen world there was always bound to be a tension between action and contemplation and that the best one could hope for was to oscillate between them, recognizing that the duty of Christian charity would often call the mystic away from the higher delights of contemplation.

Eckhart broke with this model, nowhere more clearly than in Pr. 86. For Eckhart, as Dietmar Mieth put it, "Earthly perfection consists . . . not in the unity of vision, but in the unity of working," so that "here, for the first time, a spirituality of the active life becomes visible."[235] In this sermon on Martha and Mary, as well as in a number of other places in his oeuvre,[236] Eckhart not only abandoned the notion of tension-filled oscillation between action and contemplation but daringly asserted that a new kind of action performed out of "a well-exercised ground" was superior to contemplation, at least as ordinarily conceived. Here what Reiner Schürmann called "Eckhart's this-worldliness" contrasts with the "other-worldliness" of many previous Christian mystics, especially those deeply influenced by certain forms of Platonism.[237] Although Eckhart himself often speaks of the necessity of separating from time, multiplicity, and corporality as hindrances to God, the process of detachment from *ens hoc et hoc* was required because it was the only way to find all these things in God's distinct-indistinction that is the created world.[238]

Pr. 86 is long and at times obscure, with a main line of argument concerning Martha and Mary, accompanied by numerous digressions.[239] I will concentrate on what the sermon says about the value of performing works "without a why" (though the phrase itself never appears). A brief section introduces the two women, characterizing Mary as filled with "ineffable longing" and "delight" (traditional marks of contemplation) and Martha as possessing "a well-exercised ground" (*wol geübeter grunt*) and "wise understanding" (*wisiu verstantnisse*)—typical Eckhartian terms. After a short excursus on sensual and intellectual satisfaction, the two main parts of the homily take up the roots of Martha's perfection, as well as the value of the works that she does in time. Martha tells Mary to get up and help her to care for Jesus (Luke 10:40) not out of criticism but from endearment. She believed that Mary was in danger of being overwhelmed by her desire. "Martha knew

Mary better than Mary Martha," says Eckhart, "for Martha had lived long and well; and living gives the most valuable kind of knowledge. Life knows better than pleasure or light what one can get under God in this life, and in some ways life gives us a purer knowledge than what eternal light can bestow."[240] This introduces the fundamental theme of the sermon—life, that is, actual practice, gives a higher form of knowledge than even the light of contemplative ecstasy without application to actual living (Paul's ecstasy of 2 Cor. 12 is cited as example).[241] Eckhart concludes the first half of part 1 by emphasizing that Martha was concerned that Mary not get misled by becoming "stuck" in the pleasure of contemplation.

After a second brief digression, Eckhart comes to the third and most important reason for Martha's superiority to Mary, linking it to the exegetical hook that Jesus names her twice in his address. "Martha, Martha" indicates that she possesses "everything of temporal and eternal value a creature should have" (484.14–15). Martha is one of those people "who stand in the midst of things, but not in things. They stand very near [the image of eternal light], and yet do not have less of it than if they stood up above, at the rim of eternity."[242] There is much that is obscure about this section (including the notion of the "rim of eternity"), but the essential message is that Martha makes good use of the two kinds of "means" (*mittel*), or creatures. The first is described as "work and activity in time" (*werk und gewerbe in der zît* [485.8–9]), something which, Eckhart says, does not lessen eternal happiness and is even necessary to get to God.[243] "The other means is to be empty of all this" (*daz ander mittel daz ist; blôz sîn des selben* [485:11]), that is, to attain the freedom of detachment.

Eckhart goes on to underline the relation between these two "means." Both activity and emptiness are necessary. "We have been put into time," he says, "for the purpose of coming nearer to and becoming like God through rational activity in time."[244] Paul's text about "redeeming the time" (Eph. 5:16) means that we must continually rise up to God, "not according to different images, but by means of living intellectual truth" (485.13-15). The stripping away of images (*entbilden*) in favor of the pure intellectual truth of unknowing leads us forward to the eternal light of God. Martha is not there yet: there is still some mediation in her vision of God. But she is praised for standing on the brink of the embrace of the eternal light, "on the rim of eternity."

Pauline redeeming the time is a significant aspect of Eckhart's this-worldly mysticism. Studies by Alois Haas and Niklaus Largier have shown that the relationship of time and eternity in Eckhart is not merely one of negation, as some texts taken in isolation might indicate.[245] Rather, eternity must be seen as the "fullness of time," and the soul as situated between time and eternity must learn by its "rational activity in time" to redeem the times.[246] "Eternity," as Largier says, "is what binds the temporal together in an horizon of origin and end on the one side, and on the other with an embracing presence which grounds the metaphysical model of the unfolding of being. . . ."[247] As Eckhart notes in Pr. 91, through the Incarnation God renews himself— "God brings eternity into time, and with himself brings time into eternity. This takes place in the Son, when the Son pours himself out in eternity, then all creatures are poured out with him."[248] Eckhart's christological center, therefore, requires that a person like Martha, who acts from a "well-exercised ground," must work both above time in eternity[249] and in time through *werk* and *gewerbe*.[250]

Pr. 86 continues with an important excursus, explaining three "ways" to God,[251] but for our purposes it is the return to the figure of Martha in part 3 that is of concern. In this section Eckhart explains how Martha and "all God's friends" can exist "with care" but not "in care," that is, how they relate to the concerns and troubles of everyday existence. The preacher once again emphasizes that a work done in time is as noble as any kind of communion with God save for the highest unmediated vision. Such a fruitful work has three characteristics: it is orderly, discriminating, and insightful (*ordenlîche, redelîcher, wizzentlîche*). The last of these is when one "feels living truth with delightful presence in good works" (488.17–18). Eckhart then turns to how a person who has arrived at this state, that is, a Martha, is able to work undisturbed in the midst of the concerns and troubles of the world—traditionally what earlier mystics had held to be impossible, because activity was always seen as a distraction from contemplation, not its fulfillment.

Because Martha has attained a "free mind" (*vrîen gemüete*) and lives out of "a splendid ground" (*ein hêrlîcher grunt*), she has found the "One thing necessary" (Luke 10:42), that is, God. Hence, she hopes that Mary will give up consolation and sweetness and become what she is. Two digressions help explain what this means. The first is an instruction on virtue, showing that its highest stage is reached when God gives the ground of the soul his eternal will conformed to the loving command of the Holy Spirit (490.3–4). But, as the second excursus shows, this does not mean that a person remains absolutely untouched by pleasure or suffering. Even Christ was sorrowful unto death (Matt. 26:37). As long as suffering does not cause the will to waver in its dedication to

God, or "spill over into the highest part of the spirit," however, all remains well.[252] Thus, Martha "was so essential (*weselich*) that her activity did not hinder her; work and activity led her to eternal happiness."[253] Mary sitting at the feet of Jesus is not yet the true Mary, i.e., the Mary who will one day reach the same status as Martha when she "learns life and possesses it essentially" (*daz si lernete leben, daz si ez weselich besaeze* [491.14]).

In concluding the sermon, Eckhart corrects two false understandings of what it means to be a Martha-Mary, or perfect Christian. First of all, we can never be like disembodied spirits, with our senses immune to what is pleasant or unpleasant. It is only the inward "will formed to God in understanding" that can turn pain and difficulty into joy and fruitful work. Second, we should never imagine we will attain freedom from works in this life. Mary too became active as preacher and teacher (and "washerwoman of the disciples") after Christ's ascension. Indeed, Christ himself is our ultimate model for the necessity of constant activity without a why: throughout his life "there was no part of his body that did not practice its proper virtue" (492.16).

Eckhart's model of living *sunder warumbe*, then, is not as impractical or empty of content as it may at first seem. Reading Pr. 86 helps us put his message back in context. As daring, as profound, and sometimes even as obscure as his preaching of the *rara et subtilia* were, Eckhart basically wanted his audience, simple laity as well as pious religious women and learned clerics, to do the same thing—to be so dedicated to fulfilling the will of God, so unconcerned with self, that their every action proceeds from the "well-exercised ground" in which God and human are one. "God's ground is my ground, and my ground is God's ground." Eckhart always closes his sermons with a plea for the recognition of this truth. At the end of the *Book of Divine Consolation* he has a particularly effective prayer:

> May the loving compassionate God, the Truth,
>   grant to me and to all who read this book,
> that we may find the truth within ourselves,
>   and become aware of it. Amen.[254]

Eckhart's Sources

E CKHART'S MOST CITED SOURCE by far was the Bible. For the Dominican, as for all medieval mystics, Holy Writ was not *a* source of
truth; it was *the* source. In chapter 2 I give some guidelines for
approaching Eckhart's use of the Bible, so my remarks here will focus
on the Dominican's other sources.

Meister Eckhart was a philosopher-theologian as well as a mystic
and preacher, well trained in the exacting curriculum of thirteenth-
century scholastic education. Few Christian mystics were as widely read
as he. Augustine of Hippo and John Scottus Eriugena were polymaths
for their eras, but their libraries were not as large as Eckhart's. Many of
the most important Western mystics, such as Bernard of Clairvaux,
were theologically learned, but had little philosophical training.
Bernard's contemporaries, the Victorines Hugh and Richard, were
among the best-educated masters and spiritual teachers of the twelfth
century, but they knew little or nothing of many texts that were central
for Eckhart. Among the great mystics of the thirteenth century, only
Bonaventure had an education equivalent to Eckhart's. The Franciscan's reforging of the riches of Latin theology and mysticism into a new
Franciscan mold bears comparison with Eckhart's achievement,[1] but
Bonaventure's view of the relation of philosophy and theology meant
that his mystical thought has a different relation to non-Christian
philosophical resources.[2] While no one, especially Eckhart, would want
to claim that mystical "unknowing" depends on the breadth of one's
learning, the fact that the German Dominican utilized so many
resources—philosophical, theological, and mystical—in his teaching

and preaching suggests that some reflections on Eckhart's sources may be a useful addendum to this account.

This appendix is not an attempt to give an adequate survey of the full range of Eckhart's sources and the various ways in which they shaped his thought. (Such a study would have to be the length of a substantial monograph and should not even be attempted before the "Indices" of the critical edition have been completed.)[3] Rather, my intention is to give some preliminary reflections, both general and specific, on how Eckhart's use of sources helps us to understand his thought.

With regard to the breadth of the materials that Eckhart cited (or at least arguably knew and used), a glance at the published Indices is sufficient to provide a sense of the amazing range of his reading.[4] In addition, many books and articles about Eckhart discuss his use of sources, in general or in particular.[5] In what follows, I will not attempt to discuss every author cited in the Indices, or all the treatments devoted to Eckhartian *Quellenforschung* (i.e., the determination of sources). My intentions are (1) to provide some broad reflections on how the Dominican used the resources available to him; and (2) to offer a few comments on what Eckhart especially valued in the major authors and texts that influenced him.

GENERAL OBSERVATIONS

An important task in investigating Eckhart's thought is to determine the philosophers and theologians who really made a difference for him—that is, those whose writings help us grasp aspects of his thought and development that would otherwise remain obscure, or even be miscast. This is not just an issue of identifying sources, both direct (i.e., cited by name and/or actually quoted) and indirect (i.e., summarized or cited without explicit nomination). The real problem rests in evaluating just *how* significant any citation or adaptation of an authority— Christian, pagan, Jew, or Muslim—actually is for the Dominican's mystical teaching. At the deepest level, the study of Eckhart's sources merges into the interpretation of what is most important in his thought: an interpretive task to which the counting of direct citations, paraphrased adaptations, and possible reminiscences is at best a preliminary step. In order to appreciate the difficulty of the task, it will be helpful to begin by considering some general issues about the use of *auctoritates* (i.e., authoritative *texts*) in scholastic thought.[6]

Scholastic education (and all medieval academic instruction) was bound to authoritative texts in a way difficult for us to understand today. As M.-D. Chenu put it: "From Donatus in grammar all the way up to Aristotle in metaphysics, cultural achievement came by way of the texts of authors considered as masters of right thinking and of right expression. They were 'authorities,' and their texts were 'authentic.'"[7] Medieval theology was fundamentally "text-bound," especially in the way in which it was based on line-by-line study of a few recognized textbooks (the Bible, the *Ordinary Gloss,* Peter Lombard's *Books of Sentences,* etc.). It also, to a large extent, featured what might be called a "piecemeal" outlook, in the sense that many fundamental textbooks, such as the *Ordinary Gloss,* and Lombard's *Sentences,* were compilations of authoritative passages taken out of context and absorbed into a structure created for classroom use.

The medieval scholastic way of utilizing a past thinker, therefore, was different from what we are accustomed to in scholarly discourse today. In one sense, medieval teachers were closer to their "authorities" than modern academics, because so much of their training and teaching was explicitly commentarial.[8] Scholastics began their theological studies by learning how to read and comment on texts, first the Bible and then Lombard's *Sentences.* All masters of theology taught such detailed forms of exegesis as the bread-and-butter of their academic work-load. Similar kinds of exegesis were applied to the standard school-texts in the arts, in law, and in philosophy. Training in line-by-line *lectio* produced an intimacy with the text difficult to find today. Furthermore, medieval mnemonic techniques, on which much has recently been written,[9] gave well-educated theologians like Bonaventure and Eckhart a command of the Bible and other authoritative texts, along with an ability to call up intertextual relations that probably equaled those advertised by CD-ROM search engines today.

There was, however, another side to this vanished world. Medieval mastery of the *littera* of authoritative writings was not accompanied by what is taken for granted today, that is, a historical-critical approach to texts that tries to interpret them from within their historical context, however much one may recognize that the story of the reception of a text is also a part of its meaning. It is not that medieval interpreters lacked all sense of history, or that they did not strive, when necessary, to determine the author's intention (*intentio auctoris*). But medieval commentators did not have the interests or the tools of modern historical research. Most of them showed little concern for trying to understand the world in which the text they were investigating was created.

Thomas Aquinas (actually a much better "historical" critic than Eckhart) summarized the outlook well: "The study of philosophy is not for the purpose of knowing what people have thought, but for knowing what the truth is."[10] (One can agree with this adage without condoning how little most scholastics valued the meaning of historical development.)

This lack of attention to historicity, as well as the conviction of the timelessness of all expressions of truth, encouraged the scholastic practice of citing excerpts as convenient "proof-texts" for support in argument, or merely for ornament—as a kind of icing for a cake already baked. Of course, there were many exceptions to easy proof-texting, investigations in which a passage was not only quoted but also explained at length as an integral part of an argument. Even when a passage was only brought in as a proof-text, it often represented a crucial premise or axiom to the author citing it, as we often see in Eckhart's uses of Aristotle, Augustine, or the *Book of Causes*. Nevertheless, medieval citation and exposition of authorities were quite different from what most scholars practice today.

The tendency toward a-historical treatment of texts and the practice of proof-texting to buttress arguments opened the way for the use of *auctoritates* in service of different, even opposed, positions. The conflict of *auctoritates* had been a problem from early in the scholastic project. Both the lawyers, such as Gratian, and the theologians, especially Peter Abelard in his *Sic et Non* of the 1120s, contributed to the rules for creating *concordia auctoritatum*, that is, demonstrating the essential harmony of "authorities" that overtly seemed to express different positions. These rules included insights into determining authorial intention, as well as principles for investigating the *modus loquendi* of texts and genres. Also important to resolving contradictions was the emerging conviction that authorities sanctioned by tradition, especially the Fathers, should not be summarily rejected, even if what they said could not be squared with more "modern" expressions of truth. Rather, they should be "explained with reverence" (*exponere reverenter*). Finally, intelligent interpreters also became willing to admit that "authority" was malleable. As the late twelfth-century Paris Master Alan of Lille put it: "An authority has a wax nose, that is, it can be bent to different meanings."[11] The wax nose appears to have grown longer as thirteenth-century scholastics increased the range of their reading.

Eckhart sought to work out a *concordia* among his "authorities" wherever possible. Like Thomas Aquinas, he gave a reverential *expositio* to many texts by the *sancti* and established *magistri*, and even to the *philosophi* (Aquinas himself often bent over backward to find excuses for Aristotle's disagreements with Christian doctrine). Eckhart also manipulated the wax nose of some of his favorite authorities, nowhere more so than in the case of Aquinas himself. The Meister cites his Dominican predecessor with unfeigned reverence, and only rare explicit disagreement.[12] There can be no question of how much his years of studying St. Thomas meant for the development of his thought. Nevertheless, Eckhart is not fundamentally a Thomist. He was an independent thinker who, given his historical context, was formed by a "dialogue" with Thomas, but who also used the Angelic Doctor for his own purposes. As we have seen, Eckhart was also able (knowingly or unknowingly) to cite Thomas for support when it was not really the case.[13]

One helpful suggestion for reflecting on how Eckhart approached his sources can be found in R. J. Henle's *Saint Thomas and Platonism*. Henle investigated how Aquinas utilized Platonic authorities by differentiating between a *via-positio* technique and a *positio-auctoritas* technique.[14] For Thomas, a *positio* is a philosophical claim that can be approached in two ways. The first is according to the schema of *via-positio*, in which the *positio* is considered within its original philosophical context or *via* (i.e., the empirical facts or philosophical principles and arguments upon which the assertion depends for its truth). (Henle argues that Aquinas mostly criticizes Platonism when he uses this approach). The second way is the *positio-auctoritas* technique, in which the assertion (*positio*) is detached from its proper philosophical background to become an indeterminate claim that can become a starting point (*auctoritas*) for a new argument (*via*) within the context of the different philosophical system. (According to Henle, Aquinas often utilized Platonism in this mode.) Though the technical distinction between the two approaches does not appear in Eckhart, one can detect analogous strategies.[15]

There are differences between the "visibility" of sources and authorities in the Latin and the MHG texts of Eckhart. A scholastic teacher was expected to demonstrate his expertise by frequent citation of his authorities, especially the "authentic" passages drawn from ancient councils, fathers, and saints, and from the best philosophers. More recent thinkers might be cited by name, if they had acquired some classroom use. Living figures were almost never identified, although they were often implicitly used, misused, and debated.

Eckhart's Latin works, like those of Aquinas, Bonaventure, and other great scholastics, are filled, at times almost overwhelmed, by citation.

This often makes them difficult reading today to those who do not recognize how scholastic genres were meant to function. Eckhart's MHG works, however, are different. They were meant not for assiduous classroom study but for the pulpit and then for private spiritual reading. Their audience was not so much learned clerics as a largely lay audience for whom there was little reason for much direct quoting of authorities. Nevertheless, even a cursory perusal of Eckhart's vernacular sermons and treatises demonstrates how deeply learned his preaching was and how often he referred to authorities.[16] The Dominican expected his audience to be able to understand deep philosophical-theological issues; he also appears to have believed that mentioning his sources, often by name, was not something to be restricted to his Latin works. Eckhart made the pulpit into a *cathedra magistri* (professorial chair) more than most medieval preachers. His public does not seem to have minded, given the many manuscripts containing these challenging and learned homilies.

In his MHG sermons Eckhart often refers to Christian teachers, especially Augustine (according to my count, he is named ninety-three times). Other frequently named authorities include Dionysius (sixteen times), and Gregory the Great and Bernard of Clairvaux (eleven times each). It was much rarer that a Christian preacher would name a pagan, Jewish, or Muslim authority (all generically *heidnisch* in MHG). Eckhart, however, as befits his view of the identity of philosophy and theology, not only often made use of such sources, implicitly and explicitly, but he also cited the names of his favorite non-Christian authorities in his sermons (e.g., Plato, Aristotle, Cicero, Seneca, Avicenna, etc.). Most of the Dominican's non-Christian sources, however, are hidden under the generic rubric that could include both Christians and non-Christians: *die meister sprechent.*[17]

The labors of Josef Quint and the other editors of the MHG writings have uncovered many of the sources of these anonymous references among the philosophers and theologians of antiquity and the Middle Ages. But in a number of cases it appears that Eckhart may have used the singular formula (*ein meister*) as a convenient way to introduce a self-reference.[18] In only one vernacular sermon did the Dominican refer to himself directly by name—and (not surprisingly) in a controversial area where he explicitly set himself against *all* other masters.[19] There are many places where the identity of the *meister* referred to remains to be found—Eckhart or another, past or present? Within the confines of his vernacular use of sources, Eckhart once again demonstrates his characteristic boldness and originality.

We may still question how important the search for Eckhart's sources really is. As far as the academic study of the Dominican mystic is concerned, the quest for and evaluation of the rich range of thinkers he utilized can tell us much about the background to and character of his thought. In this light, *Quellenforschung* is a necessary, if not sufficient, exercise for understanding Eckhart. But for appreciating the message of Eckhart's mysticism, the search for sources remains a secondary task—a helpful adjunct, but not integral to one's response to his invitation to find God. (This is why in this account of Eckhart's mysticism I have turned to the issue only by way of a brief appendix.) Important as Plato, Aristotle, Origen, Augustine, Proclus, Avicenna, Maimonides, Aquinas, and many others were for the Meister, he doubtless had contemporaries who knew these authorities as well as he did. But none of them did what he did with the extensive resources of high scholastic learning.

Specific Authors and Texts

In order to get some sense of the frequency of Eckhart's use of particular authors, I have adopted an inexact, but I hope helpful, procedure for tabulating his authorities. Making use of the published indices of LW 1–3, as well as the indices of DW 2, 3, 5, and my own survey of DW 1 and the still incomplete DW 4, I have compiled figures for how often Eckhart refers *by name* to particular authorities, whether directly quoting or summarizing their position. These figures are rough and sometimes inflated,[20] but in general they give us a sense of the *frequency* of Eckhart's use of authorities. Naturally, mere numeration is only part of the story. In what follows, I will also make some observations on the more complex task of assessing the significance of the major themes of the most often-cited *auctoritates* for understanding Eckhart, at least in a preliminary way.

Non-Christian Authorities[21]

Although it is customary (and not incorrect) to think of Eckhart as a Platonist/Neoplatonist in his philosophical orientation, there is no philosopher he knew better or cited more often than Aristotle. To be sure, medieval authors, following Boethius and the late Neoplatonists, claimed that there was no essential conflict between Plato and his great pupil, and important Neoplatonic works, such as the *Book of Causes,* were sometimes ascribed to Aristotle. But today we know better. Even in the Middle Ages, some authors, like Thomas Aquinas, distinguished between Aristotle's philosophy and that of the *libri Platonici*, though he strove to bring them into harmony where possible.[22] Eckhart was also aware of differences between Plato and his pupil; but where he detected these, he tended to favor Plato's view, as we shall see.

Eckhart knew something of the pre-Socratic philosophers through Aristotle's comments on them. He mentions the names and views of Empedocles, Heraclitus, and others. The only aspect of pre-Socratic philosophy that really enters into his thought, however, is the axiom that Aristotle ascribed to Anaxagoras in *Physics* 1.4 (187b): "Everything has been mixed in everything." Eckhart, and after him Nicholas of Cusa, adapted this principle to describe not only the interpenetration of all things in the universe but also the divine omnipresent transcendence. As he once put it, "In divine matters 'everything is in everything' and the greatest is in the least, and so too the fruit is in the flower."[23]

Eckhart's references to Plato are quite restricted in comparison with his hundreds of direct appeals to Aristotle and profound knowledge of the Stagirite's works.[24] He cited Plato on the goodness of the Creator, the existence of the Ideas, the immortality of the soul, and other standard doctrines associated with the teaching of the Academy. Key aspects of the Dominican's doctrine, such as his emphasis on formal causality and the negative approach to naming God, go back to Plato, even if Eckhart's actual knowledge of his writings was limited and was probably most often communicated through the summaries found in Cicero, Macrobius, Augustine, Thomas Aquinas, and others. A good measure of Eckhart's respect for Plato is shown in the vernacular sermons. Although Eckhart rarely named pagan sources in his homilies, he mentions Plato by name four times.[25] The passage from Pr. 28 discussed in chapter 2 (p. 23), in which he praises "Plato, the great cleric" [i.e., learned man], for gaining unknowing knowledge of the *grunt* beyond the realm of merely human reason, shows his immense respect for the fountainhead of Western philosophy.

Eckhart was an "Aristotelian," at least to the extent that he quoted the Greek systematician twice as often as any other non-Christian thinker. The Dominican's intimate knowledge of a large range of the Stagirite's texts and the effect it had on his thought has never been adequately explored.[26] Like all scholastics, Eckhart was dependent on Aristotle's *Categories* and more advanced logical writings for his technical forms of demonstration. Much of his cosmology is Aristotelian, and important building blocks of his philosophical psychology, epistemology, and metaphysics were also based on Aristotle.[27] It was, above all, Aristotle's conception of the unity of various forms of scientific knowledge that made him so useful to Aquinas, Eckhart, and other scholastics—however much they employed him for their own purposes.

Without going into detail on the many ways in which Eckhart used Aristotle, the contribution, as well as the limitations, of his Aristotelianism can be illustrated by a look at some vernacular sermons in which the pagan philosopher makes an appearance. In Pr. 15 Aristotle is mentioned by name seven times. Citing and summarizing both from *On the Soul* and the *Metaphysics*,[28] Eckhart presents Aristotle's teaching about the rational nature of humanity and its link to the "angels" (i.e., separated intellects that move the heavenly spheres). Aristotle's analysis of how the "detached spirits" (*abegeschaidnen gaisten*) gaze upon "pure naked being" (*luter bloss wesen*), the "What" (*was*) that is God, is praised as the height of "natural science," but Eckhart clearly sees it as only a preliminary stage to the attainment of the nameless *ainige ain* (Only One), who is found in darkness and unknowing. "The final end of being is the darkness or unknowing of the hidden Godhead whose light shines upon it [i.e., being], but this darkness does not encompass it."[29]

In two sets of parallel sermons, Prr. 20a and 20b, and 36a and 36b, Eckhart again explores the limitations of Aristotle's epistemology without ever naming him, contrasting the Stagirite's theory of knowing as an abstractive process with the higher illuminative epistemology of Plato and Augustine, who are explicitly named in Prr. 36a and b.[30] This critique of Aristotle's view of knowing did not mean that Eckhart did not utilize aspects of Aristotelian epistemology that could be incorporated into his own understanding of how the human mind functioned with regard to knowing the things of this world, but it does emphasize an essential difference between Aristotle and the Dominican.

Eckhart cites a number of other ancient authorities, notably Seneca and Cicero, fairly frequently. For the most part, these citations seem to be standard quotes from well-known authors used as proof-texts for positions that are of Eckhart's own development. A more important task is to determine what access the Dominican had to pagan Neoplatonic sources and how far these shaped his thought.

Eckhart's direct contact with ancient Neoplatonism was limited; but what was available to him, especially as combined with the forms of Christian Neoplatonism found in Augustine and Dionysius,[31] was of major moment for the evolution of his metaphysics of flow, as noted above. Eckhart certainly had heard of Plotinus, but he could not have read him in any direct way. However, handy summaries of Plotinus's teaching were available to him in a pagan Latin Neoplatonist he knew well. Macrobius, whose *Commentary on the Dream of Scipio* was a standard medieval text, was a useful author for Eckhart. He quotes him especially on his teaching on the One, often in tandem with other authorities.[32]

The role of Proclus (d. 485) in Eckhart's thought is unmistakable and unmistakably important, despite the relatively few times he mentions the Greek Neoplatonist by name. Although helpful research has been devoted to the Proclean background to Eckhart in recent years, there are still debates about how much access he had to the texts of the *Proclus Latinus* tradition.[33] Eckhart certainly read William of Moerbeke's Latin version of the *Elements of Theology*, which he cites in a number of places.[34] Recent scholarship has tended to deny him knowledge of the other texts Moerbeke translated, the *Commentary on Plato's Parmenides* and the three *opuscula*.[35] The *Book of Causes*, however, one of Eckhart's favorite texts, was the most potent source of his Procleanism.

The *Book of Causes* is an Arab reworking of Proclus's *Elements*, probably produced in the ninth/tenth century and translated into Latin toward the end of the twelfth century.[36] The work is a monotheistic and creationist adaptation of the thought of Proclus. (Its anonymous author may also have been familiar with the *Enneads* of Plotinus.) The work became required reading in the Paris Arts Faculty by 1255, and most scholastics were familiar with it.[37] The deep resonance that this work had with Eckhart's metaphysics of flow is obvious not only from his numerous citations and discussions of its axioms,[38] but also in the way in which he imitated its mode of argumentation in the *Work of Propositions*. Eckhart studied both the *Book* itself (which he sometimes called the *Lumen luminum*) and Thomas's comment on it, absorbing its view of reality into his teaching and preaching.[39] It is ironic that the last of the pagan Neoplatonists—a strong opponent of triumphant Christianity—became such an important resource for Christian theology, not only shortly after his death through the aegis of the Dionysian corpus, but especially in the late thirteenth and early fourteenth centuries, the era of "Latin Procleanism."[40] A full evaluation of the Proclean element in Eckhart is still lacking, although Werner Beierwaltes and Kurt Ruh have done much to open up the importance of Proclus and his heritage, especially as filtered through the *Book of Causes*, for understanding the Dominican.

One other anonymous work deeply imbued with Platonic elements that Eckhart pondered and cited was the *Book of the Twenty-Four Philosophers*, often ascribed to the fictional seer Hermes Trismegistus.[41] The basis of this fascinating text is a series of brief axiomatic "definitions" of God given by twenty-four anonymous philosophers. These axioms are accompanied by a commentary which appears to be part of the original composition (other commentaries were later added). Françoise Hudry, the editor, has argued that the work is a translation from a lost late antique Greek original of probable Alexandrian provenance. The Latin translation was made in the late twelfth century. Eckhart made use of fourteen of the propositions of the *Book*, both in his Latin writings and in his sermons.[42] In Pr. 9, one of the Dominican's most powerful explorations of negative theology, he demonstrates his affection for the work by beginning the sermon with a description of the *Book of the Twenty-Four Philosophers* and a free translation of several of its axioms.[43]

Eckhart was also extensively influenced by his reading of Jewish and Islamic thinkers. At least two of these, the Persian philosopher Avicenna (d. 1037) and the Jewish sage Maimonides (d. 1204), are among the most significant resources for Eckhart's thought. The Jewish Neoplatonist Ibn Gabirol (d. 1058), whose *Fountain of Life* was used and debated by many scholastics,[44] was also used by Eckhart, as was (to a lesser extent) the Arab philosopher and commentator on Aristotle, Averroes (d. 1198).

Maimonides takes pride of place among these Jewish and Islamic philosophers, who were all characterized as *heidnische meister*.[45] He appears second only to Aristotle in citations by name in the Latin works, although in the sermons he is never named and only rarely referred to anonymously.[46] The *Guide to the Perplexed*, which had been rendered into Latin in the 1240s under the title *Dux neutrorum*, was used by Thomas Aquinas and became a major resource for Eckhart. The German Dominican employed it both as an example of philosophical exegesis of the Old Testament,[47] and also as an aid in his exploration of the divine mystery. The analysis of Eckhart's teaching on the divine names from his treatise in the *Commentary on Exodus* given in chapter 5 provides a sample of how the Dominican adapted the thought of the Jewish sage for his own purposes, but is not meant to be exhaustive, as other references to Eckhart's use of Maimonides in the above chapters show.[48] What is remarkable is Eckhart's positive attitude toward the Jewish philosopher—unlike Thomas and others, he never criticizes *Rabbi Moyses*.

Less attention has been paid to the role of Ibn Gabirol (d. 1058) in

Eckhart.[49] His *Fountain of Life*, a penetrating exploration of Neoplatonic metaphysics, became a main source for Eckhart's younger confrere Berthold of Moosburg in his *Commentary on the Elements of Theology of Proclus*. Eckhart cited Gabirol in his Latin works mostly for the Jewish philosopher's emphasis on God as Absolute Unity. It is interesting to see him combining Maimonides and Gabirol with the Christian witness of Boethius to proof-text his teaching on God's oneness. In the *Commentary on Exodus* he says:

> No difference at all is or can be in the One, but "All difference is below the One," as it says in the *Fountain of Life*, Book 5. "That is truly one in which there is no number," as Boethius says. And Rabbi Moses, as mentioned above, says that God is one "in all ways and according to every respect," so that any "multiplicity either in intellect or in reality" is not found in him.[50]

Avicenna was Eckhart's major resource among Muslim thinkers, though once again little secondary literature has investigated his impact on the Dominican.[51] Eckhart's attitude toward Avicenna is a good example of a critical correlation in the sense that he used him extensively, but also felt free to criticize him on key issues. In the case of creation, for example, Eckhart adopted an Avicennan formula about creation as the giving of existence, but also criticized the Islamic thinker's view of the necessity of creation, emphasizing the sovereign freedom of the Divine Agent.[52] Eckhart was fascinated with Avicenna's discussion of the role of the "separated intelligences = angels" within the metaphysics of flow and the relation between the angels and the higher powers of the human soul. In Pr. 16b, for example, a homily in praise of St. Augustine, he quotes Avicenna's *On the Soul* in differentiating the lower and higher powers.[53] A puzzling passage for evaluating Eckhart's relation to Avicenna occurs in Pr. 18. Here the Dominican cites Avicenna as "gar ein hôher meister" in presenting the Muslim's teaching that "the highest angel [= first intelligence] is so close to the first effusion ... that he created all this world and also all the angels that are beneath him," concluding "There is good doctrine in this...."[54] The problem with this praise is that the idea of God's sharing his act of creation with any other being was contrary to Christian teaching. This Avicennan view had been attacked by Thomas Aquinas and Eckhart himself, in both his Latin and his German writings.[55] Despite some attacks on Avicenna, Eckhart used him more than he criticized him. For example, in Pr. 17, one of the Dominican's most powerful statements of the mysticism of the ground, he weaves in a good deal of Avicenna, drawn from *Metaphysics* 9.7, into his presentation.[56] The Islamic philosopher's teaching that "soul" names the powers but not the *grunt der sêle,* as well as his notion of the soul as an intelligible world, were important aspects of Eckhart's teaching on the *grunt.*

Christian Authorities[57]

Naturally, Eckhart named his Christian sources more frequently than the non-Christian ones, both in the Latin writings and in his vernacular works. Augustine is given pride of place (expressly quoted by name over seven hundred times in the LW and over ninety in DW). Other frequently cited authorities are Thomas Aquinas, Boethius, Gregory the Great, Jerome, Chrysostom, Bernard, Origen, Dionysius, and John Damascene. There is considerable difference between the citations in the LW and the DW, due to both the genre and the practice of restricted reference to contemporaries or near contemporaries. St. Thomas, for example, is often expressly referred to in the Latin works, used anonymously in many places in the MHG sermons, but only named twice in the homilies as *meister Thomas.*[58] A number of authorities, especially twelfth-century ones such as Peter Lombard, are also often utilized but seldom cited by name.[59] Albert the Great, probably because he was well known in Cologne where Eckhart did much of his preaching, is named relatively often in the vernacular, but his name (as compared with his teachings) appears rarely in the scholastic works.[60] Other contemporaries, like Dietrich of Freiburg, are never mentioned, however much they affected Eckhart's thinking.

Origen of Alexandria (d. 254), the supreme mind of pre-Constantinian Christianity, is an important and somewhat overlooked source of Eckhart's thinking.[61] Eckhart did not have a wide acquaintance with Origen—he tends to use a few select passages over and over. But the fact that he cited Origen by name, some thirty-seven times by my calculation, is arresting.[62] Even more significant is how the Dominican appealed to Origen to buttress some of the central themes of his teaching, especially the birth of the Word in the soul of the just person. The specific motif that Eckhart was most attracted to in Origen's version of the mysticism of birthing was his appeal to the "divine seed" in us. According to the *Book of Divine Consolation:* "The great master Origen describes a simile of this inner nobleman, in whom God's seed and God's image have been impressed and sown, of how the seed and the image of the divine nature that is the Son of God will appear, and man will apprehend him. . . ."[63]

The thirteenth-century Dominican was familiar with many of the great fathers and doctors who set the standards of Christian orthodoxy in the fourth and fifth centuries. Knowing no Greek, he cites from the Latin fathers and from those Greeks who became available in Latin. These *auctoritates* are more often used as proof-texts than as real discussion partners. Thus, Eckhart referred to John Chrysostom's *Homilies on the Gospel on John* a number of times in his own exposition of the spiritual Gospel and elsewhere cited a text widely read in the Middle Ages, the Pseudo-Chrysostom *Unfinished Commentary on Matthew*.[64] The indefatigable Jerome, a major authority on the meaning of Hebrew names and the interpretation of difficult biblical passages, also appears with some frequency, but as a writer to be mined for helpful hints rather than as a resource for thinking through important issues. Ambrose of Milan is also cited by Eckhart, but cannot be considered a significant source.

Augustine of Hippo is a different matter.[65] Every medieval thinker was deeply imbued with Augustine—paraphrasing Alfred North Whitehead's remark about Plato, one might say that the history of Latin theology for more than a millennium after 500 is a series of footnotes to Augustine. While Eckhart is scarcely original in having Augustine as his single most important *auctoritas* after the Bible, the German Dominican's Augustinianism, like all his thought, was original and controversial. So pervasive is Augustine in Eckhart's writing and preaching that one is easily tempted to "over-Augustinianize" him. For all that he learned from the bishop of Hippo—his most constant dialogue partner—there are too many central aspects of his thought about the soul, the Trinity, union with God, where Eckhart differs from Augustine to make him out to be some kind of *Augustinus redivivus*. For example, Augustine would doubtless have been much disturbed by Eckhart's view of the possibility of realizing indistinct union with God. To reverse the perspective, it is obvious that whole realms of Augustine's theology regarding the sacraments, ecclesiology, and history, to mention but a few, were totally lost on Eckhart. Eckhart's Augustinianism, then, is real but selective.

Eckhart was familiar with a wide range of Augustine's writings (though no one has read all of Augustine, as someone once remarked). Nonetheless, like most theologians, he has a "canon within the canon" of Augustine. It does not surprise that the list is headed by the *Confessions*, which must have been the Dominican's favorite reading after the Bible. The bishop's wedding of a transformed Platonism and a piety at once biblical and personal in this evocative work was a constant inspiration for Eckhart, both in his Latin works and in his sermons.[66] Other books that Eckhart loved to cite are *The Trinity* and *On True Religion*, as well as some exegetical treatises.[67] He did not have much interest in the bishop's anti-Pelagian writings, preferring the early *On Free Choice* to the hardening views of the later Augustine.[68] Once again, though, mere numbers do not give us the whole story about what Eckhart actually took from Augustine.

In lieu of trying to give any easy, and therefore inadequate, answer to this central question concerning Eckhart's sources, I will only refer, once again, to the many times in the previous chapters when Augustine has been invoked in order to understand what Eckhart was trying to say. For example, Eckhart appealed to Augustine on the most controversial aspect of his teaching about creation, the notion of its necessary eternity.[69] He also was convinced that Plato and Augustine's view of the highest form of knowing as an inner illumination in the ground of the soul was a level to which Aristotle and the "naturalists" had never attained.[70] His anthropology utilized many themes from Augustine, not only the specification of the three higher powers of the soul (*memoria-intellectus-voluntas*), but also the distinction between humanity being created as *imago dei* and *ad imaginem dei* (i.e., on the pattern of the Word).[71] Eckhart's functional Christology, as we have seen, centered on an axiom found in Augustine (among others)—God became man that man might become God. In adopting these Augustinian motifs in his own way, Eckhart was not acting differently from other medieval theologians.

Eckhart also disagreed with Augustine, though (again like other medievals) he tended to do so silently. For example, Augustine had seen only the "vestiges" of the Trinity in creation, while for Eckhart the very structure of reality is essentially modeled on the trinitarian processions (see chapter 5, p. 76). Therefore, Eckhart also parted company with Augustine about the role of the Incarnate Word in cosmology, advancing a form of pan-Christic ontology closer to some of the Greek Fathers, like Maximus Confessor, than Augustine's view of the Incarnation as God's response to the fall of humanity (chapter 6, p. 118).

Two of Eckhart's most significant Neoplatonic sources both lived around the turn of the sixth century: Dionysius in the East and Boethius in the West. A comparison of the two shows the shortcomings of using numbers alone to determine influence. Eckhart refers to Boethius by name more often than Dionysius in the Latin works, though less often in his sermons. As useful as Boethius was for Eckhart, especially his *Consolation of Philosophy*,[72] it is hard to deny that Dionysius is the more powerful influence. Boethius was a helpful *auctoritas*, especially because of his Neoplatonic teaching on divine unity and goodness; Dionysius, however, was the "disciple of the Apostles," an anonymous fifth-century monk whose assumption of the identity of the Dionysius of Acts 17:34 gave him quasi-scriptural authority.

Dionysius knew and used Proclus, though he was also a profound student of the Greek fathers, especially the Cappadocians. As the inventor of dialectical Christian Neoplatonism, his role in Eckhart's thought is hard to exaggerate.[73] Eckhart lived in an era that has been been described as a "Dionysian Renaissance." Although John Scottus Eriugena was well acquainted with Dionysius, the influence of the *corpus dionysiacum* in the early medieval West was relatively modest, even in the twelfth century. From the second quarter of the thirteenth century, however, powerful waves of Dionysianism are evident in the scholastic world. The two most important of these are the "affective Dionysianism" pioneered by the Victorine Thomas Gallus between 1230 and his death in 1247,[74] and what has been called the "speculative Dionysianism" ("emanative Dionysianism" might be a more appropriate name) that began with Albert the Great's lecturing on the *corpus dionysiacum* at Cologne around 1250.

The history of the emanative Dionysianism, with its rich mixture of themes drawn from the *Proclus Latinus*, the *Book of Causes*, and Arabic Aristotelianism, especially Avicenna, remains to be written.[75] So too, the full range of Dionysius's impact on Eckhart's mysticism could easily use a monograph of its own. Kurt Ruh has provided valuable remarks on the role of Dionysius in Eckhart's vernacular sermons and the sequence "Granum sinapis,"[76] but more explicit citations and appeals to Dionysius are to be found, as expected, in the Latin writings. Ruh shows that the majority of Eckhart's uses of Dionysius in his preaching (which he counts as thirty-seven in all) come from the earlier sermons found in the *Paradise of the Intelligent Soul* collection. Nevertheless, Eckhart read and employed Dionysius throughout his career. Here it will suffice to summarize some the major aspects of the Dionysian role in Eckhart that have been touched on in the above chapters to suggest something of the range of his significance for the Dominican.

Although the outward terminology of Eckhart's teaching on the Trinity is Western in orientation, using Augustine, Peter Lombard, and Aquinas, there are deep affinities between the Dominican's dynamic view of the inner trinitarian processions and Dionysius's trinitarianism (see chapter 5, pp. 79–81). Eckhart's notion of *causa essentialis* (chapter 5, pp. 101–2), of the role of the desert (chapter 6, pp. 143–44), and of the diffusion of Supreme Goodness (chapter 5, pp. 105) all owe something to Dionysius. Above all, it is in terms of his dialectical approach to God-language, the priority of unknowing (*Deus est innominabilis*) in the search for God, and the goal of indistinct union in which Eckhart learned the most from his study of Denys. These major motifs of Neoplatonic mysticism were not restricted to the Dionysian writings, but the way in which the unknown fifth-century author fused them into the first explicitly "mystical theology" (he invented the term) made him indispensable for Eckhart.

The early medieval author whom Eckhart explicitly cited most frequently by name is Gregory the Great. Gregory's *Morals on Job* and other works were favorite reading of all medieval theologians, both monastic and scholastic. As in the case of his use of Jerome, Chrysostom, and others, however, Eckhart employed Gregory for proof-texting more than being formed by him in some significant way. The same is true for the other early medieval authors he cites from time to time (e.g., Isidore of Seville, John of Damascus, Bede, etc.).

One important question concerns Eckhart's possible use of John Scottus Eriugena, the first Western dialectical Neoplatonist. The Irish savant and the German Dominican make for stimulating comparisons on many key issues concerning the whole dynamic process of *exitus* and *reditus*.[77] They used many of the same sources (Origen, Augustine, Dionysius), though Eriugena employed Greek fathers who were only names to Eckhart, and the Dominican had access to Proclus and Proclean texts unknown to the Irishman. However, evidence for any extensive use of Eriugena is problematic.[78] It is not that Eckhart could not have had access to texts of Eriugena, and we are sure that he did read one of them, Eriugena's *Homily on the Prologue of John*.[79] While we cannot exclude further direct contact between the two great dialectical Platonists, it is difficult to number Eriugena among Eckhart's key sources.

Meister Eckhart's use of twelfth-century theologians and mystics is not as significant for understanding his thought as his employment of ancient authorities, both pagan and Christian. Bernard of Clairvaux is the most important of his twelfth-century sources.[80] To be sure, Eckhart often appealed in anonymous fashion to *auctoritates* and opinions found in Peter Lombard's *Sentences*, and he also sided with the Lombard on identifying the Holy Spirit as the love in us that draws us to God (see chapter 5, p. 89). He utilized the handy compilation of patristic scriptural opinions known as the *Ordinary Gloss*, and he shows familiarity with and respect for the broad-ranging Victorine teacher

Hugh. Anselm of Canterbury and Alan of Lille are among the other twelfth-century theologians he used.[81]

What makes Bernard of Clairvaux significant for understanding Eckhart is not just the veneration Eckhart showed for him, but especially what the Dominican took from the abbot's teaching on love. Eckhart's insistence that the love which is an essential part of our way to union must be utterly spontaneous ("without a why"), totally disinterested, and without measure (see chapter 6, p. 155) is basically Bernardine in character. Eckhart also used passages from Bernard's treatment of God in *On Consideration* as proof-texts for his own more speculative and apophatic treatment of the divine nature. In the long run, the Dominican and the Cistercian present different forms of mysticism, but Eckhart's use of Bernard goes beyond mere politeness, indicating study and inner appreciation of the genius of the abbot of Clairvaux.

In considering Eckhart's use of thirteenth-century thinkers, we encounter the difficulty of assessing just how deep an impact these theologians and mystics had upon him in the absence of much direct citation. The great exception to this lack, of course, is Thomas Aquinas. Although Aquinas was not canonized until 1323, late in Eckhart's life, he had become a school text, at least for Dominicans, and therefore Eckhart did not hesitate to employ him constantly, to cite his name often (at least in the Latin works), and to treat him with the respect due to the *doctor ecclesiae* status he was not to attain officially until 1568.[82] As Alain de Libera has claimed, Eckhart was the only friar among the gifted minds of the German Dominicans of the period c. 1250-1325 who really sought to combine the heritage of Albert the Great (developed by thinkers like Ulrich of Strasbourg, Dietrich of Freiburg, and subsequently Berthold of Moosburg) with the Thomism that was becoming the party line among non-German Dominicans.[83] But Eckhart is not *really* a Thomist. Although it could well be argued that Eckhart's metaphysical mysticism might never have achieved its depth of sophistication without his ongoing re-reading and mental dialogue with Thomas, more often than not Eckhart's essential positions are rather different from those of the Angelic Doctor.

The many comparisons between Aquinas and Eckhart in the foregoing chapters provide substantiation for this claim. For example, Eckhart was deeply influenced by Aquinas's metaphysical teaching on God as *ipsum esse subsistens,* to the extent that many passages in his school texts and sermons might be directly taken from Thomas (and often quote him). Nevertheless, *esse* does not have the pre-eminence with Eckhart that it does with Aquinas, largely (as argued in chapter 5, pp.

95–98) because the German's dialectical metaphysics is different from that of Aquinas. This divergence is well illustrated by considering how the two Dominicans understand analogy. Despite Eckhart's appeal to Thomas in this area, most investigators have emphasized how different Eckhart's notion of analogy is from that of Thomas (see chapter 5, pp. 91–92). Disagreements also emerge when one considers the doctrine of creation. Eckhart could cite Aquinas with conviction in speaking about God's unique free production of all things, but his exemplaristic approach to creation, stressing formal causality rather than Thomas's efficient causality, was at the root of the difficulties his creation theology encountered at the Cologne and Avignon trials (see chapter 5, pp. 100–102). Aquinas would scarcely have agreed with Eckhart's harping on the "eternity" of creation, however much he would have admitted that *insofar as* creation is considered from the viewpoint of the eternal ideas in the mind of God, it may be thought of as eternal. The divergences between Aquinas and Eckhart extend into many other areas.[84] Despite these differences, Thomas Aquinas is for Eckhart a resource second only to Augustine. The recent studies that have done much to uncover the intellectual context of Eckhart in the world of German Dominican thought, especially that of Albert and Dietrich, cannot gainsay the fact that Eckhart cites Aquinas hundreds of times, but other Dominicans sparingly.

The past two decades, especially as a result of the publication project known as the *Corpus Philosophorum Teutonicorum Medii Aevi* under the editorship of Kurt Flasch and Loris Sturlese, have revitalized interest in Eckhart's teacher Albert the Great (d. 1280), as well as his contemporaries among the German Dominicans, such as Ulrich of Strasbourg (d. 1277), Dietrich of Freiburg (d. c. 1320), and Berthold of Moosburg (c. 1300–c. 1365). This research has also involved new consideration about what Eckhart's student, John Tauler (c. 1300–1361), has to tell us concerning the intellectual currents that shaped the Meister.[85] The most significant attempt to summarize the findings of this new stage in the search for Eckhart's sources and context has been Alain de Libera's *La mystique rhénane*, whose second edition of 1994 has been often cited here. There is no question that the new light shed on Eckhart's mileau in the vibrant intellectual world of the German Dominicans centered on the Cologne *studium* marks a significant advance in our recovery of the sources of Eckhart's thought. As pointed out above, the Meister's metaphysics of flow is rooted in part in Albert the Great's Cologne teaching and his form of Dionysianism (see, e.g., chapter 5, pp. 71–74). Although Eckhart never cites his contemporary Dietrich by

name (and rarely even indirectly), there can be no question that Eckhart knew him and his work, and that he must have engaged in discussion with him. Both Dominicans were preoccupied with the role of
intellect in achieving true *beatitudo*. How much Eckhart really took
from Dietrich and where and why he disagreed with him are part of the
new intense *Eckhart-Forschung*. It is clear that on some essential points,
such as whether human felicity resides in the active intellect, as Dietrich
held, or in the passive intellect's reception of divine inflow, as Eckhart
taught, there are important differences between the two.[86] Doubtless,
this aspect of Eckhart's heritage will become clearer as the publications
of the *Corpus* continue and spur further research.

The other side of the investigation of Eckhart's contemporary
sources that has undergone an explosion in recent years has been the
relation of the Dominican to thirteenth-century female mysticism.
This issue has been taken up more directly in this book than the philosophical roots of Eckhart's thought in German Dominican thinkers,
though both are of equal importance.[87] For the context and intention
of Eckhart's mystical preaching, we cannot afford to neglect the role of
the Dominican nuns, pious beguines, and the literature produced by
the impressive female theologians who graced the thirteenth century,
such as Beatrice of Nazareth, Hadewijch, Mechthild of Magdeburg,
and, above all, Marguerite Porete. Even more than in the case of his
relations to contemporary Dominican thinkers, however, this aspect of
the search for Eckhart's sources is fraught with difficulty. The Meister
never directly quoted a woman, nor could he have been expected to.
Careful research has proven, however, that Eckhart had read (or had
had read to him) Porete's *Mirror of Simple Souls*.[88] Not only a number
of shared themes (e.g., freedom from the virtues, living without a why,
annihilation of the created will, indistinct union, etc.), but even the verbal expression of these dangerous teachings in Pr. 52 and elsewhere,
indicate that this silent source had a real impact on Eckhart.

How far Eckhart may have been aware of other mystical writings
produced by thirteenth-century women is still a subject of research.
Although the textual links are tenuous at best, Eckhart could have
known something of Mechthild of Magdeburg's *Flowing Light of the
Godhead,* a compilation of mystical poems and visions put together by
Dominicans (and soon translated into Latin) in a convent that was
under his jurisdiction during his time as an administrator.[89] Several
times in the above chapters I have also noted intriguing parallels
between Eckhart's teaching and that found in the Middle Dutch mystic
Hadewijch,[90] though it is difficult to think that Eckhart could have had

access to her writings, especially since they appear to be little known before the mid-fourteenth century. Important as the search may be, the procedures of scholarship and citation among scholastics like Eckhart, accustomed for the most part to masking contemporary sources in anonymity, make it unlikely that we will soon reach any security about exactly what writings by women may have been known and used by Eckhart.

When all is said and done, the search for Eckhart's sources is both fascinating and frustrating. The German Dominican was widely read in many writings of the greatest theological, philosophical, and mystical teachers of antiquity and the Middle Ages. To a greater or lesser extent, they helped shape his mystical teaching in ways still only partly explored. But in the end they give us only a partial grasp Eckhart's genius.

'Notes

Preface

1. The volumes of *The Presence of God* published thus far are *The Foundations of Mysticism: Origins to the Fifth Century* (New York: Crossroad, 1991); *The Growth of Mysticism: Gregory the Great to the Twelfth Century* (New York: Crossroad, 1994); and *The Flowering of Mysticism: Men and Women in the New Mysticism (1200–1350)* (New York: Crossroad, 1998).

2. This is the title of the first of the *sprüche,* or "Sayings," ascribed to Eckhart and printed in Pfeiffer (ed., 597): Diz ist Meister Eckehart, dem got nie niht verbarc. The *sprüche* have not yet been edited in DW, so the authenticity of individual items remains in doubt.

Chapter 1
Meister Eckhart: Lesemeister and Lebemeister

1. Sprüche 8 (Pfeiffer 599.19–21) (my trans.).

2. Since 1980, the Dominican order, as well as interested individuals and groups such as the International Eckhart Society, has sought to obtain an official declaration from the papacy to acknowledge "the exemplary character of Eckhart's activity and preaching and to recommend his writings (particularly the spiritual works, treatises, and sermons) as an expression of authentic Christian mysticism and as trustworthy guides to the Christian life according to the spirit of the Gospel." Thus far, no such statement has appeared.

3. About three hundred manuscripts containing Eckhart's German sermons, both authentic and pseudonymous, survive. A few Eckhart sermons that had come to be ascribed to his follower, John Tauler, were printed in the early Tauler editions (and therefore read by Martin Luther, among others).

4. There are a number of surveys of modern Eckhart research. For older accounts, see Ingeborg Degenhardt, *Studien zum Wandel des Eckhartbildes* (Leiden: Brill, 1967); and Toni Schaller, "Die Meister-Eckhart Forschung von der Jahrhundertwende bis zum

Gegenwart," *Freiburger Zeitschrift für Philosophie und Theologie* 15 (1968): 262–316, 403–26; idem, "Zur Eckhart-Deutung der letzten 30 Jahre," *Freiburger Zeitschrift* . . . 16 (1969): 22–39. More recently, see Niklaus Largier, "Meister Eckhart: Perspektiven der Forschung, 1980–1993," *Zeitschrift für deutsche Philologie* 114 (1995): 29–98; idem, "Recent Work on Meister Eckhart: Positions, Problems, New Perspectives, 1990–1997," *Recherches de Théologie et Philosophie médiévales* 65 (1998): 147–67. In addition, Largier has compiled a very useful *Bibliographie zu Meister Eckhart* (Freiburg, Switzerland: Universitätsverlag, 1989), listing 1,491 items.

5. The bulk of Eckhart scholarship continues to be produced in German, but distinguished contributions in English and French (and to a lesser extent in Italian) demonstrate how international the interest in the German Dominican has become.

6. This is my fourth attempt to give a general account of Eckhart and his teaching, and I am conscious of the fact that there is bound to be some overlap with these earlier presentations. Nevertheless, I hope that my continuing reading of Eckhart and study of the many excellent products of the newer *Eckhartforschung* (mostly in German) have resulted in a richer and deeper presentation here. For my previous general presentations, see (a) "2. Theological Summary," in the "Introduction" to *Essential Eckhart*, 24–61; (b) "Meister Eckhart: An Introduction," in *An Introduction to the Medieval Mystics of Europe*, ed. Paul Szarmach (Albany: SUNY Press, 1984), 237–57; and (c) "Meister Eckhart," in *Medieval Philosophers: Dictionary of Literary Biography, Volume 115*, ed. Jeremiah Hackett (Detroit/London: Bruccoli Clark, 1992), 150–68.

7. The documents relating to Eckhart's life, the *Acta Eckhardiana* are now being edited by Loris Sturlese in LW 5. Among the many accounts of Eckhart's life and works, the following are indispensable: Josef Koch, "Kritische Studien zum Leben Meister Eckharts," *Archivum Fratrum Praedicatorum* 29 (1959): 1–51; and 30 (1960): 1–52; Kurt Ruh, *Meister Eckhart: Theologe. Prediger. Mystiker* (Munich: C. H. Beck, 1985); idem, "Kapitel XXXVI: Meister Eckhart," in Kurt Ruh, *Geschichte der abendländische Mystik*, vol. 3, *Die Mystik des deutschen Predigerordens und ihre Grundlegung durch die Hochscholastik* (Munich: C. H. Beck, 1996), 216–353 (hereafter *Geschichte 3*). An important recent attempt to provide an overview of Eckhart's life and thought is Loris Sturlese, "Meister Eckhart: Ein Porträt," *Eichstätter Hochschulreden* 90 (Regensburg: Pustet, 1993), part of which is available in English as "A Portrait of Meister Eckhart," *Eckhart Review* (spring 1996): 7–12. For recent discussions of Eckhart's life and work, see Niklaus Largier, "Recent Work on Meister Eckhart," 148–56.

8. See Acta n.1 (LW 5:155), and also n.11 (LW 5:162–63), which records the death of his father ("dominus Eckardus miles de Hochheim") in 1305.

9. This *Sermo Paschalis* (LW 5:136–48) already shows Eckhart's mastery of philosophical sources and impressive rhetorical skills.

10. *Sermo Paschalis* n.15 (LW 5:145.5–6): Et Albertus saepe dicebat: "hoc scio sicut scimus, nam omnes parum scimus."

11. Eckhart's brief *Collatio in Libros Sententiarum*, a sermon prologue to his commentary, can be found in LW 5:17–26. There is still debate over whether an anonymous *Sentence* commentary found in a Bruges manuscript may belong to Eckhart, or at least to his circle. See Andreas Speer and Wouter Goris, "Das Meister-Eckhart-Archiv am Thomas-Institut der Universität zu Köln: Die Kontinuität der Forschungsaufgaben," *Bulletin de philosophie médiévale* 37 (1995): 149–74.

12. For an introduction to the condemnation and the debate over its meaning and effect, see John F. Wippel, "The Condemnations of 1270 and 1277 at Paris," *Journal of Medieval and Renaissance Studies* 7 (1977): 169–201.

13. For a comparison of Eckhart's view of the relation of philosophy and theology with that of Bonaventure on the one hand and Albert and Thomas on the other, see Bernard McGinn, "*SAPIENTIA JUDAEORUM:* The Role of Jewish Philosophers in Some Scholastic Thinkers," in *Continuity and Change: The Harvest of Late-Medieval and Reformation History. Essays presented to Heiko A. Oberman on his 70th Birthday,* ed. Robert J. Bast and Andrew C. Gow (Leiden: Brill, 2000), 206–28.

14. In Ioh. n.185 (LW 3:154.14–155.7): Secundum hoc ergo convenienter valde scriptura sacra sic exponitur, ut in ipsa sint consona, quae philosophi de rerum naturis et ipsarum proprietatibus scripserunt, praesertim cum ex uno fonte et una radice procedat veritatis omne quod verum est, sive essendo sive cognoscendo, in scriptura et in natura. . . . Idem ergo est quod docet Moyses, Christus et philosophus, solum quantum ad modum differens, scilicet ut credibile, probabile sive verisimile et veritas.

15. *Die rede der underscheidunge* (RdU) is edited in DW 5:137–376. There are a number of English translations, including that found in *Essential Eckhart,* 247–85.

16. Sturlese, "A Portrait of Meister Eckhart," 8–10; Ruh, *Geschichte* 3:258–67.

17. See Sturlese, "A Portrait," 10.

18. The *Quaestiones Parisienses* (Qu. Par.) can be found in LW 5:29–71. There is an English translation by Armand Maurer, *Master Eckhart: Parisian Questions and Prologues* (Toronto: PIMS, 1974). In addition, from the same year at Paris we have Eckhart's *Sermo die b. Augustini Parisius habitus* (LW 5:89–99).

19. Qu.Par. 1 n.4 (LW 5:40.5–6): . . . quod non ita videtur mihi modo, ut quia sit, ideo intelligat, sed quia intelligit, ideo est. . . .

20. On the relation between Thomas and Eckhart, see especially Ruedi Imbach, *DEUS EST INTELLIGERE: Das Verhältnis von Sein und Denken in seiner Bedeutung für das Gottesverständnis bei Thomas von Aquin und in den Pariser Quaestionen Meister Eckharts* (Freiburg, Switzerland: Universitätsverlag, 1976).

21. On the context and significance of the Qu. Par., see the papers in *Maître Eckhart à Paris: Une critique médiévale de l'ontothéologie. Les Questions parisiennes no. 1 et no. 2* (Paris: Presses Universitaires de France, 1984). For the historical background, consult especially the essay of Eduoard Wéber in this volume, "Eckhart et l'ontothéologisme: Histoire et conditions d'une rupture," 13–83.

22. Qu.Par.1 n.11 (LW 5:46.7–10): Item: in his quae dicuntur secundum analogiam, quod est in uno analogatorum, formaliter non est in alio, ... Cum igitur omnia causata sunt entia formaliter, deus formaliter non erit ens.

23. The nature of the beatific vision was an object of considerable discussion in High Scholastic theology. See the massive study of Christian Trottmann, *La vision béatifique: Des disputes scolastiques à sa définition per Benoît XII* (Rome: École Française de Rome, 1995), who summarizes Eckhart's view on pp. 328–30.

24. Qu.Par.3, n.6 (LW 5:59.12–13): . . . intellectus, actus et habitus ipsius sint quid nobilius voluntate, actu et habitu eius. The eleven *rationes* are found in nn.6–20 (LW 5:59–64). In Pr. 70 Eckhart refers to this debate as something that happened recently (DW 3:188ff.).

25. Alain de Libera, "Les 'raisons d'Eckhart,'" in *Maître Eckhart à Paris,* 109–40. De Libera argues that Eckhart developed his position out of lines of thought he found in Aquinas and that therefore: "Eckhart ne s'est, semble-t-il, jamais *senti* en opposition réelle avec Thomas" (p. 132).

26. The collection has been edited by Philip Strauch, *Paradisus anime intelligentis (Paradis der fornunftigen sele): Aus der Oxforder Hs. Cod. Laud. Misc. 479 nach E. Sievers Abschrift,* Deutsche Texte des Mittelalters 30 (Berlin, 1919). For further information,

see Ruh, *Meister Eckhart*, 60–71; as well as his article "Paradisus animae intelligentis" ("Paradis der fornunftigen sele") in *VL* 7:298–303; and *Geschichte* 3:274–79. See also Ria van den Brandt, "Die Eckhart-Predigten der Sammlung *PARADISUS ANIME INTELLIGENTIS* näher betrachtet," in *Albertus Magnus und der Albertismus: Deutsche philosophische Kultur des Mittelalters*, ed. Maarten J. F. M. Hoenen and Alain de Libera (Leiden: Brill, 1995), 173–87; and Burkhard Hasebrink, "Studies on the Redaction and Use of the *Paradisus anime intelligentis*," in *De l'homélie au sermon: Histoire de la prédication médiévale*, ed. Jacqueline Hamesse and Xavier Hermand (Louvain-la-neuve: Université Catholique, 1993), 144–58. Hasebrink notes that the stages and redactional perspective of the editing of the *Paradisus* do not guarantee that every individual Eckhart sermon in it must date to 1303–1311, but doubtless many do.

27. Ruh, *Geschichte* 3:279: "Auf sprachliche Ebene bedeutet dies: 'Latein' und 'Deutsch' begegnen sich in einem Werk der Volkssprache."

28. Pr. 9 (DW 1:150.3–7): Niergen wonet got eigenlîcher dan in sînem tempel, in vernünfticheit, . . . diu dâ lebet in sîn aleines bekantnisse, in im selber aleine blîbende, dâ in nie niht engeruorte, wan er aleine dâ ist in sîner stilheit (trans. *Teacher and Preacher*). Much has been written on this sermon. For a general interpretation of the homily and the literature on it, see Largier 1:834–55. An insightful study of the major theme can be found in Susanne Köbele, "*BÎWORT SÎN*: 'Absolute' Grammatik bei Meister Eckhart," *Zeitschrift für deutsche Philologie* 113 (1994): 190–206.

29. Pr. 98 (DW 4:244.38–43): Dâ wirt si sô lûterlîchen ein, daz si kein ander wesen enhât dan daz selbe wesen, daz sîn ist, daz ist daz sêle-wesen. Diz wesen ist ein begin alles des werkes, daz got würket in himelrîche und in ertrîche. Ez ist ein urhap und ein grunt aller sîner götlîchen werke. Diu sêle engât ir natûre und irm wesene und irm lebene und wirt geborn in der gotheit. . . . Si wirt sô gar ein wesen, daz dâ kein under-scheit ist, dan daz er got blîbet und si sêle (my trans.). Georg Steer, the editor of DW 4, notes the many parallels between Pr. 98 and Pr. 17, a key text on the *grunt*. Eckhart had already used the term *grund/abgrund* ten times in his RdU.

30. Georg Steer, "Meister Eckharts Predigtzyklus *von der êwigen geburt*: Mutmas-sungen über die Zeit seiner Entstehung," in *Deutsche Mystik im abendländischen Zusammenhang: Neue erschlossene Texte, neue methodische Ansätze, neue theoretische Konzepte*, ed. Walther Haug and Wolfram Schneider-Lastin (Tübingen: Niemeyer, 2000), 253–81.

31. In Eccli. is edited in LW 2:231–300. On the dating of this work, see Acta n.33 (LW 5:179). There is a partial translation in *Teacher and Preacher*, 174–81.

32. Sturlese, "Meister Eckhart: Ein Porträt," 15.

33. In Eccli. n.53 (LW 2:282.3–6): Igitur omne ens creatum habet a deo et in deo, non in se ipso ente creato, esse, vivere, sapere positive et radicaliter. Et sic semper edit, ut productum est et creatum, semper tamen esurit, quia semper ex se non est, sed ab alio.

34. In Eccli. n.58 (LW 2:287.1–4): Qui ergo edit, edendo esurit, quia esuriem edit, et quantum edit, tantum esurit. . . . Edendo enim esurit et esuriendo edit et esurire sive esuriem esurit. On this text, see Donald F. Duclow, "The Hungers of Hadewijch and Eckhart," *Journal of Religion* 80 (2000): 421–41. Eckhart may be reflecting and expand-ing on Augustine, who, in *Sermo* 170.9 (PL 38:931), referred to God as *satietas insatia-bilis*.

35. Loris Sturlese, "Meister Eckhart in der Bibliotheca Amploniana: Neues zur Datierung des 'Opus tripartitum'," in *Der Bibliotheca Amploniana: Ihre Bedeutung im Spannungsfeld von Aristotelismus, Nominalismus und Humanismus*, ed. Andreas Speer,

Miscellanea Mediaevalia 23 (Berlin/New York: Walter de Gruyter, 1995), 434–46; idem, "Un nuovo manoscritto delle opere latine di Eckhart e il suo significato per la ricostruzione del testo e della storia del Opus tripartitum," *Freiburger Zeitschrift für Philosophie und Theologie* 32 (1985): 145–54; idem, "Meister Eckhart: Ein Porträt," 16–19.

36. The *Opus tripartitum* (Op.trip.) survives only in its prologues edited in LW 1: (a) *Prologus generalis* (Prol.gen. in LW 1:148–65); (b) *Prologus in opus propositionum* (Prol.op.prop. in LW 166–82); and (c) *Prologus in opus expositionum* (Prol.op.expos. in LW 1:183–84). This text is from Prol.gen. nn.3–6 (LW 1:149.3–151.12): Distinguitur igitur secundum hoc opus ipsum totale in tria principaliter. Primum est opus generalium propositionum, secundum opus quaestionum, tertium opus expositionum. Opus autem primum, quia propositiones tenet mille et amplius, in tractatus quattuordecim distinguitur iuxta numerum terminorum, de quibus formantur propositiones. . . . Opus autem secundum, quaestionum scilicet, distinguitur secundum materiam quaestionum, de quibus agitur ordine quo ponuntur in Summa doctoris egregii venerabilis fratris Thomas de Aquino, ... Opus vero tertium, scilicet expositionum, . . . subdividitur numero et ordine librorum veteris et novi testamenti, quorum auctoritates in ipso exponuntur. On the Op.trip., see the important recent study of Wouter Goris, *Einheit als Prinzip und Ziel: Versuch über di Einheitsmetaphysik des "Opus tripartitum" Meister Eckharts* (Leiden: Brill, 1997), as well as Ruh, *Geschichte* 3:290–308.

37. The treatment of the proposition *esse est deus* can be found both in Prol.gen. nn.12–22 (LW 1:156–65) and Prol.op.prop. nn.1–25 (LW 1:166–82). There is a translation of these texts in Maurer, *Master Eckhart: Parisian Questions and Prologues,* 77–105. Although the prologues are the only parts of the Op.prop. to survive, Eckhart's references to other treatises, e.g., *De bono, De natura superioris,* etc., indicate that some other propositions were probably written down, at least in a preliminary way.

38. In. Gen. I is edited in LW 1:185–444. For a partial English translation, see *Essential Eckhart,* 82–91.

39. In Sap. is edited in LW 2:303–634. A selection of passages is translated in *Teacher and Preacher,* 147–74. See especially the exegesis of Wisdom 7:27a on God as *unum* (In Sap. nn.144–57; *Teacher and Preacher,* 166–71).

40. In Ex. is edited in LW 2:1–227 and has been translated in its entirety in *Teacher and Preacher,* 41–146. Eckhart's extensive use of Maimonides in this commentary may argue for a date in the second decade of the fourteenth century when he seems to have begun using the Jewish sage more extensively.

41. In Ioh. takes up the whole of LW 3. The section on the Johannine Prologue (John 1:1–14) has been translated in *Essential Eckhart,* 122–73. An important comment on John 14:8 dealing with the Trinity can be found in *Teacher and Preacher,* 182–93.

42. The fifty-six Latin *sermones* (given Latin numeration and the abbreviations S. and SS. to distinguish them from the vernacular Prr.) are edited in LW 4. Several of these sermons have been rendered into English in James M. Clark and John V. Skinner, *Treatises and Sermons of Meister Eckhart* (New York: Harper & Brothers, 1958); *Teacher and Preacher,* 207–38; and *Meister Eckhart: Selected Writings,* selected and translated by Oliver Davies (London: Penguin, 1994), 253–65.

43. In a number of places, Eckhart refers to other parts of the *Opus expositionum* (Op.expos.), especially commentaries on the Pauline epistles. It is likely, as Ruh suggests (*Geschichte* 3:291), that Eckhart lectured on these texts, but did not have time to commit his commentaries to writing.

44. Prol.gen. n.2 (LW 1:148.5–9): Auctoris intentio in hoc opere tripartito est satisfacere pro posse studiosorum fratrum quorundam desideriis, qui iam dudum precibus

importunis ipsum impellunt crebro et compellunt, ut ea quae ab ipso audire con-
sueverunt, tum in lectionibus et aliis actibus scholasticis, tum in praedicationibus, tum
in cottidianis collationibus, scripto commendat. . . .

45. See Goris, *Einheit als Prinzip und Ziel*, 12–14 and 46.

46. Prol.gen. n.7 (LW 1:152.3–5): Advertendum est autem quod nonnulla ex
sequentibus propositionibus, quaestionibus, expositionibus primo aspectu monstruosa, dubia aut falsa apparebunt, secus autem si sollerter et studiosius pertractentur.

47. Ruh, *Geschichte* 3:293, notes the close interconnection of the three parts
demonstrated in the parallel between the first proposition (*esse est deus*), the first question (*an deus est?*), and the first commentary dealing with *In principio creavit deus
caelum et terram* (Gen. 1:1).

48. In Ioh. n.2 (LW 3:4.4–6): In cuius verbi expositione et aliorum quae sequuntur,
intentio est auctoris, sicut et in omnibus suis editionibus, ea quae sacra asserit fides
christiana et utriusque testamenti scriptura, exponere per rationes naturales
philosophorum.

49. On the relation of Latin and the vernacular in late medieval mysticism, see
Bernard McGinn, *The Flowering of Mysticism: Men and Women in the New Mysticism
(1200–1350)* (New York: Crossroad, 1998), 20–24.

50. See Kurt Ruh, "Textkritik zum Mystikerlied 'Granum sinapis,'" in *Kleine
Schriften*, vol. 2, *Scholastik und Mystik im Spätmittelalter*, ed. Volker Mertens (Berlin/
New York: Walter de Gruyter, 1984), 77–93 (a paper first published in 1964, with an
edition of the poem); idem, *Meister Eckhart*, 47–59; idem, *Geschichte* 3:282–90. See also
Alois M. Haas, "Granum sinapis—An den Grenzen der Sprache," in *Sermo Mysticus:
Studien zu Theologie und Sprache der deutschen Mystik* (Freiburg, Switzerland: Univer-
sitätsverlag, 1979), 301–29. Most recently, there is a translation and study of Alain de
Libera, *Maître Eckhart: Le grain de sènève* (Paris: Arfuyen, 1996). For an English version,
see Walshe 1:xxviii-xxxi.

51. The Latin commentary has been edited by Maria Bindschedler, *Der lateinische
Kommentar zum Granum Sinapis* (Basel: Schwabe, 1949). For passages emphasizing the
apex affectus and the influence of Gallus (and most likely Bonaventure), see, e.g., 86–88,
94–98, 128–32, 144, and 158.

52. Much has recently been written on the relation between Eckhart and Porete's
Mirror of Simple Souls. We will return to this theme in subsequent chapters.

53. For an introduction to Eckhart's preaching, see Alois M. Haas, "Meister
Eckharts geistliches Predigtprogramm," in *Geistliches Mittelalter* (Freiburg, Switzerland: Universitätsverlag, 1984), 317–37.

54. On Eckhart's encounter with women mystics in general, see Otto Langer,
*Mystische Erfahrung und spirituelle Theologie: Zu Meister Eckharts Auseinandersetzung
mit der Frauenfrömmigkeit seiner Zeit* (Munich/Zurich: Artemis, 1987); Amy Hollywood, *The Soul as Virgin Wife: Mechthild of Magdeburg, Marguerite Porete, and Meister
Eckhart* (Notre Dame: University of Notre Dame Press, 1995); and the papers in *Meister Eckhart and the Beguine Mystics: Hadewijch of Brabant, Mechthild of Magdeburg, and
Marguerite Porete*, ed. Bernard McGinn (New York: Continuum, 1994).

55. See especially the remarks in Pr. 29 (DW 2:78–79), a sermon probably given at
Cologne c. 1324–26.

56. For an introduction to these women mystics, see McGinn, *Flowering of Mysticism*, 222–65, and the literature cited there.

57. The earliest witness for Eckhart's presence in Strasbourg is in a document dated
April 14, 1314 (Acta n.38 [LW 5:182–84]).

58. See Jacqueline Tarrant, "The Clementine Decrees on the Beguines: Conciliar and Papal Versions," *Archivum Historiae Pontificiae* 12 (1974): 300–307. For the wider context, consult Robert E. Lerner, *The Heresy of the Free Spirit,* 2nd ed. (Notre Dame, Ind.: University of Notre Dame Press, 1997).

59. See Ruh, *Meister Eckhart,* 112–14; idem, *Geschichte* 3:242–43. On the persecution of beguines in Strasbourg, see Alexander Patschovsky, "Strassburger Beginenvervolgerung im 14. Jahrhundert," *Deutsches Archiv für Erforschung des Mittelalters* 30 (1974): 56–198.

60. See Acta nn.41–42 (LW 5:187–88).

61. Ruh, *Meister Eckhart,* 136; Sturlese, "Meister Eckhart: Ein Porträt," 17–18.

62. On Eckhart's new style of preaching after 1313, see Ruh, *Meister Eckhart,* 108, 111–12; idem, *Geschichte* 3:303.

63. Anne-Marie Vannier, "L'homme noble, figure de l'ouevre d'Eckhart à Strasbourg," *Revue des sciences religieuses* 70 (1996): 73–89; eadem, "Eckhart à Strasbourg (1313–1323/24)," in *Dominicains et Dominicaines en Alsace XIIIe–XXe S.,* ed. Jean-Luc Eichenlaub (Colmar: Éditions d'Alsace, 1996), 197–208.

64. See Pr. 71 (DW 3:224.5–225.1).

65. Pr. 53 (DW 2:528.5–529.2): Swenne ich predige, sô pflige ich ze sprechenne von abegescheidenheit und daz der mensche ledic werde sîn selbes und aller dinge. Ze andern mâle, daz man wider îngebildet werde in daz einvaltige guot, daz got ist. Ze drittem mâle, daz man gedenke der grôzen edelkeit, die got an die sêle hât geleget, daz der mensche dâ mite kome in ein wunder ze gote. Ze dem vierden mâle von götlîcher natûre lûterkeit—waz klârheit an götlîcher natûre sî, daz ist unsprechelich. Got ist ein wort, ein ungesprochen wort (trans. *Essential Eckhart*).

66. Pr. 6 (DW 1:105.1–2): Swer underscheit verstât von gerechticheit und vom gerehtem, der verstât allez, was ich sage (my trans.). Ruh treats this sermon as a late production, without assigning any definite date (*Meister Eckhart,* 155–57). Ruh also corrects those who mistranslate the *underscheit* of the passage.

67. Pr. 9 (DW 1:154.7–9): Ich meine daz wörtelîn "quasi," daz heizet "als," daz heizent diu kint in der schuole ein bîwort. Diz ist, daz ich in allen mînen predigen meine (trans. *Teacher and Preacher*). Eckhart explains what he means in more detail in 158.4–8. Cf. Kôbele, "*BÎWORT SÎN.*"

68. Vannier, "L'homme noble," 77 and 81–83.

69. In Ioh. n.6 (LW 3:7.12–8.1): . . . licet in analogicis productum sit descendens a producente, ... Item fit aliud in natura, et sic non ipsum principium . . . ut est in illo, non est aliud in natura, sed nec aliud in supposito.

70. In Ioh. n.19 (LW 3:16.10–11): Rursus duodecimo: iustus in ipsa iustitia iam non est genitus nec genita iustitia, sed est ipsa iustitia ingenita. This first discussion of *iustitia* and *iustus* stretches from nn.14–22 (LW 3:13–19).

71. See In Ioh. nn.46, 85, 119, 169–72, 177, 187–92, 196, 225, 252–53, 256, 316, 340–41, 416–17, 426, 435–36, 453–55, 458, 470–71, 477, 503–04, 511, 601, 620, 640, 643–44, 659–60, 731.

72. In Gen.II is edited in LW 1:447–702. The *prologus* to this work (nn.1–7 [447–56]), especially because it mentions "this book and others in the holy canon," is to be taken as a second *prologue* to the whole Op.expos. For a translation of the prologue and some other passages, see *Essential Eckhart,* 92–121.

73. Sturlese, "Meister Eckhart in der Bibliotheca Amploniana"; idem, "Meister Eckhart. Ein Porträt," 16–19.

74. Ruh, *Geschichte* 3:301–03; Goris, *Einheit als Prinzip und Ziel,* 49–51.

75. Niklaus Largier, "*Figurata locutio:* Philosophie und Hermeneutik bei Eckhart von Hochheim und Heinrich Seuse," in *Meister Eckhart: Lebensstationen—Redesituationen,* ed. Klaus Jacobi (Berlin: Walter de Gruyter, 1997), 328–32; idem, "Recent Work on Meister Eckhart," 150–51.

76. The *Liber Benedictus* appears in DW 5:1–136, with BgT on 3–61, and VeM on 109–19. There are a number of English versions (e.g., *Essential Eckhart,* 209–47). For a treatment of the issues connected with the book, see especially Ruh, *Geschichte* 3:308–23, and the literature discussed there.

77. The issue of the "authenticity" of Eckhart's sermons is a thorny one, especially because in his trial at Cologne the Dominican complained that the excerpts from sermons that had been objected to did not always reflect what he had said. There is no question that this is true. The many manuscript witnesses, and the often considerable variant readings they convey, confirm Eckhart's contention that these *reportationes* (i.e., transcriptions from notes) were often imperfect, or even mistaken. Nevertheless, recent research, especially of Georg Steer, the editor of DW 4, has encouraged the view that Eckhart had some hand in editing many of the exemplars of the sermons that come down to us; see Steer, "Zur Authentizität der deutschen Predigten Meister Eckharts," in *Eckhardus Theutonicus, Homo doctus et sanctus: Nachweise und Berichte zum Prozess gegen Meister Eckhart,* ed. Heinrich Stirnimann and Ruedi Imbach (Freiburg, Switzerland: Universitätsverlag, 1992), 127–68.

78. Ruh, *Meister Eckhart,* 135: "Eckharts Trost ist der Trost für denjenigen, der die Welt hinter sich lassen will."

79. See BgT (DW 5:8.9–9.2).

80. BgT 1 (DW 5:60.13–14): Mir genüeget, daz in mir und in gote wâr sî, daz ich spreche und schrîbe (trans. *Essential Eckhart*).

81. BgT 1 (DW 5:60.27–61.1): Ouch sol man sprechen, daz man sôgetâne lêre niht ensol sprechen noch schrîben ungelêrten. Dar zuo spriche ich: ensol man niht lêren ungelêrte liute, sô enwirt niemer nieman gelêret, sô enmac nieman lêren noch schrîben. Wan dar umbe lêret man die ungelêrten, daz sie werden von ungelêret gelêret (trans. *Essential Eckhart*).

82. *Vom abegescheidenheit* (Vab) can be found in DW 5:400–34. There are a number of translations in English, including *Essential Eckhart,* 285–94; and Walshe 3:117–29.

83. See especially Ruh, *Meister Eckhart,* 165–67; idem, *Geschichte* 3:349–51 and 355–58.

84. Walter Senner, "Meister Eckhart in Köln," in *Meister Eckhart: Lebensstationen—Redesituationen,* ed. Jacobi, 207–37.

85. As claimed by Senner, "Meister Eckhart in Köln," 229–35.

86. Joachim Theisen provides a list of fifteen sermons that he dates to 1325–1326 (*Predigt und Gottesdienst: Liturgische Strukturen in den Predigten Meister Eckharts* [Frankfurt: Peter Lang, 1990], 121–22). These include Prr. 1, 11, 12, 13, 14, 15, 18, 19, 25, 26, 37, 49, 51, 59, and 79. Senner also includes Prr. 16, 22, 28, 29, and 80 ("Meister Eckhart in Köln," 226–28). In addition, Walter Haug dates Pr. 63 to spring 1326 (*Lectura Eckhardi,* 214 n. 11); and Ruh argues that Eckhart's famous sermon on poverty of spirit (Pr. 52) is one of his last and therefore a product of the Cologne years (*Meister Eckhart,* 158). If all these ascriptions are correct, at least twenty-two of Eckhart's surviving 114 MHG sermons come from these three years.

87. Loris Sturlese is in the process of editing all the trial documents in *Acta Eckhardiana* nn.44–67 in LW 5:190 ff. For a theological account of the issues of the trial, most of what I wrote in my article "Eckhart's Condemnation Reconsidered," *The*

Thomist 344 (1980): 390–414, still stands. Further precision about issues of dating, context, and the status of the documents has been enhanced by scholarship of the past two decades. See especially Ruh, *Meister Eckhart*, 168–86; Winfried Trusen, *Der Prozess gegen Meister Eckhart: Vorgeschichte, Verlauf und Folgen* (Paderborn: Pustet, 1988); eadem, "Meister Eckhart vor seinen Richtern und Zensoren," in *Meister Eckhart: Lebensstationen—Redesituationen,* ed. Jacobi, 335–52. Also consult Oliver Davies, "Why were Eckhart's propositions condemned?" *New Blackfriars* 71 (1990): 433–45; Jürgen Miethke, "Der Prozess gegen Meister Eckhart im Rahmen der spätmittelalter Lehrzuchtverfahren gegen Dominikanertheologen," in *Meister Eckhart: Lebenstationen—Redesituationen,* ed. Jacobi, 353–75; and especially the papers in *Eckardus Theutonicus, homo doctus et sanctus: Nachweise und Berichte zum Prozess gegen Meister Eckhart,* ed. Heinrich Stirnimann and Ruedi Imbach (Freiburg, Switzerland: Universitätsverlag, 1992). Most recently, see Ruh, *Geschichte* 3:243–57; and Robert E. Lerner, "New Evidence for the Condemnation of Meister Eckhart," *Speculum* 72 (1997): 347–66.

88. For a sketch of Henry II and the background of the trial, see Davies, "Why were Eckhart's propositions condemned?" as well as his *Meister Eckhart: Mystical Theologian* (London: SPCK, 1991), 31–45. See also Friedrich Iohn, *Die Predigt Meister Eckharts,* (Heidelberg: Carl Winter, 1993), 157–68.

89. The decrees of this Chapter can be found in the *Monumenta Ordinis Praedicatorum Historica, Tomus IV, Acta Capitulorum Generalium* (Vol. II), ed. Benedict Maria Reichert (Rome: Propaganda Fidei, 1899), 160.25–161.5. The key passage reads: . . . quod in ipsa provincia [Theutonia] per fratres quosdam in praedicacione vulgari quedam personis vulgaribus ac rudibus in sermonibus proponuntur, que possint auditores faciliter deducere in errorem, idcirco damus vicariam super istis diligencius inquirendis et censura debita puniendis ac coerecendis. . . . Koch doubted that the remarks were directed against Eckhart ("Kritische Studien zum Leben Meister Eckharts," 314–16), as did Trusen (*Der Prozess gegen Meister Eckhart,* 60). However, I side with Ruh (*Meister Eckhart,* 171–72) and Davies ("Why were Eckhart's propositions condemned?" 434–35) that the language argues that Eckhart was indeed intended. A similar reprimand was issued by the General Chapter of Toulouse when Eckhart's case was still *sub judice.* This decree of May 28, 1328 (*Monumenta* IV:180.1–5) reads: Cum ex eo quod aliqui in praedicationibus ad populum conantur tractare quaedam subtilia, que non solum ad mores non proficiunt, quinimo facilius ducunt populum in errorem, precipit magister ordinis in virtute sancte obediencie de diffinitorum consilio et assensu, quod nullus de cetero presumat talia in sermonibus pertractare. . . .

90. This list, the *Processus Coloniensis I* (Proc.Col.I) has been edited by Sturlese as Acta n.46 (LW 5:197–226).

91. Sturlese is in the process of editing this text (Proc.Col.II) as Acta n.47 (LW 5:226–40 thus far).

92. The critical edition of this document in the Acta of LW 5 is still in preparation. Since Eckhart was answering two lists of extracts, it will consist of Proc.Col.I nn.75–151, and Proc.Col.II nn.1–160. For the present, the most useful edition is Théry. There is a partial translation in *Essential Eckhart,* 71–77. A complete translation, based on the older edition of Augustus Daniels, can be found in Raymond Bernard Blakney, *Meister Eckhart: A Modern Translation* (New York: Harper & Row, 1941), 258–305.

93. Théry, 186: Errare enim possum, hereticus esse non possum, nam primum ad intellectum pertinet, secundum ad voluntatem. Eckhart repeats the point often (e.g., Théry, 191, 197–98, 206).

94. Théry, 243: Solutio: totum quod dictum est, falsum et absurdum, secundum ymaginationem adversantium; verum est tamen secundum verum intellectum. . . .

95. Théry, 240: . . . vivere meum est esse dei, vel vita mea est essentia dei, quidditas dei quidditas mea. Dicendum est quod falsum est et error, sicut sonat. Verum quidem est, devotum et morale quod hominis justi, inquantum justus, totum esse est ab esse dei, analogice tamen.

96. Théry, 186: Ad evidentiam igitur premissorum, tria notanda sunt: Primum est quod li "inquantum", reduplicatio scilicet, excludit omne aliud, omne alienum etiam secundum rationem a termino.

97. Théry, 185: . . .quod juxta libertatem et privilegia ordinis nostri, coram vobis non teneor conparere nec objectis respondere. . . .

98. See Théry, 196.

99. See Ruh, *Geschichte* 3:246–47.

100. Acta n.54 (not yet edited in LW 5). The best present edition is that of M.-H. Laurent, "Autour de procès de Maître Eckhart," *Divus Thomas,* ser. III, 13 (1936): 344–46.

101. The *Votum,* Acta n.57, has not yet appeared in LW 5. The current edition is that of Franz Pelster, "Eine Gutachten aus dem Eckehart-Prozess in Avignon," in *Aus der Geisteswelt des Mittelalters: Festgabe Martin Grabmann* (Münster: Aschendorff, 1935), 1099–1124. The text in question deals with XXIIIus articulus (p. 1120): Istum articulum verifficat, quia Christus caput et nos membra, cum loquimur, in nobis loquitur. Item in Christo tanta fuit unio verbi cum carne, quod communicat sibi ydiomata, ut Deus dicatur passus et homo creator celi et ipsi Christo proprie competit quod dicatur iustus, inquantum iustus; li inquantum reduplicacio excludit omne alienum a termino. In Christo autem non esse aliud ypostaticum nisi verbi, in aliis autem hominibus verifficatur plus et minus.

102. Senner, "Meister Eckhart in Köln," 233, citing Friedrich Steill, *Ephemerides Dominicano-Sacrae* of 1691.

103. The critical text of the papal bull has not yet appeared in LW 5, but a text may be found in Laurent, "Autour du procès," 435–46. The quotations that follow are taken from the translation in *Essential Eckhart,* 77–81.

104. Lerner provides an edition of the Mainz copy ("New Evidence," 363–66).

Chapter 2
Approaching Eckhart: Controversies and Perspectives

1. Pope John Paul II quoted Eckhart in a 1985 address.

2. Heinrich Seuse Denifle, "Meister Eckeharts lateinische Schriften und die Grundanschauungen seiner Lehre," *Archiv für Literatur und Kirchengeschichte des Mittelalters* 2 (1886): 482: ". . . dass Eckehart ein unklarer Denker war, der sich die Consequenzen seiner Lehre resp. seiner Ausdrucksweise nicht bewusst war."

3. Otto Karrer, *Meister Eckehart: Das System seiner religiösen Lehre und Lebensweisheit* (Munich: Josef Müller, 1926). The best survey of the early twentieth-century Eckhart scholarship is Toni Schaller, "Die Meister-Eckhart Forschung von der Jahrhundertwende bis zum Gegenwart," *Freiburger Zeitschrift für Philosophie und Theologie* 15 (1968): 262–316, 403–26.

4. There have been a number of recent surveys of this debate. See especially Ruh, *Geschichte* 3:227–31; and Niklaus Largier, "Meister Eckhart: Perspektiven der

Forschung, 1980–1993," *Zeitschrift für deutsche Philologie* 114 (1995): 52–59. Among earlier treatments, see Frank Tobin, *Meister Eckhart: Thought and Language* (Philadelphia: University of Pennsylvania Press, 1986), 185–92; and Günter Stachel, "Streit um Meister Eckhart: Spekulativer Theologe, beinahe Häretischer Scholastiker oder grosser Mystiker?" *Zeitschrift für Katholische Theologie* 111 (1989): 57–65.

5. Heribert Fischer, "Grundgedanken der deutschen Predigten," in *Meister Eckhart der Prediger: Festschrift zum Eckhart-Gedenkjahr*, ed. Udo M. Nix and Raphael Öchslin (Freiburg: Herder, 1960), 55–59. See also idem, "Zur Frage nach der Mystik in den Werken Meister Eckharts," in *La mystique rhénane* (Paris: Presses Universitaires de France, 1963), 109–32; idem, *Meister Eckhart: Einführung in sein philosophisches Denken* (Munich: Karl Alber, 1974), 139–41.

6. C. F. Kelley, *Meister Eckhart on Divine Knowledge* (New Haven: Yale University Press, 1977), 106–13.

7. Kurt Flasch, "Die Intention Meister Eckharts," in *Sprache und Begriff: Festschrift für Bruno Liebrucks*, ed. Heinz Röttges (Meisenheim am Glan: Hain, 1974), 292–318, esp. 299–302. Flasch has restated this argument in a number of subsequent publications.

8. Kurt Flasch, "Meister Eckhart: Versuch, ihn aus dem mystischen Strom zu retten," in *Gnosis und Mystik in der Geschichte der Philosophie*, ed. Peter Koslowski (Darmstadt: Wissenschaftliche Buchgesellschaft, 1988), 94–110.

9. Burkhard Mojsisch, *Meister Eckhart: Analogie, Univozität und Einheit* (Hamburg: Felix Meiner, 1983), 11–12, 111, and 146.

10. Ruh, *Geschichte* 3:227–31; Alois M. Haas, "Aktualität und Normativität Meister Eckharts," in *Eckhardus Theutonicus, Homo doctus et sanctus: Nachweise und Berichte zum Prozess gegen Meister Eckhart*, ed. Heinrich Stirnimann and Ruedi Imbach (Freiburg, Switzerland: Universitätsverlag, 1992), 203–68; idem, *Meister Eckhart als normative Gestalt geistlichen Lebens*, 2nd ed. (Freiburg: Johannes, 1995); Largier, "Meister Eckhart: Perspektiven der Forschung," 52–59.

11. Words such as "mysticism" and "mystic," although modern, can still be useful for revealing important aspects of the religious world of medieval Christianity. For more on this issue, see Bernard McGinn, "*Quo vadis?* Reflections on the Current Study of Mysticism," *Christian Spirituality Bulletin* (spring 1998): 13–21, especially my response to Simon Tugwell (p. 17).

12. Pr. 52 (DW 2:487.5–7): Wan ich sage iu in der êwigen wârheit: ir ensît denne glîch dirre wârheit, von der wir nû sprechen wellen, sô enmuget ir mich niht verstân (trans. *Essential Eckhart*).

13. A good expression of this unity can be found in a passage from In Ioh. n.444 (LW 3:381.4–7): Patet ergo, sicut frequenter in nostris expositionibus dicitur, quod *ex eadem vena* descendit veritas et doctrina theologiae, philosophiae naturalis, moralis, artis factibilium et spectabilium et etiam iuris positivi, secundum illud Psalmi: "de vultu tuo iudicium meum prodeat" (my italics).

14. For a comparison of Aquinas and Eckhart on the relation of faith and reason as it affected their reading of Jewish philosophy, see my paper, "*SAPIENTIA JUDAEORUM.*" See also the section on "The Nature of Theology and the Role of Scripture," in "2. Theological Summary," in *Essential Eckhart*, 26–29. These previous treatments, however, do not take into account the important texts treated below in which Eckhart speaks of the insufficiency of the light of natural reason and the pagan masters who knew only this natural light.

15. In Ioh. n.185 (LW 3:155.5–7): Idem ergo est quod docet Moyses, Christus et

philosophus, solum quantum ad modum differens, scilicet ut credibile, probabile sive verisimile et veritas. In a later text in this commentary Eckhart characterizes the difference between the Old and the New Testaments as the difference between what is grasped by the *physicus* (natural scientist) and the *metaphysicus* (philosopher); see In Ioh. nn.443–44 (LW 3:380–81).

16. Pr. 9 (DW 1:152.2–5): . . . noch sint ez allez heidenischer meister wort, diu hie vor gesprochen sint, die niht enbekanten dan in einem natiurlîchen liehte; noch enkam ich niht ze der heiligen meister worten, die dâ bekanten in einem vil hoehern liehte (trans. *Teacher and Preacher*). See also Pr. 15 (DW 1:251.10–13): Dis luter bloss wesen nemmet Aristotiles ain "was." Das ist das hoechst, das Aristotiles von naturlichen kunsten ie gesprach, vnd uber das so enmag kain maister hoeher gesprechen, er sprach dann in dem hailgen gaist.

17. Pr. 101 (*Lectura Eckhardi*, 260.1–5 and 16–21). These passages will be discussed in chapter 4 below.

18. See Pr. 15 (DW 1:251.15).

19. Pr. 28 (DW 2:67.1–68.3): Nû sprichet *Plâtô*, der grôze pfaffe, der vaehet ane und wil sprechen von grôzen dingen. Er sprichet von einer lûterkeit, diu enist in der werlt niht; . . . her ûz drücket im got, der êwige vater, die vüllede und den abgrunt aller sîner gotheit. . . . [U]nd sin gebern daz ist sîn inneblîben, und sîn inneblîben ist sîn ûzgebern (trans. Walshe modified). In the notes on this passage in DW 2:67–68 Quint discusses what particular teachings of Plato Eckhart may have had in mind. Aquinas's summary of Plato's treatment of *ens/unum/summum bonum* in STh 1a, q.6, a.4 is certainly a text that Eckhart would have known, but this does not seem a likely source for the point Eckhart makes here. Others have thought that Eckhart may actually be referring to Proclus. Hans Hof (*Scintilla animae: Eine Studie zu einem Grundbegriff in Meister Eckharts Philosophie* [Lund: Gleerup, 1952], 213–15), saw the influence of the doctrine of the *unum animae* found in Proclus's *De providentia et fato,* a supposition considered "séduisant" by Alain de Libera in *La mystique rhénane d'Albert le Grand à Maître Eckhart* (Paris: Éditions du Seuil, 1994), 310 n.156. Similar teaching is found in Proclus's *Expositio in Parmenidem Platonis,* which was translated into Latin by the Dominican William of Moerbeke. (The Latin version has been edited by Carlos Steel, *Proclus: Commentaire sur le Parménide de Platon. Traduction de Guillaume de Moerbeke,* 2 vols. [Leuven: Leuven University Press; Leiden: Brill, 1982–85], and there is a translation from the Greek and Latin [where the Greek is lost] by Glenn R. Morrow and John M. Dillon, *Proclus' Commentary on Plato's "Parmenides"* [Princeton: Princeton University Press, 1987]). Steel, however, denies that Eckhart knew the work (*Commentaire* 1:34*–35*).

20. In Ioh. n.2 (LW 3:4.4–6): In cuius verbi expositione et aliorum quae sequuntur, intentio est auctoris, sicut et in omnibus suis editionibus, ea quae sacra asserit fides christiana et utriusque testamenti scriptura, exponere per rationes naturales philosophorum. It is on the basis of this text (as well as a mistaken view of mysticism) that Flasch ("Die Intention Meister Eckharts," 294–96), and Mojsisch (*Meister Eckhart,* 6–18) argue that Eckhart is a philosopher, not a mystic.

21. In Gen.II n.4 (LW 1:454.6–10): Primum est, quod non est putandum, quasi per talia parabolica intendamus probare divina, naturalia et moralia ex parabolis; sed potius hoc ostendere intendimus, quod his, quae probamus et dicimus de divinis, moralibus et naturalibus, consonant ea quae veritas sacrae scripturae parabolice innuit quasi latenter. See also In Ex. n. 211 (LW 2:178).

22. This triple division, which appears often in Eckhart's works, may have been

taken from Thomas Aquinas (see *In De Anima* I, lect. 1.7), though it is also suggested by Jerome (*Epistola* 30. 1 in PL 22:441–42), as well as in Avicenna and Albert the Great. Eckhart uses it especially in the prologue to In Gen.II, the introduction to his later exegetical writings (see nn.1, 2, 4, and 7 [LW 1:447.8, 451.3, 454.7–9, and 456.4]). It also frequently appears in the John commentary; e.g., In Ioh. nn.2–3, 125, 186, 441, 444, 477, and 509 (LW 3:4, 108, 156, 378, 381, 410, 441).

23. From this perspective, Eckhart's view bears an analogy to a position like that of Hugh of St. Victor, or Bonaventure, who argued for a special form of Christian philosophy over and above the "fallen philosophy" of natural reason. But Eckhart arrives at his position in a different way and uses it differently. He does not criticize the failings of the philosophy of natural reason, but rather absorbs it into the higher synthesis of the apophatic Christian philosophy of *unwizzen*.

24. In Ioh. n.361 (LW 3:307.1–4): Sicut enim praesumptionis est et temeritatis nolle credere, nisi intellexeris, sic ignaviae est et desidiosum quod fide credis, rationibus naturalibus et similitudinibus non investigare, ...

25. Niklaus Largier, "Intellekttheorie, Hermeneutik und Allegorie: Subjekt und Subjektivität bei Meister Eckhart," in *Geschichte und Vorgeschichte der modernen Subjektivität,* ed. Reto Luzius Fetz, Roland Hagenbüchle, and Peter Schulz (Berlin/New York: Walter de Gruyter, 1998), 462–64 and 474–82.

26. In scholarship prior to 1980, little attention was paid to Eckhart's exegesis. Among the few helpful works devoted to the topic were Josef Koch, "Sinn und Struktur der Schriftauslegungen," *Meister Eckhart der Prediger,* ed. Nix and Öchslin, 73–103; and Konrad Weiss, "Meister Eckharts biblische Hermeneutik," in *La mystique rhénane,* 95–108. The monograph of Eberhard Winkler, *Exegetische Methoden bei Meister Eckhart* (Tübingen: Mohr, 1965), is not very successful. In recent scholarship this gap has been redressed by treatments such as those of Donald F. Duclow, "Hermeneutics and Meister Eckhart," *Philosophy Today* 28 (1984): 36–43; idem, "Meister Eckhart on the Book of Wisdom: Commentary and Sermons," *Traditio* 43 (1987): 215–35. Also important is Frank Tobin, "Creativity and Interpreting Scripture: Meister Eckhart in Practice," *Monatshefte* 74 (1982): 410–18; idem, *Meister Eckhart,* 23–29. Recently a number of penetrating studies have appeared in German, such as Susanne Köbele, "*PRIMO ASPECTU MONSTRUOSA:* Schriftauslegung bei Meister Eckhart," *Zeitschrift für deutsches Altertum und deutsche Literatur* 122 (1993): 62–81; Niklaus Largier, "*FIGURATA LOCUTIO:* Hermeneutik und Philosophie bei Eckhart von Hochheim und Heinrich Seuse," in *Meister Eckhart: Lebensstationen—Redesituationen* ed. Klaus Jacobi (Berlin: Walter de Gruyter, 1997), 303–32; idem, "Intellekttheorie, Hermeneutik und Allegorie," in *Geschichte und Vorgeschichte der modernen Subjektivität,* ed. Fetz, Hagenbüchle, and Schulz, 460–86; and Wouter Goris, *Einheit als Prinzip und Ziel: Versuch über die Einheitsmetaphysik des "Opus tripartitum" Meister Eckharts* (Leiden: Brill, 1997), chap. 1.

27. In this Eckhart went against the program of Thomas Aquinas, who, although he did not deny the importance of the spiritual interpretation, argued that *sacra doctrina* should depend on the Bible's literal sense (see STh 1a, q.1, a.10).

28. An important monograph of Yossef Schwartz on the relation between Maimonides and Eckhart, especially in relation to exegesis, is forthcoming. Niklaus Largier has advanced the case for a "hermeneutical turn" in Eckhart's thinking under the influence of Maimonides during the second decade of the fourteenth century ("*FIGURATA LOCUTIO,*" 326–32). Though Eckhart may have shifted toward a more "parabolical" mode of interpretation at this time and may have begun to use Maimonides more

extensively, he was certainly familiar with the *Dux neutrorum* from his days as a student in Paris.

29. Duclow aptly uses the phrase "mystical hermeneutics" to characterize Eckhart's approach to scripture ("Hermeneutics and Meister Eckhart," 42).

30. Pr. 22 (DW 1:381.3–5): "Mich wundert," sprach ich, "daz diu geschrift alsô vol ist, daz nieman daz allerminste wort ergründen enkan" (my trans.). Parallel passages cite Augustine's authority for this, using texts such as *Confessiones* (hereafter *Conf.*) 13.24.37 (PL 32:861), and *De Genesi ad litteram* 2.5 (PL 34:249–50).

31. Pr. 89 (DW 4:38–39).

32. Pr. 51 (DW 2:465–66). The metaphor is drawn from Gregory the Great, *Moralia in Job*, "Ad Leandrum" 4 (PL 75:515A).

33. BgT 1 (DW 5:42:21–43.1): Sant Augustinus sprichet, daz der allerbest die geschrift vernimet, der blôz alles geistes suochet sin und wârheit der geschrift in ir selben, daz ist: in dem geiste, dar inne si geschriben ist und gesprochen ist: in gotes geiste (trans. Walshe). The text from Augustine is *De doctrina christiana* 3.27.38 (PL 34:80).

34. In Gen.II n.3 (LW 1:453.5–6): Nec enim aliquis scripturas intelligere putandus est, qui medullam, Christum, veritatem, latitantem in ipsis nesciet invenire. Largier points out that the centrality of the christological principle distances Eckhart from Maimonides in decisive fashion, however much he learned from the Jewish sage ("*FIG-URATA LOCUTIO*," 318–19).

35. John 1:1 (*In principio erat verbum*) is given an initial fifteen interpretations in In Ioh. nn.4–12, another seven in nn.28–39, and a moral reading in n.51 (LW 3:5–12, 22–33, and 41–43). Wisdom 8:1 (*Attingit a fine usque ad finem fortiter et disponit omnia suaviter*) receives twenty-two interpretations in In. Sap. nn.167–200 (LW 2:502–35). On this text as a paradigm of Eckhart's philosophical mysticism, see Erwin Waldschütz, "Probleme philosophische Mystik am Beispiel Meister Eckharts," in *Probleme philosophischer Mystik: Festschrift für Karl Albert zum siebigsten Geburtstag*, ed. Elenor Jain and Reinhard Margreiter (Sankt Augustin: Academia Verlag, 1991), 71–92.

36. In Ioh. n.745 (LW 3:649.3–10): Adhuc autem notandum quod talis modus loquendi, excessive scilicet, proprie competit divinis scripturis. Omne enim divinum, in quantum huiusmodi, immensum est nec ad mensuram datur. . . . Divinorum etiam est excellentia nobis ea non nude praeponi, sed sub figuris rerum sensibilium occultari.

37. For an example of this type of rewriting by translation, see the remarks on Pr. 30 dealing with the Our Father in Köbele, "*PRIMO ASPECTU MONSTRUOSA*," 68–79. However, Eckhart also engaged in similar reinterpretations through repunctuation and unusual translations at times in his Latin works. For example, rather than reading John 1:3 (*sine ipso factum est nihil*) as the traditional "without him nothing was made," he translates it as "without him what was made [*factum* as participial noun] was nothing" (In Ioh. n.53 [LW 3:44]).

38. On Eckhart's delight in word games, biblical and nonbiblical, throughout his works, see Tobin, *Meister Eckhart*, 171–79.

39. Prol.op.expos. n.5 (LW 1:184.16–18): Quinto notandum quod auctoritates principales plerumque multis modis exponuntur, ut qui legit, nunc istam rationem, nunc aliam, unam vel plures accipiat, prout iudicaverit expedire. See also In Ioh. nn.39 and 225 (LW 3:33 and 189).

40. There are, to be sure, a number of places where Eckhart does follow the narrative structure of the text. For example, in Pr. 71 (DW 3:219–22 and 230) he uses Song of Songs 3:1–4 as an account of the soul's progress to God.

41. On this aspect of Eckhart's hermeneutics, see Goris, *Einheit als Prinzip und Ziel,* 37–51.

42. Prol.op.expos. n.1 (LW 1:183.1–184.2): Primo quod in expositione auctoritatis, de qua tunc agitur, plurimae et plerumque adducuntur aliae auctoritates canonis, et illae omnes auctoritates possunt in locis suis exponi ex ista, sicut nunc ista per illas. The same point is made in Prol.gen. n.14 (LW 1:159.9–12).

43. In Ioh. n.433 (LW 3:371).

44. For the two kinds of *parabolae,* see In Gen.II, prol. n.5 (LW 2:454–55), and In Ioh. nn.174–76 (LW 3:143–45). In Gen.II n.126 (LW 1:590.6) uses the neologism *parabolizare* to describe how the Bible teaches by figures.

45. In Gen.II, prol. n.1 (LW 1:448.17–449.1): Quando ergo ex his quae leguntur intellectum alicuius mysticae significationis possumus exsculpere, . . . Eckhart also uses the terms *mystice exponere* (ibid., n.2 [452.8–9]) and *mystice consonare* (In Ex. n.222 [LW 2:185.6]).

46. In Gen.II prol. n.2 (LW 1:449.5–9): Cum ergo "sensus" etiam "litteralis, quem auctor scripturae intendit, deus autem sit auctor sacrae scripturae," ut dictum est, omnis sensus qui verus est sensus litteralis est. Constat enim quod omne verum ab ipsa veritate est, in ipsa includitur, ab ipsa derivatur et intenditur. The embedded quotation here is from Thomas Aquinas, STh 1a, q.1, a.10, but Eckhart's notion of the multiplicity of true meanings is drawn from Augustine, as the succeeding quotations from *Conf.* 12.31.42, 12.18.27, and 13.24.37, make clear (see PL 32: 844, 835–36, and 861).

47. Duclow, "Meister Eckhart on the Book of Wisdom," 234.

48. Pr. 51 (DW 2:473.5–9): Ich han gesprochenn etwan me [probable reference to DW 1:212.3–6]: die schal muoz zerbrechen, vnnd muoz sa, dass darinn ist, herauss kommen; Wann, wiltu den kernen haben, so muostu den schalen brechen. Vnd also: wiltu die natur bloss finden, so muessent die gleychnuss alle zerbrechenn, vnnd ye das es me darin trittet, ye es dem wesen naeher ist. So wenn das sy dass ein findet, da es alles eyn ist, da bleibet sy <in> dem einigen <ein> (trans. Walshe modified). See the insightful analysis in Köbele, "*PRIMO ASPECTU MONSTRUOSA,*" 64–67; cf. Duclow, "Meister Eckhart on the Book of Wisdom," 40–41; and Largier, "*FIGURATA LOCUTIO,*" 323–26.

49. In his apophatic exegesis, Eckhart bears comparison with John Scottus Eriugena, though the Irish thinker's exegetical principles come at these issues from another perspective. On Eriugena's exegesis, see Bernard McGinn, "The Originality of Eriugena's Spiritual Exegesis," in *Iohannes Scottus Eriugena: The Bible and Hermeneutics,* ed. Gerd Van Riel, Carlos Steel, and James McEvoy (Leuven: Leuven University Press, 1996), 55–80.

50. On Eckhart the preacher, see especially Joachim Theisen, *Predigt und Gottesdienst: Liturgische Strukturen in den Predigten Meister Eckharts* (Frankfurt: Peter Lang, 1990); Burkhard Hasebrink, *Formen inizitativer Rede bei Meister Eckhart: Untersuchungen zur literarische Konzeption der deutschen Predigt* (Tübingen: Niemeyer, 1992); Friedrich Iohn, *Die Predigt Meister Eckharts: Seelsorge und Häresie* (Heidelberg: Carl Winter, 1993); and the various papers in *Lectura Eckhardi.*

51. Ruh, *Geschichte* 3:324: "Eckharts deutsches Predigtwerk steht zweifellos in der Mitte seines Schaffens. Er hat sich auch selbst mehr als Prediger denn als Professor und Gelehrter verstanden."

52. Eckhart analyzes three essential characteristics of the preacher (*vitae puritas, intentionis sinceritas, opinionis aut famae odoriferae suavitas*) in his In Eccli. nn.2–5 (LW 2:231–34). The passage cited here is from n.4 (233.3–4): Sic praedicator verbi dei, quod

est "dei virtus et dei sapientia," non debet sibi esse aut vivere, sed Christo quem praedicat ... Eckhart goes on analyze the relation between Christ and the preacher through the invocation of *quasi,* the adverb that is one of his key terms for absolute dependence leading to inner identity: Christus vitis, praedicator *quasi vitis* (233.5–11). See Susanne Köbele, "*BÎWORT SÎN:* 'Absolute' Grammatik bei Meister Eckhart," *Zeitschrift für deutsche Philologie* 113 (1994): 203.

53. Theisen, *Predigt und Gottesdienst,* 550: "Die Intention seiner Predigt ist es grundsätzlich, die Aktualität des gefeierten Geheimnisses aufzuzeigen und die Gemeinde in diese Aktualität einzubeziehen."

54. Reiner Schürmann, *Meister Eckhart: Mystic and Philosopher* (Bloomington: Indiana University Press, 1978), 89, 106–7. The same point is made by Duclow, "Hermeneutics and Meister Eckart," 38–39. See also Hasebrink, *Formen inzitativer Rede,* 57–58.

55. Ruh analyzes how Eckhart's preaching strives to identify both the speaker and the audience in the oneness of the ground (*Geschichte* 3:352–53).

56. In Eccli. n.69 (LW 299.2–3): "Praedica" quasi praedic, id est prius intus dic; vel "praedica," id est prodic vel produc extra, ut "luceat coram hominibus." A comparable interpretation is found in Pr. 30 (DW 2:93–94 and 97–98).

57. Pr. 2 (DW 1:41.5–7): Möhtet ir gemerken mit mînem herzen, ir verstüendet wol, waz ich spriche, wan ez ist wâr und diu wârheit sprichet ez selbe (trans. *Essential Eckhart*).

58. Eckhart claims to be speaking out of, or in the name of, Divine Truth in a number of places. For example, in Pr. 48 (DW 2:415.4–5): Ich spriche ez bî guoter wârheit und bî êwigen wârheit und bî iemerwerdender wârheit ... (repeated in 420.5–6). Such formulas are especially evident in the noted poverty sermon, Pr. 52 (DW 2:487.5–7, 490.6, 491.9, and 506.1–3). In a passage in Pr. 66 (DW 3:113–14) he invites his hearers to realize the Divine Truth within each of them.

59. Pr. 64 (DW 3:90.4–7): Ich wil üch sagen, wie ich der läute gedenck: ich fleiss mich des, das ich mein selbs vnd aller menschen vergesse, vnd füge mich für sy in ainicheit. das wir in ainicheit beleiben, des helf vns got. Amen (trans. Walshe). Alois M. Haas puts it well: "The speaker [Eckhart] understands himself as a witness of the unity to which he directs others" ("Schools of Late Medieval Mysticism," in *Christian Spirituality: High Middle Ages and Reformation,* ed. Jill Raitt [New York: Crossroad, 1987], 147).

60. The great literary critic Erich Auerbach devoted some pregnant pages to Eckhart's language in his *Literary Language & Its Public in Late Latin Antiquity and the Middle Ages* (Princeton: Princeton University Press, 1965), 330–32. Among the most important contributions of the 1980s were two essays of Alois M. Haas collected in his *Geistliches Mittelalter* (Freiburg, Switzerland: Universitätsverlag, 1984): "Meister Eckhart und die Sprache. Sprachgeschictliche und sprachtheologische Aspekte seines Werkes" (pp. [193–214]), and "Meister Eckhart und die deutsche Sprache" (pp. [215–37]). Also significant is Walter Haug, "Das Wort und die Sprache bei Meister Eckhart," in *Zur deutschen Literatur und Sprache des 14. Jahrhunderts: Dubliner Colloquium 1981,* ed. Walter Haug, Timothy R. Jackson, Johannes Janota (Heidelberg: Carl Winter, 1983), 25–44. In English the penetrating comments of Tobin, *Meister Eckhart,* chaps. 3 and 5, summarize and expand upon his earlier papers in this field. Literature of the 1990s will be mentioned in what follows.

61. An older example of such analysis of entire sermons can be found in Schürmann, who studied Prr. 2, 17, 26, 16b, 71, 76, 30, and 52 (*Meister Eckhart*). For recent

examples, see Hasebrink, *Formen inzitativer Rede* (detailed treatment of Prr. 12, 30, and 49); and Iohn, *Die Predigt* (only Prr. 1 and 6). Suzanne Köbele in her book *Bilder der unbegriffenen Wahrheit: Zur Struktur mystischer Rede im Spannungsfeld von Latein und Volkssprache* (Tübingen/Basel: Francke, 1993) compares the parallel Latin and MHG sermons, Pr. 21 and SS. XXXVII and XXXVIII, and Pr. 20a and S. VIII). See also Ruh, *Geschichte* 3 (treating Prr. 22, 2, 39, 6, and 52); and the sermons presented and commented on in *Lectura Eckhardi* (Prr. 4, 12, 16b, 17, 18, 19, 48, 52, 63, 71, 101, and S. IV).

62. Alois M. Haas lays out the general modes of mystical language that he applied to Eckhart in the papers referred to above. (See also idem, "Mystische Erfahrung und Sprache," in *Sermo Mysticus: Studien zu Theologie und Sprache der deutschen Mystik* [Freiburg, Switzerland: Universitätsverlag, 1979], 18–36; and idem, "Das mystische Paradox," in *Das Paradox: Eine Herausforderung des abendländische Denkens*, ed. Paul Geyer and Roland Hagenbüchle [Tübingen: Stauffenberg, 1992], 273–89.)

63. On the "appellative text function" that invites the hearer to identify himself as the subject of the thematized divine knowledge set forth in the sermon, see Hasebrink, *Formen*, 36–48; and *Lectura Eckhardi*, 240. On the way in which Eckhart's sermons effect their own transcendence or self-destruction, see *Formen*, 134–36 and 265–68.

64. See the summary in Hasebrink, *Formen*, 260–63.

65. See the summary in Hasebrink, *Formen*, 263–65. In his study of Pr. 12, Hasebrink shows how 37 of the 81 sentences in the sermon express conditional relations (see pp. 104–36).

66. See Tobin, *Meister Eckhart*, esp. chap. 5.

67. See also Pr. 9 (DW 1:154.11–155.1): Daz aller eigenlîcheste, daz man von gote gesprechen mac, daz ist wort und wârheit. Got nante sich selber ein wort.

68. Tobin, *Meister Eckhart*, 87; cf. vii, 89, 158–59. See also the reflections of Haug, "Das Wort und die Sprache bei Meister Eckhart," 34–35.

69. See Tobin, *Meister Eckhart*, 158–67.

70. See ibid., 167–71. For an example of a chiastic text in the German works, see, e.g., Pr. 30 (DW 2:94.6–7): Got ist in allen dingen. Ie mê er ist in den dingen, ie mê er ist ûz den dinge: ie mê inne, ie mê ûze, ie mê ûze, ie mê inne. In the Latin works, the most distinctive chiastic passages are in the dialectical texts, such as presentation of *unum* as distinct indistinction in In Sap. nn.154–55 (LW 2:489–91).

71. Important recent discussions of the relation of German and Latin in Eckhart can be found in Burkhard Hasebrink, "GRENZVERSCHIEBUNG: Zu Kongruenz und Differenz von Latein und Deutsche bei Meister Eckhart," *Zeitschrift für deutsches Altertum und deutsche Literatur* 121 (1992): 369–98; and Köbele, *Bilder der unbegriffenen Wahrheit*, chap. 2. For the wider perspective on Latin and German in the late Middle Ages, see *Latein und Volkssprache im deutschen Mittelalter 1100–1500*, ed. Niklaus Henkel and Nigel F. Palmer (Tübingen: Niemeyer, 1992).

72. Haug, "Das Wort und die Sprache," 39: ". . . im Prinzip könnte man sich seine Predigten genausogut lateinisch wie deutsch denken. . . ."

73. See the critique of these authors in Köbele, *Bilder*, 171–73.

74. Kurt Ruh, *Meister Eckhart: Theologe. Prediger. Mystiker* (Munich: C. H. Beck, 1985), 45: "Es ist, um es auf eine Formel zu bringen, der spirituelle Mehrwert der Volkssprache, der Eckhart deren Gebrauch in den 'Reden der Unterweisung' afdrängte." See also pp. 192–95. The term *Mehrwert* had already been used by Alois M. Haas in relation to the vernacular of Mechthild of Magdeburg (*Sermo Mysticus*, 79–81).

75. Köbele, *Bilder*, 10: "Das inhaltlich Neue der mystischen Aussage ist an das Medium der Volkssprache eng gebunden."

76. Hasebrink, "GRENZVERSCHIEBUNG," 372–77.

77. Ibid., 379–98, as illustrated through an analysis of parallel German and Latin sermons (Pr. 25–27 and S. VI.1; Pr. 18 and S. XXXVI; and Pr. 17 and S. LV.4). The interchanges between Latin and German, evident both within Eckhart's oeuvre, and in the later Latin translations of German sermons and German versions of Latin works, is evidence for this exchange of boundaries. Hasebrink's conclusion is worth citing: ". . . die Volkssprache erlangt einen neuen Gebrauchswert, dessen Höhe, darin liegt die Ironie der Grenzverscheibung, durch die Vereinbarkeit von Kongruenz und Differenz zum Lateinischen bestimmt wird. Die Volkssprache wird bei Eckhart zu einem zugleich literarisierten, klerikalen, wissenschaftlichen und selbstreflexiven Sprachmedium, das die transzendierenden und negierenden Bewegungen des Denkens an sich selbst erfährt."

78. Haas, "Meister Eckhart und die deutsche Sprache," *Geistliches Mittelalter,* [237]: "Er [Eckhart] hat eine Theologie des Wortes, aber keine der deutschen Sprache."

79. Köbele, *Bilder,* 13 and 51 uses this term, thanking K. Ruh for suggesting it.

80. Despite the many excellences of Köbele's *Bilder,* she often speaks as if only the vernacular sermons are dangerous, or near heresy (e.g., pp. 144–47, 164–69, and 197).

81. This will be discussed in more detail in chap. 3 below. In this connection Köbele's claim (e.g., *Bilder,* 179, 184, 190–95) that Eckhart's Latin language adheres to a hierarchical model that is analogical, causal, and static seems to me to be an inadequate reading of the full range of his Latin writings. The same exaggerated contrast is found in Köbele's essay *"BÎWORT SÎN,"* 203–6.

Chapter 3
Eckhart and the Mysticism of the Ground

1. For a treatment of these female mystics, see Bernard McGinn, *The Flowering of Mysticism: Men and Women in the New Mysticism (1200–1350)* (New York: Crossroad, 1998), chaps. 5 and 6.

2. According to Alois M. Haas ("Meister Eckhart und die deutsche Sprache," in *Geistliches Mittelalter* [Freiburg, Switzerland: Universitätsverlag, 1984], [218–19], "die deutsche Mystik" was first used by Karl Rosenkranz, a student of G. W. F. Hegel, in 1831. The term was used by Wilhelm Preger in his classic work *Geschichte der deutschen Mystik im Mittelalter: Nach den Quellen untersucht und dargestellt,* 3 vols. (Leipzig: Dörffling & Franke, 1874–93). In the twentieth century it has been employed in scores of studies, both early and late. For example, Joseph Bernhart used it to characterize Eckhart and his followers in his *Die philosophische Mystik des Mittelalters von ihren antiken Ursprüngen bis zur Renaissance* (Munich: Reinhard, 1922), chap. 8. It continues to be used in recent summaries of late medieval mysticism, such as Alois M. Haas, "Deutsche Mystik," in *Geschichte der deutschen Literatur, III/2, Die deutsche Literatur im späten Mittelalter 1250–1370,* ed. Ingeborg Glier (Munich: C. H. Beck, 1987), 234–305.

3. The term appears most often in French literature, e.g., Jeanne Ancelet-Hustache, *Master Eckhart and the Rhineland Mystics* (New York: Harper, 1957; French original, Paris, 1956). See also the collection of papers in *La mystique rhénane* (Paris: Presses Universitaires de France, 1963), and the recent summary of Alain de Libera, *La mystique rhénane d'Albert le Grand à Maître Eckhart* (Paris: Éditions du Seuil, 1994). "Rhineland mysticism" has sometimes been expanded into the rather cumbersome descriptive term, "rhéno-flamand," as in Louis Cognet, *Introduction aux mystiques rhéno-flamands* (Paris: Desclée, 1968).

4. Carl Greith, *Die deutsche Mystik im Prediger-Orden (von 1250–1350)* (Freiburg-im-Breisgau: Herder, 1861); and Kurt Ruh, *Geschichte 3*.

5. This characterization also goes back to the nineteenth century. Josef Bach, in dependence on Franz von Baader, entitled his book on Eckhart *Meister Eckhart: Der Vater der deutschen Speculation* (Vienna: Braumüller, 1864). Another early use of the term was that of Henry Delacroix, *Essai sur le mysticisme spéculatif en Allemagne au quatorzième siècle* (Paris: Alcan, 1900).

6. Josef Quint, "Mystik und Sprache: Ihr Verhältnis zueinander, insbesondere in der spekulativen Mystik Meister Eckeharts," in *Altdeutsche und altniederländische Mystik,* ed. Kurt Ruh, Wege der Forschung 23 (Darmstadt: Wissenschaftliche Buchhandlung, 1964), 113–51 (a paper originally published in 1953).

7. E.g., Fernand Brunner, "Maître Eckhart et le mysticisme speculatif," *Revue de théologie et de philosophie* 3 (1970): 1–11.

8. On the interaction of love and knowledge in Christian mysticism, see Bernard McGinn, "Love, Knowledge and *Unio mystica* in the Western Christian Tradition," in *Mystical Union in Judaism, Christianity, and Islam: An Ecumenical Dialogue,* ed. Moshe Idel and Bernard McGinn (New York: Continuum, 1996), 59–86.

9. See, for example, Alois M. Haas's argument for the usefulness of the term *Fundamentalmystik* in relation to Eckhart in "Die Aktualität Meister Eckhart: Ein Klassiker der Mystik (ca. 1260–1328)," in *Gottes Nähe: Religiöse Erfahrung in Mystik und Offenbarung. Festschrift zum 65. Geburtstag von Josef Sudbruck SJ,* ed. Paul Imhoff S.J. (Würzburg: Echter, 1990), 84. Haas also discusses attempts to place Eckhart within "die deutsche Mystik" in "Die deutsche Mystik, 5.1, Das Verhältnis von Sprache und Erfahrung," in *Sermo Mysticus: Studien zu Theologie und Sprache der deutschen Mystik* (Freiburg, Switzerland: Universitätsverlag, 1979), 136–67.

10. See Bernard McGinn, *The Growth of Mysticism: Gregory the Great through the Twelfth Century* (New York: Crossroad, 1994), 154–57.

11. Choosing *grunt* as the central category for this account is not meant to reduce the importance of the many other mystical terms and metaphors found in Eckhart and his followers (e.g., *vernünfticheit, bild, geburt, durchbrechen, einicheit, abegescheidenheit,* etc.). My treatment is designed to show how seeing these terms from the perspective of *grunt* helps reveal the riches of their content in new ways.

12. For the notion of *Sprengmetapher,* see Hans Blumenberg, "Paradigmen zu einer Metaphorologie," *Archiv für Begriffsgeschichte* 6 (1960): 7–142; idem, "Beobachtungen an Metaphern," *Archiv für Begriffsgeschichte* 15 (1971): 161–214; idem, "Ausblick auf eine Theorie der Unbegrifflichkeit," in *Theorie der Metapher,* ed. Anselm Haverkamp (Darmstadt: Wissenschaftliche Buchgesellschaft, 1983), 438–54. Blumenberg also employs the term "absolute Metapher." For applications to Eckhart, see Susanne Köbele, *Bilder der unbegriffenen Wahrheit: Zur Struktur mystischer Rede im Spannungsfeld von Latein und Volkssprache* (Tübingen/Basel: Francke, 1993), 17–18, 66–67, and 181–91; and Alois M. Haas, "The Nothingness of God and its Explosive Metaphors," *The Eckhart Review* no. 8 (1999): 6–17.

13. See Blumenberg, "Paradigmen," 131–36; idem, "Beobachtungen," 170–71.

14. Eckhart has a formulation close to this in speaking of the relation of God and creation in Pr. 13a, though here he uses *boden* rather than *grunt* (DW 1:225.4–5): Got suochet nicht vsser im selber, das alle creaturen habint, das hat got alzemale in ime. Er ist der boden, der reif aller creaturen.

15. This point has been emphasized by Erwin Waldschütz in his important monograph *Denken und Erfahren des Grundes: Zur philosophischen Deutung Meister Eckharts*

(Vienna-Freiburg-Basel: Herder, 1989), especially part 3, chap. 4 (pp. 324–49) on the *Grunderfahrung.* I prefer to use the term "consciousness of the ground" to avoid the ambiguities present in the term "experience."

16. The most recent semantic survey of the terminology of *grunt* and related words in selected German mystics can be found in Michael Egerding, *Die Metaphorik der spät-mittelalterlichen Mystik,* 2 vols. (Paderborn: Schöningh, 1997) 2:279–309. Egerding lists ninety-two appearances of *grunt* in Eckhart, but a survey of eighteen of the eventual twenty-six sermons to appear in DW 4 provides another thirty-seven appearances for a total of 129. Given other possibly authentic works, and some uses missed by Egerding, I surmise that Eckhart used *grunt* and its related terms 140–150 times. Suso employs the term seventy-nine times according to Egerding, while Tauler uses it no fewer than 414 times!

17. For example, in the thirty-two sermons not included in DW that appear in Pfeiffer, *grunt* appears at least thirty times. Particularly important are Pf. LXI (ed., 194–95) with ten appearances; Pf. LXXI (ed., 224–26) with 5; and Pf. XCIII (ed., 303–5) with eight.

18. On the *centro del alma* in the Spanish mystics, see Léonce Reypens, "Ame (structure)," in DS 1:461–63. John of the Cross occasionally uses the term *fondo* as the equivalent of *centro,* e.g., "la intima sustancia del fondo del alma" (*Living Flame of Love,* str. 3, v. 3); "en el centro y fondo de mi alma" (*Living Flame,* c.4, vv.1–2, t.2).

19. The literature is so extensive that I will mention only a few of most important treatments. Among older discussions of *grunt* in Eckhart, see Benno Schmoldt, *Die deutsche Begriffssprache Meister Eckharts: Studien zur philosophischen terminologie des Mittelhochdeutschen* (Heidelberg: Quelle & Meyer, 1954), 49–62; Bernward Dietsche, "Der Seelengrund nach den deutschen und lateinischen Predigten," in *Meister Eckhart der Prediger: Festschrift zum Eckhart-Gedenkjahr,* ed. Udo M. Nix and Raphael Öchslin (Freiburg: Herder, 1960), 200–258; and Heribert Fischer, "Fond de l'Ame, I, Chez Maitre Eckhart," in DS 5:650–61. Recent analyses include Burkhard Mojsisch, *Meister Eckhart: Analogie, Univozität und Einheit* (Hamburg: Felix Meiner, 1983), 131–44; Otto Langer, "Meister Eckharts Lehre vom Seelengrund," in *Grundfragen christliche Mystik,* ed. Margot Schmidt and Dieter R. Bauer (Stuttgart/Bad Cannstatt: frommann-holzboog, 1987), 173–91; Waldschütz, *Denken und Erfahren des Grundes;* Burkhard Hasebrink, "GRENZVERSCHIEBUNG: Zu Kongruenz und Differenz von Latein und Deutsche bei Meister Eckhart," *Zeitschrift für deutsches Altertum und deutsche Literatur* 121 (1992): 369–98; Köbele, *Bilder der unbegriffenen Wahrheit,* 171–91; and Peter Reiter, *Der Seele Grund. Meister Eckhart und die Tradition der Seelenlehre* (Würzburg: Königshausen & Neumann, 1993).

20. A classic study of Tauler's use of *grunt* is Paul Wyser, "Taulers Terminologie vom Seelengrund," in *Altdeutsche und altniederländische Mystik,* ed. Kurt Ruh, Wege der Forschung 23 (Darmstadt: Wissenschaftliche Buchhandlung, 1964), 324–52. See also Louise Gnädinger, "Der Abgrund ruft dem Abgrund: Taulers Predigt Beati oculi (V 45)," in *Das "Einig Ein": Studien zur Theorie und Sprache der deutschen Mystik,* ed. Alois M. Haas and Heinrich Stirnimann (Freiburg, Switzerland: Universitätsverlag, 1980), 167–207; eadem, *Johannes Tauler: Lebenswelt und mystische Lehre* (Munich: C. H. Beck, 1993), 181–93 and 241–51. Also useful is Loris Sturlese, "Tauler im Kontext: Die philosophischen Voraussetzungen des 'Seelengrundes' in der Lehre des deutschen Neo-platonikers Berthold von Moosburg," *Beiträge zur Geschichte der deutschen Sprache und Literatur* 109 (1987): 390–426.

21. Herman Kunisch, *Das Wort "Grund" in der Sprache der deutschen Mystik des 14.*

und 15. Jahrhunderts (Osnabrück: Pagenkämper, 1929). Kunisch's work is valuable for its collection of materials, but is insufficient in many ways, most notably for its overemphasis on the courtly language of the *grund des herzens* as a source for mystical uses (see pp. 11–14), and its undervaluing of the central role of Eckhart (e.g., 1, 15, 42–43, and 93) in developing the mysticism of the ground.

22. Köbele, *Bilder*, 173: "Von der Sekundärliteratur sieht man sich bei dieser Frage im Stich gelassen, wenn nicht in die Irre geführt."

23. What follows is based on the summary found in Köbele, *Bilder*, 174–75, citing appropriate MHG dictionaries.

24. Egerding (*Die Metaphorik*, 279–82) lists and discusses thirty-nine uses of these words in Mechthild's *Das fliessende Licht der Gottheit*. These texts can be found in Hans Neumann, ed., *Mechthild von Magdeburg: Das fliessende Licht der Gottheit*, 2 vols. (Munich: Artemis, 1990–93).

25. E.g., *Das fliessende Licht* I 8.3, VI 2.34, VI 16.25.

26. Ibid., I 5.19 and II 16.2.

27. Ibid., I 8.4, I 9.2.

28. Mechthild's contemporary, David of Augsburg, shows an even less developed use of *grunt*-language (Egerding, *Die Metaphorik*, 282–83). He employs *gruntlôs* of God, but never uses *grunt*.

29. For Hadewijch's use of *afgront* to describe the interpenetration of the infinitely hungry divine and human abysses, see especially Letter 18, as discussed in McGinn, *Flowering of Mysticism*, 211–19. Hadewijch is usually dated to c. 1250, but recently some studies have argued that a dating in the early fourteenth century may be preferable; see Wybren Scheepsma, "Hadewijch und die *Limburgse sermoenen*: Überlegung zu Datierung. Identität und Authentizität," in *Deutsche Mystik im abendländischen Zusammenhang*, ed. Walter Haug and Wolfram Schneider-Lastin (Tübingen: Niemeyer, 2000), 683–702. If these arguments hold up, Hadewijch would be a contemporary, not a predecessor, of Eckhart's view of the identity of ground between God and human. On the relations between Hadewijch and Eckhart, see Saskia Murk-Jansen, "Hadewijch and Eckhart: Amor intelligere est," in *Meister Eckhart and the Beguine Mystics: Hadewijch of Brabant, Mechthild of Magdeburg, and Marguerite Porete*, ed. Bernard McGinn (New York: Continuum, 1994), 17–30.

30. Joseph Van Mierlo, *Hadewijch: Brieven*, 2 vols. (Antwerp: N.V. Standaard, 1947), Letter 18.69–70 (1:154–55): Siele ist een wech vanden dore vaerne gods in sine vriheit, Dat es in sinen gront di niet gheraect en can werden, sine gherakene met hare diepheit. . . .

31. On the mid-fourteenth-century "publication" of Hadewijch's works, see Kurt Ruh, *Geschichte der abendländische Mystik*: vol. 2, *Frauenmystik und Franziskanische Mystik der Frühzeit* (Munich: Beck, 1993), 161–63.

32. On this conversation, see McGinn, *Flowering of Mysticism*, 22–24.

33. The point is emphasized by Köbele (*Bilder*, 176–80), against positions advanced by scholars such as Fischer, Schmoldt, and Mojsisch, who seek to reduce the meaning of *grunt* to its Latin "equivalents." Another example of this approach is Wyser ("Taulers Terminologie vom Seelengrund," 344), who claims that Augustine's mysticism of introversion reflected in the term *abditum mentis* lies at the basis of German mysticism's concentration on the *grunt*.

34. On the importance of the "Grunderfahrung" as demanding communication to others, see Waldschütz, *Denken und Erfahren des Grundes*, 328–29.

35. See Martin Grabmann, "Die Lehre des hl. Thomas von Aquin von der *scintilla*

animae in ihre Bedeutung für die deutsche Mystik des Predigerordens," *Jahrbuch für Philosophie und spekulativen Theologie* 14 (1900): 413–27. Among later discussions, see, e.g., Hieronymus Wilms, "Das Seelenfünklein in der deutschen Mystik," *Zeitschrift für Aszese und Mystik* 12 (1937): 157–66; Endré von Ivanka, "Apex mentis: Wanderung und Wandlung eines stoischen Terminus," *Zeitschrift für katholischen Theologie* 72 (1950): 129–76; and Hans Hof, *Scintilla animae: Eine Studie zu einem Grundbegriff in Meister Eckharts Philosophie* (Lund: Gleerup, 1952). For a good treatment in English on Eckhart's teaching on the "spark of the soul," see Frank Tobin, *Meister Eckhart: Thought and Language* (Philadelphia: University of Pennsylvania Press, 1986), 126–40. There are useful surveys of traditional terminology relating to the soul and its structure in the DS; see especially Léonce Reypens, "Ame (structure)," DS 1:433–69; Aimé Solignac, "NOUS et MENS," DS 11:459–6; idem, "Synderesis," DS 14:1407–12.

36. Reypens, "Ame (structure)," DS 1:434: ". . . le père de l'introversion et le grand théoreticien de l'image de Dieu dans l'âme, saint Augustin."

37. S. XLIX.1, n.507 (LW 4:422:12–13). In the same sermon Eckhart speaks of the ". . . superius in anima, ubi vertex animae nectitur lumini angelico" (n.505 [LW 4:421.10–11]). In a text from In Ioh. n.679 (LW 3:593.4–7) Eckhart uses both *abditum mentis* and *supremus animae* jointly, citing Augustine's *De Trinitate*. Another passage, this one from In Gen.II n.149 (LW 1:606.1), identifies this "high point" with intellect: Supremum autem animae in nobis intellectus est. On the *supremum animae* and *videre Deum facie ad faciem* (the Jacob story in Gen. 32:30), see In Gen.II n.219 (LW 1:697–98).

38. E.g., S. IX, n.98 (LW 4:93.6): . . . in abdito animae, ubi solus deus illabitur. Eckhart here identifies this *abditum* with the soul's essence. The same teaching can be found in MHG sermons, e.g., Pr. 72 (DW 3:252.1–6). For *abditum mentis vel cordis*, see S. XLVII.1, n. 488 (LW 4:403.14); and In Sap. n.95 (LW 2:429.3). That the *abditum animae* could acquire something of the dynamics of the *grunt* is shown by a passage in In Ioh. n.320, where Eckhart interprets the *hic* (= Nicodemus) of John 3:2 as referring to the ground of the soul that seeks out Jesus: Hic notat indivisionem, unionem, unitatem; indicat animae, ubi lucet, fulget lux divina, sapit, dulcescit suavitas divina, scaturit fons divinae largitatis: in intimo et abdito animae, ut docet Augustinus . . . (LW 3:268.5–8). In several sermons Tauler explicitly equates the *grund der sêle* with the Augustinian *abditum mentis;* see Wyser, "Taulers Terminologie vom Seelengrund," 337–41. For *abditum mentis* in Augustine, see, e.g., *De Trinitate* 14.7.9 and 15.21.40 (PL 42:1043 and 1088). For the relation between *grunt der sêle* and *(nuda) essentia animae*, see Hasebrink, "GRENZVERSCHIEBUNG," 394–96.

39. E.g., In Gen.II nn.139–40, 143, and 153 (LW 1:605–08, 612, and 623). See also S. XXIV, n.249 (LW 4:228). Insofar as *ratio superior* is understood as a power of the soul, it should be distinguished from the *grunt;* see Reiter, *Der Seele Grund*, 421–23.

40. For *synderesis*, see, e.g., In Gen.II nn. 164, 168, 190, 197, and 199 (LW 1:634, 638, 662, 669, 671–72); and Pr. 20a and 20b (DW 1:331–34, and 348–49). For the wider use of the term, see Heinrich Appel, "Die Synteresis in der mittelalterlichen Mystik," *Zeitschrift für Kirchengeschichte* 13 (1982): 535–44.

41. *Scintilla animae* occurs in Eckhart's Latin defense as a translation of *vunkelîn* from Pr. 2. See Proc.Col.I n.69 (LW 5:223); and the repetition in Proc.Col.II, n.121.

42. On this term, see Hélène Merle, "*DEITAS:* Quelques aspects de la signification de ce mot d'Augustin à Maître Eckhart," in *Von Meister Dietrich zu Meister Eckhart*, ed. Kurt Flasch (Hamburg: Felix Meiner, 1984), 12–21, who argues that Gilbert of Poitiers'

logical distinction between *deus (quod est)* and *deitas (quo est)* is helpful for understanding Eckhart's doctrine of the *deus absconditus.*

43. On the relation of *grunt* to *causa, principium,* and *ratio,* see Schmoldt, *Die deutsche Begriffssprache Meister Eckharts,* 49–54.

44. See Proc.Col.I n.56 (LW 5:217). The sermon text reads: . . . die tugent, die da haisset demuetikait, du ist ain wurtzel in dem grund der gothait (DW 1:247.2–3), which the Latin renders as ". . . quod virtus habet radicem in fundo divinitatis. . . ."

45. This was suggested by Wyser, "Taulers Terminologie vom Seelengrund," 334. Dionysius uses the phrase *puthmên pantokratikos* twice in *De divinis nominibus,* in chap. 4 (PG 3:700B) and chap. 10 (937A). These were translated in a variety of ways, including *omnipotens fundus* by Robert Grosseteste (see *Dionysiaca,* ed. Philippe Chevallier, 2 vols. [Paris: Desclée, 1937] 1:168, 483). In chap. 9 (913B) Dionysius also commented on the *profundum* ascribed to God in Eph. 3:18 (for the translations, see *Dionysiaca* 1:406, 465).

46. See the treatment of *principium* in chapter 5 below. The most detailed study of the relation between *grunt* and *principium* is found in Waldschütz, *Denken und Erfahrung des Grundes,* Teil II, *Denken von Grund und principium,* 107–285.

47. In Eccli. n.12 (LW 2:241.11–242.1): Principium autem, sicut et li primum, relationem importat ordinis et originis.

48. Pr. 69 (DW 3:179.2–6): Vernünfticheit . . . brichet in den grunt, dâ güete und wârheit ûzbrichet, und nimet ez *in principio,* in dem beginne, . . . (trans. *Teacher and Preacher*). See also Pr. 18 (DW 1:302.6–7): . . . und der sun treit sie [the soul] vürbaz ûf in sînen ursprunc [= *principio*], daz ist in dem vater, in den grunt, in daz êrste, dâ der sun wesen ine hât. . . . The term also appears in Pr. 22, though not as a translation for *grunt;* see Pr. 22 (DW 1:389.1): 'In principio' daz sprichet als vil ze tiutsche als ein angenge alles wesens. . . .

49. In Ioh. nn.14–27 (LW 3:13–22).

50. In Sap. nn.144–57 (LW 2:481–94). Even in the Latin commentaries, however, there are places where Eckhart speaks of the soul's desire for indistinction in the *unum;* e.g., in commenting on Wisdom 18:14 in In Sap. n.282 (LW 2:614.13–615.1): Deus autem indistinctus est, et anima amat indistingui, id est unum esse et fieri cum deo. In n.283 (LW 2:615–16) Eckhart interprets the same passage as teaching the birth of the Word in the soul. On Eckhart's understanding of *unum,* see Wouter Goris, *Einheit als Prinzip und Ziel: Versuch über die Einheitsmetaphysik des "Opus tripartitum" Meister Eckharts* (Leiden: Brill, 1997); and Bernard McGinn, "Meister Eckhart on God as Absolute Unity," in *Neoplatonism and Christian Thought,* ed. Dominic O'Meara (Albany: SUNY Press, 1982), 128–39.

51. God as Absolute Unity is found in a number of the vernacular sermons, though the dialectical development is rare. In Pr. 10, however, there is an important discussion of oneness as the negation of negation in relation to the ground (DW 1:173.1–9).

52. S. XXIX (LW 2:263–70). There is a translation in *Preacher and Teacher,* 223–27. On this sermon, see Goris, *Einheit als Prinzip und Ziel,* 82–88.

53. S. IV, n.28 (LW 2:28.5–8): Tertio, sicut deus est in se indistinctissimus secundum naturam ipsius, utpote vere unus et propriissime et ab aliis distinctissimus, sic et homo in deo indistinctus ab omnibus, quae in deo sunt, . . . et simul distinctissimus ab omnibus aliis.

54. Pr. 13 (DW 1:218.5–6): . . . der himelische vater der gebirt in mich sîn glîch, und von der glîcheit sô kumet ûz ein minne, daz ist der heilige geist (my trans.).

55. Pr. 13 (DW 1:219.3–5): Und ie denne ein ieglich dinc edeler ist, ie staetlicher ez

loufet. Der grunt jaget sie alliu. Wîsheit und güete und wârheit leget etwaz zuo; ein enleget niht zuo dan den grunt des wesens (my trans.). On the importance of this passage, see Waldschütz, *Denken und Erfahrung des Grundes*, 208–15. Eckhart often refers to God as love "hunting" or "pursuing" all things, and all things "hunting" him in return. See, Pr. 59 (DW 2:633.4–8); Prr. 63, 65, 69, 79 (DW 3:75–76, 95, 171–72, 368); Pr. 101 (Pfeiffer, 8); BgT (DW 5:32); RdU 5 (DW 5:200). In the Latin works, see S. VI n.54 (LW 4:52).

56. Waldschütz summarizes (*Denken und Erfahrung des Grundes*, 213): "Die Rückkehr des Seienden meint wirklich nichts anders als den Grund selbst so sein zu lassen, dass er in seinem Gründen immer gegenwärtig sein kann—und so das Seiende selbst zu sich kommt. Zu dieser Erfüllung 'jagt' der Grund alle Dinge: Er jagt sie, weil und insofern er ihnen innerlichst ist, und er jagt sie zum Ziel, nämlich dem Grund-Sein für anderes."

57. Eckhart uses *abgrunt/abgründicheit* four times to describe the *gotheit* or *got* (DW 1:194.5; DW 2:68.1 and 84.7; DW 5:238.4–5), and twice to characterize *wesen* (DW 2:84.7 and 493.5).

58. For the development of mystical meanings of *abyssus*, see Bernard McGinn, "The Abyss of Love," in *The Joy of Learning and the Love of God: Studies in Honor of Jean Leclercq*, ed. E. Rozanne Elder (Kalamazoo: Cistercian Publications, 1995), 95–120.

59. Ibid., 97–100.

60. Ibid., 103–10 and the texts cited there.

61. Ibid., 110–12.

62. Pr. 42 (DW 2:309.3–7): Nû wizzet: alliu unser volkomenheit und alliu unser saelicheit liget dar ane, daz der mensche durchgange und übergange alle geschaffenheit und alle zîtlicheit und allez wesen und gange in den grunt, der gruntlôs ist. Wir biten des unsern lieben herren got, daz wir ein werden und innewonen, und ze dem selben grunde helfe uns got. Âmen. (my trans.). Eckhart often insists that it is only the power of "intellect" (*vernünfticheit/bekantnisse*) that penetrates into the ground; see, e.g., Pr. 7 (DW 1:122.10–123.5), and Pr. 66 (DW 3:113.1–3).

63. Pr. 54b (DW 2:565.13–566.2): wan swer komen wil in gotes grunt, in sîn innerstez, der muoz ê komen in sînen eigenen grunt, in sîn innerstez. wan nieman enmac got erkennen, er enmüeze ê sich selben erkennen (my trans.). See the parallel in Pr. 54a (DW 2:550.4–551.2): Suln wir iemer komen in den grunt gotes und in sîn innerstez, sô müezen wir ze dem êrsten komen in unsern eigenen grunt und in unser innerstez in lûterer dêmüeticheit. The relation between humility and *grunt*, as Waldschütz points out (*Denken und Erfahrung des Grundes*, 184–85), must be understood in an ontological way.

64. Eckhart, of course, often concentrates his exposition on the anthropological side of his dialectic. On the *grunt der sêle*, see, e.g., Pr. 17 (DW 1:281–93), and Pr. 101 (as found in *Lectura Eckhardi*, 250–54).

65. E.g., Pr. 15 (DW 1:253.5–6): . . . da gottes grund vnd der sele grund ain grund ist. It is interesting that Eckhart could use the same formula to express ultimate beatitude; see, e.g., Pr. 39 (DW 2:257.2–3): . . . wan des gerehten saelicheit und gotes saelicheit ist éin saelicheit, wan dâ ist der gerehte saelic, dâ got saelic ist. For more on the relation between *grunt* and *saelicheit* in Eckhart, see Pr. 45 (DW 2:363.3–7, and 373.4–7).

66. What I mean by "fused identity" here is close to what Michael A. Sells discusses in relation to Plotinus in his *Mystical Languages of Unsaying* (Chicago: University of Chicago Press, 1994), 22–27.

67. Pr. 5b (DW 1:90.8–9): Hie ist gotes grunt mîn grunt und mîn grunt gotes grunt. Hie lebe ich ûzer mînem eigen, als got lebet ûzer sînem eigen (trans. *Essential Eckhart*). There are a number of other such "fused-identity formulas" in the German sermons; e.g., Pr. 28 (DW 2:67.1–69.4), using both *grunt* and *einicheit;* Pr. 48 (DW 2:415.4–9); Pr. 80 (DW 3:378.2–5); Pr. 98 (DW 4:243.35–244.44); etc. In the sermons edited by Pfeiffer, see especially LXI (ed., 194–95), and LXXI (ed., 225.34–226.13). For a list of texts and discussion, see Reiter, *Der Seele Grund,* 450–51 and 484–533.

68. This form of relation between God and the soul is found especially in those Latin texts that use the word *illabor* to indicate God's movement into the soul's depth (e.g., Sermo IX, n. 98 [LW 4:93.6]). But the same formulae can also be found in German sermons, e.g., Pr. 10 (DW 1:162.4–6), Pr. 76 (DW 3:252.1–6).

69. See Langer, "Eckharts Lehre von Seelengrund," 183–90, arguing against the view of B. Mojsisch.

70. Much has been written about the *vunkelîn,* or "uncreated something." A classic account remains that of Hof, *Scintilla animae.*

71. See the treatment in the following chapter.

72. The history has been expounded by Hugo Rahner, "Die Gottesgeburt: Die Lehre der Kirchenväter von der Geburt Christi aus den Herzen der Kirche und der Gläubigen," in *Symbole der Kirche: Die Ekklesiologie der Väter* (Salzburg: Müller, 1964), 7–41. See also Dietmar Mieth, "Gottesschau und Gottesgeburt: Zwei Typen Christlicher Gotteserfahrung in der Tradition," *Freiburger Zeitschrift für Theologie und Philosophie* 27 (1980): 204–23.

73. Pr. 48 (DW 2:420.7–421.3): . . . ez wil in den einvaltigen grunt, in die stillen wüeste, dâ nie underscheit îngeluogete weder vater noch sun noch heiliger geist; . . . wan dirre grunt ist ein einvaltic stille, diu in ir selben unbeweglich ist, und von dirre unbewegelicheit werdent beweget alle dinc und werdent enpfangen alliu leben, diu vernunftliclîche in in selben sint (trans. *Essential Eckhart*). On this sermon, see the commentary by Burkhard Mojsisch in *Lectura Eckhardi,* 156–62.

74. E.g., Pr. 51 (DW 2:470.3–6).

75. E.g., Pr. 69 (DW 3:178.2–180.2). In Pr. 52, especially in the third section (DW 2:499.9–505.9), similar language is used with regard to *durchbrechen,* though *grunt* is not employed. Another daring expression of indistinct union beyond the Persons of the Trinity without *grunt* language can be found in Pr. 83 (DW 3:448).

76. Pfeiffer LVI (ed. 179–81). Originally rejected by Josef Quint as belonging to Eckhart, the homily was later translated and seemingly accepted by Quint in his *Meister Eckehart: Deutsche Predigten und Traktate* (Munich: Carl Hanser, 1963), 271–73. It has been translated by both Walshe (2:79–82), and Davies (*Meister Eckhart: Selected Sermons,* 232–34) and accepted as authentic.

77. Pf. LVI (ed. 181.3–6): Dô ich stuont in dem grunde, in dem boden, in dem river und in der quelle der gotheit, dâ fragete mich nieman, war ich wolte oder waz ich tête: dâ enwas nieman, der mich frâgete. Dô ich flôz, dô sprâchen al crêatûren von got. As Burkhard Mojsisch has shown, in his "'Ce moi': La conception du moi de Maître Eckhart," *Revue des sciences religieuses* 70 (1996): 27–28, *got* as used by Eckhart is a relational term employed of the Creator, and therefore not an ultimate term for the hidden divinity. Thus, *got* must be left behind (see, e.g., Pr. 52) in the releasement that some have spoke of as Eckhart's "mystical atheism." On "mystical atheism," see Gerald Hanratty, "The Origin and Development of Mystical Atheism," *Neue Zeitschrift für Systematische Theologie* 30 (1988): 1–17, although I believe that the author's contention that Eckhart is the source of the mystical atheisms of the nineteenth century is seriously

mistaken. See also Reiner Schürmann, *Meister Eckhart: Mystic and Philosopher* (Bloomington: Indiana University Press, 1978), 213.

78. Pf. LVI (ed. 181.16–18): Swenne ich kume in den grunt, in den boden, in den river und in die quelle der gotheit, sô frâget mich nieman, wannen ich kome oder wâ ich sî gewesen. Dâ vermiste mîn nieman, daz entwirt (trans. Davies).

79. The dialectical character of Eckhart's thought means that from different perspectives any of the major themes of his thought can be given a certain priority. Thus, Waldschütz (*Denken und Erfahrung des Grundes,* 351) is not incorrect in claiming "Gottesgeburt ist höchster und letzter Vollzug der Grunderfahrung," without necessarily contradicting my insistence that in another sense identity in the *grunt* is deeper than the *gottesgeburt.*

80. Eckhart's views on *unio mystica* will be discussed in more detail in chap. 6. For a sketch of the history of understandings of union, see McGinn, "Love, Knowledge, and *Unio mystica,*" especially 71–80 on Eckhart and his contemporaries and followers.

81. See Bernard McGinn, *The Foundations of Mysticism: Origins to the Fifth Century* (New York: Crossroad, 1991), 232–43.

82. Bernard of Clairvaux, *De diligendo Deo* 10.28 (*S. Bernardi Opera,* ed. Jean Leclercq et al., 8 vols. [Rome: Editiones Cistercienses, 1957–77] 3:143.15–24).

83. For a treatment of Porete and her teaching on union, see McGinn, *Flowering of Mysticism,* 244–65; and Sells, *Mystical Languages of Unsaying,* chaps. 5 and 7.

84. On the historical contacts, see Edmund Colledge and J. C. Marler, "'Poverty of Will': Ruusbroec, Eckhart and the Mirror of Simple Souls," in *Jan van Ruusbroec: The Sources, Content, and Sequels of His Mysticism,* ed. Paul Mommaers and N. de Paepe (Leuven: Leuven University Press, 1984), 14–47; as well as the papers of Maria Lichtmann, Amy Hollywood, and Michael Sells in *Meister Eckhart and the Beguine Mystics,* 65–146.

85. Pr. 5b (DW 1:93.7). See the note on this text in Largier 1:803–07. To say that *grunt* has a special ability to express Eckhart's notion of indistinct union is not to deny that the Dominican often uses other terms, such as *wesen* and *isticheit* in parallel ways (e.g., Prr. 6, 52, 77, 83 [DW 1:106.1–3, DW 2:492.3–7 and 504.2, DW 3:340.8–10 and 447.5 ff.]). Identity formulas using birthing language are also found, e.g., Prr. 4, 22, and 38 (DW 1:72.8–73.1, and 382.3–383.1; DW 2:228.1–3).

86. Köbele, *Bilder,* 187: . . . *grunt* hat . . . keine andere "Bedeuting" als die Identität des göttlichen Grundes mit dem Grund der Seele. Diese Identität ist eine dynamische Identität."

87. B. Mojsisch refers to this fused identity as a "univocal-transcendental relationship of correlation" (*Meister Eckhart,* 135). E. Waldschütz equates *Grund-Sein* with *In-Beziehung-Sein* (*Denken und Erfahrung des Grundes,* 173, 201, 215, and especially 342–48) and stresses the event-identity of the *grunt* (e.g., 139–40, 164–66). See also Bernhard Welte, *Meister Eckhart: Gedanken zu seinem Gedanken* (Freiburg: Herder, 1979), 110–26.

88. For the history of these symbols, see Bernard McGinn, "Ocean and Desert as Symbols of Mystical Absorption in the Christian Tradition," *Journal of Religion* 74 (1994): 155–81 (pp. 167–72 on Eckhart). Evagrius Ponticus (c. 390) appears to have been the first to use ocean or sea as a symbol for fusion with God, while John Scottus Eriugena (c. 870) has the earliest usage of the expression the "desert of the divine nature."

89. For a list of the uses of desert language in Eckhart and the other German mystics, see Egerding, *Die Metaphorik,* 2:722–26.

90. E.g., Gottfried von Strassburg, *Tristan,* lines 2498–2508: nu warte ich allenthalben mîn/ und sihe niht lebendes umbe mich./ dise grôze wilde die fürht'ich:/ swar ich min ougen wende,/ da ist mir der werlde ein ende;/ swâ ich mich hin gekêre,/ dan sihe ich ie nimêre/ niwan ein toup gevilde/ unde wüeste unde wilde,/ wilde velse und wilden sê./ disiu vorhte tuot mir wê (*Gottfried von Strassburg, Tristan,* ed. Reinhold Bechstein and Peter Ganz, 2 vols. [Wiesbaden: Brockhaus, 1978]). I wish to thank Frank Tobin for bringing this text to my attention.

91. The mutuality is especially brought out in passages from Pr. 29 (DW 2:76.2–77.4) and from VeM (DW 5:119.1–7). In the Latin works, see In Gen.II n. 149 (LW 1:618.12–619.1). *Grunt* and *einoede* are used together in Pr. 10 (DW 1:171.12–15), and Pr. 48 (DW 2:420.9–110).

92. Pr. 7 (DW 1:123.1–3): . . . vernünfticheit nimet got, als er in ir bekant ist; dâ enkan si in niemer begrîfen in dem mer sîner gruntlôsicheit (my trans.).

93. Pr. 17 (DW 1:281.12–282.3): . . . swer dâ schrîbet von beweglîchen dingen, der enrüeret die natûre noch den grunt der sêle niht. Swer nâch der einvalticheit und lûterkeit und blôzheit die sêle, als si in ir selber ist, nennen sol, der enkan ir enkeinen namen vinden (trans. Walshe). Cf. Pr. 17 (DW 1: 284.5); Pr. 77 (DW 3:337–38); Pr. 83 (DW 3:440.5–6); and Pr. 98 (DW 4:236.11–237.13). Pr. 17 parallels S. LV.4 (LW 4:458–65), which treats the same verse from John 12:25. For a discussion of the two homilies, see Hasebrink, "GRENZVERSCHIEBUNG," 393–97; and Loris Sturlese, "Predigt 17: 'Qui odit animam suam,'" in *Lectura Eckhardi,* 75–96. In several sermons Eckhart says that the soul in its essence, like God, has no name; e.g., Prr. 3, 7 (DW 1:53–56, 123–24); Pr. 38 (DW 2:237). See also the discussion of the unnameable ground of the soul as a desert in Pr. 28 (DW 2:66.2–7).

94. For the negative anthropology of Eriugena, see McGinn, *Growth of Mysticism,* 104–6.

95. See, e.g., RdU 23 (DW 5:293.5–7): . . . sunder diu hoehste hoehe der hôchheit liget in dem tiefen grunde der dêmüeticheit. Wan ie der grunt tiefer ist und niderr, ie ouch diu erhoeunge und die hoeher und unmaeziger ist. . . . The RdU speaks of the *abgrunde gotes* (238.4–5) and the *grunde der sêle* (219.8, 255.8, 256.7), but does not yet use fused identity formulae.

96. Largier, "Negativität, Möglichkeit, Freiheit. Zur Differenz zwischen der Philosophie Dietrichs von Freiberg und Eckharts von Hochheim," in *Dietrich von Freiberg: Neue Perspektiven seiner Philosophie, Theologie und Naturwissenschaft,* ed. Karl-Hermann Kandler, Burkhard Mojsisch, Franz-Bernard Stamkötter (Amsterdam/Philadelphia: B. R. Gruner, 1998)," 158–62.

97. Pr. 54a (DW 2:560.6–7): Ie man die wurzel und den kernen und den grunt der gotheit mê erkennet ein, ie man mê erkennet alliu dinc (my trans.).

98. Pr. 39 (DW 2:256.3–4): Und dar umber ganc in dînen eignen grunt, und dâ würke, und din werk, diu dû würkest, dui sint alliu lebendic. See also Pr. 5b (DW 1:90.6–12). On working "out of the ground," see Waldschütz, *Denken und Erfahrung des Grundes,* 140–42, and 173–85.

99. Pr. 16b (DW 1:276.3–5): Dû solt alle tugende durchgân und übergân und solt aleine die tugent nemen in dem grunde, dâ si ein ist mit götlîcher natûre (my trans.). On this sermon, see S. Köbele, "Predigt 16b: 'Quasi vas auri solidum,'" in *Lectura Eckhardi,* 43–74. The same insistence on taking virtue "in the ground" is found in RdU 21 (DW 5:282.4). *Grunt* has a special relation to the virtue of humility. For example, in Pr. 55 Eckhart says: "Ie mê der mensche in den grunt rehter dêmuot gesenket wirt, ie mê er gesenket wirt in den grunt götlîches wesens" (DW 2:582–3–4). For Eckhart's teach-

ing on the relation of virtues to the *grund,* see Dietmar Mieth, "Die theologische trans-position der Tugendethik bei Meister Eckhart," in *Abendländische Mystik im Mittelalter,* ed. Kurt Ruh (Stuttgart: J. B. Metzler, 1986), 63–69.

100. Pr. 86 (DW 3:481.11). See the treatment below in chapter 6.

101. This will be treated in more detail in chapter 6 below.

102. Pr. 67 makes the connection between *grunt* and Christ more explicitly than any other Eckhartian homily. In Pr. 24, however, a discussion of the soul's oneness in the ground of the Trinity leads immediately into a treatment of Christ's assumption of total humanity through the Incarnation (DW 1:419–20).

103. Pr. 67 (DW 3:133.2–8): Ez ist diu wesenlich vernünfticheit gotes, der diu lûter blôz kraft ist *intellectus,* daz die meister heizent ein enpfenclîchez. . . . Dar obe nimet si êrste die lûter *absolûcio* des vrîen wesens, daz dâ sunder dâ, dâ ez ennimet noch engi-bet; ez ist diu blôze isticheit, diu dâ beroubet ist alles wesens und aller isticheit. Dâ nimet si got blôz nâch dem grunde dâ, dâ er ist über allez wesen. Waere dâ noch wesen, sô naeme si wesen in wesene; dâ enist niht wan éin grunt (my trans.).

104. Pr. 67 (DW 3:134.5–8): . . . daz ich in dem selben understantnisse habe des per-sônlîche wesens, daz ich daz persônlich wesen selber sî, alzemâle lougenlîche mîn selbes verstantnisses alsô, als ich nâch geistes art éin bin nâch dem grunde alsô, als der grunt selbe ein grunt ist . . . (my trans.). Part of the difficulty of this complex sermon is try-ing to understand what Eckhart means by the technical terms he is creating: *persônliche wesen* (twelve times); *understantnisse* (five times); *persônlicheit* (twice); *understôz* (three times).

105. On the importance of *entbilden,* see Wolfgang Wackernagel, YMAGINE DENUDARI: *Éthique de l'image et métaphysique de l'abstraction chez Maître Eckhart* (Paris: Vrin, 1991).

106. Pr. 67 (DW 3:135.11–15): Wan denne got [= Christ, a common MHG use] in dem grunde des vaters êwiclîche inneblîbende ist und ich in im, ein grunt und der selbe Kristus, ein understandicheit mîner menscheit, sô ist si als wol mîn als sîn an einer understandicheit des êwigen wesens, daz beidiu wesen lîbes und sêle volbrâht werden in éinem Kristô, éin got, éin sun (my trans.).

107. See chapter 6 below for more on this.

108. See Quint, "Mystik und Sprache," 141–51, with a treatment of *grunt* on pp. 141–43. According to Quint, "Und so wächst denn, aus innersten Denk- und Sprach-not hervorgetrieben, zur adäquaten Benennung des innersten Seinsgrundes der Seele wie des göttlichen Urgrundes ein mystisches Wortfeld, das weithin durch *metapho-rische,* bildliche Ausdrücke das sprachlich auszusagen versucht, was begrifflich nicht zu fassen ist" (p. 141).

Chapter 4
The Preacher in Action: Eckhart on the Eternal Birth

1. These sermons can be found in Pfeiffer I–IV (ed., 3–30), though in incorrect order. In the critical text in DW 4 they will appear as follows: Pr. 101 (= Pf. I), Pr. 102 (= Pf. II), Pr. 103 (= Pf. IV), Pr. 104 (= Pf. III). I will cite the sermons by number and line from the forthcoming critical edition of Georg Steer in DW 4. I thank Prof. Steer for his kindness in making this text available to me. Pr. 101, along with an illuminating study, can be found in Georg Steer, "Predigt 101: 'Dum medium silentium tenerent omnia,'" in *Lectura Eckhardi,* 247–88. Steer further analyzes this preaching treatise in

"Meister Eckharts Predigtzyklus *von der êwigen geburt.* Mutmassungen über die Zeit seiner Entstehung," in *Deutsche Mystik im abendländischen Zusammenhang,* ed. Walter Haug and Wolfram Schneider-Lastin (Tübingen: Niemeyer, 2000), 253–81. I will use the translation of the sermons in Walshe 1:1–47, unless otherwise noted.

2. Pr. 104A.519–22: : . . . gesaget gelêrten und erliuhteten liuten, die von gote und von der geschrift gelêret und erliuhtet sint (cf. Pf. 23.29–30). See also the comments in Pr. 101.7–10 and 112–15.

3. Steer ("Meister Eckharts Predigtzyklus," 263–66) also notes some significant similarities of language and theme with the RdU, such as the use of the term *gemüete* for mind (26 times in RdU; 5 times in the cycle), which later largely falls out of the Meister's vocabulary (only 3 times in all other sermons and treatises).

4. See Steer, "Meister Eckhart's Predigtzyklus," for links between the cycle and interpretations found in the Wisdom commentary. The relation between Pr. 101 and Eckhart's In Sap. has also been studied by Donald F. Duclow, "Meister Eckhart on the Book of Wisdom: Commentary and Sermons," *Traditio* 43 (1987): 228–32.

5. Steer, "Predigt 101," 279–80.

6. The use of ground language is somewhat uneven over the four sermons: Pr. 101 (12 times), Pr. 102 (14 times), Pr. 103 (once), Pr. 104 (6 times).

7. Pr. 52 (DW 2:486–506). Matthew 5:3 was a favorite Eckhart text. For other treatments in the vernacular works, see, e.g., RdU 3 and 23 (DW 5:195–96, 297–301); BgT 1 (DW 5:22, 29, and 42); and Pr. 79 (DW 3:365).

8. The Introit from the the Old Latin version of the Bible reads "Dum medium silentium tenerent omnia et nox in suo cursu medium iter haberet, omnipotens sermo tuus, Domine, de caelis a regalibus sedibus venit." Eckhart silently added Job 4:12: "Porro ad me dictum est verbum absconditum." He then translated this into MHG as: . . . 'dô alliu dinc wâren enmitten in einem swîgenne, dô kam von oben her nider von dem küniclîchen stuole' 'in mich ein verborgen wort' (Pr. 101.10–11, my trans.). Eckhart commented on the Vg version ("Cum enim *quietem silentium* contineret omnia") in In Sap. nn.279–85 (LW 2:611–19, translated in *Teacher and Preacher,* 171–74). But even in his Latin commentary the Dominican eventually introduced the liturgical version of the passage to bring his reading in conformity with that presented in Pr. 101. See In Sap. n.285 (LW 2:618.5–8): Et hoc est quod cantat ecclesia: "dum medium silentium tenerent omnia", id est: dum omnia tenerent ipsum medium, et omne medium silentium, id est silens. Medium enim ut sic silentium est exuta iam ratione medii, sicut multa et omnia unum sunt in uno et in deo. Steer ("Meister Eckharts Predigtzyklus," 272–76) notes that four of the seven readings proposed for Wisdom 18:14 in the commentary are related to texts found in the Christmas sermon cycle.

9. Joachim Theisen summarizes this aspect of Eckhart's preaching as follows: "Eckhart spricht in den Predigten von der Heilsgeschichte stets unter dem Aspekt der Liturgie. Nicht das historische Geschehen interessiert ihn, sondern die jeweiligen heilsgeschichtliche Bedeutung, die sich in der Gegenwart der liturgischen Feier entfaltet" (*Predigt und Gottesdienst,* 552).

10. Pr. 101.15–16: Daz êrste ist, wâ got der vater spreche sîn wort in der sêle und wâ dirre geburt stat sî und wâ si dises werkes enpfenchlic sî (Walshe trans. modified). This part will be treated in Pr. 101.36–106 and taken up in more depth in Pr. 102.

11. Pr. 101.33–35: . . . oder daz man sich entziehe und ledic mache von allen gedenken und von allen worten und werken . . . , und daz man sich zemâle halte in einem lûtern gotlîdenne. . . . This question is treated in Pr. 101.107–202 and explored in more detail in Prr. 103 and 104.

12. Issue three takes up the least space (see Pr. 101.203–24 and Pr. 103.39–106), but it is touched upon in other places in the cycle.

13. Pr. 10133–35: Ich wil iu dise rede bewaeren mit natiurlîchen reden, daz ir ez selber möhtet grîfen, daz ez also ist, wie ich doch der schrift mê gloube dan mir selber. Aber ez gât iu mê în und baz von bewaerter rede. The point is also made in the roughly contemporary Prol.op.prop. n.16 (LW 1:176.8).

14. Pr. 101.196–98: Wan die vom dem adel der sêle schriben, die enwâren noch niht naeher komen dan sie ir natiurlîchen vernunft truoc. Sie enwâren nie in den grunt komen. Des muoste in vil verborgen sîn und blîben unbekant. The criticism is repeated in a sharper form in Pr. 101.207–9: Alle die wârheit, die alle meister ie gelêrten mit irer eigen vernunft und verstantnisse oder iemer mê suln biz an den jüngsten tac, die verstuonden nie daz allerminste in disem wizzenne und in disem grunde.

15. Pr. 10137–54: Ach, herre, wâ ist daz swîgen und wâ ist diu stat, dâ diz wort îngesprochen wirt? . . . Ez ist in dem lûtersten, daz diu sêle geleisten mac, in dem edelsten, in dem grunde, jâ in dem wesene der sêle, daz ist in dem verborgensten der sêle. . . . Wan daz enist von natûre nihtes enpfenclich dan aleine des götlîchen wesens âne allez mittel. Got gât hie in die sêle mit sînem allen, niht mit sînem teile. Got gât hie in den grunt der sêle. The term *grunt* appears six times in this passage.

16. Pr. 101.82–83: Got würket in der sêle âne mittel, bilde oder glîchnisse, jâ in dem grunde, dâ nie bilde înkam dan er selber mit sînem eigenen wesene. Because the soul can have images of things outside it, but no image of itself, in this context Eckhart also reaffirms his negative anthropology—Und dar umbe sô ist der sêle kein dinc als unbekant als ir selber (Pr. 101.65).

17. As Steer points out ("Predigt 101," 275–76), Eckhart differs markedly from Thomas Aquinas here in denying any form of *species intelligibilis* in the procession of the Son from the Father (e.g., STh 1a, q.14, a.2).

18. Pr. 101.92: Und in der wâren einunge liget alliu iriu saelicheit.

19. Eckhart makes the transition by means of a second interjection, an objection put by a questioner representing Avicenna (see *Metaphysica* 9.7), who claims that there is nothing in the soul but the images that enable it to become a *saeculum intellectuale/vernünftigiu werlt.* Eckhart decisively rejects this, because it would make true beatitude (i.e., union with God) impossible. See also In Gen.I n.115 (LW 1:270.13–271.1), and Pr. 17 (DW 1:289.1–8), and the discussion in Steer, "Predigt 101," 276–77.

20. Pr. 101.112–17. Eckhart's caution here, especially with regard to absorbing *aller tugenden wesen,* is reminiscent of Marguerite Porete's teaching about "saying good-bye" to the virtues while preserving their inner meaning (see Bernard McGinn, *The Flowering of Mysticism: Men and Women in the New Mysticism [1200–1350]* [New York: Crossroad, 1998], 253–54).

21. Pr. 101.118–21: Als dâ alle die kreft sint *abegezogen* . . . sô dû alle dîne krefte ie mê maht *geziehen* in ein vergezzen aller dinge und ir bilde. . . (my italics).

22. Paul's rapture is mentioned also in the early RdU 10 in the course of a discussion of "inwardness, devotion, jubilation [i.e., the *iubilus* experience], and ecstasy" (DW 5:219–24). For more on Eckhart's references to Paul's ecstasy, see chapter 6.

23. Robert K. C. Forman, *Meister Eckhart: Mystic as Theologian* (Rockport: Element Books, 1991), chap. 5. Forman discusses nine passages from the German works and two from the Latin, including these texts from Pr. 101 (pp. 98–101).

24. Forman, *Meister Eckhart,* 115–25.

25. Pr. 101.137–50.

26. Pr. 101.151: Nû möhtest dû sprechen: Swaz got würket âne bilde in dem grunde und in dem wesene, ...

27. Pr. 101.155–60: Daz unwizzen ziuhet sie in ein wunder und tuot sie disem nâchjagen, wan si bevindet wol, daz es ist und enweiz aber niht, wie noch waz ez ist. Wenne der mensche weiz der dinge sache, alzehant, sô ist er der dinge müede und suochet aber ein anderz ze ervane und ze wizzene und quilet und jâmert iemer mê alsô nâch wizenne und enhât doch kein bîblîben. Dar umber, diz unbekante bekantnisse daz enthaltet sie bî disem blîbende und tuot sie disem nâchjagen (my trans.). This may be the earliest vernacular appearance of *docta ignorantia,* a phrase that goes back to Augustine (see *Ep.* 130.14.28 [PL 33:505]). The importance of unknowing/not-knowing is a constant throughout Eckhart's works; see, for example, the analysis of poverty of spirit as "knowing nothing" in Pr. 52 (DW 2:494–97), and the conclusion of Pr. 83 (DW 3:448).

28. See, e.g., Pr. 9 (DW 1:157–58) on the three kinds of *wort;* and the discussion in Pr. 53 (DW 3:528–31). This will be taken up in more detail in chapter 5.

29. Pr. 101.171–73: . . . dô er wider kam, dô was ez im nihtes niht vergezzen. Mêr: ez was im sô verre inne in dem grunde, dar sîne vernunft niht înkomen enmohte. Ez waz ihm bedecket.

30. Pr. 101.176–90.

31. Pr. 101.192–96: . . . eyâ, herre, ir wellet der sêle irn natiurlîchen louf umbekêren und wider ir natûre tuon. Ir natûre ist, daz si durch die sinne neme und in bilden. Wellet ir den orden umbekêren? Nein! Waz weist dû, waz adels got geleget habe in die natûre, diu noch niht alliu geschriben ensint, mêr: noch verborgen? (my trans.)

32. Pr. 101.209–12: Wie daz ez doch ein unwizzen heize und ein unbekantheit, sô hât ez doch mê inne dan allez wizzen und bekennen ûzwendic disem. Wan diz unwizzen daz reizet und ziuhet dich von allem wizzenden dingen und ouch von dir selber (my trans.).

33. Pr. 101.212–20. Rather daringly, Eckhart asserts that a person who has attained this form of "establishment" (*der hie inner rehte stüende*) can never be separated from God, by either mortal or venial sin.

34. See Rahner, "Die Gottesgeburt: Die Lehre der Kirchenväter von der Geburt Christi aus dem Herzen der Kirche und der Gläubigen." For twelfth-century uses, see also Bernard McGinn, *The Growth of Mysticism: Gregory the Great to the Twelfth Century* (New York: Crossroad, 1994), 283–84, and 331–32.

35. Pr. 102.3–5: . . . daz disiu êwige geburt geschiht in der sêle in aller der wîse, als si geschihet in der êwikeit, noch minner noch mê, wan ez ist éiniu geburt. Und disiu geburt geschihet in dem wesene und in dem grunde der sêle.

36. Eckhart's treatment here does not address the issue of the angels, who are also *vernünftigen crêatûren.*

37. Pr. 102.28–68. This section contains the most uses of the language of *grunt* in the whole cycle—it appears nine times.

38. Pr. 102.66–68: Disiu geburt enmac niht bestân mit vinsternisse der sünden, aleine si doch niht engeschihet in den kreften sunder in dem wesene und in dem grunde der sêle. The relationship between this "light" and grace, which Eckhart would later insist is needed to help the soul realize the birth, is unclear here. On grace in Eckhart, see chapter 6.

39. Pr. 102.99–100: In mir enmac keine wîse sîn crêatûrliches wizennes, daz niht enhindere, alsô als got alliu dinc weiz âne hindernisse, alsô als die saeligen tuont (my trans.).

40. Pr. 102.121–23: Hie muoz er komen in ein vergezzen und in ein nihtwizzen. Ez muoz sîn in einer stille und in eime swîgenne, dâ diz wort sol gehoeret werden.

41. Pr. 27 (DW 2:53.4–5): Des vaters sprechen ist sîn gebern, des sunes hoeren ist sîn geborn werden (trans. Walshe). The same teaching is found in the Latin works, e.g., In Ioh. n.641 (LW 3:557.5–10).

42. Pr. 102.130–34: Man sol hie komen in ein überformet wizzen. Noch diz unwizzen ensol niht komen von unwizzenne, mêr: von wizzenne sol man komen in ein unwizzen. Danne suln wir werden wizzende mit dem götlichen wizzenne und danne wirt geadelt unde gezieret unser unwizzen mit dem übernâtiurlîchen wizzenne. Und hie in disem, dâ wir uns halten lîdende, dâ sîn wîr volkomener, dan ob wir wührten (my trans.). According to Steer ("Predigt 101," 268), this is the only place where Eckhart uses the term *überformet wizzen*.

43. On the difference between Dietrich's and Eckhart's teaching on the intellect and *beatitudo*, see especially Niklaus Largier, "*Intellectus in deum ascensus*. Intellekttheoretische Auseinandersetzungen in Texten der deutschen Mystik," *Deutsche Vierteljahrsschrift für Literaturwissenschaft und Geistesgeschichte* 69 (1995): 423–71.

44. Pr. 102.141–42: Und dar umbe suln wir in dem êwigen lebene vil sêliger sîn in der kraft des hoerennes dan in der kraft des sehennes.

45. Pr. 102.152–57: Und als got ist almehtic an dem wirkenne, alsô ist die sêle abgründic an dem lîdenne, und dar umbe wirt si überformet mit gote und in gote. Got der sol würken und diu sêle lîden, er sol sich selben bekennen unde minnen in ir, si sol bekennen mit sîner bekantnüsse und sol minnen mit sîner minne, und dar umbe ist si vil sêliger mit dem sînen dan mit dem iren, und alsô ist ouch ir sêlikeit mè gelegen in sînem würkenne denne in dem iren (my trans.). For parallel texts in Marguerite Porete, especially in her discussion of the fifth and sixth stages of the soul's itinerary to annihilation in chap. 118 of the *Mirror of Simple Annihilated Souls*, see McGinn, *Flowering of Mysticism*, 259–61.

46. See McGinn, *Flowering of Mysticism*, 216–17. In other passages, however, Eckhart emphasizes a mutual *durchbrechen* that is closer to the beguine; see, e.g., Pr. 29 (DW 2:76.2–77.4).

47. Steer, "Predigt 101," 264; idem, "Meister Eckharts Predigtzyklus."

48. Pr. 103.9–10: . . . solt dû dise edele geburt vinden, sô muost dû alle menige lâzen und muost wider in den ursprunc und in den grunt komen, dà dû ûz komen bist.

49. Pr. 103.47–49: Sîn name enist niht dan ein mügelich enpfenclicheit, diu zemâle wesennes niht enmangelt noch ouch darbende ist, mêr: alleine ein mügelich enpfenclicheit, in dem dû volbrâht solt werden (Walshe trans. modified).

50. The combination of the metaphors of climbing the heights with the emptiness of the desert is also found in strophe 4 of the *Granum sinapis:* Dez puntez berk/ stîg âne werk,/ vorstenlichkeit!/ der wek dich treit/ in eine wûste wunderlîch.

51. Pr. 103.68–70: Daz wâre wort der êwicheit wirt aleine gesprochen in der êwicheit, dâ der mensche verüestet und verellendet ist sîn selbes und aller manicvalticheit (Walshe modified). In this context Eckhart cites Hosea 2:14, a text that was his biblical signature for the desert motif. See Bernard McGinn, "Ocean and Desert as Symbols of Mystical Absorption in the Christian Tradition," *Journal of Religion* 74 (1994): 168, and chapter 6 below.

52. Pr. 103.72–73: . . . in der verworfenheit und in der wüeste und in der ellendicheit aller crêatûren. On Mechthild's sense of estrangement (*verworfenheit*), see Bernard McGinn, "Suffering, emptiness and annihilation in three beguine mystics," in *Homo Medietas: Aufsätze zu Religiosität, Literatur und Denkformen des Menschen vom*

Mittelalter bis in die Neuzeit. Festschrift für Alois Maria Haas zum 65. Geburtstag, ed. Claudia Brinker-von der Heyde and Niklaus Largier (Frankfurt: Peter Lang, 1999), 162–69.

53. On the history of the theme of mystical desolation and how it contrasts with Eckhart's usual way of using the desert and divine hiddenness, see Bernard McGinn, "*Vere tu es Deus absconditus:* The Hidden God in Luther and Some Mystics" (forthcoming). See also Alois M. Haas, "'. . . DAS PERSÖNLICHE UND EIGENE VERLEUGNEN': Mystische *vernichtigkeit und verworfwenheit sein selbs* im Geiste Meister Eckharts," in *INDIVIDUALITÄT: Poetik und Hermeneutik XIII*, ed. Manfred Frank and Anselm Haverkamp (Munich: Fink, 1988), 106–22.

54. Pr. 103.95–96: . . . und grôz guot in dich güzze, sô er dich alsô ledic und blôz vindet (my trans.).

55. Pr. 103.108–9: Daz bevinden en ist niht in dînem gewalt, mêr: ez ist in dem sînem. Sô ez im vüeget. Er mac sich zöugen, sô er wil, und mach sich verbergen, sô er wil. Eckhart supports this by citing the "Spirit breathing where it will" from John 3:8. (He later gives a purely natural reading of this text in In Ioh. nn.331–34 [LW 3:280–83]).

56. These three hindrances (*zît/menige/materie* [Pr. 103.125–26]) occur elsewhere in Eckhart's sermons; see, e.g., Pr. 11 and 12 (DW 1:178ff. and 193ff.).

57. Pr. 103.126–38: Wenne disiu geburt in der wârheit geschehen ist, sô enmügen dich alle crêatûren niht gehindern, mêr: sie wîsent dich alle ze gote und ze dirre geburt. . . . jâ, alliu dinc werdent dir lûter got, wan in allen dingen sô enmeinest noch enminnest dû niht dan lûter got. Rehte als ob ein mensche lange die sunne anesaehe an dem himel, waz er dar nâch saehe, dâ bildete sich diu sunne inne (Walsh trans. modified). The second sign, engendering many good images in one instant, is treated in Pr. 104 and will be discussed below. Other signs of the birth are being able to act and love "without a why," as Eckhart says in BgT 1 (DW 5:43.20–25), and grieving for nothing that has happened to us, even sin (Pr. 76 in DW 3:325–28).

58. Pr. 103.155–57: Mit der minne überwindest dû in allerschierest und mit der minne beladest dû in allersêrest. Dar umbe enlâget got mit keinen dingen sô sêre an uns als der minne.

59. Pr. 103.176–77: Dar umbe warte aleine disem angele, sô wirst dû saeliclîche gevangen, unde ie gevangener, ie vrîer.

60. Steer, "Meister Eckharts Predigtzyklus," 264–66.

61. Pr. 104A.5–8: . . . der êwigen gebürte, diu zîtlich ist worden unde noch tegelîche geborn wirt in der sêle innerstem und in irme grunde âne allen zuoval (my trans.).

62. Pr. 104A.23–25: Und daz muoz geschehen mit grôzem gewalt, daz alle krefte zerücke suln getriben werden und irs werkes abegân.

63. It is important to keep in mind that in this part of the sermon Eckhart is talking about the faculty or power of the intellect and not about the soul's ground. Hence, although at first glance some of what he says here seems to be at odds with statements made in the previous sermons, if we keep in mind that he is talking about the *effect* that the eternal birth, which happens in the ground, has upon the external powers, we will see that he is really only filling in the picture for his students.

64. The active and passive intellects were scholastic commonplaces derived from Aristotle's *De anima* 3.18 (430a). This distinction was well known to Eckhart; see, e.g., Pr. 18 (DW 1:303), Pr. 37 (DW 2:220.1–221.1), In Sap. n.93 (LW 2:427), S. X n. 109 (LW 4:102). This passage, with its threefold distinction, seems original to Eckhart and is not repeated elsewhere, but it can be compared with Pr. 71 (DW 3:215.4–11) where Eck-

hart distinguishes the *suochende vernünfticheit* (i.e., active intellect) from a higher *ander vernünfticheit, diu dâ niht ensuochet.* For more on intellect in Eckhart, see chapter 5.

65. Pr. 104A.54–75: Aber diu mügelîche vernunft diu luoget ze in beiden: waz got gewürken müge und der geist gelîden, daz daz ervolget werde nâch mügelicheit. . . . Und ê diz anegevangen werde von dem geiste und von gote volbrâht, sô hât der geist ein anesehen dar zuo und ein mügelich erkennen, daz ez allez wol geschehen mac und möhte, und daz heizet diu mügelîche vernunft, aleine si doch vil versûmet werde und niemer ze vruht enkome (Walshe trans. modified). In Pr. 103 Eckhart denied the possibility of any preparation or cooperation on our part with regard to the birth (Pr. 103.85–88). This need not contradict the above passage, *if* we allow that here the Dominican is speaking about a stage *prior* to the work of the birth itself. It is also possible that he is merely reflecting good Augustinian and Thomistic grace doctrine—we can do nothing for salvation *on our own;* all cooperative grace presupposes God's operative grace.

66. Pr. 104A.75–79: Sô sich aber der geist üebet nach sîner maht in rehten triuwen, sô underwindet sich sîn gotes geist und des werkes und denne sô schouwet unde lîdet der geist got (Walshe trans. modified).

67. Pr. 104A.126–28: Wan got enist niht ein zerstoerer der nâtûre, mêr: er volbringet sîe. . . . Eckhart also speaks of grace not destroying, but fulfilling nature in RdU 22 (DW 5:288–89). This is good Thomistic doctrine; e.g., STh 1a, q.1, a.8c: Cum enim gratia non tollat naturam, sed perficit. . . .

68. The text of this passage in Pfeiffer has *der heilige Thomas,* but Steer has shown that the better manuscripts have the original *Meister Thomas,* thus showing that the sermon was written before Thomas's canonization in 1323. Pr. 104A.155–59: Meister Thomas sprichet, dâ sî daz würkende leben bezzer dan daz schouwende leben, dâ man in der würklicheit ûzgiuzet von minne, daz man îngenommen hât in der schouwunge. This passage refers to STh 2a2ae q.182, a.2: Potest tamen contingere quod aliquis in operibus vitae activae plus meretur quam alius in operibus vitae contemplativae; puta si propter abundantiam divini amoris, ut eius voluntas impleatur propter ipsius gloriam, interdum sustinet a dulcedine divinae contemplationis ad tempus separari.

69. Pr. 86 (DW 3:481–92). See the discussion at the end of chapter 6 below.

70. Pr. 104A.159–73: Alsô in dirre würklicheit enhât man anders niht dan eine schouwelicheit in gote. Daz eine ruowet in dem andern unde volbringet daz ander.

71. In concluding (Pr. 104A.199–209), Eckhart has strong words of criticism for those who care only for the contemplative life and neglect the active.

72. Pr. 104A.236–43: Sehet, allez daz diu würkende vernunft tuot an einem nâtiurlîchen menschen, daz selbe und verre mê tuot got in einem abegescheiden menschen. Er nimet im abe die würkende vernunft und setzet sich selber an ir stat wider und würket selber dâ allez daz, daz diu würkende vernunft solte würken. This is the only time that the word *abegescheiden* appears in these sermons.

73. Pr. 104A.319–30: Dar umbe gerüeret diu vernunft niemer in disem lebene. . . . Got offenbâret sich niemer sô sêre in disem lebene, ez ensî nochdenne ein niht gegen dem, daz er ist. Wie daz diu wârheit sî in dem grunde, si ist aber bedecket unde verborgen der vernunft.

74. Pr. 104A.374–78: . . . waz denne in dir geborn wirt und dich begrîfet, . . . daz enist alzemâle niht dîn, ez ist alzemâle dînes gotes. . . .

75. Pr. 104A.396–403: Rehte alsô ist ez in der sêle. Got der gebirt in der sêle sîne geburt unde sîn wort, und diu sêle enpfaehet ez und gibet ez vürbaz den kreften in maniger wîse, nû in einer begerunge, nû in guoter meinunge, nû in minnewerken, nû

in dankbaerkeit, oder swie ez dich rüeret. Ez ist allez sîn und niht dîn mit nihte. Eckhart again appeals to Paul to support this position, citing Rom. 8:26 and 1 Cor. 12:13. On the use of *geburt* as meaning "Son" and not "birth," see Pr. 75 (DW 3:299.1–9), and the remarks in Steer, "Predigt 101," 286.

76. The proper understanding of the relation between outer and inner works was a major theme of the RdU; see especially RdU 7, 16, 21, and 23 (DW 5:210–11, 247–48, 275–76, and 290–309). An interesting comparison could be made between RdU 23 (DW 5:290–92) and Prr. 103–4.

77. Pr. 104A.567–70: Dû solt haben ein ûferhaben gemüete, niht ein niderhangendez, mêr: ein brinnendez, und daz in einer lîdender swîgender stilheit.

78. Pr. 104A.579–85: Daz wir hie dirre ruowe und disem inwendigen swîgenne alsô volgen, daz daz êwic wort in uns gesprochen werde und verstanden, daz wir einez werden mit im, des helfe uns der vater und daz selbe wort und ir beider geist. Amen.

Chapter 5
The Metaphysics of Flow

1. The term "metaphysics of flow" was used by Alain de Libera to characterize the philosophy of Eckhart's teacher, Albert; see *Albert le Grand et la philosophie* (Paris: Vrin, 1990), chap. 4. Although Eckhart's thought differs from Albert in particulars, the term also describes his metaphysics.

2. *Poems of Gerard Manley Hopkins*, 3rd ed. (London: Oxford University Press, 1948), no. 116.

3. Pr. 53 (DW 2:530.3–4). For a collection of texts on *exitus* and *reditus*, see "2. Theological Summary," in *Essential Eckhart*, 30.

4. For a brief introduction to the history of *exitus-reditus* in Christian thought, see Paul Rorem, "Procession and Return in Thomas Aquinas and His Predecessors," *Princeton Seminary Bulletin* 13 (1992): 147–63.

5. Eckhart uses Eccli. 1:7 at least thirteen times in his Latin works, though only sparingly in the vernacular writings.

6. On the "Granum sinapis," see especially Alois M. Haas, "Granum sinapis—An den Grenzen der Sprache," in *Sermo Mysticus: Studien zu Theologie und Sprache der deutschen Mystik* (Freiburg, Switzerland: Universitätsverlag, 1979), 301–29.

7. Obviously, *ebullitio* involves formal, or exemplary, causality along with efficient and final. *Bullitio* is purely formal.

8. Sermo XLIX.3, n.511 (LW 4:425.14–426.12): *IMAGO.* Nota quod imago proprie est emanatio simplex, formalis transfusiva totius essentiae purae nudae, . . . Est ergo emanatio ab intimis in silentio et exclusione omnis forinseci, vita quaedam, ac si imagineris rem ex se ipsa et in se ipsa intumescere et bullire in se ipsa necdum cointellecta ebullitione. . . . Primus, . . . quo quid producitur a se et de se ipso et in se ipso naturam nudam . . . , eo siquidem modo quo bonum est diffusivum sui. . . . Secundus gradus est quasi ebullitio sub ratione efficientis et in ordine finis, quo modo producit quid a se ipso, sed non de se ipso. Aut ergo de alio quolibet, et dicatur factio; aut de nihilo, et est tertius gradus productionis, qui dicitur creatio. On the teaching regarding *imago* in this sermon, see Donald F. Duclow, "'Whose Image is This?' in Eckhart's *Sermones*," *Mystics Quarterly* 15 (1989): 29–40. For more on the difference between *productio* in God and outside God, see In Gen.II nn.8–10 (LW 1:479–91).

9. One of the first to note the importance of *bullitio-ebullitio* in Eckhart was

Vladimir Lossky, *Théologie négative et connaissance de Dieu chez Maître Eckhart* (Paris: Vrin, 1960), 116–20. There are useful remarks in Lyndon P. Reynolds, "*Bullitio* and the God beyond God: Meister Eckhart's Trinitarian Theology," *New Blackfriars* 70 (1989): 169–81, 235–44.

10. This *reditio completa* of the divine nature upon itself was central to Eckhart's dynamic view of the *emanatio* within God (i.e., *bullitio*, not *ebullitio*). It occurs in many places in his Latin works; e.g., here in In Ex. nn.16–17 (LW 2:22–23), and also In Ex. n.74; In Eccli. n.10; In Sap. n.5 (LW 2:77, 239, 326–27); In Ioh. n.222 (LW 3:186); and S. XLIX.2 and S. LII (LW 4:425 and 438). Eckhart often cited the *auctoritas* of *Liber de causis* 15: "Omnis sciens qui scit essentiam suam [i.e., substantia divina] est rediens ad essentiam suam reditione completa" (see *Le LIBER DE CAUSIS: Édition établie à l'aide de 90 manuscrits avec introduction et notes,* ed. Adriaan Pattin [Leuven: Uitgave van "Tijdschrift voor Filosofie," n.d.], 79). The notion is ultimately derived from Proclus's *Elements of Theology,* prop. 83 (see *Proclus: The Elements of Theology,* ed. E. J. Dodds, 2nd ed. [Oxford: Clarendon Press, 1963], 76–79).

11. In Ex. n.16 (LW 2:21.7–22.1): . . . puritatem affirmationis excluso omni negativo ab ipso deo indicat; rursus ipsius esse quandam in se ipsum et super se ipsum reflexivam conversionem et in se ipso mansionem sive fixionem; adhuc autem quandam bullitionem sive parturitionem sui—in se fervens et in se ipso et in se ipsum liquescens et bulliens, lux in luce et in lucem se toto se totum penetrans, et se toto super se totum conversum et reflexum undique. . . .

12. S. XXV.1, nn.258–59 (LW 4:236.2–237.2): Secunda gratia procedit a deo sub ratione et proprietate personalis notionis. . . . Rursus deus sub ratione boni est principium ebullitionis ad extra, sub ratione vero notionis est principium bullitionis in se ipso, quae se habet causaliter et exemplariter ad ebullitionem. . . . Adhuc prima gratia consistit in quodam effluxu, egressu a deo. Secunda consistit in quodam refluxu sive regressu in ipsum deum.

13. In Io. n.564 (LW 3:492.9–11): . . . unum fons est primo primae emanationis, filii scilicet et spiritus sancti a patre aeterna processione; bonum autem fons est secundae, ut sic dicamus, temporalis productionis creaturae. . . .

14. Pr. 38 (DW 2:243.5–24.1): Ich spriche etwenne von zwein brunnen. . . . Ein brune, dâ diu gnâde ûz entspringet, ist, dâ der vater ûzgebirt sînen engebornen sun; . . . . Ein ander brunne ist, dâ die crêatûren ûz gote vliezent . . . (my trans.). The grace referred to in the former case is obviously *gratia gratum faciens.*

15. Pr. 35 (DW 2:180.5–7): Der êrste ûzbruch und das êrste ûzsmelzen, dâ got ûzsmilzet, dâ smilzet er in sînen sun, und dâ smilzet er wider in den vater (Walshe trans.). For comparable passages, see, e.g., Prr. 3 and 7 (DW 1:54, 123).

16. For an introduction to Eckhart's MHG terminology on the Trinity as the source of all emanation, see Kurt Ruh, "Die trinitarische Spekulation in deutscher Mystik," in *Kleine Schriften,* vol. 2, *Scholastik und Mystik im Spätmittelalter,* ed. Volker Mertens (Berlin/New York: Walter de Gruyter, 1984), 33–36. Key terms are also treated in Michael Egerding, *Die Metaphorik der spätmittelalterlichen Mystik,* 2 vols. (Paderborn: Schöningh, 1997), vol. 2, especially under *brechen* (pp. 129–33), *brunne* (pp. 139–42), *smelzen* (pp. 524–25), and *vliessen* (pp. 633–43).

17. For other appearances of *bullitio-ebullitio,* see, e.g., S. XXV n.263 (LW 4:239–40); and In Sap. n.283 (LW 2:615–16).

18. The most complete presentation of Albert's metaphysics of flow is to be found in his treatise *De causis et processu universitatis a Prima Causa,* edited by Winfried Fauser in *Alberti Magni Opera Omnia* (Monasterii Westfalorum: Aschendorff, 1993),

vol. 17, part 2. For the use of *ebullitio* to describe the emanative process, see Albert's *De animalibus* XX.2.1, as found in *Albertus Magnus: De animalibus libri XXVI,* ed. Hermann Stadler, Beiträge zur Geschichte der Philosophie des Mittelalters 16 (Münster: Aschendorff, 1920), 1306–8.

19. For Dietrich of Freiberg's use of *ebullitio,* see Alain de Libera, *La mystique rhénane d'Albert le Grand à Maître Eckhart* (Paris: Éditions du Seuil, 1994), 196–97. Sample texts can be found in his *De intellectu et intelligibili* 1.5.2 and 1.8.2. See *Dietrich von Freiberg. Opera Omnia,* ed. Burkhard Mojsisch et al. (Hamburg: Felix Meiner, 1977–), 1:139, 142.

20. Berthold of Moosburg used *ebullitio* to characterize how the first species of Eriugena's *natura* flows into the primordial causes of the second species in his comment on a passage from the *Clavis physicae,* the twelfth-century abridgment of John Scottus Eriugena's *Periphyseon.* See Berthold, *Expositio super Elementationem theologicam Procli,* ed. Loris Sturlese, Maria Rita Pagnoni-Sturlese, and Burkhard Mojsisch (Hamburg: Felix Meiner, 1984–), prop. 18B (47.123–28), with reference to *Honorius Augustodunensis. Clavis physicae,* ed. Paolo Lucentini (Rome: Edizioni di Storia e Letteratura, 1974), 126–27. For Berthold's use of *ebullitio,* see de Libera, *La mystique rhénane,* 353–56, 362–64, and 384.

21. See Thomas Aquinas, *In III Sent.* d.27, q.1, a.1, ad 4: . . . dicitur amor extasim facere et fervere, quia fervet, *extra se ebullit,* et exhalet. Aquinas here is putting together passages from Dionysius's *De divinis nominibus* 4.13 (PG 3:711A) and *De caelesti hierarchia* 7.1 (PG 3:205C).

22. Marguerite Porete, *Le Mirouer des simples ames,* ed. Romana Guarnieri and Paul Verdeyen (Turnhout: Brepols, 1986), chap. 64 (pp. 186–87): Haec sola dongeria amoris, dicit Amor, dant sibi profundationem et cumulationem et attingentiam bullitionis amoris [French: boillon de amour], iuxta testimonium ipsiusmet amoris.

23. A good treatment of *principium* and the role of "principial knowing" (i.e., seeing all things from the divine perspective) can be found in C. F. Kelley, *Meister Eckhart on Divine Knowledge* (New Haven: Yale University Press, 1977). See also Erwin Waldschütz, *Denken und Erfahrung des Grundes: Zur philosophischen Deutung Meister Eckharts* (Vienna/Freiburg/Basel: Herder, 1989), part 2.

24. In Ioh. n.342 (LW 3:291.4–8) Unum autem per se principiat et dat esse et principium est intra. Et propter hoc proprie non producit simile, sed unum et idem se ipsum. . . . Hinc est quod in divinis personis emanatio est formalis quaedam ebullitio [*sic*], et propter hoc tres personae sunt simpliciter unum et absolute. The use of *ebullitio* here goes against all Eckhart's other formulations and hence I consider it a scribal error and translate as *bullitio.* Alain de Libera accepts *ebullitio* ("L'être et le bien: Exode 3,14 dans la théologie rhénane," in *Celui qui est: Interprétations juives et chrétiennes d'Exode 3.14,* ed. Alain de Libera and Emilie Zum Brunn [Paris: Cerf, 1986], 155–56).

25. See In Eccli. n.12 (LW 2:241–42).

26. In Ioh. n.656 (LW 3:570.13–571.2): Item secundo: filius est principium de principio, pater "principium sine principio"; oportet ergo filium adire patrem qui fons est totius deitatis, ut ibi accipiat quod fluat, secundum illud Eccl. 1: "ad locum unde exeunt flumina, revertuntur, ut iterum fluant." The characterization of the Father as *principium sine principio* and the Son as *principium de principio,* often repeated by Eckhart, was first advanced by Augustine, *Contra Maximinum* 2.17.4 (PL 42:784), and was common among the scholastics. Augustine also describes the Father as "principium . . . totius divinitatis" in *De Trinitate* 4.20.29 (PL 42:908). Eckhart cites this elsewhere; e.g., In Ioh. n.568 (LW 3:495); S. II nn.4 and 10 (LW 4:7 and 11).

27. In Ioh. nn.546–76 (LW 3:477–506), to be treated below.

28. In Gen.I nn.3–7 (LW 1:186–91). Eckhart also analyzes the verse in the Prol.gen. nn.14–22 (LW 1:159–65).

29. Here Eckhart agrees with a major theme of Thomas Aquinas's teaching on creation as found, for example, in STh 1a, q.46, a.1, especially ad 6, and ad 9.

30. In Gen.I n.7 (LW 1:190.1–12): Rursus tertio principium, in quo *deus creavit caelum et terram*, est primum nunc simplex aeternitatis, ipsum, inquam, idem nunc penitus, in quo deus est ab aeterno, in quo etiam est, fuit et erit aeternaliter personarum divinarum emanatio. . . . Simul enim et semel quo deus fit, quo filium sibi coaeternum per omnia coaequalem deum genuit, etiam mundum creavit.

31. Eckhart often used Ps. 61:12, both in this sense (e.g., In Ioh. n.73 [LW 3:61], Pr. 30 [DW 2:98]) and with other connotations; see, e.g., In Gen.II n.16 (LW 1:486); In Ex. n.97 (LW 2:101); In Ioh. nn.163, 486, 639 (LW 3:135, 418, 555); Pr. 53 (DW 2:536).

32. See STh 1a, q.45, a.6; and the *Commentarium in Epistolam ad Romanos* cap. 1, lect. 6.

33. See "In agro dominico" arts. 1 and 3, both drawn from In Gen.I n.7 (LW 1:190–91). The second article, taken from In Ioh. n.216 (LW 3:187) also deals with the eternity of the universe.

34. E.g., Augustine, *De Trinitate* 6.10.12 (PL 42:932); and Thomas Aquinas, STh 1a, q.46, a.7.

35. On the a priori aspect of Eckhart's trinitarianism, see Reynolds, "*Bullitio* and the God beyond God," 170–71, 240–41.

36. S. IV (LW 4:22–32). The Romans verse forms the theme of the sermon, being repeated ten times. As expressing proper attributes of the three Persons, see especially nn.21–22 (LW 4:23–24). For a commentary on this sermon, see Bernard McGinn, "Sermo IV," in *Lectura Eckhardi*, 289–316.

37. Werner Beierwaltes, "Unity and Trinity East and West," in *Eriugena East and West*, ed. Bernard McGinn and Willemien Otten (Notre Dame, Ind.: University of Notre Dame Press, 1995), 211.

38. In Sap. n.28 (LW 2:348.9–11): Sic ergo omnis actio naturae, moris et artis habet de sui integritate tria, puta generans, genitum et amorem gignentis ad genitum et geniti ad gignentem. . . . A more detailed development can be found In Ioh. nn.361–67 (LW 3:306–12).

39. Eckhart's comment on Gen. 1:1 takes up In Gen.II nn.8–40 (LW 1:479–507) and treats three themes: (1) "productio sive emanatio filii et spiritus sancti a patre aeternaliter"; (2) "item productio sive creatio generalis totius universi ab uno deo temporaliter"; and (3) "et plura quantum ad proprietates tam creatoris quam creaturarum" (n.8 [LW 1:479.4–7]). For other texts dealing with *principium* in this work, see In Gen.II nn. 49–50 and 111–12 (LW 1:517–18, 576–78).

40. The entire comment on John 1:1 takes up In Ioh. nn.4–51 (LW 3:5–43). The key passages are nn.4–14, 19–21, and 28–51. There is an English translation in *Essential Eckhart*, 123–40. For a commentary with references to secondary literature, see Largier 2:835–67.

41. In Ioh. n.6 (LW 3:8.1–5): Arca enim in mente artificis non est arca, sed est vita et intelligere artificis, ipsius conceptio actualis. Quod pro tanto dixerim, ut verba hic scripta de divinarum personarum processione doceant hoc ipsum esse et inveniri in processione et productione omnis entis naturae et artis. Although his topic here is the divine *bullitio*, the inner unity of *bullitio* and *ebullitio* allows Eckhart to refer to the trinitarian aspect of all making often in his commentary (e.g., In Ioh. nn.7, 10–11, 13,

14–22, 25, 30–31, 36–37, 46, etc). This parallelism is found throughout Eckhart's writings.

42. On *reductio* in Bonaventure's theology, see Bernard McGinn, *The Flowering of Mysticism: Men and Women in the New Mysticism (1200–1350)* (New York: Crossroad, 1998), 91–92.

43. In the course of this explanation, Eckhart provides an exemplary summary of his teaching on the *emanatio* in the Trinity in n.35 (LW 3:29–30).

44. In Ioh. n.45 (LW 3:37.8–9): Notandum quod res omnes universi non erant "ante constitutionem mundi" nihil, sed esse quoddam virtuale habebant. . . . In the history of Christian thought the concept of the virtual existence of all things in the Divine Word goes back at least as far as Origen (e.g., *De principiis* 1.4.3–5). Thomas Aquinas put it as follows: . . . esse rei quod habet in Verbo, non est aliud ab esse Verbi; . . . unde hoc modo cognoscere creaturam in Verbo non esset cognitio creaturae, sed magis Creatoris (*De veritate* q.8, a.16c).

45. E.g., In Ioh. nn.73–74, 134–39, 336–38, 359, 362–63, 479, 562, 566–69, and 573 (LW 3:61–62, 115–17, 284–87, 304, 307–8, 411–12, 489, 494–97, and 500). For appearances elsewhere, see In Ex. nn.28 and 265 (LW 2:32, 213–14); In Eccli. nn.9, 12, 56–57 (LW 2:237–38, 241, 284–86); In Sap. nn.161–62, 175, 193 (LW 2:497–98, 510–11, 529); SS. II and XV (LW 4:8, 145–46).

46. Pr. 22 (DW 1:382.3–6): "'In principio.' Hie ist uns ze verstânne geben, daz wir ein einiger sun sîn, den der vater êwiclîche geborn hât ûz dem verborgenen vinsternisse der êwigen verborgenheit, inneblîbende in dem êrsten beginne der êrsten lûterkeit, dui dâ ist ein vûlle aller lûterkeit" (trans. *Essential Eckhart*). Later in the sermon Eckhart says: "'In principio' daz sprichet als vil ze tiutsche als ein angenge alles wesens, als ich sprach in der schuole; ich sprach noch mê: ez ist ein ende alles wesens, wan der êrste begin ist durch des lesten endes willen" (389.1–3).

47. BgT 1 (DW 5:30–34). A key passage reads: Ein [i.e., the Father] ist *begin* âne allen *begin*. Glîchnisse [i.e., the Son] ist *begin* von dem einen aleine und nimet, daz ez *begin* ist, von dem und in dem einen. Minne [i.e., the Holy Spirit] hât von ir natûre, daz si vluizet und urspringet von zwein als ein (30.13–16; my italics).

48. For an introduction to Eckhart's view of the Trinity, see Bernard McGinn, "A Prolegomenon to the Role of the Trinity in Meister Eckhart's Mysticism," *Eckhart Review* (spring 1997): 51–61; and the longer German version, "Sermo IV," in *Lectura Eckhardi*, 289–316. In the large literature relating to Eckhart's view of the Trinity, I have found the following especially helpful: R.-L. Oechslin, "Eckhart et la mystique trinitaire," *Lumière et vie* 30 (1956): 99–120; idem, "Der Eine und Dreieinige in den deutschen Predigten," in *Meister Eckhart der Prediger: Festschrift zum Eckhart-Gedenkjahr,* ed. Udo M. Nix and Raphael Öchslin (Freiburg: Herder, 1960), 149–66; Reynolds, "*Bullitio* and the God beyond God"; Alain de Libera, "L'Un ou la Trinité," *Revue des sciences religieuses* 70 (1996): 31–47; and Rainer Haucke, *Trinität und Denken: Die Unterscheidung der Einheit von Gott und Mensch bei Eckhart* (Frankfurt: Peter Lang, 1986).

49. For some aspects of this issue, see Bernard McGinn, "The God beyond God: Theology and Mysticism in the Thought of Meister Eckhart," *Journal of Religion* 61 (1981): 1–19.

50. The three treatises on the Trinity are found in In Ioh. nn.358–67, 511–18, and 546–76 (LW 3:303–12, 442–48, and 477–506). The last has been translated into English in *Teacher and Preacher,* 182–93. S. IV can be found in LW 4:22–32 and is available in *Teacher and Preacher,* 207–12. In addition, there are many other passages in the Latin works of importance for Eckhart's trinitarianism. These occur not only in the John

commentary (e.g., nn.4–27, 32–36, 40–50, 56–60, 82, 160–66, 187–98, 411–14, 422–25, 437–38, 468–69, 641, 656), but also throughout Eckhart's biblical expositions; e.g., In Gen.II nn.9–20, 44, 48–51, 179–80, 214–17; In Ex. nn.16, 28, 56, 62–65, 70–72); In Eccli. nn.11–12, 23; In Sap. nn.27–29, 64–67, 89, 192; see also SS. II nn.3–18, XXXV nn.357–63, XXXVI nn.366–67, and XLIX n.512.

51. At least thirty-four of Eckhart's MHG sermons contain discussions of the Trinity. Among the most important are Pr. 10 (DW 1:173); Prr. 35, 47, 49 (DW 2:180–81, 394–96, 433–35); Prr. 67, 83 (DW 3:132–34, 446–48). See also BgT 1.1 (DW 5:30–34, 41–42).

52. It is customary in Latin theology to distinguish two *processiones* in God, the procession of the Son from the Father by way of *generatio,* and the procession of the Holy Spirit from both Father and Son by *spiratio.*

53. By Eckhart's time, scholastics generally made a threefold distinction among the attributes ascribed to God, distinguishing (1) *common or essential* attributes (i.e., those predicated of all three Persons, such as infinity); (2) *proper or personal* (often *notio personalis* in Eckhart) attributes (those that are peculiar to one Person, such as "begotten" of the Son); and (3) *appropriated* attributes (those that are really common to all three Persons, but that are traditionally ascribed to one or the other Person). For a classic discussion of appropriated attributes, see Aquinas, STh 1a, q.39, a.8.

54. For some comments on the Dionysianism of Eckhart's view of the Trinity, see de Libera, "L'Un ou la Trinité?"

55. Pr. 10 (DW 1:173.1–5): Ich predigete einest in latîne, und daz was an dem tage der drîvalticheit, dô sprach ich: der underscheit kumet von der einicheit, der underscheit in der drîvalticheit. Diu einicheit ist der underscheit, und der underscheit ist diu einicheit. Ie der underscheit mêr ist, ie diu einicheit mêr ist, wan das ist underscheit âne underscheit (my trans.). Josef Quint in his note to this passage suggests that Eckhart has S. II n.14 in mind, but the same teaching is also found in S. IV. On this sermon, see the remarks in W. Goris, *Einheit als Prinzip und Ziel: Versuch über die Einheitsmetaphysik des "Opus tripartitum" Meister Eckharts* (Leiden: Brill, 1997), 228–37.

56. S. XI n.118 (LW 4:112.5–6): Deus autem est ab omni numero proprie eximitur. Est enim unus sine unitate, trinus sine trinitate, sicut bonus sine qualitate, ... There are many parallels in the Latin texts, and also in the MHG sermons, e.g., Pr. 38 (DW 2:234). God's freedom from all number is part of the wider aseity which also frees him from place (*locus*) and time (*tempus*). Because God is *illocalis* (e.g., In Sap. n.133 [LW 2:471]), he can be described as the *locus omnium* (e.g., In Ioh. nn.199–205 [LW 3:168–73]; S.V n.51 [LW 4:48]). Eckhart's thought on God as the "place" of all things makes for interesting comparisons with the thought of Eriugena and Maimonides. See Yossef Schwartz, "'Ecce est locus apud me': Maimonides und Eckharts Raumvorstellung als Begriff des Göttlichen," in *Raum und Raumvorstellungen im Mittelalter,* ed. Jan A. Aertsen and Andreas Speer (Berlin/New York: Walter de Gruyter, 1998), 348–64.

57. Pr. 38 (DW 2:234) speaks of the Godhead having distinction without number or quantity even if there were a hundred Persons there. (A similar formulation is found in Par.an., No. 4 [ed. 15.18–20].) Two important hyperbolic passages in the Wisdom commentary make the same point. In Sap. n.38 (LW 2:360.1–3) says: Hinc est quod tres personae in divinis, quamvis sint plures, non tamen multa, sed unum, etiam si essent personae mille (see also In Sap. n.112 [LW 2:449]).

58. In Ex. n.60 (LW 2:66.6): Nulla igitur in ipso deo distinctio esse potest aut intelligi. This passage was part of a long text singled out as art. 23 in the bull of condemnation. The "absolute Oneness" of God will be taken up in greater detail below.

59. Pfeiffer LVI (ed. 180.15–16): Nû wil ich aber sprechen daz ich nie gesprach: got unde gotheit hât underscheit als verre als himel und erde (trans. Walshe). This sermon was not originally accepted as authentic by Quint, but has been considered as such by Walshe and O. Davies (*Meister Eckhart: Selected Writings,* 232–34). It will appear in DW 4.

60. An important issue on which Eckhart is not always clear is the relation between the hidden Godhead, or "God beyond God," suggested by some vernacular texts (e.g., Prr. 48, 67, 83, Pfeiffer LVI) and the *divina essentia* and *deitas* of the Latin writings. L. Reynolds argues that "we should be wary of attributing to Eckhart the belief that there is some distance or distinction between the essence and the Persons, or of assuming that when Eckhart does distinguish between the Trinity and the hidden Godhead he is distinguishing between the Persons and the essence" (*"Bullitio* and the God beyond God," 178, cf. 236). It is true that Eckhart does not make an explicit identification of the *gotheit* of the MHG sermons and the *deitas* or *essentia divina.* It is also true that the kind of radical formulations found in the MHG sermons are generally absent from the Latin works. However, (1) the passage cited from Pr. 10 indicates that Eckhart *thought* he was propounding the same teaching in both the Latin and the vernacular sermons; (2) the distinction of Persons and essence (*deitas*) is strongly, if dialectically, expressed in places in the John commentary (e.g., In Ioh. nn.562, 564); and (3) Reynolds himself admits that Eckhart's teaching suggests that "there is a non-relative aspect" in God (art., 236, 242–43).

61. Pr. 24 (DW 1:419.4–5): . . . wan in dem grunde götlîches wesens, dâ die drîe per-sônen éin wesen sint, dâ ist si ein nâch dem grunde (trans. Walshe).

62. In Pr. 2, Eckhart uses the language of "looking into the *einic ein*" beyond the three Persons (DW 1:43–44), though the sermon also speaks of the *grunde* earlier (31.1–3). Pr. 48 explicitly speaks of the "simple ground" into which the distinct Person never gazed (DW 2:420–21). Pr. 69 (DW 3:178–80) and Pfeiffer LVI (ed., 181) talk of getting rid of "God" by breaking through into the ground. Only two sermons contain such radical formulae without using *grunt*—Pr. 52 (DW 2:499–505) and Pr. 83 (DW 3:447–48). One of Eckhart's most memorable images in his MHG sermons is that of "taking God naked as he is in his dressing room" (e.g., Prr. 11, 37, 40, 59 [DW 1:183–84; DW 2:217, 274, 636]). This too may be thought of as a way of presenting the break-through beyond the distinction of Persons into the naked ground of the Godhead.

63. S. IV n.30 (LW 2:31.1–8): In summa nota quod omne quod de trinitate beata scribitur aut dicitur, nequaquam sic se habet aut verum est. . . . Verum quidem est quod est aliquid in deo respondens trinitati quam dicimus et ceteris similibus. Passages like this can be paralleled throughout Eckhart's Latin and German works (e.g., Pr. 51 [DW 2:467.7–10]).

64. Eckhart's notion of God as "pure possibility," what Pr. 48 describes as the "sim-ple silence, in itself immovable, and by this immovability all things are moved" (DW 2:421), is different from Aquinas's notion of the divine nature as pure act, *ipsum esse subsistens.* The *grunt* is not really the Aristotelian-Thomistic notion of *potentia* either, at least insofar as it lies "beyond" potency understood as a correlative term.

65. Eckhart's view of the divine relations that constitute the three Persons seems to privilege the unity of the divine substance or essence more than that of Thomas Aquinas, at least to the extent that In Ex. nn.63–65 (LW 2:67–70) describes the relations as "as it were standing on the outside," citing without disapproval the suspect view of Gilbert of Poitiers. However, Reynolds (*"Bullitio* and the God beyond God," 178–80) argues that the difference between Aquinas and Eckhart here is at best slight.

66. In Ex. n.28 (LW 2:34.1–4): Rursus potentia generandi in patre est essentia potius quam paternitas, ut dicunt meliores. Propter quod deus pater generat filium deum, sed non generat ipsum patrem. Dat filio esse dei, esse patris, sapere et posse patris, non tamen quod sit pater, sed quod sit filius, relatione oppositus patri. Among the *meliores* signaled out by Eckhart is Thomas Aquinas (STh 1a, q.41, a.5). Eckhart discusses this dictum elsewhere, e.g., In Ex. n.56 (LW 2:61); In Ioh. nn.43 and 468–69 (LW 3:36 and 401); S. II n.6 (LW 4:8). He considered the principle important enough to cite it as one of the examples of *inquantum* predication in his Cologne Defense (Théry, 186).

67. In Ex. n.56 (LW 2:61.6–7): Dicimus tamen vere et proprie quod pater generat, non essentia, filius generatur, non essentia.

68. Attributing *unitas/unum* to the Father, as Eckhart notes (nn.546, 556–57, 562), has been approved by the saints and teachers, especially by Augustine, who is the source of the trinitarian triad of appropriated terms *unitas-aequalitas-connectio/nexus* (see *De doctrina christiana* 1.5.5 [PL 34:21]). Eckhart often appeals to this form of trinitarian language by ascribing *unitas* to the Father; e.g., In Gen.II nn.12 and 215 (LW 1:483, 691); In Ioh. nn.360, 513, 668 (LW 3:305–6, 444, 581). For a history of the development of the triad, see Bernard McGinn, "Does the Trinity Add Up? Transcendental Mathematics and Trinitarian Speculation in the Twelfth and Thirteenth Centuries" (forthcoming).

69. The notion of "property" (*proprietas*) corresponds to the MHG *eigenschaft,* one of the most frequent terms in Eckhart's vocabulary. In general it can be said that the Dominican tends to use *proprietas/eigenschaft* positively when ascribed to God, at least the trinitarian God, but negatively when used of creatures as signifying their particular being (*esse hoc et hoc*). Of course, God too becomes *âne eigenschaft* in the *grunt* (e.g., Pr. 2 [DW 1:43.4–5]). For a study of the MHG uses, see Frank Tobin, "Eckhart's Mystical Use of Language: The Contexts of *eigenschaft,*" *Seminar* 8 (1972): 160–68.

70. In Ioh. n.562 (LW 3:489.1–490.3): Haec quattuor praemissa idem sunt et convertuntur realiter quantum ad suppositum sive subiectum, distinguuntur autem ab invicem propria ratione sive proprietate uniuscuiusque; ratio enim entis est quid abiectum et indistinctum et ipsa sua indistinctione ab aliis distinguitur. Quo etiam modo deus sua indistinctione ab aliis distinctis quibuslibet distinguitur. Hinc est quod ipsa essentia sive esse in divinis ingenitum est et non gignens. Ipsum vero unum ex sui proprietate distinctionem indicat . . . et propter hoc personale est et ad suppositum pertinet cuius est agere. . . . Ex quo patet quod [si] unum sive unitas est post [ens] primum principium omnis emanationis, nihil addens super ens nisi solam negationem negationis. . . . Verum autem ex sui proprietate, cum sit quaedam adaequatio rei et intellectus et proles genita cogniti et cognoscentis, ad filium pertinet, genitum quidem, non gignentem. . . .

71. In Io. n.564 (LW 3:492.3–11): Primum est quod ens sive esse est ingenitum nec gignens nec genitum, sine principio nec ab alio; unum vero est sine principio, ingenitum, sed gignens; verum autem est genitum, sed non gignens, habens principium ab alio; bonum autem est ab alio, habens principium, non genitum, tamen non gignens, sed creans, creata extra in esse producens. . . . Unum fons est primo primae emanationis, filii scilicet et spiritus sancti a patre aeterna processione; bonum autem fons est secundae, ut sic dicamus, temporalis productionis creaturae. . . .

72. See, e.g., In Io. nn.512–13 (LW 3:443–45); In Gen.II nn.12–15 and 215 (LW 1:483–86, 690–91); BgT 1 (DW 5:30).

73. The ascription of *ens* to the Father also occurs in the midst of the third trini-

tarian treatise in the John commentary; see In Io. n.568 (LW 3:496)—a sign that Eckhart was not really concerned about consistency.

74. In Ioh. n.360 (LW 3:304.14–315.4): . . . quod indivisa sunt opera horum trium in creaturis, quarum sunt unum principium. Propter quod in creaturis ens respondens patri, verum respondens filio, bonum respondens appropriate spiritui sancto convertuntur et unum sunt, distincta sola ratione, sicut pater et filius et spiritus sanctus sunt unum, distincta sola relatione. What Eckhart seems to mean here is that *insofar* as he is efficient cause, God is one principle, so that the differing terms *ens-verum-bonum* in creatures are distinct "by reason alone" (*sola ratione*), that is, they are really one in the concrete creature and are distinguished only by different concepts in the mind. There is an (imperfect) parallel between this and the three divine Persons, who are really one in the divine essence, but who are also "distinct by relation alone" (*sola relatione*), that is, *really* distinct insofar as they are different Persons.

75. In Ioh. n.360 (LW 3:305.9–306.2): Nec obstat quod ab Augustino unitas patri appropriatur ratione quidem prioritatis sive fontalis diffusionis et originis, quia has rationes positivas, scilicet prioritatis et huiusmodi, non significat li unum.

76. This would conform to the dialectical treatment of *unum* found In Sap. nn.144–57 (LW 3:481–94).

77. In Ioh. n.556 (LW 3:485.5–7): . . . unum ipsum est negatio negationis, negationis, inquam, quam multitudo omnis qui opponitur unum includit; negatio autem negationis medulla, puritas et geminatio est affirmati esse, Exodi 3, "ego sum qui sum."

78. Pr. 75 (DW 3:293.5–294.2, and 299.3): . . . und alsô liget er kindes als ein vrouwe, diu geborn hât. . . . Pr. 29 (DW 2:86.4–5) uses similar language: Er [the Father] gebirt in nû und hiute. Dâ ist kintbette in der gotheit, dâ werdent sie "getoufet in dem heiligen geiste."

79. See Pr. 40 (DW 2:278).

80. Pf. CIII (ed., 336.23–29): Diu dritte vrâge ist: wâ diu vaterlicheit hât muoterlîchen namen? . . . Dâ sich persônlich verstentnisse heldet zuo der einicheit der nâtûre und gemeinet sich dâ mite, dâ hât diu veterlicheit muoterlîchen namen unde wirket muoterlich werk, wan daz ist eigentlich ein muoterlich werk, daz si enpfâhe dâ daz êwic wort entspringet. In dem wesenlîchen gehügenisse dâ hât diu muoterlicheit vaterlîchen namen und wirket veterlich werk (trans. Walshe)

81. Pr. 71 (DW 3:224.5–7): Ez dûhte einen menschn als in einem troume—ez was ein wachender troume—wie ez swanger würde von niht als ein vrouwe mit einem kinde, und in dem nihte wart got geborn; dér was diu vruht des nihtes (my trans.).

82. Pr. 26 (DW 2:31.5–32.1): Si [die oberste teile der sêle] enwil nit got, als er der heilige geist ist und als er der sun ist, und vliuhet den sun. Si enwil ouch nit got, als er got ist. War umbe? Dâ hât er namen, und waerent tûsent göt, si brichet iemermê durch. si wil in dâ, dâ er niht namen enhât: si wil etwaz edelers, etwaz bezzers dan got, als er namen hât. Waz wil si denne? Si enweiz: si wil in, als er vater ist.

83. Pr. 51 (DW 2:469.9–10): . . . so muoss er geberen sein bild bleibende in im selber grund, das bilde, also als es ewigklich ist gewesen in im (forme illius), daz ist sein form bleybend in im selber (my trans.). It is interesting to see Eckhart use both Latin and MHG here.

84. Pr. 51 (DW 2:470.3–10): . . . vnd doran benueget den vater nit, er ziehe wider in die erstekeit, in das innestes, in den grund vnnd in den kernen der vetterlicheit, da er ewigklich ist inne gewesen in im selber in der vatterschaft vnnd da er gebraucht sein selbs in dem, der vatter als der vatter sein selbs in dem einigen ein. . . . Diss ist das aller best, vnd ich han mich darinn vertoeret. Darumb: alles, das die natur geleisten mag, das

schlüsset sy darzuo, daz stürtzet in die vatterschaft, das sy ein sey vnd ein sun sey vnd entwachse allem dem andern vnd al ein sey in der vaterschafft . . . (my trans.).

85. Pr. 70 (DW 3:197.4–6): Nû spriche ich: "wir suln in bekennen rehte, als er sich selben bekennet" in den widerbilde, daz aleine bilde gotes ist und der gotheit, niht der gotheit dan als vil, als si der vater ist (*Teacher and Preacher* trans. modified). On this passage, see the comments in Largier 2:680–81.

86. S. II n.8 (LW 4:9.11–12): . . . quia processus ille est ad intra, tum quia intellectualis, tum quia nihil est deo extra, ... On Thomas Aquinas's teaching regarding the *emanatio intelligibilis* in God, see STh 1a, q.27, a.1. The difference between *generatio* and all forms of *alteratio*, or change, is an important theme in Eckhart (see, e.g., In Ioh. n.409 [LW 3:348]).

87. Much has been written on Eckhart's teaching on the *verbum*. See especially, Émilie Zum Bruun and Alain de Libera, *Métaphysique du Verbe et théologie négative* (Paris: Beauchesne, 1984).

88. Eckhart's teaching on silence is laid out in detail in the sermon cycle on the eternal birth (Prr. 101–4) discussed above. An important mini-treatise in praise of silence can be found in Pr. 95 (DW 4:192–95). On this theme, see Marco Vannini, "*Praedica Verbum:* La *generazione* della parola dal silenzio in Meister Eckhart," in *Il Silenzio e La Parola da Eckhart a Jabès*, ed. Massimo Baldini and Silvano Zucal (Trent: Morcelliana, 1987), 17–31.

89. In Ioh. n.488 (LW 3:420.11–421.3). Eckhart also quotes Job 33:15–16, and Augustine, *Confessiones* 9.10.24 to confirm God's speaking in the midst of darkness and silence. For a similar vernacular use of Wisdom 18:14, see Pr. 73 (DW 3:266).

90. In Ioh. n.488 (LW 3:421.3–8).

91. In Gen.I n.77 (LW 1:239): . . . verbum, quod est in silentio paterni intellectus, verbum sine verbo aut potius super omne verbum.

92. See especially the comment on *dixitque deus* (Gen. 1:3) in In Gen.II nn.48–51 (LW 1:516–20), where Eckhart shows that God's creative speaking must be understood in light of John 1:1. The same teaching is found in the MHG works; e.g., Pr. 53 (DW 2:535.1–2): Alle crêatûren sint ein sprechen gotes.

93. In Gen.II n.49 (LW 1:519.11–13): Effectus enim in sua causa analoga latet, absonditur, tacet, non loquitur nec auditur, nisi dicatur et producatur verbo intus generato et concepto vel extra prolato. Eckhart refers to the Augustinian distinction between the *verbum interius* and the *verbum exterius* in a number of other places in his Latin works; e.g., In Gen.II nn.111–12 and 148 (LW 1:576–78, 617), In Ioh. n.537 (LW 3:468).

94. Eckhart's teaching on silence has been studied by Karl Albert, "Meister Eckhart über das Schweigen," in *Festschrift für Lauri Seppänen zum 60. Geburtstag* (Tampere: Universität Tampere, 1984), 301–9; and especially Kurt Ruh, "Das mystische Schweigen und die mystische Rede," in *Festschrift für Ingo Reiffenstein zum 60. Geburtstag* (Göppingen: Kümmerle, 1988), 463–72.

95. Pr. 9 (DW 1:157.3–8): Ez ist ein vürbrâht wort, daz ist der engel und der mensche und alle crêatûren. Ez ist ein ander wort, bedâht und unvûrbrâht [not vûrbrâht as in Quint], dâ bî mac ez komen, daz ich mich bilde. Noch ist ein ander wort, daz dâ ist unvürbrâht und unbedâht, daz nimer ûzkumet, mêr ez ist êweclich in dem, der ez sprichet; ez ist iermermê in einem enpfâhenne in dem vater, der ez sprichet, und inneblîbende (trans. *Teacher and Preacher*). Both Tobin (*Teacher and Preacher*, 261 n. 23) and Walshe (2:156 n. 13) argue for "unvûrbrâht" as the better reading to indicate the nature of the human *verbum interius* as contrasted with the divine.

96. The Word that remains eternally within is equivalent to what Eckhart speaks of as "the eternal Word [being] the medium and image itself that is without medium and without image" in Pr. 69 (daz êwic wort ist daz mittel und daz bilde selber, daz dâ ist âne mittel und âne bilde [DW 3:168.8–10]). For a discussion of this aspect of Eckhart's thought, see Zum Bruun and de Libera, *Métaphysique du Verbe*, 172–94, on "Le 'Verbe non dit.'"

97. Pr. 9 (LW 1:158.5–7): Dâ sol diu sêle sîn ein bîwort und mit gote würken ein werk, in dem înswebenden bekantnisse ze nemenne ir saelicheit in dem selben, dâ got saelic ist (*Teacher and Preacher*).

98. Pr. 53 (DW 2:529.6–530.1): Got ist ein wort, daz sich selber sprach. . . . Got ist gesprochen und ungesprochen. Der vater ist ein sprechende werk, und der sun ist ein spruch würkende (trans. Walshe). On this elegant chiastic formula, see the discussion in Frank Tobin, *Meister Eckhart: Thought and Language* (Philadelphia: University of Pennsylvania Press, 1986), 169. Eckhart's teaching on the Father's speaking of the *wort*, and the relation of the Word and silence is found throughout his sermons. For some other important examples, see, e.g., Prr. 1 and 19 (DW 1:15–17, 312); Prr. 30, 36a, and 49 (DW 2:97–98, 189–91, 433–38). See also Pfeiffer CIII (ed., 335–36).

99. It is on this basis that Eckhart can speak of the human soul as co-creator with God; see, e.g., Pr. 52 (DW 2:502–04).

100. Robert K. C. Forman, *Meister Eckhart: Mystic as Theologian* (Rockport: Element Books, 1991), chap. 5, and 166.

101. The discussions of the Holy Spirit in the Latin works are too numerous to list here, but it is instructive to note how often the Spirit's role comes up in the vernacular sermons (see, e.g., Prr. 1, 10, 11, *15*, 18, 20b, *23*, *27*, 29, 37, 41, 53, 65, 69, 76, 81, *82*, 85, 92, with the more important treatments italicized). A. de Libera rightly stresses the importance of Eckhart's doctrine of the Holy Spirit (*La mystique rhénane*, 287–95).

102. On S. IV and the Holy Spirit, see McGinn, "A Prolegomenon to the Role of the Trinity," especially 57–58.

103. S. IV nn.22–23 (LW 4:24.5–11): . . . nota primo quod in ipso spiritu sancto sic sunt omnia, ut quod in ipso non est, necesse sit esse nihil. . . . Secundo nota quod sic *in ipso sunt omnia*, ut si aliquid sit non in ipso spiritu sancto, spiritus sanctus non est deus. In the first form Eckhart, in unusual fashion, takes John 1:3 (*sine ipso factum est nihil*) as referring to the Spirit and not to the Word.

104. S. IV n.28 (LW 4:27.10–28.1): Ubi notandum quod cum dicimus omnia esse in deo, sicut ipse est indistinctus in sui natura et tamen distinctissimus ab omnibus, sic in ipso sunt omnia distinctissime simul et indistincta.

105. S. IV n.24 (LW 4:25.3–5): Tertio, quod sic *in ipso sunt omnia*, ut pater in filio non sit nec in patre filius, si pater non sit unum, id ipsum cum spiritu sancto, aut filius id ipsum quod sit spiritus sanctus.

106. In Ioh. n.438 (LW 3:376.2–5): Li in quantum autem reduplicatio est; reduplicatio vero, sicut ipsum vocabulum testatur, dicit nexum et ordinem duorum; dicitur enim reduplicatio duorum replicatio, plica et nexus duorum. Sic spiritus, tertia in trinitate persona, nexus est duorum, patris et filii.

107. The distinction between *amor concomitans* and *amor spiratus* is discussed in several places. See, e.g., In Ioh. nn.165–66 and 364 (LW 3:136–37 and 308–10), and In Sap. n.28 (LW 2:348–49).

108. See, e.g., S. IV n.25 (LW 4:26); In Ioh. n.506 (LW 3:437–38); Pr. 41 (DW 2:287.7–8); etc.

109. Pr. 27 (DW 2:41.4–42.2): . . . daz die besten meister sprechent, daz diu minne,

mit der wir minnen, ist der heilige geist. Êtliche wâren, die wolten ez widersprechen. Daz ist iemer wâr: alle die bewegede, dâ wir beweget werden ze minne, dâ beweget uns niht anders wan der heilige geist (trans. Walshe slightly modified). See the note on this text in Largier 1:954–56. Other passages in Eckhart make the same case: e.g., Sermo XI n.113 (LW 4:106); Pr. 10 (DW 1:168); Pr. 65 (DW 3:97). There are, however, some texts that seem to go against it; e.g., Pr. 63 (DW 3:74), on which see the remarks of Haug in *Lectura Eckhardi*, 213–14. Peter Lombard's teaching can be found in *Sententiarum Libri IV* I, dist. 17, cap. 1 and 6 (*Magistri Petri Lombardi Sententiae in IV Libris Distinctae*, 3rd ed. [Grottaferrata: Editiones Collegii S. Bonaventurae ad Claras Aquas, 1971], 142 and 149). Thomas Aquinas denies the Lombard's view in STh 2a.2ae, q.23, a.2; but Albert the Great sided with the Lombard (see *In I Sent.* dist. 17, L–R). On this aspect of Eckhart's teaching, see Édouard Wéber, "Eléments néoplatoniciens en théologie mystique au XIIIième siècle," in *Abendländische Mystik im Mittelalter: Symposium Kloster Engelberg*, ed. Kurt Ruh (Stuttgart: Metzler, 1986), 196–207.

110. In Ioh. n.506 (LW 3:437.12–438.2): . . . eo quod una sit facies et imago in qua deus nos videt et nos ipsum, secundum illud: "in lumine tuo videbimus lumen." Sic enim et idem amor est spiritus sanctus quo pater filium diligit et filius patrem, quo deus nos diligit et nos deum.

111. In Ex. n.34 (LW 2:3–10): Licet autem de diversis nominibus dei notaverim in diversis locis. . . . Primo quid philosophi quidam de hoc senserint et quidam Hebraeorum de his attributionibus. Eckhart's treatise on the Divine Names can be found in nn.34–78 and 143–84 of In Ex. (LW 2:40–82, and 130–58). There is a translation in *Teacher and Preacher*, 53–70, and 90–102. In addition to the study of this treatise in the "Introduction. 2. Meister Eckhart on Speaking about God," in *Teacher and Preacher*, 15–30, see the remarks in Tobin, *Meister Eckhart*, 67–78; and Goris, *Einheit als Prinzip und Ziel*, 156–83.

112. Eckhart's early *Sermo die b. Augustini Parisius habitus* (probably 1302) sketches out a theory of two ways of knowing God that remained undeveloped in later works. In nn.4–14 (LW 5:92–99) he distinguishes (1) cognitio "*per speculum et in aenigmate*" (see 1 Cor. 13:12), which operates according to three modes: *ablatio-eminentia-causa*; and (2) cognitio per speculum et in lumine, a specialis irradiatio of grace, that also has three modes: (a) *ad occulta vel futura pronuntiandum* (i.e., prophecy); (b) *ad meritorie operandum* (i.e., workings of grace); and (c) *in exstasi mentis* (i.e., enjoyment of God). For a study of this theory, see Goris, *Einheit als Prinzip und Ziel*, 183–88.

113. For what follows, see Bernard McGinn, "Meister Eckhart on God as Absolute Unity," in *Neoplatonism and Christian Thought*, ed. Dominic O'Meara (Albany: SUNY Press, 1982), 130–35; and Alain de Libera, "À propos de quelques théories logiques de Maître Eckhart: Existe-t-il une tradition médiévale de la logique néo-platonicienne?" *Revue de théologie et de philosophie* 113 (1981): 1–24.

114. Eckhart's most detailed discussion of secundum adiacens and tertium adiacens predication occurs in the Prol.op.prop. nn.1–8 and 25 (LW 1:166–70, 181). See also In Ex. n.15 (LW 2:20); In Sap. n.20 (LW 2:341–42); In Ioh. nn.97, 377 (LW 3:83–84, 321). For a history of the distinction, though one that does not mention Eckhart, see Gabriel Nuchelmans, *Secundum/tertium adiacens: Vicissitudes of a logical distinction* (Amsterdam: Koninklijke Nederlandse Akademie, 1992).

115. E.g., Thomas Aquinas, STh 1a, q.13, a.5; *In Perihermeneias* bk. 2, chap. 10, lect. 2, nn.2–5.

116. Tabula prologorum in op. trip. n.4 (LW 1:132.4–6): Primum est quod solus deus proprie est et dicitur ens, unum, verum et bonum. Secundum est quod omne

quod est ens, unum, verum aut bonum, non habet hoc a se ipso, sed a deo et ab ipso solo.

117. Much has been written about Eckhart's view of analogy. Among the early treatments, see Lossky, *Théologie négative et connaissance de Dieu*, "Index des thèmes," 426; Josef Koch, "Zur Analogielehre Meister Eckharts," in *Mélanges offerts à Etienne Gilson* (Paris: Vrin, 1959), 327–50; and Fernand Brunner, "L'analogie chez Maître Eckhart," *Freiburger Zeitschrift für Philosophie und Theologie* 16 (1969): 333–49. For more recent studies, see especially Alain de Libera, *Le problème de l'être chez Maître Eckhart: Logique et métaphysique de l'analogie* (Geneva: Cahiers de la Revue de théologie et de philosophie, 1980); Burkhard Mojsisch, *Meister Eckhart: Analogie, Univozität und Einheit* (Hamburg: Felix Meiner, 1983), chap. 3; and Reiner Manstetten, *Esse est Deus: Meister Eckharts christologische Versöhnung von Philosophie und Religion und ihre Ursprünge in der Tradition des Abendländes* (Munich: Karl Alber, 1993), 284–302.

118. In Eccli. n.53 (LW 2:282.1–5): . . . analogata nihil in se habent positive radicatum formae secundum quam analogantur. Sed omne ens creatum analogatur deo in esse, veritate et bonitate. Igitur omne ens creatum habet a deo et in deo, non in se ipso ente creato, esse, vivere, sapere positive et radicaliter. Among the other formal discussions of analogy in Eckhart, see In Gen.I n.128 (LW 1:282–83); In Ex. n.54 (LW 2:58–60); In Sap. n.44 (LW 2:367); In Ioh. nn.5–6, 86, 97, 182–83, 492 (LW 3:7, 74, 84, 150–52, 405); and Qu.Par. 1, n.11 (LW 5:46–47). Analogy is often employed in the MHG works, but rarely reflected upon in a formal way.

119. Dietmar Mieth, *Die Einheit von Vita Activa und Vita Passiva in den deutschen Predigten und Traktaten Meister Eckharts und bei Johannes Tauler* (Regensburg: Pustet, 1969), 136: "Analogie ist also nicht wie bei Thomas ein Bezugsverhältnis, sondern ein Abhängigkeitsverhältnis; Analogie erklärt nicht, was ist, sondern wodurch es ist."

120. See Tobin, *Meister Eckhart*, 64; and de Libera, "À propos de quelques théories," 15.

121. The pioneering character of Lossky's *Théologie négative* is nowhere more evident than in its recognition of the importance of Eckhart's dialectic (see "Index des thèmes" under "Dialectique," on p. 431). Also significant was the insightful article of Maurice de Gandillac, "La 'dialectique' du Maître Eckhart," in *La mystique rhénane* (Paris: Presses Universitaires de France, 1963), 59–94; and the reflections in Reiner Schürmann, *Meister Eckhart: Mystic and Philosopher* (Bloomington: Indiana University Press, 1978), 176–92.

122. "In agro dominico," art. 26, drawing on a passage in Pr. 4 (DW 1:69–70).

123. "In agro dominico," appended art. 2, drawn from Pr. 9 (DW 1:148).

124. Ultimately, this form of language is based on Plato's *Parmenides*, but for the history of mysticism the story can begin with Neoplatonic developments from Plato. For reflections on this component of the history of Western mysticism, see Bernard McGinn, *The Foundations of Mysticism: Origins to the Fifth Century* (New York: Crossroad, 1991), 44–61 (on Plotinus and Proclus), and 157–82 (on Dionysius); as well as idem, *The Growth of Mysticism: Gregory the Great to the Twelfth Century* (New York: Crossroad, 1994), 88–118 on Eriugena.

125. For some reflections on Eckhart's place in the history of Platonic dialectic, see McGinn, "Meister Eckhart on God as Absolute Unity," 136–39.

126. On Eckhart's use of these sources, see especially Kurt Ruh, *Geschichte* 3:17–56, and 280–90, building on his earlier studies, "Dionysius Areopagita im deutschen Predigtwerk Meister Eckharts, Perspektiven der Philosophie," *Neues Jahrbuch* 13 (1987): 207–23; and "Neuplatonische Quellen Meister Eckhart," in *Contemplata aliis*

tradere: Studien zum Verhältnis von Literatur und Spiritualität, ed. Claudia Brinker, Urs Herzog, Niklaus Largier, and Paul Michel (Frankfurt: Peter Lang, 1995), 317–52. On the relation to Proclus, see Werner Beierwaltes, "Primum est dives per se: Meister Eckhart und der 'Liber de causis,'" in *On Proclus and his Influence in Medieval Philosophy,* ed. E. P. Bos and P. A. Meijer (Leiden: Brill, 1992), 141–69.

127. E.g., In Ex. nn.112–19 (LW 2:110–17). The dialectical use of similarity/dissimilarity is where Eckhart is closest to Dionysius, who employs the same language in *De divinibus nominibus* 9.6–7 (PG 3:913C–916A). See the comment of Thomas Aquinas on this passage, *De divinis nominibus expositio* cap. 9, lect. 3.

128. E.g., In Eccli. n.58 (LW 2:286–87).

129. E.g., Pr. 14 (DW 1:237); RdU 23 (DW 5:293–94).

130. E.g., In Eccli. n.54 (LW 2:283); In Ioh. n.12 (LW 3:11); Pr. 30 (DW 2:94).

131. E.g., In Sap. n.132 (LW 2:469–70).

132. E.g., In Ioh. n.425 (LW 3:360–61).

133. The three most complex are (1) In Ex. nn.113–19 (LW 2:110–17; translated in *Teacher and Preacher,* 81–83); (2) In Eccli. nn.42–61 (LW 2:270–90; in *Teacher and Preacher,* 174–81); and (3) In Sap. nn.144–57 (LW 2:481–94; *Teacher and Preacher,* 166–71). For other appearances, see In Gen.I n.173 (LW 1:318); In Ex. nn.40, 102, 104–7 (LW 2:45, 104, 106–7); In Sap. nn.38–39, 52, 60, 282 (LW 2:359–60, 379, 388, 614–15); In Ioh. nn.99, 103, 197, 562, 634 (LW 3:85, 88–89, 166–67, 489, 551–52). Distinction/indistinction language appears often in Eckhart's Latin sermons; e.g., SS. II, IV, X, XXIX, XXX, XXXIV, XXXVII, XLIV (LW 4:9, 27–28 and 31, 98–100, 265, 278, 299, 320–21, 368).

134. See Prr. 10, 13b, 14 (DW 1:173, 225, 237); Prr. 28, 30, 36a, 50 (DW 2:67–68, 94, 189, 459–60); Prr. 63, 77 (DW 3:82, 338 and 340); VeM and RdU 23 (DW 5:115 and 293–94).

135. Many students of Eckhart have recognized the importance of this aspect of his thought, though not all have given it the same name. H. Hof, for example, preferred the term "Analektik" (i.e., speech that leads "above") (*Scintilla animae: Eine Studie zu einem Grundbegriff in Meister Eckharts Philosophie* [Lund: Gleerup, 1952], 155–58). B. Mojsisch speaks of Eckhart's "objektive Paradoxtheorie" (*Meister Eckhart,* 86–87).

136. On this text see McGinn, "Meister Eckhart on God as Absolute Unity," 132–34. A detailed discussion can be found in Goris, *Einheit als Prinzip und Ziel,* 209–28. Many other students of Eckhart have also treated the passage; see especially Lossky, *Théologie négative,* 261–65; Mojsisch, *Meister Eckhart,* 86–95; and Manstetten, *Esse est Deus,* 218–24. Rather than give the full Latin for all the quotations used here, I will cite only the most important and invite the reader to consult the text in LW. The following outline may be helpful.

God as One (In Sap. nn.144–57)

I. **God Is One (nn.144–55)**

  A. Three arguments that God is One (= indistinct) (nn.144–46)

  B. The meaning of One (n.147)

    —negative moment: indistinction

    —positive moment: fullness

  C. The Relation of the One and the Many (nn.148–51)

    —the One as negation of negation (n.148)

    —authorities on the One and number (Macrobius, Boethius, Proclus)

D. Two new arguments that God is one (nn.152–53)
E. The Dialectic of Distinction/Indistinction (nn.154–55)
   —three arguments for God's distinction (n.154)
   —three arguments for God's indistinction (n.155)
II. Because God Is One He Can Do All Things (nn.156–57)
   A. The Fundamental Argument (n.156)—based on the *Liber de causis,*
      prop. 17
   B. Three Further Arguments (n.157)

137. Eckhart has two definitions of *unum*. The more usual, nondialectical definition, taken from Aristotle (*Metaphysics* 10.9 [1054a23]) is "unum est indivisum in se,
divisum ab aliis" (e.g., In Sap. n.39 [LW 2:360.11–12]; In Ioh. n.550 [LW 3:480.9]; S. LV
n.540 [LW 4:453.10–11]; Pr. 21 [DW 1:357.7–12]). The second, his own dialectical definition, whose negative pole is *indistinctum* and whose positive pole is *negatio negationis* (e.g., Prol.op. prop. nn.6, 12, 15 [LW 1:169, 172, 175]), is what is expounded here.
A. de Libera holds that Eckhart adheres only to an Aristotelian concept of *unum* (*La
mystique rhénane,* 386–87, and 435–36 n.170), but this seems to me to neglect the con-
ceptual difference between *indivisum in se* and *indistinctum*.

138. The relationship between *esse* and *unum* is also expounded in the first of the
propositions (*esse est Deus*) discussed in Prol. op.prop. nn.5–6, 9–12, 15 (LW 1:168–69,
171–72, 175–76).

139. "Omnis enim multitudo uno participat" (In Sap. n.151 [LW 2:488]). This
axiom is the first proposition of Proclus's *Elementatio theologica* (ed. Dodds, 2–3), and
was a favorite authority for Eckhart, who also cites it, e.g., In Gen.I n.114 (LW 1:269);
In Gen.II n.15 (LW 1:485); In Ex. n.101 (LW 2:103); In Sap. nn.39, 293 (LW 2:360, 629).
Eckhart, probably following Aquinas, distinguished the author of the *Liber de causis*
from Proclus, although recognizing the dependence of the former on the latter (see In
Ioh. n.396 [LW 3:337]).

140. In the critical edition this key sentence reads: Et e converso, quanto distinctius,
tanto indistinctius, quia distinctione sua *distinguitur* ab indistincto (In Sap. n.154 [LW
2:490.5–6]). But, as W. Goris has effectively argued (*Einheit als Prinzip und Ziel,*
224–28), if the subject is God, as it appears is the case, then the verb should be *indis-
tinguitur*. Hence, the translation given here.

141. In Ex. n.73 (LW 2:75–76) says that the truth of an affirmative proposition sub-
sists in the identity (= indistinction) of terms, while the truth of a negative one stands
in the distinction of terms. Hence, the *negatio negationis* fuses both forms of predication into one, a formally negative expression of positive fullness, or "what the One signifies when expressed negatively" (In Ex. n.74). Eckhart explicitly affirms this in In
Eccli. n.63 (LW 2:293.1–2): . . . unum transcendens in voce quidem negatio est sed in
significato, cum sit negatio negationis, est mera affirmatio.

142. On the *negatio negationis,* see Prol.op.prop. nn.6, 12, 15 (LW 1:169, 172, 175);
In Gen.I n.158 (LW 1:306, in the form *privatio privationis*); In Ex. nn.16, 74 (LW 2:21,
76–78); In Eccli. nn.60, 63 (LW 2:289, 293); In Sap. n.147 (LW 2:485–86); In Ioh.
nn.207–8, 556, 611, 692 (LW 3:175–76, 485, 533, 608); SS. X n.111, XXXVII n.375 (LW
4:104, 320). In the MHG sermons we find it explicitly featured in Pr. 21 (DW 1:361.10
and 363.1–7), and implicitly appearing in Pr. 44 (DW 2:348.1–2). The extent to which
Eckhart may have been aware of Proclus's use of *negatio negationis* is disputed. Thomas
Aquinas (e.g., *Quodlibet* X, q.1, a.1, ratio 3) and Dietrich of Freiburg also used the term,
but only to express a being of reason, not the inner nature of God. Goris correctly

describes *negatio negationis* as the "operator" of the transcendentals in Eckhart's thought—". . . kann die *negatio negationis* hier als Operator der Gottesattributen auftreten: Sie negiert jene Dimension der Vielheit und legt die *perfectiones* in ihrer *göttlichen* Reinheit frei" (*Einheit als Prinzip und Ziel,* 376). See his discussions on pp. 197–206, 215–18, which contend that Eckhart adapted his metaphysical understanding of the term from Henry of Ghent's *Summa quaestionum ordinarium* a.25, q.1, and a.73, q.11, ad 2. See also Lossky, *Théologie négative,* 304–6; and de Libera, *La mystique rhénane,* 435–36 (note 170). Eckhart's *in quantum* principle of reduplication can be seen as expressing the dialectical outlook evident in the *negatio negationis.*

143. For a sketch of the background, see Harry A. Wolfson, "St. Thomas on the Divine Attributes," as well as some of the other essays reprinted in *Studies in the History of Philosophy and Religion,* 2 vols., ed. Isadore Twersky and George H. Williams (Cambridge, Mass.: Harvard University Press, 1973, 1977).

144. Tallying the implied as well as the explicit citations of any author in Eckhart will produce different results. By my count, the In Ex. has 85 references to Maimonides' *Dux neutrorum,* compared to 77 for Augustine and 73 for Aquinas. For the relation between Maimonides and Eckhart, see Josef Koch, "Meister Eckhart und die jüdische Religionsphilosophie des Mittelalters," *Jahresbericht der Schleschischen Gesellschaft, Philosophisch-psychologische Sektion* 101 (1928): 134–48; Hans Liebeschütz, "Meister Eckhart und Moses Maimonides," *Archiv für Kulturgeschichte* 54 (1972): 64–96; B. McGinn, "Introduction. 2. Meister Eckhart on Speaking about God," in *Teacher and Preacher,* 15–30; idem, "'*SAPIENTIA JUDAEORUM*'"; Reudi Imbach, "Ut ait Rabbi Moses: Maimonidische Philosopheme bei Thomas von Aquin und Meister Eckhart," *Collectanea Franciscana* 60 (1990): 99–116; Yossef Schwartz, "'*Ecce est locus apud me':* Maimonides und Eckharts Raumvorstellung als Begriff des Göttlichen," and "Metaphysiche oder theologische Hermeneutik? Meister Eckhart in den Spuren des Maimonides und des Thomas von Aquin" (forthcoming).

145. E.g., In Ex. nn. 61, 78 (LW 2:66, 81).

146. The point that *esse* is not a *dispositio,* crucial for Eckhart's argument, is evident from In Ex. nn.40, 44, 48, 51, 53, 74, 158, 161–69.

147. David Burrell, *Knowing the Unknown God: Ibn Sina, Maimonides, Aquinas* (Notre Dame: University of Notre Dame Press, 1986), chap. 3, especially 46–47.

148. VeM (DW 5:115.7–11): In underscheide envindet man noch ein noch wesen noch got noc raast noch saelicheit noch genüegede. Bis ein, daz dû got mügest vinden! Und waerlîche, waerest dû rehte ein, sô blibest dû ouch ein in underscheide und underscheit würde dir ein und enmöhte dich iezent nihtes niht hindern (my trans.).

149. The issue of the role of the transcendentals in Eckhart's thought has been often discussed. For a good brief analysis, see Werner Beierwaltes, *Platonismus und Idealismus* (Frankfurt: Klostermann, 1972), 37–67. More detailed considerations can be found in older works (especially Lossky, *Théologie négative*), and in more recent studies, such as Goris, *Einheit als Prinzip und Ziel;* and Manstetten, *Esse est Deus.*

150 Eckhart gives priority to *esse* as a divine predication in many other texts besides the Prol.op.prop. The Dominican's teaching on *esse* has been the subject of considerable study. Two important treatments are Karl Albert, *Meister Eckharts These vom Sein* (Saarbrücken: Universitäts- und Schilbuchverlag, 1976); and Manstetten, *Esse est Deus.*

151. Without attempting to provide an exhaustive list of the other discussions of God as *unum* in the Latin works, see the following: (1) In Gen.I nn.10–13, 84, 158 (LW 1:193–97, 243–44, 306); (2) In Gen.II nn.10–12, 73–74, 179, 215 (LW 1:481–83, 538–40, 649, 690–91); (3) In Ex. nn.57–61, 74, 91, 101, 134, 138 (LW 2:62–66, 77–78, 94, 103,

123, 126); (4) In Eccli. nn.60, 63 (LW 2:289, 293); (5) In Sap. nn.38, 99, 107, 110, 219, 287, 293 (LW 2:359–60, 434–35, 443, 446–47, 553–54, 620–21, 628–29); (6) In Ioh. nn.24, 67, 114, 195, 207–08, 320, 329, 342, 360, 513–18, 526, 546–65, 692 (LW 3:20, 55–56, 99–100, 164, 75–76, 268, 278–79, 291, 305, 444–48, 456–57, 477–93, 608); (7) SS. X n.103–07, XXIX, XXXVII n.377, XLIV nn.438–39, XLVIII n.503 (LW 4:98–101, 263–70, 322–23, 367–69, 419).

152. For some of the sermons in which Eckhart speaks about the divine *einicheit* and *einig ein* see, e.g., Prr. 13, 15, 19, 21, 23 (DW 1:219, 245, 314, 361–68, 401–2); Prr. 28, 29, 51 (DW 2:63, 76–77 and 88, 472–73); Prr. 64, 67, 71, 83 (DW 3:88–90, 130, 221–24, 442 and 447–48). There are also important passages in the BgT (DW 5:30–31, 34, 46–47) and in the VeM (DW 5:114–15 and 119).

153. Qu.Par.1 n.4 (LW 5:4–7): Tertio ostendo quod non ita videtur mihi modo, ut quia sit, ideo intelligat, sed quia intelligit, ideo est, ita quod deus est intellectus et intelligere et est ipsum intelligere fundamentum ipsius esse. On *esse* and *intelligere* in Eckhart and their relation to Aquinas, the classic work is R. Imbach, *Deus est intelligere: Das Verhältnis von Sein und Denken in seiner Bedeutung für das Gottesverständnis bei Thomas von Aquin und in den Pariser Quaestionen Meister Eckharts* (Freiburg, Switzerland: Universitätsverlag, 1976). See also John Caputo, "The Nothingness of the Intellect in Meister Eckhart's 'Parisian Questions,'" *The Thomist* 39 (1975): 85–115; and Emilie Zum Brunn, "Dieu n'est pas être," in *Maître Eckhart à Paris: Une critique médiévale de l'ontothéologie. Les Questions parisiennes no. 1 et no. 2* (Paris: Presses Universitaires de France, 1984), 84–108.

154. Qu.Par. 2 n.2 (LW 5:50.1–5): Prima est, quia intellectus, in quantum intellectus, nihil est eorum quae intelligit, ... Si igitur intellectus, in quantum intellectus, nihil est, et per consequens nec intelligere est aliquod esse. The nothingness of the human intellect, that is, its quality as a *tabula rasa* which must be free of all forms and images in order to know, is, of course, the reason why it is truly *imago dei* and capable of unity in the ground; see Tobin, *Meister Eckhart,* 131–36, and the discussion below.

155. The logic of the argument would be: (a) *esse* is the first of creatures and God cannot be a creature; (b) but *intellectus/intelligere* is "nothing" of the creatures it knows; therefore (c) God can be said to be *intellectus.*

156. S. XXIX nn.300 and 304 (LW 4:266.11–12, 270.1–2): Ubi nota quod unitas sive unum videtur proprium et proprietas intellectus solius. . . . Deus enim unus est intellectus, et intellectus est deus unus. Another important sermon on the relation of *esse* and *intelligere* is S. XI (LW 4:105–15), on which see Zum Bruun, "Dieu n'est pas être," 105–8.

157. The distinction between God as the *esse* that is *indistinctum/absolutum/simpliciter* and creatures as *esse hoc et hoc* is one of the most frequent themes in Eckhart. Karl Albert counts sixty-five appeals to it in the course of the Op.trip. alone; see "Die philosophische Grundgedanke Meister Eckharts," *Tijdschrift voor Philosophie* 27 (1965): 321 note 5. Thomas Aquinas had spoken of the difference between the *esse universale* of God and the *esse hoc vel tale* of creatures (e.g., STh 1a, q.45, a.5c), a passage that may provide a source for this theme in Eckhart.

158. Pr. 91 (DW 4:92.7–9): Got enist niht wan ein lûter wesen, und diu creâtûre ist von nihte und hat ouch ein wesen von den selben wesene (my trans.). For some other appearances, see Prr. 3, 7, 8, 23 (DW 1:55–57, 122, 131, 397); Prr. 37, 39, 45, 54a (DW 2:216, 262, 372, 553–54); Prr. 67, 77, 86 (DW 3:135, 339–41, 488); and BgT (DW 5:28–29).

159. To choose just a few examples from Eckhart's preaching. In the Latin sermons,

God is said to be beyond being in SS. XI, XXIV, and XXIX (LW 4:112, 226, 270). In the MHG sermons we find such formulations as that in Pr. 9 (DW 1:146.1–2): Ich spraeche als unrehte, als ich got hieze ein wesen, als ob ich die sunnen hieze bleich oder swarz. In Pr. 71 God is *wesen âne wesen* (DW 3:231.1–3); in Pr. 82 he is *wesen weselôs* (DW 3:431.3–4); and in Pr. 83 *ein vber swebende wesen und ein vber wesende nitheit* (DW 3:442.1–2).

160. On *bonum* as a not fully divine transcendental, see Goris, *Einheit als Prinzip und Ziel*, 379–81.

161. Augustine, *De trinitate* 8.3.4 (PL 42:949): Bonum hoc et illud; tolle hoc et illud et vide ipsum bonum, si potes; ita Deum videbis. Eckhart cites this, for example, in the BgT 2 (DW 5:25.1–3), In Gen.II n.65 (LW 1:532), In Sap. n.98 (LW 2:432–34), and S. LV n.546 (LW 4:457).

162. Pr. 71 (DW 3:222.7–8): Daz vierde: daz si [the soul] vil lîhte wânde, daz er keinen namen anders enhabe wan minne; si nennet alle namen in der minne.

163. See Goris, *Einheit als Prinzip und Ziel*, 52–53, 376–78. J. A. Aertsen agrees, arguing that Eckhart unifies the Aristotelian position of the "transcendentality of the first" with the Platonic notion of the "transcendence of the first" ("Ontology and Henology in Medieval Philosophy [Thomas Aquinas, Meister Eckhart and Berthold of Moosburg]," in *On Proclus and His Influence in Medieval Philosophy*, ed. E. P. Bos and P. A. Meijer [Leiden: Brill, 1992], 132–39). Long before, Vladimir Lossky recognized that there is no *unum* beyond *esse indistinctum* in Eckhart (*Théologie négative*, 63–64).

164. A. de Libera puts it well: "Si aucune *pré*-sence ne nous livre Dieu, l'entrée dans l'unique-Un nous délivre de la présence" (*La mystique rhénane*, 286).

165. In Gen.I n.41 (LW 1:216.7–10): Sunt enim duae causae, propter quas res sunt nobis difficiles ad cognoscendum, vel quia excedunt proportionem nostri intellectus propter eminentiam sui esse, . . . vel quia deficiunt ab esse sive ab ente, quod est obiectum intellectus. See Aristotle, *Metaphysics* II.1 (993b 7–11).

166. In Ex. nn.39–40 (LW 2:44–46).

167. In Gen.I n.270 (LW 1:409).

168. S. VIII n.84 (LW 4:80): Nota primo quod dicit *homo quidam* [Lk. 14:16] sine nomine, quia deus est nobis innominabilis propter infinitatem omnis esse in ipso. Characterizing God as *innominabilis* goes back to Dionysius (e.g., *De divinis nominibus* 1.6 [PG 3:596]), a passage that Eriugena and Sarrazin translate as "mirabile nomen, quod est super omne nomen, quod est innominabile" (PL 122:1117). The affirmation of the unnameability of God (*innominabilis-indicibilis/namelôs-âne name*) is found often in Eckhart's preaching; e.g., SS. IV n. 30, IX n.96, LV n.547 (LW 4:31, 92, 458); Prr. 7, 16, 17, 20a (DW 1:122, 253, 284, 328–30); Prr. 26, 36a, 38 (DW 2:31, 188–89, 237); Prr. 71, 77, 80, 82, 83 (DW 3:221–22, 337, 380–83, 431, 441); Pr. 95 (DW 4:189–91). Conversely, taking a term from the Hermetic treatise *Asclepius* III.20a, Eckhart also spoke of God as *omninominabilis;* e.g., In Gen.I n.84 (LW 1:243–44), In Ex. n.35 (LW 2:41–42), S. VIII n.88 (LW 4:84), Pr. 71 (DW 3:222). For a study of this aspect of Eckhart's God-language, see Lossky, *Théologie négative*, 17–26, 60–64.

169. Pr. 23 (DW 1:402.2): Er ist nihtes niht; Pr. 71 (DW 3:223.1–2): Got ist ein niht, und got ist ein iht; Pr. 83 (DW 3:443.7): . . . got ist vngewordene istikeit vnd sin vngenanten nitheit. . . . On Eckhart's neologism *istikeit*, signifying *esse existentiae*, see Meinrad Morard, "Ist, istic, istikeit bei Meister Eckhart," *Freiburger Zeitschrift für Philosophie und Theologie* 3 (1956): 169–86, who lists fourteen uses of *istikeit*, and three of *ist* and seven of *istic* in the same sense.

170. The treatise on naming God can be found in the comment on the word

"aperuit" of the base text "Os suum aperuit" (Prov. 31:26) for Pr. 95b (DW 4:185.106–198.290). The tract is structured around three questions: (1) Do you know what God is? (2) Why does scripture give God so many names? And (3) is God to be praised or should we keep silence? The passage cited comes from the answer to this third question. See 193.220–24: Ie man sîn mê luogent, ie man in mê lobet. Ie man im mê unglîches zuoleget, ie man sînem bekantnisse naeher kumet, als ich ein glîchnisse sagen wil. And 194:237–195.242: Als diu sêle in daz bekantnisse kumet, daz got alsô unglîch ist allen natûren, sô kumet si in ein wunder und wirt wider getriben und kumet in ein swigen. Mit der stille senket sich got in die sêle, und mit der gnâde wirt si begozzen, . . . (my trans.).

171. Pr. 22 (DW 1:389.6–8): Waz ist daz leste ende? Ez ist diu verborgen vinsternisse der êwigen gotheit und ist unbekant und wart nie bekant und enwirt niemer bekant. Got blîbet dâ in im selber unbekant, . . . (trans. *Essential Eckhart*).

172. Eckhart's four major discussions of creation are: (1) Prol. gen. nn.12–22 (LW 1:156–65); (2) In Gen.I nn.1–28 (LW 1:185–206); (3) In Gen.II nn.8–40 (LW 1:479–507); (4) In Sap. nn.19–40 (LW 2:339–62). Among other important treatments, see Prol.op.prop. nn.11 and 23 (LW 1:171–72, 179–80); In Gen.I n.112 (LW 1:265–67); In Gen.II nn.53 and 69 (LW 1:521, 535–38); In Ioh. nn.213–22 (LW 3:179–86). For analyses of Eckhart's teaching on creation, see Bernard McGinn, "Do Christian Platonists Really Believe in Creation?" in *God and Creation: An Ecumenical Symposium*, ed. David B. Burrell and Bernard McGinn (Notre Dame, Ind.: University of Notre Dame Press, 1990), 197–223; and Alois M. Haas, "Seinsspekulation und Geschöpflichkeit in der Mystik Meister Eckharts," in *Sein und Nichts in der abendländischen Mystik*, ed. Walter Strolz (Freiburg: Herder, 1984), 33–58.

173. E.g., Prol.gen. n.16 (LW 1:160); In Gen.I n.14 (LW 1:197); In Sap. n.19 (LW 2:340). See Avicenna, *Metaphysica* VI.2.

174. E.g., Prol.gen. n.12 (LW 1:157); In Gen.II n.9 (LW 1:480); In Sap. n.25 (LW 2:345); In Ioh. n.56 (LW 3:47).

175. To cite but one example, see Pr. 71 (DW 3:217.6–7): Got vluizet in alle crêatûren, und blîbet er doch unberüeret von in allen.

176. In Sap. nn.25–26 (LW 2:345–46). Eckhart often says that the granting of *esse* is the purpose of creation, but, since *esse* contains all other qualifications, he could use other formulations to express the divine intent. For example, In Sap. n.197 (LW 2:531) describes the unity of the universe as God's intent, while Pr. 60 (DW 3:11–12) says that God created all things so that they can attain final *ruowe*.

177. In Ioh. n.514 (LW 3:445.3–4): Restat ergo videre quomodo esse sub ratione sive proprietatis unius principium est et ab ipso procedit universitas et integritas totius entis creati. The linking of *esse* and *unum* to understand creation is also evident In Ex. n.97 (LW 2:100), where Eckhart cites Maimonides concerning the two fundamental beliefs (*duae principalitates*): "scilicet quod creator est et quod unus est."

178. In Gen.I n.3 (LW 1:186.12–87.1): De primo sciendum est quod principium, in quo *creavit deus caelum et terram*, est ratio idealis. Et hoc est quod Ioh. 1 dicitur: "in principio erat verbum"—graecus habet logos, id est ratio. . . .

179. See In Gen.I n.4 (LW 1:187–88).

180. On *causa essentialis*, see Burkhard Mojsisch, "'Causa essentialis' bei Dietrich von Freiburg und Meister Eckhart," in *Von Meister Eckhart zu Meister Dietrich*, ed. Kurt Flasch (Hamburg: Meiner, 1984), 106–14; idem, *Meister Eckhart*, 24–29.

181. In Ioh. n.31 (LW 3:25.8–10): Et tale agens, principium scilicet in quo est logos, ratio, est agens essentiale nobiliori modo praehabens suum effectum, et est habens

causalitatem super totam speciem sui effectus. Eckhart often returns to the *causa essentialis* in the commentary; see, e.g., nn.38, 45, 139, 195, 239 (LW 3:32–33, 37–38, 117, 163, 200). See also In Gen.II n.47 (LW 1:515); In Sap. nn.21, 71, 132 (LW 2:342, 400–401, 470).

182. In Gen.II n.45 (LW 1:512.13–14): . . . quia omne verum agens essentiale semper est spiritus et vita. . . .

183. S. II n.6 (LW 4:8.4–9): Carissimi, in causis essentialibus, etiam secundoprimis, causa se tota descendit in causatum, ita ut quodlibet sit in quolibet modo quolibet, sicut De causis dicitur [cf. *Liber de causis,* prop.12]. In causis autem primordialibus sive originalibus primo-primis, ubi magis proprie nomen est principii quam causae, principium se toto et cum omnibus suis proprietatibus descendit in principiatum.

184. E.g., In Sap. n.170 (LW 2:505.10–11): . . . agens enim sive efficiens secundum genus causarum est causa extrinsica, forma vero est causa rei intrinseca.

185. S. IV n.21 (LW 4:24.2–3): . . . notandum quod li *ex* non est causa efficiens proprie, sed potius ratio causae efficientis. The *ratio causae* is explored in great detail in many texts, especially In Ioh. nn.4–14, and In Gen.II n.2–14.

186. S. XXIII n.223 (LW 4:208.5–11): Non est ergo imaginandum quod deus creavit extra se et quasi iuxta se caelum et terram in quodam nihilo. Omne enim quod fit in nihilo, utique fit nihil. . . . Sed e converso creando vocat cuncta ex nihilo et a nihilo ad esse.

187. In Sap. n.122 (LW 2:459.1–2): Non enim imaginandum, sicut plurimi autumnant, quasi deus extra se et a se, non in se creaverit aut produxerit omnia, sed a se et in se creavit. . . . Cf. Prol.gen. n.17 (LW 1:160.13–62.12); In Eccli. n.49 (LW 2:207.11–208.11).

188. S. XXIII n.222 (LW 4:208.1–2): . . . secundo quod creavit et quievit a creando ad modum aliorum artificum, secundum planum litterae quae dicit: 'requievit deus die septimo ab universo opere.'"

189. Pr. 30 (DW 2:94.3–9): . . . daz alle crêatûren ûzvliezent und doch inneblîbent, daz ist gar wunderlich; . . . Ie mê er ist in den dingen, ie mê er ist ûz den dingern: ie mê inne, ie mê ûze, und ie mê ûze, ie mê ine. Ich hân ez etwenne mê gesprochen, daz got alle dise werlt schepfet nû alzemâle. Allez, daz got ie geschuof sehs tûsent jâren und mê, dô got die werlt machete, die schepfet got nû alzemâle (trans. Walshe). *Creatio continua* is spoken of elsewhere in the MHG works; e.g., Pr. 38 (DW 2:231–32), and BgT (DW 5:44), and it is especially emphasized in the Latin writings; e.g., Prol.gen. nn.18 and 21 (LW 1:162–63 and 165); In Gen.I n.20 (LW 1:201); In Sap. nn.33 and 292 (LW 2:354, 627); In Ioh. nn.411–12 and 582 (LW 3:349–50, 510). Mieth summarizes the importance of the role of *creatio continua* (*Die Einheit von Vita Activa und Vita Passiva,* 215): "In der Fruchtbarkeit der gottgeeinten Seele vollziehen sich 'creatio continua' und 'incarnatio continua,' die in dem Ereignis der Gottesgeburt zusammengefasst sind."

190. See especially In Ioh. nn.213–19 (LW 3:180–84), which makes considerable use of Augustine, *Confessiones* 11.10–13.

191. Along with the passages from *Conf.* 11, in the Cologne trial Eckhart twice cited *Conf.* 1.6.3 (PL 32:665) in his defense (see Théry, 206, 208). He also quotes this passage in In Ioh. nn.580, 638 (LW 3:508, 554).

192. In Ioh. n.323 (LW 3:271): Adhuc autem, quia creatio exterior subiacet tempori quod facit vetus. . . . See also In Gen.II n.62 (LW 1:529); In Ex. n.85 (LW 2:88); S. XV n.155 (LW 4:147–48).

193. For a brief summary on *esse virtuale/esse formale,* see Tobin, *Meister Eckhart,* 59–62. My concentration here on the distinction between *esse virtuale* and *esse formale*

as fundamental to Eckhart's understanding of the being of creatures means that a number of other aspects of his metaphysics of creation will be left out of account. Among these are: (1) the analysis of the extrinsic and intrinsic principles of created being (In Gen.I n.24, In Gen.II nn.21–34); and (2) the difference between *ens reale* and *ens cognitivum* (see In Gen.I n.25, In Gen.II n.202, In Ioh. nn.514–540).

194. In Sap. n.21 (LW 2:342.9–12): Omnia autem sunt in deo tamquam in causa prima intellectualiter et in mente artificis. Igitur non habent esse suum aliquod formale, nisi causaliter educantur et producantur extra, ut sint.

195. Eckhart appeals to the *esse virtuale/esse formale* distinction often in his Latin writings; see In Gen.I nn.77, 83 (LW 1:238–39, 242); In Gen.II nn.35, 45, 52, 62 (LW 1:503, 512, 520, 528–30); In Ex. n.175 (LW 2:151); In Sap. nn.22, 32, 127 (LW 2:343, 352–53, 465); In Ioh. nn.37–38, 45, 342 (LW 3:31–33, 37, 290–91); SS. VIII nn.89–90, IX n.102 (LW 4:84–87. 96–97); Qu.Par. 1 nn.8–11 (LW 5:45–47).

196. See, e.g., In Gen.I nn.2 and 14 (LW 1:186, 197–98).

197. Pr. 57 (DW 2:600–02). On the history of the mirror as a mystical image, see Margot Schmidt, "Miroir," DS 10:1290–1303.

198. In Ex. n.121 (LW 2:114.6–115.2): E converso nullo modo formae rerum sunt in deo formaliter, rationes autem rerum et formarum sunt in deo causaliter et virtualiter. . . . Sic igitur res creata et eius forma, per quam habet nomen, est in re ipsa, nequaquam in deo. . . . Manet ergo dissimilitudo, et deficit fundamentum similitudinis in utroque termino, deo scilicet et creatura.

199. In Ex. n.122 (LW 2:115.3–4): Adhuc autem formae rerum non essent a deo productae, nisi in ipso essent. Omne enim, quid fit, fit a simili.

200. In Ex. n.117 (LW 2:112.7–9): Rursus etiam nihil tam dissimile et simile coniunctim alteri—de tertio—quam deus et creatura. Quid enim tam dissimile et simile alteri quam id, cuius dissimilitudo est ipsa similitudo, cuius indistinctio est ipsa distinctio.

201. *Votum theologicum* (ed. Pelster, 1109.32–38): Unde idem nunc eternitatis est, quo Deus mundum creavit et quo Deus est et quo Deus filium sibi coeternum generavit, nec sequitur quod si creacio Dei accio sit eterna, quod mundus sit eternus, quia Deus sic produxit mundum de novo et ex tempore, et in nunc temporis, quod mundus et eius creacio passio est in tempore seu nunc temporis et creacio passio non est in Deo sed in creatura. Eckhart mounted a similar defense during the Cologne trial (see Théry, 186–87, 194, 208). At Avignon we can also read the rebuttal of the inquisitors (Pelster, 1110–11).

202. For a more detailed discussion, see McGinn, "Do Christian Platonists Really Believe in Creation?" 202–4.

203. In the Latin works, see, e.g., Prol.op.prop. n.22 (LW 1:178); In Ex. nn.29, 40, 135 (LW 2:34, 45, 124); In Sap. n.34 (LW 2:354); In Ioh. nn.215, 308 (LW 3:181, 256); S. XXXI n.323 (LW 4:283). In his sermons Eckhart sometimes uses neologisms to express the nothingness of created being, such as *nulleitas* (S.XV n.158 [LW4:150.5]) and *nihileitas* (S. XXXVII n.375 [LW 4:321.1]).

204. Proc.Col.I (Théry, 207): Praeterea, dicere mundum non esse nichil in se, et ex se, sed esse quid modicum, manifesta blasphemia est. See also Théry, 205; Pelster, 1112–13.

205. Thomas Aquinas, STh 1a2ae q.109, a.2, ad 2: Unaquaeque autem res creata, sicut esse non habet nisi ab alio, et in se considerata est nihil. See also Eriugena, *Periphyseon* III (PL 122:640AB): Nihil enim aliud nos sumus, in quantum sumus, nisi ipsae rationes nostrae aeternaliter in deo substitutae.

206. See In Gen.I n.146 (LW 1:299). In Frank Tobin's insightful formulation, "creatures . . . exist at the nondimensional intersection of nothingness and infinity" (*Meister Eckhart*, 188).

207. See Annick Charles-Saget, "Non-être et Néant chez Maître Eckhart," in *Voici Maître Eckhart*, Textes et études réunis par Emilie Zum Brunn (Paris: Jérôme Millon, 1994), 318. On Eckhart's differing uses of *nihil/niht*, see also Beverly Lanzetta, "Three Categories of Nothingness in Meister Eckhart," *Journal of Religion* 72 (1992): 248–68; and Burkhard Mojsisch, "*Nichts* und *Negation*: Meister Eckhart und Nikolaus von Kues," in *Historia philosophiae medii aevi: Studien zur Geschichte der Philosophie des Mittelalters*, ed. Burkhard Mojsisch (Amsterdam: G. R. Grüner, 1991), 2:675–93.

208. The axiom *bonum est diffusivum sui* is found in many Neoplatonic sources, not least in Dionysius, *De divinis nominibus* 4.1 (PG 3:693B). Eckhart cites it both in his Latin sermons (e.g., S. XLIX n.511 [LW 4:426.8]) and in his vernacular preaching (e.g., Pr. 9 [DW 1:149.1–2]). In the Proc.Col. II n.39 (Théry, 242) he refers to Dionysius as the source: "Bonitas non sinit ipsum sine germine esse, sicut dicit Dionysius." It should be noted that a more frequently used axiom from the *Liber de causis*, prop. 21: Primum est dives per se . . . (ed. Pattin, 92), really says the same thing, that is, the Primal freely gives of itself. (Eckhart cites prop. 21 at least thirty times.)

209. In Gen.I n.12 (LW 1:195.10–12): Tertio et melius dico quod re vera ab uno uniformiter se habente semper unum procedit immediate. Sed hoc unum est ipsum totum universum, quod a deo procedit, unum quidem in multis partibus universi, ... See also In Gen.I nn.13–14 (LW 1:196–98).

210. E.g., SS. XXVIII n.287; XLIV n.445 (LW 4: 258, 372).

211. In Gen.II n.17 (LW 1:487.7–10): Primo, quod numerus et divisio semper imperfectorum est et ex imperfectione oritur. In se ipso etiam imperfectio est, cum sit casus sive processus ad extra unum, quod cum ente convertitur. See the discussion in nn.16–19 (LW 1:486–89), as well as In Gen.I n.26 (LW 1:205–06); In Ex. n.141 (LW 2:128–29); and In Sap. n.38 (LW 2:446).

212. On *malum* as privation, see especially In Sap. nn.14–16, 53–56, 197, 228–33 (LW 2:334–37, 380–83, 531–32, 563–67); SS. XXI nn.201–03, XXVIII n.290 (LW 4:186–88, 260). Without denying this traditional view, in the *Commentary on John* Eckhart takes a different tack, placing greater emphasis on how the privation of evil can only exist and be seen *in* what is good; e.g., In Ioh. nn.75, 81, 91 (LW 3:63, 69–70, 78–79). On the nature of sin specifically, see In Ioh. n.306 (LW 3:254).

213. S. VIII n.90 (LW 4:86.6–9): Ipsummet nihil, radix malorum, privationum et multitudinis, absconditur in esse ipso vero et pleno. Ratio, quia est in illo secundum modum illius, aut potius est in illo et est illud, secundum illud: "quod factum est, in ipso vita erat."

214. In Ioh. n.494 (LW 3:426.4–6): Adhuc autem in omni opere, etiam malo, malo, inquam, tam poenae quam culpae, manifestatur et relucet et aequaliter lucet gloria dei. This forms art. 4 of "In agro dominico." Articles 5 and 6 are taken from the same passage. In addition, two other articles dealing with sin drawn from the MHG works were also condemned (art. 14 from BgT 1 [DW 5:22.5–9], and art. 15 paraphrasing RdU 12 [DW 5:232–35]). Eckhart discusses sin in a number of his MHG sermons; e.g., Pr. 32 (DW 2:146–47); Pr. 74 (DW 3:278); Pr. 96 (DW 4:218); Pr. 102 (Pfeiffer, 11–13). For more on Eckhart's teaching on sin, see "2. Theological Summary," in *Essential Eckhart*, 44–45.

215. E.g., S. XVII (LW 4:158).

216. On the three levels of created being, see In Ioh. nn.63–64, 83, 89 (LW 3:144–45, 153, 155–56).

217. Eckhart loved to talk about the angels, especially in his MHG sermons, though little attention has been paid to this aspect of his thought. See Frank Tobin, "Meister Eckhart and the Angels," in In hôhem prîse: A Festschrift in Honor of Ernst S. Dick, ed. Winder McConnell (Göppingen: Kümmerle Verlag, 1989), 379–93; and Thomas Renna, "Angels and Spirituality: The Augustinian Tradition to Eckhardt," Augustinian Studies 16 (1985): 29–37. As with Thomas Aquinas, consideration of angels allowed Eckhart to make important observations about the nature of the intellect.

218. In Gen.II n.151 (LW 1:621.5–11): ... sic eodem modo per omnia deus loquitur omnibus quae sunt. Loquitur, inquam, omnibus et omnia. Sed alia ipsum audiunt, ipsi respondent sub proprietate esse, qua scilicet deus est esse et ab ipso esse omnium. Alia vero ipsum audiunt et suscipiunt verbum dei, ut est vita prima et vera; et ista sunt viventia omnia. Suprema vero in entibus ipsum audiunt deum non solum per esse et in esse, aut per vivere et in vivere, sed per intelligere et in ipso intelligere. Intellectio enim et locutio illic idem. This passage, with its use of esse omnium shows that Eckhart's source for the three levels of creation is probably Dionysius, De divinis nominibus 5.1 (PG 3:816B).

219. Pr. 90 (DW 4:57–70). See especially 66.132–67.150, where Eckhart says: Und swenne der mensche dar zuo kumet, daz er sich ein mit gote vindet, denne aller êrste kêret er alliu dinc ze irn êrsten sachen (66.139–43).

220. Two central expositions of Eckhart's general anthropology are (1) the account of the Fall, exegeting Gen. 3:1 (In Gen.II nn.135–65 [LW 1:601–35]), translated in Essential Eckhart, 108–21; and (2) Pr. 83 (DW 3:437–48).

221. Eckhart's general anthropology is based on Augustine, though there are important differences in the way in which the two thinkers understand the effects of the Fall (e.g., there is little of Augustine's emphasis on concupiscentia in Eckhart). For a brief sketch of the Western medieval doctrine of humanity as imago Dei, see Bernard McGinn, "The Human Person as Image of God, II, Western Christianity," in Christian Spirituality, I, Origins to the Fifth Century, ed. Jean Leclercq, Bernard McGinn, John Meyendorff (New York: Crossroad, 1985), 312–30.

222. In Gen.II nn.135–37 and 145, citing Augustine, De Trinitate 12.13.20 et al. (see PL 42:1008–1009).

223. In Gen.II n.153 (LW 1:623.11–12): Hoc dictum est de homine ratione intellectus quantum ad rationem superiorem, qua est "caput" animae et "imago dei."

224. In Gen.II n.113 (LW 1:579.6): Notandum quod homo id quod est per intellectum est.

225. A recent rereading of Eckhart's MHG sermons has shown me that no other theme, not even the birth of the Word in the soul, appears more frequently than bild and vernunft. (A) Image comes in for discussion in Prr. 1, 2, 3, 5b, 6, 9, 10, 16a, 16b, 17, 20a, 20b, 22, 23, 24, 30, 32, 40, 43, 44, 45, 50, 51, 57, 67, 69, 70, 72, 77, 78, 83, 89, 101, 102 (I have italicized the more important treatments). In addition, Pfeiffer LXXVII (ed., 249–51) has a significant commentary on Gen. 1:26. (B) Intellect is treated even more often; see Prr. 1, 3, 4, 6, 8, 9, 10, 13, 15, 16b, 17, 18, 19, 20b, 21, 22, 23, 26, 32, 34, 36a, 36b, 37, 38, 42, 43, 45, 52, 53, 54a, 59, 61, 66, 67, 68, 69, 70, 71, 72, 73, 75, 76, 80, 83, 90, 101–4. Naturally, both motifs have attracted a large literature. For introductions to Eckhart's teaching on bild, see Alois M. Haas, "Meister Eckhart: Mystische Bildlehre," in Sermo Mysticus: Studien zu Theologie und Sprache der deutschen Mystik (Freiburg,

Switzerland: Universitätsverlag, 1979), 209–37; and Loris Sturlese, "Mysticism and Theology in Meister Eckhart's Theory of the Image," *Eckhart Review* (March 1993): 18–31. A more detailed consideration can be found in W. Wackernagel, *YMAGINE DENUDARI: Éthique de l'image et métaphysique de l'abstraction chez Maître Eckhart* (Paris: Vrin, 1991), chaps. VI–X. Eckhart's teaching on intellect and *imago* has been the subject of several important treatments in the last decades; see, e.g., Kurt Flasch, "Procedere ut imago: Das Hervorgehen des Intellekts aus seinem göttlichen Grund bei Meister Dietrich, Meister Eckhart und Berthold von Moosburg"; and Burkhard Mojsisch, "'Dynamik' der Vernunft bei Dietrich von Freiberg und Meister Eckhart," (both in *Abendländische Mystik im Mittelalter*, ed. Kurt Ruh [Stuttgart: Metzler, 1986], 116–44); Mojsisch, *Meister Eckhart*, 74–81; A. de Libera, *La mystique rhénane*, 250–77; and N. Largier, "'*Intellectus in deum ascensus:* Intellekttheoretische Auseinandersetzungen in Texten der deutschen Mystik," *Deutsche Vierteljahrsschrift für Literaturwissenschaft und Geistesgeschichte* 69 (1995): 423–71. These studies have demonstrated that there is a complex relation between Eckhart's teaching on image and intellect and that of his predecessors, notably Dietrich.

226. The key texts on *imago* in the Latin works are (1) In Gen.I nn.115–20 (LW 1:270–76), exegeting Gen.1:26, *faciamus hominem ad imaginem et similitudinem nostram;* (2) In Sap. n.143 (LW 2:480–81) on Wisdom 7:26, *imago bonitatis illius;* (3) In Ioh. nn.23–26 (LW 3:19–21) on Col. 1:15, *imago dei invisibilis;* (4) S. XLIX nn.505–12 (LW 4:421–28) on Matthew 22:30, *Cuius est imago haec et superscriptio?*

227. In Gen.I n.115 (LW 1:270.4–13): Quantum ad nunc autem sciendum quod creatura rationalis sive intellectualis differt ab omni creatura quae citra est, quod ea quae citra sunt producta sunt ad similitudinem eius quod in deo est et habent ideas sibi proprias in deo, . . . natura vero intellectualis ut sic potius habet ipsum deum similitudinem quam aliquid quod in deo sit ideale. Ratio huius est quod "intellectus ut sic est, quo est omnia fieri," non hoc et hoc determinatum ad speciem. The quotation is from Aristotle, *De anima* 3.18 (430a14). On the significance of this passage, see Goris, *Einheit als Prinzip und Ziel*, 245–51.

228. In Gen.I n.115 (LW 1:272.1–2): De ratione enim imaginis est quod sit expressiva totius eius plene, cuius imago est, non expressiva alicuius determinati in illo. Cf. S. XLIX nn.505, 509–12 (LW 4:421, 424–28).

229. Qu.Par. 2 n.2 (LW 5:50.1–5): Prima est, quia intellectus, in quantum intellectus, nihil est eorum quae intelligit, ... Si igitur intellectus, in quantum intellectus, nihil est, et per consequens nec intelligere aliquod esse. The same point is made in the MHG sermons; e.g., Pr. 69 (DW 3:171.1–2). On this important theme, see Caputo, "Nothingness of the Intellect in Mesiter Eckhart's 'Parisian Questions.'"

230. In Ioh. n.549 (LW 3:479.3–480.1): Homo autem creatus est ad imaginem totius substantiae dei, et sic non ad simile, sed ad unum. . . . (N)on sufficit recursus ad simile, sed recurrit ad unum unde exivit, et sic solum sibi sufficit.

231. In Ioh. nn.23–26 (LW 3:19–21) specifies the following nine marks of image as image: (1) It receives nothing of its own from the subject in which it is found, but only from the object it images. (2) It receives its existence from the object it images. (3) It receives the whole existence of the object it images insofar as this object is an exemplar. (4) It is one and is an image of only one thing. (5) It is in the exemplar. (6) The image and the exemplar are one. (7) The begetting of an image is a formal emanation. (8) Image and exemplar are simultaneous. (9) Image and exemplar have mutual knowledge. These nine characteristics should be compared to the eight listed in S. XLIX nn.509–10 (LW 4:424–25).

232. Pr. 40 (DW 2:277.7–10): Und dar umbe: als man sprichet, daz der mensche mit gote ein sî und nâch der einicheit got sî, sô nimet man in nâch dem teile des bildes, an dem er gote glîch ist, und niht nâch dem, und er geschaffen ist (trans. *Teacher and Preacher*).

233. Pr. 16b (DW 1:263–76). There are two English versions: Walshe 1:123–28; and that of Frank Tobin in *Teacher and Preacher*, 275–79 (I use the Tobin translation here, unless otherwise noted). See the discussion of Susanne Köbele in *Lectura Eckhardi*, 52–74; and Bruce Milem, "Meister Eckhart and the Image: Sermon 16b," *Eckhart Review* (spring 1999): 47–59, as well as the notes in Largier 1:905–12.

234. Pr. 16b (DW 1:265.4): Dâ treget diu sêle daz götlîche bilde und ist gote glîch.

235. Pr. 16b (DW 1:268.3–6): Ir sult wizzen, daz daz einvaltic götlîche bilde, daz in die sêle gedrücket ist in dem inigsten der natûre, âne mittel sich nemende ist; und daz innigste und daz edelste, daz in der natûre ist, daz erbildet sich aller eigenlîchest in daz bilde der sêle, ...

236. Pr. 16a (DW 1:268.9–11): Hie ennimet daz bilde niht got, als er ein schepfer ist, sunder ez nimet in, als er ein vernünftic wesen ist, und daz edelste der natûre erbildet sich aller eigenlîchest in daz bilde (Tobin trans. modified).

237. Eckhart used this text often, citing it seventeen times in the John commentary and another eight times in the LW and DW according to the indices published thus far.

238. Pr 16b (DW 1:272.11–273.6): Her umbe ist daz aleine ein gereht mensche, der alliu geschaffeniu dinc vernihtet hât und an einer glîchen linien âne allez ûzluogen in daz êwige wort gerihtet stât und dar în gebildet und widerbildet in der gerehticheit. Der mensche nimet, dâ der sun nimet und ist der sun selber. Ein geschrift sprichet: "nieman bekennet den vater dan der sun," und dâ von, wellet ir got bekennen, sô sult ir niht aleine glîch sîn dem sune, sunder ir sult der sun selber sîn (Tobin trans. modified). There are similar expressions of absolute identity with the Son as *imago Dei* elsewhere; see, e.g., Pr. 44 (DW 2:328–44, and 349), Pr. 51 (DW 2:472), and Pr. 70 (DW 3:197–98).

239. Pr. 16a (DW 1:259.22–29): alsoe sprekic oec van den beelde der sielen. dat daer ute gaet, dat es, dat daer in blijft, ende dat daer in blijft, dat es, dat daer ute gaet. Dir beelde es die sone des vad, ende dit beelde benic selue, ende dit beelde es die wisheit (trans. Walshe). See the Latin article in Proc.Col.I n.62 (LW 5:220–21).

240. Sturlese, "Mysticism and Theology in Eckhart's Theory of the Image," 18–25.

241. Proc. Col. I n.127 (forthcoming in LW 5; Théry, 202): Quod autem in fine dicitur: quod ego sum illa ymago, error est et falsum. Non enim quidquam creatum est ymago, sed ad ymaginem creati sunt angelus et homo. Ymago enim proprie, et similitudo non est proprie facta nec opus nature.

242. Pr. 72 (DW 3:243:1–2): Daz dritte ist inwendic in dem geiste, daz bekennet sunder bilde und glîchnisse, und diz bekantnisse glîchet sich den engeln (my trans.).

243. Pr. 70 (DW 3:194.13–195.2): Sol ich got bekennen âne mittel und âne glîchnisse, sô muoz got vil nâhe ich werden und ich vil nâhe got, alsô gar ein, . . . (trans. *Teacher and Preacher*).

244. Pr. 70 (DW 3:197.2–198.2): Gotes eignschaft ist, daz er sich selben bekennet sunder "kleine" und sunder diz und daz. Alsô bekennet der engel got, als er sich selben bekennet. . . . Nû spriche ich: "wir suln in bekennen rehte, als er sich selben bekennet" [cf. 1 Cor. 13:12] in dem widerbilde, daz aleine bilde ist gotes und der gotheit, niht der gotheit dan als vil, als si der vater ist. Rehte als vil wir dem bilde glîch sîn, in dem bilde alliu bilde ûzgevlozzen und gelâzen sint, und in dem bilde widerbildet sîn und glîche îngetragen sîn in daz bilde des vaters, als verre als er daz in uns bekennet, als verre

bekennen wir in, als er sich selben bekennet (trans. *Teacher and Preacher* modified). A similar teaching is found in Pr. 72, where Eckhart also preaches the necessity of going beyond all images of this and that to "the Son . . . as an image of God above all images, . . . an image of his concealed Godhead" (DW 3:244.4–245.1: . . . der sun ist ein bilde gotes obe bilde; er ist ein bilde sîner verborgenen gotheit). The perfect mutuality of the knowledge between God and the soul at this level is well expressed in Pr. 10 (DW 1:162.2–4): Daz selbe bekantnisse, dâ sich got selben inne bekennet, daz ist eines ieglîchen abegescheidenen geistes bekantnisse und kein anderz.

245. Pr. 69 (DW 3:159–80). For literature on this important sermon and a commentary, see Largier 2:666–75.

246. Pr. 69 (DW 3:169.1–5): Ein kraft ist in der sêle, daz ist vernünfticheit. Von êrste, sô diu gotes gewar wirt und gesmecket, sô hât si vünf eigenschefte an ir. Daz êrste ist, daz si abescheidet von hie und von nû. Daz ander, daz si nihte glîch enist. Daz dritte, daz si lûter und unvermenget ist. Daz vierde, daz si in ir selber würkende oder suochende ist. Daz vünfte, daz si ein bilde ist (trans. *Teacher and Preacher*).

247. Pr. 69 (DW 3:176.4–175.5): . . . in dem hât ir die predige alzemâle: bilde und bilde ist sô gar ein und mit einander, daz man keinen underscheit dâ verstân enmac. . . . Ich spriche mê: got mit sîner almehticheit enmac keinen underscheit dâ verstân, wan ez wirt mit einander geborn und stirbet mit einander (trans. *Teacher and Preacher*).

248. Pr. 69 (DW 3:178.3–179.7): Vernünfticheit diu blicket în und durchbrichet alle die winkel der gotheit und nimet den sun in dem herzen des vaters und in dem grunde und setzet in in irn grunt. Vernünfticheit diu dringet în; ir engenüeget niht an güete noch an wîsheit noch an wârheit noch an gote selber. . . . Si engeruowet niemer; si brichet in den grunt, dâ güete und wârheit ûzbrichet, und nimet ez *in principio,* in dem beginne, dû güete und wârheit ûzgânde ist, ê ez dâ deheinen namen gewinne, ê ez ûzbreche (my trans.).

249. Pr. 52 (DW 2:502.7–9): . . . wan in dem selben wesene gotes, dâ got ist obe wesene und ob underscheide, dâ was ich selbe, dâ wolte ich mich selben und bekante mich selben ze machenne disen menschen (trans. *Essential Eckhart*). Eckhart repeats this in several guises in what follows (DW 2:503–05). In addition, see Pr. 22 (DW 1:380–81); Pr. 30 (DW 2:94–96); and Pr. 91 (DW 4:84).

250. See Pr. 13 (DW 1:220.4–8): Ein kraft ist in der sêle, von der ich mêr gesprochen hân—und waere diu sêle alliu alsô, sô waere si ungeschaffen und ungeschepflich. Nû enist des niht. An dem andern teile sô hât si ein zuosehen und ein zuohangen ze der zît, und dâ rüeret si geschaffenheit und ist geschaffen—vernünfticheit: dirre kraft enist niht verre noch ûzer (trans. Walshe). Note that Eckhart's qualifications expressed in the sermon text did not make it into the condemned article. In the Cologne proceedings this text is found in Proc. Col. I n.59 (LW 5:218). Many other texts in the MHG sermons have similar language about an uncreated something or power in the soul; see, e.g., Prr. 2, 7, 10, 11, 12 22, 24 (DW 1:32–35 and 39–45, 123–24, 171–73, 182–84, 197–98, 380–81, 417–18); Prr. 26, 27, 28, 29, 30, 40, 42, 46, 48, 50 (DW 2:30 and 34, 52–53, 66, 88, 95–97, 277, 306–8, 382, 418–20, 459–60); Prr. 68, 76, 84 (DW 3:141, 315–16, 462); Pr. 95 (DW 4:186). The same teaching is propounded in the Latin works, as clearly expressed In Sap. n.24 (LW 2:344.6–345.1): Si quid esset vivens aut intelligens, non habens esse aliquod praeter et extra vivere et intelligere, ipsum esset ut sic increabile. Cf. In Gen.I n.112 (LW 1:267), In Sap. nn.32, 94 (LW 2:353, 428); S. XXIX nn.301, 304 (LW 4:267–68, 269–70).

251. Eckhart's response can be found in Proc.Col.I n.137 (LW 5, forthcoming;

Théry, 201): . . . dixi . . . ut esset intellectus, sicut ipse deus intellectus est, qui utique intellectus purus est, increatus, nulli nichil habens commune. Filium quidem suum unigenitum quem generat, qui est ymago, vestivit se ipso ut esset increatus, immensus, qualis et pater. Hominem autem utpote creatum, fecit ad ymaginem, non ymaginem, et vestivit non se ipso, sed secundum se ipsum. For another response on "petia vel pars anime sit increabilis," see Théry, 214–15. In the sermon that he preached in his defense at Cologne in February 13, 1327, Eckhart mounted a similar argument, here invoking the language of *concreatum* to describe the soul as *ad imaginem*. Eckhart said: Et quod aliquid sit in anima, si ipsa tota esset talis, ipsa esset increata, intellexi verum esse et intelligo etiam secundum doctores meos collegas, si anima esset intellectus essentialiter. Nec unquam dixi, nec sensi, quod aliquid sit in anima, quod sit aliquid anime, quod sit increatum et increabile, quia tunc anima esset pecia [= petia] ex creato et increato, cuius oppositum scripsi et docui, nisi quis vellet dicere: increatum vel non creatum, id est, non per se creatum sed concreatum. On this text, see Tobin, *Meister Eckhart*, 133.

252. The best short account of these terms and their relation to Eckhart's teaching on the intellect is in Tobin, *Meister Eckhart*, 126–40. Other studies are H. Hof, *Scintilla animae;* and Klaus Kremer, "Das Seelenfunklein bei Meister Eckhart," *Trierer theologische Zeitschrift* 97 (1988): 8–38.

253. S. XXXVI n.364 (LW 4:313.9–10): Et ut totum, quod est animae unum, quaerat in hac, venit Jesus. On the role of the *unum animae* in Eckhart's preaching and its connection with Proclus, see A. de Libera, *La mystique rhénane*, 278–84.

254. On this see Mojsisch, *Meister Eckhart*, 131–32; and Wackernagel, *YMAGINE DENUDARI*, 45–48 and 131–32.

Chapter 6
Going without a Way: The Return to the Ground

1. My translation from the edition in Alois M. Haas, "An den Grenzen der Sprache," in *Sermo Mysticus: Studien zu Theologie und Sprache der deutschen Mystik* (Freiburg, Switzerland: Universitätsverlag, 1979), 304.

2. Among the works devoted to Eckhart's Christology, see Bardo Weiss, *Die Heilsgeschichte bei Meister Eckhart* (Mainz: Matthias Grünewald Verlag, 1965), chaps. 2–4; Richard Schneider, "The Functional Christology of Meister Eckhart," *Recherches de théologie ancienne et médiévale* 35 (1968): 291–332; Dietmar Mieth, *Christus—Das Soziale im Menschen* (Düsseldorf: Patmos, 1972); Alois M. Haas, "Jesus Christus—Inbegriff des Heils und verwirkliche Transzendenz im Geist der deutschen Mystik," in *Epiphanie des Heils. Zur Heilsgegenwart in indischer und christlicher Religion* (Vienna: Institut für Indologie der Universität Wien, 1983), 193–216; idem, *Meister Eckhart als normative Gestalt geistlichen Lebens*, 2nd ed. (Freiburg: Johannes Verlag, 1995), especially chap. 4; and Alain de Libera *La mystique rhénane d'Albert le Grand à Maître Eckhart* (Paris: Éditions du Seuil, 1994), 250–59. Specifically on Eckhart's soteriology, see Irmgard Kampmann, *"Ihr sollt der Sohn selber sein": Eine fundamentaltheologische Studie zur Soteriologie Meister Eckharts* (Frankfurt: Peter Lang, 1996).

3. For an introduction, see Ewert Cousins, "The Humanity and Passion of Christ," in *Christian Spirituality, II, High Middle Ages and Reformation*, ed. Jill Raitt in collaboration with Bernard McGinn and John Meyendorff (New York: Crossroad, 1987), 375–91.

4. For an overview of the history of *imitatio Christi*, see Giles Constable, *Three Studies in Medieval Religious and Social Thought* (Cambridge: Cambridge University Press, 1995), part 2.

5. For example, in interpreting John 1:43, where Jesus tells Philip "Come, follow," rather than relating the passage to the *imitatio Christi* motif as most authors did, Eckhart's In Ioh. nn.227–48 (LW 3:190–207) provides a long sermon on the universal following God as *esse*—one that doesn't even mention Christ!

6. Pr. 90 (DW 4:43–71). In DW 4:66–70 Eckhart adopts Aquinas's teaching on the four modes of Christ's knowledge (see STh 3a, qq.9–12; and in *Compendium theologiae* bk. 1, chap. 216) as a springboard for a treatment of what Christ teaches us through our participation in these modes. A few other places briefly touch on technical christological issues; e.g., the brief mention of the *esse personale hypostaticum ipsius verbi* (depending on Thomas Aquinas, STh 3a, q.2, a.5) in the Prol.op.prop. n.19 (LW 1:177); and the distinction of the three states of humanity assumed by the Word in S. V nn.42–43 (LW 4:42–43).

7. In the MHG sermons alone, for example, the following contain discussions of Christ (more important treatments in italics): Prr. 1, 5a, *5b*, 20a, 20b, *22*, 23, *24*, 25, *29*, 30, 40, 41, *46*, *47*, *49*, 55, 59, *67*, 78, 86, 87, *90*. In the treatises, see BgT (DW 5:48–49); RdU (DW 5:246–49, 253–54, 259, 270–72); and the doubtfully authentic VAbe (DW 5:414, 430–31). Christology is a frequent topic in the Latin commentaries, especially the John commentary.

8. See Schneider, "Functional Christology of Meister Eckhart"; and Haas, "Jesus Christus."

9. Eckhart's commentary on John 1:1–18 takes up nn.4–198 (LW 3:5–167) of this, his longest, work.

10. The earliest appearance of the axiom "God became man so that man might become God" is in Irenaeus, *Adversus haereses* 3.19.1 (PG 7:939AB); but it can be found in various forms in many other Fathers, e.g., Athanasius, *De incarnatione* 8 (PG 25:110). Eckhart may well have been familiar with it through texts in Augustine; e.g., Sermo 13 (PL 39:216). The related formula used here (*homo est per gratiam quod Deus est per naturam*) is based on a passage found in Maximus Confessor, *Ambigua* (PG 91:1088C), and is paraphrased by Eriugena, *Periphyseon* V (PL 122:880A): Animadverte, quod ait [i.e., Maximus], totus homo manens secundum animam et corpus per naturam, et totus factus Deus secundum animam et corpus per gratiam. Similar formulae, however, can be found in many authors.

11. Pr. 29 (DW 2:84.1–2): Warumbe ist got mensche worden? Dar umbe, daz ich got geborn würde der selbe (trans. Walshe). See also Prr. 25, 30, 46 (DW 2:14–16, 98, 378–83); Pr. 67 (DW 3:134–35).

12. The formula *filius per naturam-filius per gratiam* occurs in Augustine's *Tractatus in Ioannem* 75.1 (PL 35:1829): Quamvis ergo nos Filius Dei suo Patri adoptaverit filios, et eumdem Patrem nos voluerit habere per gratiam, qui ejus Pater est per naturam. . . . For a more detailed exposition of the distinction in the commentary on the Prologue, see n.123 (LW 3:107). Similar appeals to the distinction of sonships can be found throughout In Ioh.; e.g., nn.117, 368, and 455 (LW 3:101–2, 312–13, and 389).

13. See, e.g., BgT 1 (DW 5:37–38), and such homilies as Pr. 40 (DW 2:277), and Pr. 59 (DW 2:378). In the Latin writings, see SS. XLII n.422, LII n.523 (LW 4:355, 437–38). The same theme is implied when Eckhart discusses how we are co-heirs with Christ in In Eccli. n.41 (LW 2:269–70), S. XII n.126, and S. LV n.556 (LW 4:120 and 465).

14. E.g., Proc.Col. I n.61 (LW 5:219) and Eckhart's response in Théry, 201–2. The largest group of such texts is from Proc.Col. II—arts. 7, 15, 24–26, 27, 29, 39, 53, 57, 59 (Théry, 214, 219–20, 226–29, 229–35, 235–36, 242–44, 259, 264–65, 266–68). See also Votum Theologicum from Avignon, art. XVII-XVIII, and XXI-XXIII (Pelster ed., 1117, 1119–21). For a study of these texts, see Karl G. Kertz, S.J., "Meister Eckhart's Teaching on the Birth of the Divine Word in the Soul," *Traditio* 15 (1959): 339–63, though I believe that Kertz misunderstands the import of the distinction of sonships by failing to see that they represent only one pole of Eckhart's dialectical thought about our relation to Christ.

15. Proc.Col.II (Théry, 268): Non est ergo putandum quod alius sit filius quo Christus ejus filius est, et alius quo nos nominamur et simus filii dei, sed id ipsum et is ipse, qui Christus filius est naturaliter genitus, nos filii dei sumus analogice cui coherendo, utpote herenti, coheredes sumus.

16. The 2 Corinthians text is used three more times and explained in greater length in the commentary on v. 14 (In Ioh. nn.119–120 [LW 3:103–5]). It is cited frequently elsewhere: e.g., In Gen.I n.301 (LW 1:440); In Gen.II nn.130, 141, 219 (LW 1:596, 609–10, 697–98); In Sap. n.45 (LW 2:368); In Ioh. nn.155, 505, 575 (LW 3:128, 436, 504); S. XLIX nn.507–8 (LW 4:423); Prr. 6 and 23 (DW 1:110, 397–98); Pr. 41 (DW 2:296); BgT 1 (DW 5:32); RdU 20 (DW 5:266).

17. In Ioh. n.117 (LW 3:101.14–102.2): Parum enim mihi esset *verbum caro factum* pro homine in Christo, supposito illo a me distincto, nisi et in me personaliter, ut et ego essem filius dei.

18. Besides its frequent presence in the Defense, Eckhart also used the *inquantum* principle in sermons discussing Christ's Sonship and ours, e.g., Pr. 22 (DW 1:381–82), and Pr. 40 (DW 2:272–81).

19. In Ioh. n.118 (LW 3:103.12–14): Ait ergo: *verbum caro factum est* in Christo, *et habitavit in nobis,* quando in quolibet nostrum filius dei fit homo et filius hominis fit filius dei. Eckhart emphasizes the necessary connection between the two sonships by appealing to John 16:2 ("I will see you *again*"), arguing that the first "seeing" is the Incarnation and the second is the Son's dwelling in us (see nn.117 and 119).

20. In Ioh. n.125 (LW 3:108.9–13): . . . *plenum gratiae et veritatis* inclusive, supposita veritate semper historiae, continere et docere rerum naturalium, moralium et artificialium proprietates. Notandum ergo quod universaliter et naturaliter in omni opere naturae et artis verbum caro fit et habitat in illis quae fiunt sive in quibus verbum caro fit.

21. In Ioh. n.185 (LW 3:154.8–14): Rursus notandum quod, quia "verbum caro factum est," ut habitaret in nobis, ut supra expositum est, . . . congrue subiciendum videtur quod dei sapientia sic caro fieri dignata est, ut ipsa incarnatio quasi media inter divinarum personarum processionem et creaturarum productionem utriusque naturam sapiat, ita ut incarnatio ipsa sit exemplata quidem ab aeterna emanatione et exemplar totius naturae inferioris. Eckhart goes on to draw the conclusion from this that there can be no difference in the *content* of philosophy and theology, only in the way the truth is apprehended (LW 3:155.5–7).

22. On this aspect of Eckhart's thought, see Haas, *Meister Eckhart als normative Gestalt,* 94–96.

23. S. XXV n.253 (LW 4:232.2–3): . . . Ioh. 16: "exivi a patre et veni in mundum" per creationem, non tantum per incarnationem. This notion of what was later to be called the absolute predestination of Christ is also found in Pfeiffer LXXVII (ed. 250.22–26):

Ez stêt in dem buoche Moysi geschriben, daz Âdam wêre der êrste mensche, den got ie geschuof. Und ich spriche, daz Kristus wêre der êrste mensche, den ie got geschuof. Alse wie? Ez sprichet ein meister: daz êrste in der meinunge ist daz beste von den werken.

24. Proc.Col.II, art. 27 (LW 5:234): Vicesimus septimus articulus sic dicit: Deus nihil dat extra se. Ipse semper dat ex aeternitate, non in tempore. Deus nihil habet facere cum tempore, sed ipse solum dat et operatur ex aeternitate. This seems to reflect a text from Pr. 5a (DW 1:77.18–78.1): Sin gab ist zemol einfaltig und volkommen on teilen und nit in zyt, alles in der ewikeit. . . . The point appears more fully in Prol.gen. nn.17–19; e.g.: Ubi notandum quod omne quod deus creat, operatur vel agit, in se ipso operatur vel agit (LW 1:161.3–4). Eckhart's defense of art. 27 has not yet appeared in LW 5, so I will use the edition in Théry, 229–35.

25. Proc.Col.II (Théry, 230): Hinc est quod opus creationis, nature, ordinatur ad opus recreationis et gratie, materiale ad formale, materia ad formam, passivum ad activum, mulier ad virum.

26. Proc.Col.II (Théry, 231): Patet ergo manifeste omne quod in premissis quatuor articulis dicitur, scilicet quod humanam naturam assumpsit verbum ex intentione prima, hanc tamen naturam, scilicet in Christo, propter totam speciem humanam. Assumendo igitur ipsam naturam, in ipso et per ipsum contulit gratiam filiationis et adoptionis omnibus hominibus, michi, tibi et cuilibet participantibus univoce et equaliter ipsam naturam, secundum illud: *verbum caro factum est,* in Christo scilicet, *et habitavit in nobis.*

27. Proc.Col.II (Théry, 232–34).

28. Pr. 46 (DW 2:378–86); I will cite the translation of F. Tobin in *Teacher and Preacher,* 304–6.

29. Pr. 46 (DW 2:380.5–381.2): Wan als daz wâr ist, daz got mensche worden ist, als wâr ist daz, daz der mensche got worden ist. Und alsô ist diu menschlîche natûre über-bildet in dem, daz si worden ist daz götlîche bilde, daz dâ bilde ist des vaters.

30. The sermon concludes (DW 3:384–86) with a fourth point illustrating the transformation by an examination of the relation between the just person and Justice.

31. Pr. 49 (DW 2:427–51). I will use the translation found in Walshe 2:285–97, who numbers this sermon as 89, following Pfeiffer.

32. For other treatments of the relation between Mary's birth and our own, see, e.g., Prr. 22, 23, 78, etc.

33. The four conditions that Eckhart advances (DW 2:429–31) are based on Gregory's *Homilia in Evangelia* bk. I, Hom. 18, n.1 (PL 76:1150B).

34. Pr. 49 (DW 2:435.6–8): Sehet, her umbe sprichet der vater diz wort williclîche und niht von willen, und natiurlîche und niht von natûre.

35. Pr.49 (DW 2:435.8–9): In disem worte sprichet der vater mînen geist und dînen geist und eines ieglîchen menschen geist glîch dem selben worte.

36. On suffering in Eckhart, see especially Donald F. Duclow, "'My Suffering is God': Meister Eckhart's *Book of Divine Consolation,*" *Theological Studies* 44 (1983): 570–86; and Alois M. Haas, "'Trage Leiden geduldiglich': Die Einstellung der deutschen Mystik zum Leiden," *Zeitwende* 57, no. 3 (1986): 154–75.

37. Pr. 49 (DW 2:440.10–11): Daz ist in der wârheit; wan dô der lîchame von pîne an dem kriuze starp, dô lebete sîn edel geist in dirre gegenwerticheit.

38. For other discussions of Christ's external suffering, see the treatises, RdU 20 (DW 5:270–72), and especially the doubtfully authentic treatise VAbe (DW 5:411–22). It is in the latter text where Eckhart uses the analogy of the moving door (= outer

powers) and the immobile hinge (= inner ground) to help explain why Christ did not suffer within (5:421–22). For a full treatment of the role of suffering in Christ and in the just person the teaching of Pr. 86 also needs to be taken into account (see below).

39. Eckhart often proposes Christ's suffering and death as the example for all Christians, using Matt. 10:37 ("Deny yourself and come follow me") and Matt. 16:24 ("If anyone wishes to come after me, let me take up his cross and follow me"), as well as related texts in Luke 9:23 and 14:27. The most extended treatment is in S. XLV nn. 459–68 (LW 4:380–87; translated in *Teacher and Preacher*, 230–33), but see also S. LV nn.545–46 (LW 4:456–57). For some appearances in the vernacular works, see, e.g., Prr. 10, 15 (DW 1:170, 224); Pr. 59 (DW 2:628, 630); Pr. 76 (DW 3:326); and BgT (DW 5:45). There are many other texts that propose Christ's suffering as a model without citing these specific biblical verses; e.g., S. XIII n.149 (LW 4:140).

40. Pr. 49 (DW 2:445.7–9): . . . und alles sînes lidennes sol in dünken als kleine, rehte als ein tropfe wazzers gegen dem wilden mer. Als kleine solt dû ahten alles dînes lîdennes gegen dem grôzen lîdenne Jêsû Kristî.

41. Pr. 49 (DW 2:446.5–7): . . . sunder er sol got lâzen mit im würken allez, daz er wil, oder als dû niht ensîst: alsô gewaltic sol got sîn in allem dem, daz dû bist, als in sîner eigenen ungeschaffenen natûre. The motif of utter surrender to God even if he should damn us (*resignatio ad infernum*), based on Romans 9:3, was a popular one with late medieval mystics. Eckhart makes use of it often: In Ex. n.270 (LW 2:217); In Ioh. n.79 (LW 3:67); S. VI n.67 (LW 4:65); Prr. 4, 6, 12 (DW 1:63–64, 100 and 103, 195–97); Pr. 25 (DW 2:10–11); RdU 10 (DW 5:223); and especially BgT 1 (DW 5:14–15, 21, 25, and 40).

42. Pr. 49 (DW 3:449.3–5): Kristus, unser herre, der ist aleine unser ende, dem wir nâchvolgen suln, und unser zil, under dem wir blîben suln und mit dem wir vereinet werden suln glîch aller sîner êre, als und diu einunge zuogehoeret.

43. At this point we might well ask what role the resurrection plays in Eckhart's teaching. The Meister rarely refers to Christ's physical resurrection, but insofar as his resurrection is the source of our own, one can say that it does have a place in his teaching (see, e.g., the early texts in the *Collatio in Libros Sententiarum* n.8 [LW 5:24–25]), and the *Sermo paschalis* of 1294 [LW 5:136–48]). Among the later MHG sermons, see especially Pr. 35 (DW 2:173–83), preached for the Easter Vigil, as well as the sermons delivered on Easter Sunday (Prr. 55–56) and the Octave of Easter (Prr. 36a-36b). See also the difficult Pr. 67 (DW 3:126–38), where the Dominican teaches (the only place in his works) that the most complete union with God will not be realized until the resurrection of the body (see especially 3:134–35).

44. On the BgT, see Duclow, "My Suffering is God," especially 575–82. Suffering, of course, is also a major theme of Eckhart's preaching; see, e.g., Prr. 2, 4, 6, 8, 11, 12, 13 (DW 1:36–38, 61–64, 103, 127–28, 188, 200–201, 214); Prr. 30, 49, 51, 59 (DW 2:106, 430–47, 476, 630–31); Prr. 62, 68 (DW 3:63, 145); Pr. 94 (DW 4:142–45). There are also important considerations in RdU (DW 5:225, 229, 257–58, 271–72).

45. BgT (DW 5:54.3): . . . mîn leit in gote ist und mîn leit got ist.

46. BgT (DW 5:49.6–8): Gotes sun von natûre wolte von gnaden, daz er durch lîden möhte, und du wilt gotes sun werden und niht mensche, daz du niht enmügest noch endürfest lîden durch got noch durch selben (trans. Walshe) There is a similar passage in DW 5:48.5–8. Eckhart's teaching here shows similarities to Hadewijch's insistence that the best way to follow Jesus is to live both God *and* man (i.e., the suffering Christ); see Bernard McGinn, *The Flowering of Mysticism: Men and Women in the New Mysticism (1200–1350)* (New York: Crossroad, 1998), 219–21.

47. Among Eckhart's sermons, we find frequent discussion of the purpose of the Incarnation; see, e.g., Prr. 5a, 25, 29, 30, 38; S. XII; Pfeiffer LXXV; etc.

48. See Pr. 22 (DW 1:377.12–379.1): "Vrouwe, daz ir nû gloubet, daz ich iuch liep hên, sô hân ich mich iu glîch gemachet; ich enhân ouch niht dan éin ouge." Diz ist der mensche, der kunde gar kûme glouben, daz in got sô lip hâte, biz als lanc daz got im selber ein ouge ûz stach und an sich name menschlîche natûre (trans. *Essential Eckhart*). Eckhart tells the same story in In Ioh. n.683 (LW 3:598–99).

49. For discussions of Christ taking on common human nature and not a human person, beside the texts utilized above, see, e.g., Prr. 5b, 24, and 41. In the Latin writings, e.g., Prol.op.prop. n.19 (LW 1:177); In Ioh. nn.288–91 (LW 3:241); and SS. XX n.199, XXV n.263, and LII n.523 (LW 4:184, 240, and 437).

50. For some examples, see Pr. 2, and the other vernacular sermons cited below. The theme is frequent in the Latin sermons; see, SS. XX, XXII, XLII, XLIV.1, and LII.

51. "In agro dominico," art. 11, as drawn from Pr. 5a (DW 1:77.10–13). Article 12 is taken from Pr. 24 (DW 1:421–22). Here Eckhart explicitly states that he taught this position at Paris, presumably between 1311 and 1313. A number of other articles, especially 13 and 20–22, deal with the related question of the identity between the Eternal Word and the just person, though they do not explicitly mention the Incarnate God-man.

52. See especially In Ioh. nn.352–55, and the long commentary on Jn. 4:38 in nn.381–404 (LW 3:298–301 and 324–43).

53. E.g., Proc.Col.II, art. 29 (Théry, 235–36); and the Votum at Avignon, art. XXIII (ed. Pelster, 1120–21).

54. Here I differ from Kertz, "Meister Eckhart's Teaching on the Birth of the Divine Word in the Soul," especially 345–50, who misses the importance of the identity motif.

55. Pr. 38 (DW 2:231.3–232.1): Waere aber, daz zît diu sêle berüeren möhte, sô enmöhte got niemer in ir geborn werden, und si enmühte niemer in gote geborn werden. . . . Daz ist daz nû der êwichkeit, dâ diu sêle in gote alliu dinc niuwe und vrisch und gegenwertic bekennet und in der lust, als diu ich iezuo gegenwertic hân (trans. Walshe). The same interpretation of Galatians 4:4 is found in Prr. 4, 11, and 24 (DW 1:74, 177–78, 422–23). See also In Ioh. n.293 (LW 3:245).

56. In Ioh. nn.683–91 (LW 3:598–607) has a brief interpretation of the passion narrative during which the Meister says almost nothing about the details of Jesus' suffering that fascinated most of his contemporaries. He discusses only five of the eighty-two verses in John 18–19, and most of his attention is taken up with one verse: John 18:38, when Pilate asks Christ, "What is truth?"

57. See, e.g., Prr. 1, 49, and 86; and RdU 16–18. In the Latin works, S. LV.3 is important.

58. See RdU 17 (DW 5:253–55).

59. While the essence of the *imitatio passionis* rests in complete abnegation and stripping off of all created reality, the most detailed treatment of Matthew 16:24, that found in S. XLV (LW 4:374–87), also has much to say about how "devout remembrance of the Lord's Passion" in a more concrete and practical sense can help lead to this goal.

60. S. XLVII n.485 (LW 4:400.14): Unde ut daret [Deus] totum se, assumpsit totum me.

61. VAbe (DW 5:433.1–3): Daz snelleste tier, iuch treget ze dirre volkomenheit, daz ist lîden, wan ez niuzet nieman mê êwiger süezicheit, dan die mit Kristô stânt in der groesten bitterkeit (trans. *Essential Eckhart*).

62. "In agro dominico," art. 25, drawn from In Ioh. n.728 (LW 3:636–37).

63. Eckhart, of course, emphasizes the reciprocity of love of God and love of neighbor in a number of places; e.g., In Ex. n.99 (LW 2:101–2); In Ioh. n.290 (LW 3:242); SS. XXX n.307, XL nn.390 and 393 (LW 4:272, 336 and 338). Similar insistence is often found in the MHG sermons that treat love—one of Eckhart's most common themes. On love in the vernacular sermons, see Prr. 4, 5a, 5b, 12, 22 (DW 1:67–68, 79, 87–88, 195–97, 385–87); Prr. 27, 28, 29, 30, 32, 39, 40, 41, 45, 57 (DW 2:41–50, 59–60, 79–82, 101–6, 145, 264, 273, 285–87, 371–72, 605–6); Prr. 60, 61, 63, 65, 71, 73, 74, 75, 76, 82, 83 (DW 3:13–14, 44–45, 74ff, 95–103, 222, 267–69, 284–86, 292ff, 328, 426–27, 448); Prr. 92, 103 (DW 4:129–31; Pfeiffer 29–30); BgT (DW 5:15, 25); RdU 10 and 15 (DW 5:218–24, 240–44); VAbe (DW 5:402–3, 432). For an introduction to Eckhart's doctrine of love, see Bernard McGinn, "St. Bernard and Meister Eckhart," Cîteaux 31 (1980): 373–86.

64. Pr. 12 (DW 1:195.1–5): Hâst dû dich selben liep, sô hâst dû alle menschen liep als dich selben. Die wîle dû einen einigen menschen minner liep hâst dan dich selben, dâ gewünne dich selben nie liep in der wârheit, dû enhabest denne alle menschen liep als dich selben, in einen menschen alle menschen, und der mensche ist got und mensche . . . (trans. Walshe).

65. S. LVI n.557 (LW 4:466.5–8): Unde oportet omnia reducere et tingere in sanguine Christi, mediante ipso filio in patrem, sicut omnia operatur pater per filium, ut refluxus effluxui respondeat.

66. S. LII n.523 (LW 4:437.7–11): Deus assumpsit vestem nostram, ut vere, proprie et per substantiam sit homo et homo deus in Christo. Natura autem assumpta communis est omni homini sine magis et minus. Ergo datum est omni homini filium dei fieri, per substantiam quidem in ipso, in se autem adoptive per gratiam.

67. On grace in Eckhart, see Edouard-Henri Wéber, "La théologie de la grâce chez Maître Eckhart," Revue des sciences religieuses 70 (1996): 48–72; V. Lossky, Théologie négative et connaissance de Dieu chez Maître Eckhart (Paris: Vrin, 1960), 175–97; F. Tobin, Meister Eckhart: Thought and Language (Philadelphia: University of Pennsylvania Press, 1986), 105–15; W. Goris, Einheit als Prinzip und Ziel: Versuch über die Einheitsmetaphysik des "Opus tripartitum" Meister Eckharts (Leiden: Brill, 1997), 249–51, and chap. 8 passim; and Largier 2:904–13, commenting on S. XXV. This Latin sermon (LW 4:230–44), Eckhart's most sustained treatment of grace, has been translated in Teacher and Preacher, 216–23. The context in which Eckhart formulated his doctrine of grace in MHG has been analyzed by Georg Steer, Scholastische Gnadenlehre in mittelhochdeutschen Sprache (Munich: Beck, 1961), 13–15 on Eckhart.

68. Treatments of grace are found in most of Eckhart's works. I. Latin Works: In Gen.II n.145 (LW 1:613); In Ex. nn.13, 275 (LW 2:19, 222); In Sap. nn.214, 272–74 (LW 2:550, 602–4); In Ioh. nn.179, 326, 500–501, 521, 544, 592–94, 709 (LW 3:147–48, 274, 431–32, 449–50, 474–75, 516–17, 621); SS. II nn.15–18, IX nn.96–102, XV n.159, XVII n.179, XX n.200, XXV, XXXII n.328, XLIV n.437, XLIX n.508, LII n.523 (LW 4:16–20, 92–97, 151–52, 167–68, 185, 230–44, 286–87, 367, 423, 437). II. German Works: Prr. 7, 11, 21, 24 (DW 1:124, 177, 366–67, 419); Prr. 33, 38, 43, 44, 52 (DW 2:151, 241–45, 325–27, 346–47, 501–2); Prr. 66, 67, 70, 73, 75, 76, 80, 81, 82, 86 (DW 3:109–10 and 118, 134, 196, 262–63 and 267, 297–98, 318–20, 381, 398–404, 428–30, 490); Prr. 96, 103 (DW 4:213–19; Pfeiffer, 27). See also RdU (DW 5:265, 272, 307–8).

69. See the comments in Tobin, Meister Eckhart, 107–8, 111.

70. See S. XXV n.258 (LW 4:237–38). We have commented above on how Eckhart uses the traditional distinction between gratia gratis data and gratia gratum faciens in his own way.

71. In Sap. nn.272–74 (LW 2:602–4).

72. In Sap. n.273 (LW 2:603.7–9): . . . quod gratia gratum faciens, quae et super-naturalis dicitur, est in solo intellectivo, sed nec in illo, ut res est et natura, sed est in ipso ut intellectus et ut naturam sapit divinam, ... On grace as supernatural, see also S. XXV nn. 264 and 268. In his MHG works Eckhart also insists that grace is given only to the soul's essence; see, e.g., Pr. 11 (DW 1:177.4–8): Der sêle engenüeget ouch enkeine wîs niht, der sun gotes enwerde denne in ir geborn. Und dâ entspringet gnâde. Gnâde wirt dâ îngegozzen. Gnâde enwürket niht; ir werk ist ir gewerden. Si vliuzet ûz dem wesene gotes und vliuzet in daz wesen der sêle und niht in die krefte. The supernatural, but still created, status of grace is emphasized in Pr. 81, where Eckhart speaks of grace as *ein antlütze gotes* and uses the following analogy: . . . wan diu gnâde heltet sich ze gote als der schîn der sunnen ze der sunnen . . . (DW 3:400.12–13).

73. S. II n.18 (LW 4:20.6–7): Sic ergo in solo deo, sapientia dei, filio, est omnis gra-tia, quia sine merito sunt eius dona omnia et sui solius. The entire S. II.2 nn. 16–18 speaks of the double gratuity of grace, both of creation (*gratia gratis data*) and recre-ation (*gratia gratum faciens*)

74. S. XXV n.266 (LW 4:241–42) says that the soul can receive grace only insofar as it is an *imago* ordered to God, not in its created status as *ens hoc et hoc*. Although grace is received in the essence of the soul as intellect, in Pr. 33 (DW 2:152–54) and elsewhere Eckhart allows that grace overflows to work in all the powers—will, reason, and the irascible power.

75. See STh 1a2ae, q.109, aa.2–8; q. 111, aa.2–3. Of course, in q. 109, a.1 Aquinas also recognizes the necessity of grace in elevating the mind to know supernatural truths.

76. Pr. 38 (DW 2:244.6–8): Gnâde enwürket kein werk, si ist ze zart dar zuo; werk ist ir als verre, als der himel ist von der erden. Ein innesîn und ein anehaften und ein einen mit gote, daz ist gnâde, . . . (trans. Walshe).

77. Pr. 96 (DW 4:215.33–35): Daz ander, daz si die sêle machet gote glîch und drücket gotes glîchnisse in die sêle und machet sie gotvar, daz si sich den den tiuveln erbiutet vür einen got, daz ist von der edelkeit der gnâde. The adjective *gotvar* is also used in Prr. 43, 54b (DW 2:328–29, 568), and Prr. 81, 82 (DW 3:400, 429).

78. Pr. 96 (DW 4:218.51–52): Alsô bringet diu gnâde die sêle in got und bringet die sêle über sich selber und beroubet sie ir selbes und alles des, daz crêatûre ist, und vere-inet die sêle mit gote (my trans.). The axe example (DW 4:217–18) is adapted from Aristotle, *De anima* II.1 (412b).

79. S. XXV n.263 (LW 4:240.2–5): Item respectu suscipientis gratiam gratia est con-firmatio, configuratio sive potius transfiguratio animae in deum et cum deo. Secundo dat esse unum cum deo, quod plus est assimilatione.

80. Pr. 21 (DW 1:367.3–5): Ich spriche: gnâde eneiniget niht die sêle mit gote, si ist ein volbringen; daz ist ir werk, daz si die sêle wider ze gote bringet (trans. *Teacher and Preacher*). See also Pr. 52 (DW 2:501–2), where Eckhart speaks about Paul as going beyond the work of grace.

81. Pr. 82 (DW 3:427–31).

82. S. IX n.102 (LW 4:96.8–97.2): Nota, si tantum bonum est gratia unius hominis, quantum bonum omnis hominis, omnium angelorum tot specierum, quantum bonum ibi vivere, immo in ipso *deo omnis gratiae*, ubi iam gratia non gratia formaliter, sed vir-tualiter sicut calor in caelo, ubi iam nec bonum nec suave nec esse, sed supra "in regione et regno dissimilitudinis" infinitae. Eckhart's reversal of the famous Platonic-Augustinian phrase of the *regio dissimilitudinis* (*Confessiones* 7.10.16 [PL 32:742]),

which in the tradition had always been applied to the sinful realm of fallen humanity, is striking.

83. Pr. 43 (DW 2:326.1–2): Gnâde engeworhte nie dehein guot werk, daz ist: si engeworhte nie dehein werk; si vliuzet wol ûz an üebunge einer tugend (trans. Walshe).

84. Pr. 70 (DW 3:196.2–12): Daz lieht der sunnen ist kleine wider dem liehte der vernünfticheit, und diu vernünfticheit ist kleine wider dem liehte der gnâde. . . . Daz lieht der gnâde, swie groz ez ist, ez ist doch kleine wider dem götlîchen liehte. . . . Wenne aber diu gnâde wirt volbrâht ûf daz hoehste, sô enist ez niht gnâde, ez ist ein götlich lieht, dar inne man got sihet. . . . Dâ enist kein zuoganc, dâ ist ein dar komen (trans. Walshe modified). For more on the superiority of the light of grace over the light of natural intellect, see Pr. 73 (DW 3:262–63).

85. Pr. 75 (DW 3:299.9–300.3): Suln wir dar în komen, sô müezen wir klimmen von natiulîchem liehte in daz lieht der gnâde und dar inne wahsen in daz lieht, daz der sun selber ist. Dâ werden wir geminnet in dem sune von dem vater mit der minne, diu der heilige geist ist, . . . (trans. Walshe modified).

86. Eckhart does not use the language of created and uncreated grace, so I have avoided it in this presentation. However, his insistence on the virtual existence of grace in God is much like what many others referred to as uncreated grace. See Wéber, "La théologie de la grace," 57–60.

87. On the Eucharist, see RdU 20 (DW 5:262–74); on confession, RdU 21 (DW 5:274–75).

88. To be sure, Eckhart was not totally silent on the sacraments. See, for example, the reflections on the Eucharist in Prr. 20a and 20b (DW 1:326–45), and SS. V and XL n.402 (LW 4:33–49, 343). (S. V is largely a summary of Aquinas's eucharistic theology.) Eckhart also sometimes preached on devout practices; see the *collatio* on bearing the cross in S. XLV nn.464–68 (LW 4:384–87). D. Mieth suggests that both the strength and something of the weakness of Eckhart's spirituality lie in this lack of attention to the concrete forms of piety (*Die Einheit von Vita Activa und Vita Passiva in den deutschen Predigten und Traktaten Meister Eckharts und bei Johannes Tauler* [Regensburg: Pustet, 1969], 159–64, 173, 178).

89. For Eckhart's teaching on prayer, see the essay of Freimut Löser, "'Oratio est cum deo confabulatio': Meister Eckharts Auffassung vom Beten und seine Gebetspraxis," in *Deutsche Mystik in abendländischen Zusammenhang,* ed. Walter Haug and Wolfram Schneider-Lastin (Tübingen: Niemeyer, 2000), 283–316. There are brief but apt remarks in Ian Almond, "How *Not* to Deconstruct a Dominican: Derrida on God and 'Hypertruth,'" *Journal of the American Academy of Religion* 68 (2000): 338–40. Almond concludes: "Eckhart's prayers do not 'direct,' they *de-limit;* they do not 'determine,' they *empty.* Far from invoking the very concept of the God Eckhart deemed idolatrous, Eckhart's prayers initiate the breakthrough to the nameless, silent darkness of the God-head" (p. 340).

90. "In agro dominico" art. 7: Item quod petens hoc aut hoc, malum petit et male, quia negationem boni et negationem Dei petit, et orat deum sibi negari. This is an adaptation of In Ioh. n.611 (LW 3:534.2–4). The other condemned article relating to prayer concerns not taking or asking anything from God. See art. 9 drawn from Pr. 6 (DW 1:112.6–9).

91. On "asses," e.g., Pr. 52 (DW 2:489); on "merchants," e.g., Pr. 16b (DW 1:272–74).

92. Major discussions of prayer can be found in both the Latin and the MHG sermons. See, e.g., SS. XIII nn.147–50, XXIV nn.231–33, and XLVII n.409 (LW 4:138–41, 215–17, and 404–5); and Prr. 53 and 59 (DW 2:543, 624–26); Prr. 62, 63, 65, 67, and 68

(DW 3:60–61, 81, 102, 131, and 145); and RdU (DW 5:188, 190–91). Eckhart also wrote a commentary on the "Lord's Prayer," probably an early work, that can be found in LW 5:109–29. In addition, there is an extensive discussion in the doubtfully authentic Vab (DW 5:414–16, and 426–27). For a more complete listing and discussion of texts, see Löser, "'Oratio est cum deo confabulatio.'"

93. On these four prayers, see Löser, "'Oratio est cum deo confabulatio.'"

94. On God's presence as *esse*, see, e.g., In Ex. n.163 (LW 2:143), and In Ioh. n.97 (LW 3:84).

95. Pr. 4 (DW 1:70.2–3): Alle crêatûren hânt kein wesen, wan ir wesen swebet an der gegenwerticheit gotes (my trans.).

96. Tobin, *Meister Eckhart*, 144, puts this well: "One who merely has an intellectual grasp of all this is still far from the truth. We have to be like this truth to understand it. . . . Paradoxically, it is only by living in such a way that we become the truth do we understand the truth."

97. RdU 6 (DW 5:205.10–211.1): Der got alsô in wesenne hât, der nimet got götlîchen, und dem liuhtet er in allen dingen; . . . . In im blicket got alle zît, in im ist ein abegeschieden abekêren und ein înbilden sînes geminneten gegenwertigen gotes (trans. Walshe).

98. RdU 12 (DW 5:234.5–7): Got ist ein got der gegenwerticheit. Wie er dich vindet, alsô nimet er und enpfaehet dich, niht, waz dû gewesen sîst, sunder waz dû iezunt bist (trans. Walshe). For more on presence, see RdU 7, 21 (DW 5:210–12, 276).

99. Pr. 13a (DW 1:224.12–13): Got ist vber ellu ding ein instan in sich selber vnd sin instan enthaltet alle creaturen (trans. Walshe). See Pr. 3 (DW 1:56).

100. Pr. 9 (DW 1:155.9–10): . . . meinet einen menschen, der hie zuo komen wil, der sol got alle zît bî und gegenwertic sîn . . . (trans. *Teacher and Preacher*). In the same sermon see also 156.11–157.7. Many other sermons deal with the presence theme, e.g., Prr. 5b, 24 (DW 1:93, 418–19 and 423); Prr. 42, 49, 56 (DW 2: 301, 437, 589); Pr. 68 (DW 3:142); and Pr. 97 (DW 4:228).

101. For Eckhart's use of these terms, see the materials gathered in Michael Egerding, *Die Metaphorik der spätmittelalterlichen Mystik*, 2 vols. (Paderborn: Schöningh, 1997), vol. 2, specifically *abescheiden* (pp. 24–28), *brechen* (pp. 129–33), and *gebern* (pp. 219–29).

102. There are many treatments of detachment in Eckhart's mysticism. See especially Denys Turner, *The Darkness of God: Negativity in Christian Mysticism* (Cambridge: Cambridge University Press, 1995), chap. 7, "Eckhart: detachment and the critique of desire." Also helpful are Alois M. Haas, "'. . . DAS PERSÖNLICHE UND EIGENE VERLEUGNEN': Mystische *vernichtigkeit und verworffenheit sein selbs* im Geiste Meister Eckharts," in *Individualität: Poetik und Hermeneutik XIII*, ed. Manfred Frank and Anselm Haverkamp (Munich: Fink, 1988), 106–22; Niklaus Largier, "Repräsentation und Negativität: Meister Eckharts Kritik als Dekonstruktion," in *Contemplata aliis tradere: Studien zum Verhältnis von Literatur und Spiritualität*, ed. C. Brinker, U. Herzog, et al. (Frankfurt: Lang, 1995), 371–90; idem, "Penser la finitude: Création, détachment et les limites de la philosophie dans la pensée de maître Eckhart," *Revue des sciences religieuses* 71 (1997): 458–73; and Marie-Anne Vannier, "Déconstruction de l'individualité ou assomption de la personne chez Eckhart?" in *Individuum und Individualität im Mittelalter*, ed. Jan. A. Aertsen and Andreas Speer (Berlin: Walter de Gruyter, 1996), 622–41.

103. Detachment, that is, "cutting off" (*abescheiden*), appears very often in the MHG sermons; see, e.g., Prr. 2, 7, *10*, 11, *12*, 15, 21, 23, *27*, 28, 29, 30, 38, 42, 43, 44, 46,

48, *52,* 53, 54a, 57, 60, 61, 67, 68, 69, 73, 74, 75, *77, 103, 104* (with the more significant appearances italicized). Both the RdU and the BgT also offer numerous treatments (e.g., DW 5:28–29, 114, 194–98, 200, 205–6, 224–31, 244–45, 275–76, 280–84, 290–309). In addition, we have the treatise, *Von abegescheidenheit* (Vab) edited in DW 5:377–437. Even if the work is not by the Meister himself, it is hard to deny that, at least in large part, it is close to his teaching.

104. On the importance of *entbilden,* see Wackernagel, *YMAGINE DENUDARI.*

105. These terms (*abegescheidenheit* and *glâzenheit*) appear as synonyms in RdU 21 (DW 5:283.8).

106. See Mieth, who says: "So ist die Abgeschiedenheitslehre nichts anders als eine Lehre von der Freiheit . . . " (*Die Einheit von Vita Activa und Vita Passiva,* 152).

107. Vab (DW 5:413.3–4): Und dû solt wizzen: laere sîn aller crêatûre ist gotes vol sîn, und vol sîn aller crêatûre ist gotes laere sîn (trans. *Essential Eckhart*).

108. In Ioh. n.397 (LW 3:338.10–11): Secundo patet quod quanto quid reliquerit plura et est pauperior, tanto invenit plura; et quod reliquerit, invenit nobilius et purius. Cf. In Ioh. n.290 (LW 3:242), and S. XXXVII n.375 (LW 4:320–21).

109. The relation of Eckhart's "deconstruction" to contemporary philosophies of deconstruction, especially that of Jacques Derrida, has received considerable attention lately. See John D. Caputo, "Mysticism and Transgression: Derrida and Meister Eckhart," in *Derrida and Deconstruction,* ed. Hugh J. Silverman (London: Routledge, 1989), 24–39; Largier, "Repräsentation und Negativität"; Marius Buning, "Negativity Then and Now: An Exploration of Meister Eckhart, Angelus Silesius and Jacques Derrida," *Eckhart Review* (spring 1995): 19–35; and most recently, Almond, "How *Not* to Deconstruct a Dominican."

110. RdU 3 (DW 5:191–96). The translations are my own unless otherwise noted.

111. DW 5:193.3: Dar umbe hebe an dir selber an ze dem êrsten und lâz dich.

112. Dw 5:196.4: Nim dîn selbes war, und swâ dû dich vindest, dâ lâz dich; daz ist daz aller beste.

113. Alois M. Haas, *NIM DIN SELBES WAR. Studien zur Lehre von der Selbsterkenntnis bei Meister Eckhart, Johannes Tauler und Heinrich Seuse* (Freiburg, Switzerland: Universtätsverlag, 1971), chap. 1, especially 20–75. Haas shows how Eckhart's view conflicts with that of Thomas Aquinas, who denied that the soul can know itself *per essentiam* (see STh 1a, q.87, a.1, and *De veritate* q.10, a.8).

114. DW 5:205.2–4: Diz waerlîche haben gotes liget an dem gemüete und an einem inniclîchen vernünftigen zuokêrene und meinenne gotes, niht an einem staeten anegedenkene in einer glîchen wîse, wan daz waere unmügelich der natûre. . . .

115. Dw 5:279.7–8: Ze keiner wîse enist unsers stânnes in disem lebene, noch nie menschen enwart, swie verre er ouch ie kam (trans. Walshe).

116. DW 5:281.5–8: Got gegap sich nie noch engibet sich niemer in deheinen vremden willen. Niht engibet er sich dan in sîn selbes willen. Swâ got sînen willen vindet, dâ gibet er sich în und laezet sich in den mit allem dem, waz er ist (trans. Walshe).

117. DW 5:282.11–283.4: Als lange lerne man sich lâzen, biz daz man niht eigens enbeheltet. . . . Man sol sich selber und mit allem dem sînen in einem lûtern entwerdenne willen und begerennes legen in den guoten und liebesten willen gotes mit allem dem, daz man wellen und begern mac in allen dingen.

118. On the relation between Porete and Eckhart's Pr. 52, see Edmund Colledge and J .C. Marler, "'Poverty of Will': Ruusbroec, Eckhart and the Mirror of Simple Souls," in *Jan van Ruusbroec: The Sources, Content, and Sequels of His Mysticism,* ed. Paul Mommaers and N. de Paepe (Leuven: Leuven University Press, 1984); Kurt Ruh, *Meister Eck-*

hart: Theologe. Prediger. Mystiker (Munich: C. H. Beck, 1985), 99–104; Michael A. Sells *Mystical Languages of Unsaying* (Chicago: University of Chicago Press, 1994), chap. 7; Hollywood, *The Soul as Virgin Wife. Mechthild of Magdeburg, Marguerite Porete, and Meister Eckhart* (Notre Dame: University of Notre Dame Press, 1995), chap. 7; and the papers of Lichtmann, Hollywood, and Sells in *Meister Eckhart and the Beguine Mystics: Hadewijch of Brabant, Mechthild of Magdeburg, and Marguerite Porete,* ed. Bernard McGinn (New York: Continuum, 1994).

119. The text of Pr. 52 can be found in DW 2:486–506. For a commentary and bibliography, see Largier 1:1050–60.

120. On the soul becoming "free of God," compare Pr. 52 (DW 2:492.7 and 493.8) with Porete's *Mirouer* chap. 92 (ed. 258–60).

121. Sells, *Mystical Languages of Unsaying,* 193.

122. Pr. 52 (DW 2:506.1–3): Wer dise rede niht enverstât, der enbekümber sîn herze niht dâ mite. Wan als lange der mensche niht glîch enist dirre wârheit, als lange ensol er dise rede niht verstân: wan diz ist ein unbedahtiu wârheit, diu dâ komen ist ûz dem herzen gotes âne mittel (trans. *Essential Eckhart*).

123. For a treatment of the virtues in Eckhart, see Dietmar Mieth, "Die theologische Transposition der Tugendethik bei Meister Eckhart," in *Abendländische Mystik im Mittelalter,* ed. Kurt Ruh (Stuttgart: J. B. Metzler, 1986), 63–79.

124. Turner, *Darkness of God,* 179.

125. Vab (DW 5:411.12–412.6): Hie solt dû wizzen, daz rehtiu abegescheidenheit niht anders enist, wan der geist alsô unbeweglich stande gegen allen zuovellen liebes und leides, êren, schanden und lasters. . . . Wan daz got ist got, daz hât er von sîner unbeweglîchen abegescheidenheit, und von der abegescheidenheit hât er sîne lûterkeit und sîne einvalticheit und sîne unwandelbaerkeit (trans. *Essential Eckhart*).

126. Pr. 27 (DW 2:43.6–44.1): . . . daz diu minne, mit der wir minnen, diu sol sîn alsô lûter, alsô blôz, alsô abegescheiden, daz si niht ensol geneiget sîn weder ûf mich noch ûf mînen vriunt noch neben sich (trans. Walshe). The triple formula (*lûter-blôz-abegescheiden*) occurs eight times in the sermon.

127. Pr. 27 (DW 2:45.10–46.2): Und ist, daz dîn minne alsô lûter, alsô abegescheiden, alsô blôz ist in ir selber, daz dû niht anders enminnest dan güete und got, sô ist daz ein sicher wârheit, daz alle tugende, die alle menschen ie geworhten, die sint dîn alsô volkomenlîche, als ob dû sie selber geworht haetest, . . . (trans. Walshe).

128. Three of the condemned articles (arts. 7, 8, and 9) can be said to be conclusions from pure detachment insofar as they are expressions of the detached person's inability to desire or pray for any reward.

129. On compelling God in the MHG sermons, see, for example, Prr. 14, 20a (DW 1:235, 328); Prr. 25, 26, 40, 41, 43, 51 (DW 2:8–9, 29 and 34–35, 280–81, 296–97, 319, 476); Prr. 63, 65, 73 (DW 3:81–82, 97–98, 269); Prr. 93, 102, 103 (DW 4:132; and Pfeiffer 15.30–40 and 27.25–30).

130. Pr. 48 (DW 2:415.1–3): Ze glîcher wîs alsô spriche ich von dem menschen, der sich selben vernihtet hât in im selben und in gote und in allen crêatûren: der mensche hât die niderste stat besezzen, und in den menschen muoz sich got alzemâle ergiezen, oder er enist niht got (trans. *Essential Eckhart*).

131. On the "I" in Eckhart, see Burkhard Mojsisch, *Meister Eckhart: Analogie, Univozität und Einheit* (Hamburg: Felix Meiner, 1983), 118–20; idem, "'Ce moi': La conception du moi de Maître Eckhart. Une contribution aux 'Luminaries' du Moyen-Age," *Revue des sciences religieuses* 70 (1996): 18–30; Haas, "'. . . DAS PERSÖNLICHE UND

EIGENE VERLEUGNEN': Mystische *vernichtigkeit und verworffenheit sein selbs* im Geiste Meister Eckharts"; Largier, "Intellekttheorie, Hermeneutik und Allegorie: Subjekt und Subjecktivität bei Meister Eckhart"; and Marie-Anne Vannier, "Déconstruction de l'individualité ou assomption de la personne chez Eckhart?" in *Individuum und Individualität im Mittelalter,* ed. Jan A. Aertsen and Andreas Speer (Berlin/New York: Walter de Gruyter, 1996), 622–41.

132. Pr. 28 (DW 2:68.4–5): "Ego," daz wort "ich," enist nieman eigen dan got aleine in sîner einicheit (my trans.). See also Pr. 77 (DW 3:341); In Ex. nn.14 and 264 (LW 2:20 and 213); and S. XXII n.213 (LW 4:197–99).

133. Pr. 52 (DW 2:503.6–504.3): In mîner geburt, dâ wurden alliu dinc geborn, und ich was sache mîn selbes und aller dinge; und haete ich gewolt, ich enwaere niht, noch alliu dinc enwaeren niht; und enwaere ich niht, sô enwaere ouch got niht. Daz got got ist, des bin ich ein sache ... (trans. *Essential Eckhart* modified). For a comparable text, see Pr. 83 (DW 3:44.4–8). In the same Pr. 28 in which Eckhart says that *ich* belongs only to God, he goes on to say: "'Vos,'" daz wort sprichet als vil als 'ir,' daz ist ir ein sît in der einicheit, daz ist: daz wort 'ego' und 'vos,' 'ich' und 'ir,' daz meinet die einicheit" (68.5–69.2). For more on the transcendental "I" in this sermon, see 63.3–7.

134. BgT 1 (DW 5:11.12–14): ... sô müezen sie ir selbes entbildet werden und in got aleine überbildet und in gote und ûz gote geborn werden (my trans.). For other appearances of *entbilden* in the BgT, see DW 5:12.22, 21.8, 27.6, 112.19, and 116.16. See the discussion of these texts in Wackernagel, *YMAGINE DENUDARI,* 66–78.

135. RdU 21 (DW 5:281.8–9): Und ie wir mêr des unsern entwerden, ie mêr in disem gewaerlîcher werden (my trans.). Eckhart also uses *entwerden* in 283.3.

136. Wackernagel, *YMAGINE DENUDARI,* 78: "Il plus haut degré de l'*Entbildung* consiste donc en une vision dépouillée de la conscience réflexive, et il débouche dans une sorte d'inconnaissance de l'âme elle-même, dans le fond de la déité."

137. Pr. 2 is found in DW 1:21–47 (translations are my own unless otherwise noted). Much has been written on this sermon; see, e.g., Reiner Schürmann, *Meister Eckhart: Mystic and Philosopher* (Bloomington: Indiana University Press, 1978), 3–47; Ruh, *Meister Eckhart,* 143–49; M. Sells, "The Pseudo-Woman and the Meister," in *Meister Eckhart and the Beguine Mystics,* 136–40; Hollywood, *The Soul as Virgin Wife,* chap. 6. See also the comments and notes on further literature in Largier 1:759–72.

138. See Bernard McGinn, "The Language of Love in Jewish and Christian Mysticism," in *Mysticism and Language,* ed. Steven T. Katz (New York: Oxford University Press, 1992), 202–35.

139. There is an exception in Pr. 22, where Eckhart speaks of the Son's penetration into the hidden chamber of the Fatherhood using the erotic language of the Song (DW 1:387–88).

140. Eckhart was not the first to give attention to the motif of the virgin wife, a theme that can be found as early as Origen (see Bernard McGinn, *The Foundations of Mysticism: Origins to the Fifth Century* [New York: Crossroad, 1991], 125); but no previous mystic had developed it as fully.

141. DW 1:24.4–6: ... "unser herre Jêsus Kristus der gienc ûf in ein bürgelîn und wart enpfangen von einer juncvrouwen, diu ein wîp was." It should be noted that Eckhart suppresses the name of Martha, although here, as in Pr. 86, she serves as the type of the person who has combined action and contemplation and thus is superior to her purely contemplative sister. Similarly, the Virgin Mary is not named, although she is, of course, the exemplar of the whole motif of the fruitful virgin, and the sermon was

preached for the feast of the Assumption. The failure to mention the names may be Eckhart's way of suggesting to his hearers that each of them must become a Martha and a Virgin Mary.

142. Pr. 2 (DW 1:24.8–25.2): Juncvrouwe ist alsô vil gesprochen als ein mensche, der von allen vremden bilden ledic ist, alsô ledic, als er was, dô er niht enwas.

143. Pr. 2 (DW 1:27.1–9): Nû merket und sehet mit vlîze! Daz nû der mensche iemer mê juncvrouwe waere, sô enkaeme keine vruht von im. Sol er vruhtbaere werden, sô muoz daz von nôt sîn, daz er ein wîp sî. Wîp ist daz edleste wort, daz man der sêle zuo gesprechen mac, und ist vil edeler dan juncvrouwe. Daz der mensche got enpfaehet in im, daz ist guot, und in der enpfenclicheit ist er maget. Daz aber got vruhtbaerlich in im werde, daz ist bezzer; wan vruhtbaerkeit der gâbe daz ist aleine dankbaerkeit der gâbe, und dâ ist der geist ein wîp in der widerbernden dankbaerkeit, dâ er gote widergebirt Jêsum in daz veterlîche herze.

144. DW 1:31.1–3: . . . ûz dem aller edelsten grunde; noch baz gesprochen: jâ, ûz dem selben grunde, dâ der vater ûz gebernde sîn êwic wort, dar ûz wirt si vruhtbaere mitgebernde.

145. DW 1:32.6–9: Wan der êwige vater gebirt sînen êwigen sun in dirre kraft âne underlâz, alsô daz disiu kraft mitgebernde ist den sun des vaters und sich selber den selben sun in der einiger kraft des vaters.

146. DW 1:39.4–40.3: . . . ez enist weder diz noch daz; nochdenne ist ez ein waz, daz ist hoeher boben diz und daz dan der himel ob der erde. . . . Ez ist von allen namen vrî und von allen formen blôz, ledic und vrî zemâle, als got ledic und vrî ist in im selber.

147. "Diu selbe kraft dar abe ich gesprochen hân" discussed in 40.4–41.7 must be intellect and not the nameless power as the parallels of language to the previous discussion of intellect show. In translating it would be helpful if a new paragraph were begun here lest the reader confuse the two.

148. DW 1:43.9–44.2: Sunder als er ist einvaltic ein, âne alle wîse und eigenschaft: dâ enist er vater noch sun noch heiliger geist in disem sinne und ist doch ein waz, daz enist noch diz noch daz. This passage was excerpted in the Cologne list; see Proc.Col.I n.69 (LW 5:223–24), and Eckhart's response in Théry, 183–84.

149. Most of Eckhart's MHG sermons mention the birth of the Word, and many make it their major theme. Among the treatments (with more important analyses italicized), see especially Prr. 2, 3, 4, 5a, 5b, 6, 10, 11, 12, 13, 14, 16b, 18, 19, 22, 24, 25, 26, 28, 29, 30, 31, 37, 38, 39, 40, 41, 42, 43, 44, 46, 49, 50, 54b, 59, 75, 76, 84, 86, 87, 91, 98, 91, and 101–4. In addition, the BgT has a number of important considerations (see DW 5:9–11, 26, 33, 35, 41–46). The birthing motif is less prevalent in the Latin works, but still found in such passages as In Gen.II nn.180, 191 (LW 1:650, 663); In Sap. nn.55, 67, 279–88 (LW 2:383, 395, 611–22); In Ioh. nn.118–19, 341, 573 (LW 3:103–4, 290, 500); SS. VI nn.57–59, XL n.405, XLII nn.422–23, XLIV n.441, LI n.518, LV n.544 (LW 4:56–59, 344–45, 355–56, 433, 455–56). The literature on this aspect of Eckhart's mysticism is too extensive to even begin to summarize. An older study that still repays consultation is Shizuteru Ueda, Die Gottesgeburt in der Seele und der Durchbruch zur Gott: Die mystische Anthropologie Meister Eckharts und ihre Konfrontation mit der Mystik der Zen-Buddhismus (Gütersloh: Mohn, 1965).

150. Hugo Rahner, "Die Gottesgeburt: Die Lehre der Kirchenväter von der Geburt Christi aus den Herzen der Kirche und der Gläubigen," in Symbole der Kirche: Die Ekklesiologie der Väter (Salzburg: Müller, 1964).

151. Von Balthasar, Glory of the Lord. A Theological Aesthetics V. The Realm of Metaphysics in the Modern Age (San Francisco: Ignatius, 1991), 33.

152. For a brief account, see Colledge, "1. Historical Data," in *Essential Eckhart*, 7–9.

153. Eckhart generally uses the verbal form *durchbrechen*, though his followers, like John Tauler, often employ the noun *durchbruch*. "Breaking-through" language is less frequent in the MHG sermons than the other two motifs of detaching and birthing (I count sixteen sermons where it appears). The essential treatments, including those where the verb does not appear, but the concept is present, are Pr. 2 (DW 1:43–44), Pr. 7 (DW 1:122), Pr. 12 (DW 1:196–97, on "leaving God for God"), Pr. 22 (DW 1:388, on "going into the secret chamber"), Pr. 26 (DW 2:31–32), Pr. 29 (DW 2:76–77), Pr. 31 (DW 2:121, 144), Pr. 48 (DW 2:420–21, on going into the desert), Pr. 49 (DW 2:448–50), Pr. 51 (DW 2:473), Pr. 52 (DW 2:504–5), Pr. 60 (DW 3:60), Pr. 69 (DW 3:178–80), and Pr. 81 (DW 3:401). There are also important appearances in two sermons not yet in DW 4, but which many Eckhart scholars accept as authentic, Pfeiffer LVI (ed. Pfeiffer, 181), and Jostes 82 (in Franz Jostes, *Meister Eckhart und seine Jünger: Ungedruckte Texte zur Geschichte der deutschen Mystik* [Freiburg, Schweiz: Universitätsbuchhandlung, 1895], 94). O. Davies has translated both these sermons in *Meister Eckhart: Selected Writings*, 232–35 and 241–51.

154. For a good expression of this mutuality, see John D. Caputo, "Fundamental Themes of Eckhart's Mysticism," *The Thomist* 42 (1978): 224.

155. Pr. 52 (DW 2:504.6–505.1): Mêr: in dem durchbrechen, dâ ich ledic stân mîn selbes willen und des willen gotes und aller sîner werke und gotes selben, sô bin ich ob allen crêatûren und enbin weder got noch crêatûre, mêr: ich bin, daz ich was und daz ich blîben sol nû und iemermê (trans. *Essential Eckhart*). Similar passages can be found in Prr. 2, 22, 49, etc. One rather different formulation, noted above, is the passage in Pr. 26 (DW 2:31–32) where Eckhart speaks of breaking-through into the Father *insofar as* he is the ground.

156. Pr. 69 (DW 3:179.2–180.1): Vernünfticheit diu dringet în; ir engenüeget niht an güete noch an wîsheit noch an wârheit noch an gote selber. . . . Si brichet in den grunt, dâ güete und wârheit ûzbrichet, und nimet ez *in principio*, ... Aber vernünfticheit diu scheidet diz allez abe und gât în und durchbrichet in die wurzeln . . . (trans. Walshe).

157. Pr. 29 (DW 2:76.2–77.2): Dirre geist muoz übertreten alle zal und alle menige durchbrechen, und er wirt von gote durchbrochen; und alsô, als er mich durchbrichet, alsô durchbriche ich in wider. Got leitet disen geist in die wüestunge und in die einicheit sîn selbes, dâ er ein lûter ein ist und in im selben quellende ist (trans. Walshe).

158. What follows summarizes a development treated in more detail in Bernard McGinn, "Ocean and Desert as Symbols of Mystical Absorption in the Christian Tradition," *Journal of Religion* 74 (1994): 155–81. See also Belden C. Lane, *The Solace of Fierce Landscapes: Exploring Desert and Mountain Spirituality* (New York/Oxford: Oxford University Press, 1998); and Andrew Louth, *The Wilderness of God* (Nashville: Abingdon, 1991).

159. On God as desert, see *Jean Scot: Commentaire sur l'évangile de Jean,* ed. Édouard Jeauneau, SC 180 (Paris: Cerf, 1972), 140.

160. *Thomas Gallus: Commentaires du Cantique des Cantiques,* ed. Jeanne Barbet (Paris: Vrin, 1967), 67: Desertum est invia et singularis eterne Trinitatis supersubstantialis solitudo, de quo *Exo.* 5: *Deus Hebraeorum vocavit nos ut eamus viam trium dierum in desertum; De div. nom.* 13f.

161. For a survey of these uses, see McGinn, "Ocean and Desert," 167–72, especially the use in the MHG Sequence "Granum sinapis."

162. VeM (DW 5:119.2–7): Wer ist danne edeler wan der einhalp geborn ist von

dem hoehsten und von dem besten, daz crêatûren hât, und anderhalp von dem innigsten grunde götlîcher natûre und des einoede? Ich, sprichet unser herre in dem wîs-
sagen Osee, wil die edeln sêle vüeren in ein einoede, und ich wil dâ sprechen in ir herze
ein mit einem, ein von einem, ein in einem und in einem ein êwiclîche. Amen (trans.
Essential Eckhart). For a comparable passage in the Latin works, see In Gen.II n.149
(LW 1:618.12–619.1).

163. Here I shall treat only the second part of this sermon, Jostes 82 (ed. 91–98),
using the translation of O. Davies. Friedrich Schulze-Maizier gave the sermon this title
(*Meister Eckharts deutsche Predigten und Traktate* [Leipzig: Insel Verlag, 1932]). This
homily, like Pr. 52, has a number of resonances with Marguerite Porete's *Mirror,* including the motif of the three deaths of the soul (see *Mirror* chaps. 54, 60–64, 73, 87, 131;
and the discussion in McGinn, *Flowering of Mysticism,* 257–59).

164. See A. de Libera, *La mystique rhénane,* 242–48. The history of *mors mystica* has
been surveyed by Alois M. Haas, "MORS MYSTICA: Ein mystologisches Motiv," in
Sermo Mysticus, 392–480, treating Eckhart on pp. 449–58 (though without mention of
this sermon). For other passages on the *mors mystica* in Eckhart, see, e.g., Prr. 49 and
56 (DW 2:445–46, 589); Pr. 84 (DW 3:462–65); Prr. 95 and 97 (DW 4:195–96, 234–36).
On mystical death in the Jewish tradition, see Michael Fishbane, *The Kiss of God: Spiritual and Mystical Death in Judaism* (Seattle/London: University of Washington Press,
1994).

165. Jostes 82 (93.15): Hie verlust die sele all dink, got und all creaturen.

166. Jostes 82 (93.20–26): . . . wann als lang als di sele got hat und got bekent und
got weiz, so ist si verre von got. . . . Und daz ist die meist ere, di die sele got tut, daz ist,
daz si got im selbe lazze und ste (si) sein ledik.

167. Jostes 82 (94.2–3): . . . so leuhtet ir daz ungeschaffen bild, in dem sich di sele
vindet noch ir ungeschaffenheit. . . .

168. Jostes 82 (94.13–18): . . . so durchbricht di sele ir ewigen bild, uf daz si kum, da
got ist reich in einikeit. Dar um spricht ein meister, daz der sele *durchbruch* edeler sei
denn ir aufluz. . . . Diz durchbrechen daz ist der ander tot dez geistes, der ist vil mer denn
der erst. The quotation from the "Meister" (Eckhart himself?) is also found in Pr. 52 (DW
2:504.4), though in Pr. 52 the more usual verbal form of breaking-through is employed:
Ein grôz meister sprichet, daz sîn *durchbrechen* edeler sî dan sîn ûzvliezen. . . .

169. Jostes 82 (94.28–30): Als di sele durchbricht und sich verleust in irm ewigen
bild, daz ist daz sterben, daz die sele stirbet in got.

170. This is my reading of the obscure passage (Jostes, 95.5–12) in which it seems
that the term *natur* should be understood as the Father's personal property, while *wesen*
signifies the divine nature or Godhead.

171. Jostes 82 (95.28–36): . . . so enphint di sele ir selbs und get ir eygen weg und
ensucht got nimmer; und allhie so stirbet si iren hohsten tot. In disem tot verleuset di
sele alle begerung und alle bild und alle verstentnuzz und alle form und wirt beraubt
aller wesen. . . . Wann diser geist ist tot und ist begraben in der gotheit, wann di gotheit
enlebt nieman anders dann ir selber.

172. Jostes 82 (96.4–5): Als nu di sele also sich verleuset in aller weis, als hie gesagt
ist, so vindet di sele daz, daz si daz sel ist, daz si gesucht hat sunder zugank.

173. Jostes 82 (97.4–6): Got ist dor um worden ein ander ich, uf daz ich wurd ein
ander er. Also spricht sant Augustinus: Got ist mensch worder, uf daz der mensch got
wurd (my trans.). The reference to Augustine is probably Ep. 342 (PL 39:1534), as
noted by Davies.

174. In Ioh. n.547 (LW 3:477.10–11): . . . omne autem desiderium et eius quies est uniri deo. . . .

175. Almost everything written on Eckhart touches in one way or another on his teaching about mystical union; however, there are few explicit considerations. One useful study is Richard Kieckhefer, "Meister Eckhart's Conception of Union with God," *Harvard Theological Review* 71 (1978): 203–25. Since Eckhart mentions union in almost every sermon and throughout his Latin works, I will not try to give a list of even the most significant passages.

176. Pr. 83 (DW 3:443.5–7): Dv solt alzemal entzinken diner dinisheit vnd solt zer fliesen in sine sinesheit vnd sol din din vnd sin sin éin min werden als genzlich, das dv mit ime verstandest ewiklich sin vngewordene istikeit vnd sin vngenanten nitheit (my trans.). On this text, see Meinrad Morard, "Ist, istic, istikeit bei Meister Eckhart," *Freiburger Zeitschrift für Philosophie und Theologie* 3 (1956): 172–75.

177. Pr. 40 (DW 2:274.10–12): Aber zwischen dem menschen und gote enist niht aleine niht underscheit, sunder dâ enist ouch kein menige; dâ enist niht wan ein (trans. *Teacher and Preacher*). There are many such expressions in Eckhart's corpus; e.g., Pr. 9 (DW 1:106.1–3); Prr. 58, 59 (DW 2:614–16, 631–32).

178. Over and over again, Eckhart repeats that union must be *sine medio/âne mittel*. For a few typical expression, see In Gen.II n.146 (LW 1:615); In Sap. nn.282–84 (LW 2:614–16); Prr. 62, 76, 81 (DW 3:64, 323–24, 400–01).

179. For a sketch of the development of the two, see Bernard McGinn, "Love, Knowledge and *Unio mystica* in the Western Christian Tradition," in *Mystical Union in Judaism, Christianity, and Islam: An Ecumenical Dialogue*, ed. Moshe Idel and Bernard McGinn (New York: Continuum, 1996), 75–78 on Eckhart.

180. Pr. 25 (DW 2:11.1–4): Swenne der wille alsô vereinet wirt, daz ez wirt ein einic ein, sô gebirt der vater von himelrîche sînen eingebornen sun in sich in mich. War umbe in sich in mich? Dâ bin ich ein mit im, er enmac mich ûzgesliezen niht, und in dem werke dâ enpfaehet der heilige geist sîn wesen und sîn werden von mir als von gote. War umbe? Dâ bin ich in gote (Walshe trans. modified).

181. The language of indistinction has been explored above and occurs often in Eckhart's descriptions of union. Eckhart speaks of union as "substantial" or "essential" (*weselîch*, etc.); see, e.g., Pr. 76 (DW 3:320.5–6): . . . âne allen underscheit werden wir daz selbe wesen und substancie und natûre, diu er [got] selber ist; and Pr. 76 (DW 3:327.3–4): Und ich bin wol übergesast in daz götlich wesen, sô wirt got mîn und swaz er hât.

182. In Sap. n.282 (LW 2:614.13–615.1): Deus autem indistinctus est, et anima amat indistingui, id est unum esse et fieri cum deo.

183. Eckhart employs John 17:21 to ground his teaching on indistinct union in In Sap. n.44 (LW 2:366); In Ioh. nn.130, 383, 548 (LW 3:112, 326, 478); Pr. 46 (DW 2:383, 388); Prr. 64, 65 (DW 3:88–90, 100–101); BgT 1 (DW 5:33)

184. S. XXX n.314 (LW 4:276.7–8): Unum autem, non unus, omnes sancti in deo. See S. XLIV n.441 (LW 4:369.12–13): . . . omnes tamen "in eandem imaginem" transformantur et in ipso filio deo unum sunt.

185. On the higher union to come in heaven, see Pr. 7 (DW 1:119), and Pr. 39 (DW 2:265–66). As Tobin puts it (*Meister Eckhart*, 114) in commenting on the latter text: ". . . even in heaven the human spirit exists in a condition including both the birth as a state implying utter oneness with the divine existence, and the birth as an incomplete and ongoing process."

186. Pr. 5b (DW 1:93.6–94.1): Ganc dîn selbes alzemâle ûz durch got, sô gât got alzemâle sîn selbes ûz durch dich. Dâ disiu zwei ûzgânt, swaz dâ blîbet, daz ist ein einvaltigez ein. In disem ein gebirt der vater sînen sun in dem innersten gequelle. Dâ blüejet ûz der heilige geist, ... (my trans.).

187. Pr. 12 (DW 1:201.5–8): Daz ouge, dâ inne ich got sihe, daz ist daz selbe ouge, dâ ine mich got sihet; mîn ouge und gotes ouge daz ist éin ouge und éin gesiht und éin bekennen und éin minnen (trans. *Teacher and Preacher*). For another appearance, see Pr. 69 (DW 3:175.5). In Pr. 10 the same formula is applied to knowledge (DW 1:162.2–4) and to love (168.4–7). A basis for this formulation in Aristotelian theory of vision occurs often in the Latin works, see, e.g., In Gen.II n.33 (LW 1:501); In Ex. n.125 (LW 2:116–17); In Ioh. nn.107, 505 (LW 3:91–92, 436).

188. Pr. 76 (DW 3:310.3–4): Ez ist ze wizzenne, daz daz ein ist nâch dingen: got bekennen und von gote bekant ze sîne und got sehen und von gote gesehen ze sînne (trans. Walshe). This sermon is one of Eckhart's most profound expositions of the theme of our one Sonship in the divine essence.

189. In Ioh. n.506 (LW 3:437.12–13): ... eo quod una sit facies et imago in qua deus nos videt et nos ipsum, ... See the whole passage in nn.506–9 (LW 3:437–41) and the parallel texts noted there.

190. This has been well put by a number of Eckhartian scholars; see, e.g., Mieth, *Die Einheit von Vita Activa und Vita Passiva*, 215; Turner, *Darkness of God,* 171–72; Tobin, *Meister Eckhart,* 186–92; Kieckhefer, "Meister Eckhart's Conception of Union," 211–14.

191. See McGinn, *Flowering of Mysticism,* 13–14.

192. Pr. 66 (DW 3:113.8–114.2): Ich spriche aber mê—erschricket niht, wan disiu vröude diu ist iu nâhe, und si ist in iu—ez enist iuwer keinez sô grop noch sô kleine von verstantnisse noch sô verre, er enmüge dise vröude in im vinden in der wârheit, als si ist, mit vröude und mit verstânne, ê daz ir tâlanc ûz dirre kirchen komet, jâ, ê daz ich tâlanc gepredige; er mac ezals waerlîchen in im vinden und leben und haben, als daz got got ist und ich mensche bin! (trans. Walshe modified). Eckhart goes so far as to repeat this almost word-for-word later in the sermon (118.13–119.6).

193. Paul's rapture, described as an *exstasis mentis,* already appears in one of Eckhart's earliest works, e.g., *Sermo in die B. Augustini* n.6 (LW 5:94–95). He gives it an extended treatment in S. XXII nn.213–16 (LW 4:197–203), largely quoting Thomas Aquinas. In the vernacular sermons, Eckhart refers to it a number of times: Pr. 23 (DW 1:404–7); Prr. 61, 80, 86 (DW 3:36–40, 381, 483 and 486–87); Prr. 101, 102, 104 (Pfeiffer 8, 11–12, 17–18). In addition, Eckhart discusses the rapture of St. Benedict in Pr. 73 (DW 3:259).

194. On the uses of the terms *gezücket/enzücket,* see the fifteen passages studied by Robert K. C. Forman, *Meister Eckhart: Mystic as Theologian* (Rockport: Element Books, 1991), 95–125. Other appearances can now be added; e.g., Pr. 87 (DW 4:22.22). A comparable term is *gerucket/ergerucket* as used in Pr. 75 (DW 3:297–98).

195. The term *gebrûchenne/gebrûchunge* and its Dutch equivalents played a considerable role in mystics like Hadewijch and Mechthild. Eckhart uses the terms a number of times, for example, in Prr. 49, 52, 59 (DW 2:447, 492 and 493 and 497, 626); Prr. 84, 86 (DW 3:465, 487); Pr. 90 (DW 4:62). It also appears in RdU 20 (DW 5:270).

196. Pr. 41 (DW 2:291.9–292.1): Sie minent got umbe iht anders, daz got niht enist. Und eht in wirt, daz sie dâ minnent, sô enruochent sie umbe got niht. Ez sî andâht oder lust oder swaz dir wol kaeme; ez enist allez got niht, swaz dâ geschaffen ist (Walshe trans. modified).

197. Pr. 6 (DW 1:99–115). This sermon has the distinction of being the one from which the largest number of incriminating articles were taken during the Cologne proceedings. The theme of *justitia* occurs less often in the MHG texts than in the Latin, but see also Prr. 10, 16b, 24 (DW 1:161 and 174, 272–73, 421–22); Prr. 28, 29, 39, 41, 46 (DW 2:62–63, 82, 251–63, 288–89, 384–85); BgT 1 (DW 5:9–13, 18).

198. "In agro dominico" arts. 8, 9, and 10, all condemned as heretical, are taken from Pr. 6 (DW 1:100.4–6, 112.6–9, and 110.8–111.6). In addition, art. 22, said to be rash, etc., is taken from 109.7–110.2: Der vater gebirt sînen sun âne underlâz, und ich sprich mêr: er gebirt mich sînen sun und den selben sun. Ich spriche mêr: er gebirt mich niht aleine sînen sun; mêr: er gebirt mich sich und sich mich und mich sîn wesen und sîn natûre. In dem innersten quelle dâ quille ich ûz in dem heiligen geiste, dâ ist éin leben und éin wesen und éin werk. Allez waz got würket, daz ist ein; dar umbe gebirt er mich sînen sun âne allen underscheit.

199. Pr. 6 (DW 1:113.7–114.5): Got und ich, wir sint ein. Mit bekennenne nime ich got in mich, mit minnenne gân ich in got. . . . Got und ich wir sint ein in disem gewürke; er würket, und ich gewerde (my trans.). For more on union as an activity in which God works and the soul passively receives the working, see, e.g., Pr. 48 (DW 2:416–17); Pr. 83 (DW 3:447). Eckhart summarizes the essence of *beatitudo* realized in the birth of the Son in the soul in S. IX n.100 (LW 4:95.3–4) as follows: Quae gloria sive beatitudo consistit in uno eodem active in deo, passive in anima. In Pr. 21 Eckhart seems to contradict the notion that union is an activity by saying that love does not really unite us to God, because it unifies in work but not in being (*minne eneiniget niht; si einiget wol an einem werke, niht an einem wesene* [DW 1:360.3–4]). The contradiction disappears if we think of Eckhart as talking about a human work here, not as the divine work done in us when we are unified in the God in whom there is no distinction between *wesen* and *werke*.

200. S. XI n.115 (LW 4:109.1–2): . . . in essentia, ut intellectiva, sic copulatur sui supremo deo, secundum Rabbi Moysen, sic est 'genus dei.'" The reference to Maimonides is to *Guide* 3.53. On intellect and union, see also In Ioh. nn.673, 697 (LW 3:587–88, 612).

201. S. XXIX n.304 (LW 4:270.1–5): Deus enim unus est intellectus, et intellectus est deus unus. . . . Ascendere igitur ad intellectum, subdi ipsi, est uniri deo.

202. On knowledge rather than love as uniting us with God, see, for example, Prr. 7, 9, and 21 ((DW 1:122–23, 152–53, 360–63). In S. VI n.64 (LW 4:62–63) Eckhart analyzes the relation between *voluntas/caritas* and *intellectus/beatitudo* as that between a *dispositio* and a *forma substantialis,* asserting: Iterum per ipsam solam [caritatem] boni sumus, intellectu autem nudo et supernudo non boni, sed beati sumus (62.4–5). Cf. In Ioh. n.697 (LW 3:612).

203. Eckhart's opponents, who placed true *beatitudo* in reflexive knowing, seem to have included John Quidort and Durandus of St. Pourçain. See Alain de Libera, "On Some Philosophical Aspects of Meister Eckhart's Teaching," *Freiburger Zeitschrift für Philosophie und Theologie* 45 (1998): 160–63; and Largier 2:786–88.

204. VeM (DW 5:116.28–117.2): . . . wan daz êrste, dâ saelicheit ane geliget, daz ist, sô diu sêle schouwet got blôz. Dâ nimet si allez ir wesen und ir leben und schepfet allez, daz si ist, von dem grunde gotes und enweiz von wizzenne niht noch von minne noch von nihte alzemâle. Si gestillet ganze und aleine in dem wesen gotes, si enweiz niht dan wesen dâ und got (my trans.).

205. VeM (DW 5:118.23–24): . . . und herwider komen daz ist wizzen und bekennen, daz man got bekennet und weiz. Eckhart also insisted on the direct nature of the

vision of beatitude in his John commentary; see In Ioh. nn.108, 678–79 (LW 3:93, 594).

206. Pr. 60 (DW 3:22.2–23.1): Cherubîn bezeichent die wîsheit, daz ist die bekantnisse; diu treget got in die sêle und leitet die sêle an got. Aber in got enmac si sie niht bringen. . . . Sô tritet diu oberste kraft her vür—daz ist diu minne—und brichet in got und leitet die sêle mit der bekantnisse und mit allen irn kreften in got und vereinet si mit gote; und dâ würket got obe der sêle kraft, niht als in der sêle, sunder als in gote götlich (Walshe trans. modified). There is a comparable passage in S. VI n.52 (LW 4:51).

207. A. de Libera argues for two conceptions of union in Eckhart, an earlier intellectualist view, and a later "Proclean" view centering on the One (*La mystique rhénane*, 278–79 and 312 n.176), but it is not at all evident that the difference is chronological.

208. Pr. 71 (DW 3:215.9–11): . . . ein ander vernünfticheit, diu dâ niht ensuochet, diu dâ stât in irm lûtern einvaltigen wesene, daz dâ begriffen ist in dem liehte (trans. *Teacher and Preacher*).

209. See Prr. 39, 43 (DW 2:265.1–266.3, 329.3–330.3); Pr. 52 (DW 2:495.6–496.5); Pr. 83 (DW 3:448.1–9).

210. Pr. 7 (DW 1:122.8–123.3): Ich spriche: noch bekantnisse noch minne eneiniget niht. . . . Minne nimet got under einem velle, ... Des entuot vernünfticheit niht; vernünfticheit nimet got, als er in ir bekant ist; dâ enkan si in niemer begriffen in dem mer sîner gruntlôsicheit (trans. *Teacher and Preacher* modified).

211. Pr. 42 (DW 2:304.1–2): Dâ diu verstantnisse und diu begerunge endet, dâ ist ez vinster, dâ liuhtet got (trans. Walshe).

212. Eckhart even used the example of the transformation of the bread and wine into the eucharistic body and blood of Christ as a model for this process. See Pr. 6 (DW 1:110.8–111.7), a passage condemned as heretical in art. 10 of "In agro dominico." See also RdU (DW 5:265–66, 268–69).

213. S. LIV n. 532 (LW 4:448.3–8): Sic anima, ut deum videat, debet primo deo configurari per transfigurationem. . . . Secundo debet exaltari et depurari. Tertio eximi ab omni imperfecto. . . . Item debet eximi et transcendere se ipsam, ut natura est, ... Item eximi a corpore et materia, ut possit super se redire et deum intus in se ipsa invenire. For a similar text in Latin, see In Sap. n.64 (LW 2:392). Many of the MHG sermons take divinization as a main theme; e.g., Prr. 6, 40, 44, etc.

214. In Ex. n.247 (LW 2:201.7–11): Adhuc autem secundo proprium est deo, ut non habeat quare extra se aut praeter se. Igitur omne opus habens quare ipsum ut sic non est divinum nec fit deo. . . . Qui ergo operatur quippiam non propter deum, non erit opus divinum, utpote habens quare, quod alienum est deo et a deo, non deus nec divinum. For comparable passages in other Latin works, see S. IV n.21 (LW 4:22–23), and In Ioh. n.50 (LW 3:139).

215. Pr. 41 (DW 2:293.1–2): Alsus sô wirt der sun in uns geborn: daz wir sî sunder warumbe und werden wider îngeborn in dem sune (my trans.).

216. On Beatrice, see McGinn, *Flowering of Mysticism*, 166–74, and the literature cited there. *The Seven Manners of Loving* survives both in the original Middle Dutch, and in a reworked Latin form in the *Vita Beatricis* composed by her confessor. The Dutch text can be found in *Beatrijs van Nazareth: Seven Manieren van Minne*, ed. Léonce Reypens and Jan van Mierlo (Leuven: S.V. de Vlaamsche Boekenhalle, 1926).

217. *Beatrijs van Nazareth: Seven Manieren van Minne*, "Dander maniere der minnen" (7.4–6): . . . allene met minnen, sonder enich waeromme ende sonder eneghen loen van gratien van glorien . . . (my trans.).

218. See, for example, Marguerite's *Mirror*, chaps. 81, 93, 134, and 135 (ed. Guarnieri, 232–33, 260, 394, 397), and the discussion in McGinn, *Flowering of Mysticism*, 257, 264.

219. The language of *âne warumbe* and its cognates is more often employed in the MHG works, but is also found in the Latin writings. (I) MHG: Prr. 1, 5a, 5b, 6, 12 (DW 1: 9, 80–81, 90 and 92, 113 and 115, 199–200); Prr. 26, 27, 28, 29, 39, 41, 59 (DW 2:26–27, 45–46, 59, 77 and 80, 253–54 and 266, 289 and 293, 625–26); Pr. 62 (DW 3:66–67); BgT 1 (DW 5:43–44); RdU 21 (DW 5:282). (II) Latin: In Ex. n.247 (LW 2:201); In Eccli. n.59 (LW 2:287–88); In Sap. n.187 (LW 2:523); In Ioh. n.50 (LW 3:41); SS. IV n.21, VI n.59 (LW 4:22–23, 58). Many Eckhart scholars have treated this aspect of his thought; see especially John D. Caputo, *The Mystical Element in Heidegger's Thought* (Athens, Oh.: Ohio University Press, 1978), chap. 3, "The Rose is Without a Why."

220. Pr. 12 (DW 1:199–200). See In Eccli. n.59 (LW 2:287.12–13): Exemplum posset poni, si dicatur aliquis currere propter currere.

221. Pr. 28 (DW 2:59.6–7): Wer nû wonet in der güete sîner natûre, der wonet in gotes minne, und diu mine enhât kein warumbe (my trans.).

222. In Ioh. n.734 (LW 3:641.3–7): Amans enim ut sic non quaerit amari. Alienum est ipsi omne quod non est amare. Hoc solum novit, liberum est, sui gratia est. . . . Amat, ut amet, amorem amat. This is close to Bernard's noted passage in *Super Cantica* 84.4 (*Opera* 2:300.5–6): Amo, quia amo; amo, ut amem. See also S. VI n.75 (LW 4:71.9–10): Amans vere et verus amor nisi amare nescit.

223. Bernard, *De diligendo Deo* 1.1 (*Opera* 3:119.19): Causa diligendi Deum, Deus est; modus, sine modo diligere. Eckhart cites this at least five times: In Ioh. nn.369, 414 (LW 3:314, 351); Pr. 9 (DW 1:144); Pr. 82 (DW 3:430–31); and in the Cologne Defense (Théry, 238). On the influence of Bernard on Eckhart, see McGinn, "St. Bernard and Meister Eckhart," especially 382–84; and Georg Steer, "Bernhard von Clairvaux als theologische Authorität für Meister Eckhart, Johannes Tauler und Heinrich Seuse," in *Bernhard von Clairvaux. Rezeption und Wirkung im Mittelalter und in der Neuzeit*, ed. Kaspar Elm (Wiesbaden: Harrassowitz, 1994), 249–59.

224. In Ioh. n.307 (LW 3:255.2–3): Bonitas autem principaliter et formaliter ut moralis consistit in actu interiori. . . . See In Gen.II nn.131, 165–66 (LW 1:596, 634–36); In Eccli. n.26 (LW 2:253); In Sap. nn.117, 224 (LW 2:453–54, 559); In Ioh. nn.380, 583–86 (LW 3:323–24, 510–13). The same teaching can be found in the MHG works, e.g., BgT 1 (DW 5:38–40), and RdU 16 (DW 5:247–48).

225. These are the four conclusions that Eckhart reaches on the basis of his longest treatment of the relation of interior and exterior act, In Gen.II n.165. This passage was the source for two of the four condemned articles on the relation of the interior and exterior work; see "In agro dominico" arts. 16 and 17.

226. In Proc.Col.I (Théry, 195) Eckhart incorrectly cites STh 1a2ae, q.20, a.4, as holding the same view he had advanced.

227. RdU 6 (DW 5:203.9–12): Aber dû solt in den werken ein glîchez gemüete haben und ein glîchez getriuwen und eine glîche minne ze dînem gote und einen glîchen ernst. Entriuwen, waere dir alsô glîch, sô enhinderte dich nieman dînes gegenwertigen gotes (my trans.). This message is found in many places in Eckhart; e.g., RdU 17 (DW 5:250–55); Pr. 5a and 5b (DW 1:82, 91). On interior intention in Eckhart, see Amy Hollywood, "Preaching as Social Practice in Meister Eckhart," in *Mysticism and Social Transformation*, ed. Janet K. Ruffing (Syracuse: Syracuse University Press, 2001), 85–90.

228. Pr. 104A.159–73: Dâ enist niht dan einez, wan man engrîfet niergen dan in dem selben grunde der schouwunge und maht daz vruhtbaere in der würkunge, und dâ wirt diu meinunge der schouwunge volbrâht. . . . Alsô in dirre würklicheit enhât man anders niht dan eine schouwelicheit in gote: daz eine ruowet in dem andern und volbringet daz ander (my trans.).

229. Pr 62 (DW 3:56–69) is one of only three sermons which are not based on a scriptural text. Some manuscripts describe it as a *collatio,* that is, an evening talk given to the brethren.

230. On the difference between *credere Deum, credere Deo,* and *credere in Deo,* see STh 2a2ae, q.2, a.2.

231. Pr. 62 (DW 3:59.3–4): Ein mensche ensol nihtes suochen, noch verstân noch wizzen noch innicheit noch andâht noch ruowe, wan aleine gotes wille (trans. Walshe).

232. Pr. 62 (DW 3:68.3–6): Ein mensche sol in allen sînen willen ze gote kêren und got aleine meinen, und gange alsô vür sich hin, und enhabe niht vorhte, sô daz er iht gedenke, ob im reht sî, daz er im unrehte tuo (trans. Walshe).

233. Mieth, *Die Einheit von Vita Activa und Vita Passiva.* See also the commentary in Largier 2:739–47, as well as Alois M. Haas, "Die Beurteilung der Vita contemplativa und vita activa in der Dominikanermystik des 14. Jahrhunderts," in *Gottleiden-Gottlieben. Zur volkssprachlichen Mystik im Mittelalter* (Frankfurt: Insel, 1989), 97–108; and Blake R. Heffner, "Meister Eckhart and a Millennium with Mary and Martha," in *Biblical Hermeneutics in Historical Perspective,* ed. Mark S. Burrows and Paul Rorem (Grand Rapids: Eerdmans, 1991), 117–30.

234. For some aspects of the early development, see B. McGinn, "Asceticism and Mysticism in Late Antiquity and the Middle Ages," in *Asceticism,* ed. Vincent L. Wimbush and Richard Valantasis (New York: Oxford, 1995), 58–74. The importance of the theme among almost all Christian mystics can be seen by consulting the indices under "Contemplation: action and contemplation" in the already published three volumes of B. McGinn, *The Presence of God.*

235. Mieth, *Die Einheit,* 190: "Die irdische Vollkommenheit besteht . . . nicht in der Einheit der Schau, sondern in der Einheit des Wirkens"; 201: ". . . hier zum erstenmal eine Spiritualität des aktiven Lebens sichtbar wird." On the ways in which Eckhart broke with what Mieth calls *Kontemplationmystik;* see pp. 154–64, 171–84, 191–98. On Eckhart's model as one of integration, see pp. 207–18.

236. Other important texts on the relation between action and contemplation include RdU 23 (DW 5:290–309, esp. 291); Pr. 75 (DW 3:302); and Pr. 104.

237. Schürmann, *Meister Eckhart,* 47.

238. Mieth captures this well (*Die Einheit,* 131): "Kreatur ist kein Weg zu Gott; sie ist zugleich der einzige Weg zu Gott."

239. The text of Pr. 86 is found in DW 3:481–92. I will generally use F. Tobin's translation (*Teacher and Preacher,* 338–45), but with some modifications. Mieth provides a helpful outline (*Die Einheit,* 188 note 224). This is a modified version:

Part I. The Contrast between Martha and Mary (481.1–482.2)
    Digression A: Satisfaction of Sense and Intellect (482.3–13)
Part II. The Root of Martha's Perfection (483.14–488.6)
    —gives three reasons for Martha's superiority over Mary
    Digression B: Being Called by Christ (484.1–13)
    Digression C: Soul's Three Paths to God (486.10–488.6)

Part III. The Value of Martha's Works Done in Time (488.7–492.18)
　—five themes are taken up: (a) the value and qualities of works done in time;
　(b) how Martha lives from the *grunt;* (c) Martha as an example of learning life;
　(d) what to do with disturbance; (e) the need for works
　Digression D: On Virtue and 3 Kinds of Will (489.17–490.6)
　Digression E: Suffering and Joy (490.7–491.5)
　240. Pr. 86 (DW 3:482.17–483.1): Marthâ bekante baz Mariên dan Marîa Marthen, wan si lange und wol gelebet hâte; wan leben gibet daz edelste bekennen. Leben bekennet baz dan lust oder lieht allez, daz man in disem lîbe under gote enpfâhen mac, und etlîche wîs bekennet leben lûterer, dan êwic lieht gegeben müge.
　241. Along with Paul, Eckhart mentions *heidnischen meister* (483.4) as proving this. Perhaps he has Proclus in mind.
　242. Pr. 86 (DW 3:485.5–7): . . . und die liute stânt bî den dingen und niht în den dingen. Sie stânt vil nâhe und enhânt es nit minner, dan ob sie stüenden dort oben an dem umberinge der êwicheit.
　243. Eckhart says that *werk* means the external practice of the virtues, while *gewerbe* indicates their internal rational observance (485.9–11).
　244. Pr. 86 (DW 3:485.11–13): Wan der umber sîn wir gesetzet in die zît, daz wir von zîtlîchem vernünftigem gewerbe gote naeher und glîcher werden.
　245. Alois M. Haas, "Meister Eckharts Auffassung von Zeit und Ewigkeit," in *Geistliches Mittelalter*, 339–55 (363–69 on *plenitudo temporum*); Niklaus Largier, *Zeit, Zeitlichkeit, Ewigkeit: Ein Aufriss des Zeitproblems bei Dietrich von Freiburg and Meister Eckhart* (Frankfurt: Peter Lang, 1989).
　246. On the soul as created between time and eternity, see Pr. 23 (DW 1:404–5); Prr. 32, 47 (DW 2:133–34, 404–5); and Pr. 95 (DW 4:180). Eckhart took this idea from one of his favorite texts, the Pseudo-Augustinian *De spiritu et anima* 47 (PL 40:814).
　247. Largier, *Zeit, Zeitlichkeit, Ewigkeit*, 123–24: "Die Ewigkeit ist vielmehr das, was das Zeitliche einbindet in einen Horizont von Ursprung und Ende einerseits, in eine umfassende Präsenz andererseits, die gründet im metaphysisischen Modell der Entfaltung des Seienden, ...
　248. Pr. 91 (Dw 4:96.102–05): Dar zuo hât got einen heimlichen rât vunden und hât sich selber verniuwet dâ mite, daz er die êwicheit hât brâht in die zît und mit sich hât brâht die zît in die êwicheit. Daz ist geschehen an dem sune, wan dô sich der sun entgôz in die êwicheit, dô wurden alle crêatûren mite entgozzen (my trans.).
　249. See, e.g., Pr. 39 (DW 2:261–62); Pr. 77 (DW 3:335–36).
　250. For another passage on the value of works done in time, see Pr. 5b (DW 1:91–92 and 94–95). On the christological character of Eckhart's view of the relation between time and eternity, see Haas, "Meister Eckharts Auffassung," 355–56.
　251. The *drî wege in got* (Digression C: 486.10–488.6) constitutes a mini-treatise on union with God. The three ways are: (1) Seeking God in creatures through activity (*gewerbe*) and love. (2) The "pathless path" (*wec âne wec*) of intellectual ecstasy of which Peter is taken as an example. Eckhart equates this with standing on the "rim of eternity," and says that Paul's experience in 2 Cor. 12 was a higher state. (3) The highest state, which involves "seeing God without medium in his 'ownness'" (*in einicheit got sehende in sînesheit* [487.14–15]).
　252. In this section Eckhart speaks of a man accused of heresy (*der kaeme und spraeche, er waere ein ketzer* [490.18]), who still experiences a flood of grace that leaves

266 ⌒ NOTES TO PAGES 161–164

him indifferent to either joy or suffering. This may reflect Eckhart's own situation in Cologne in late 1326 and after, and thus may provide a clue for dating the sermon.

253. Pr. 86 (DW 3:491.6–7): Marthâ was sô weselich, daz sie ir gewerp niht enhinderte; werk und gewerp leitte sie ze êwiger saelde.

254. BgT 1 (DW 5:61.10–12): Der minniclîche, milte got, diu wârheit, gebe mir und allen den, die diz buoch suln lesen, daz wir die wârheit in uns vinden und gewar werden. Âmen (trans. Walshe).

Appendix
Eckhart's Sources

1. See Bernard McGinn, *The Flowering of Mysticism: Men and Women in the New Mysticism (1200–1350)* (New York: Crossroad, 1998), 87–112.

2. See McGinn, "*SAPIENTIA JUDAEORUM*." This claim about Bonaventure's mystical writings abstracts from the much-debated issue concerning how far his theological writings, despite a growing opposition to pagan philosophy, used Aristotle and other philosophical resources. See, e.g., Fernand Van Steenberghen, *La philosophie au XIIIe siècle* (Louvain/Paris: Publications Universitaires, 1966), chap. 5, "Saint Bonaventure et la Philosophie."

3. At present, we have published Indices for DW 2, 3, and 5; and LW 1, 2, and 3.

4. For a brief attempt to summarize Eckhart's sources on the basis of the findings of the editors of LW 1, see Konrad Weiss, "Meister Eckharts philosophische und theologische Autoritäten," *Studia Theologica* 21 (1967): 13–19. Weiss notes that the indices to LW 1 cite 327 works by 128 authors—a hint of the breadth of the Dominican's reading. For a rather different general attempt to relate some major themes of Eckhart's thought to the theological tradition he inherited, see Edouard-Henri Wéber, "Maître Eckhart et la grande tradition théologique," in *Eckardus Theutonicus, homo doctus et sanctus. Nachweise und Berichte zum Prozess gegen Meister Eckhard*, ed. Heinrich Stirnimann and Ruedi Imbach (Freiburg, Switzerland: Universitätsverlag, 1992), 97–125.

5. Niklaus Largier, *Bibliographie zu Meister Eckhart* (Freiburg, Switzerland: Universitätsverlag, 1989), lists fifty items directly dealing with the investigation of Eckhart's sources (## 676–725). Many important treatments can be found in other contributions to Eckhart research.

6. Surveys of the use of *auctoritates* in scholasticism can be found in chap. 16, "Authentica et Magistralia," in M.-D. Chenu, *La théologie au douzième siècle* (Paris: Vrin, 1957), 351–65; and the expansion and application of this in chap. 4, "The Procedures of Documentation," in the same author's *Toward Understanding St. Thomas* (Chicago: Regnery, 1964), 126–55. On the way in which the scholastic understanding of *auctoritas* influenced literary theories of authorship, see A. J. Minnis, *Medieval Theory of Authorship*, 2nd ed. (Philadelphia: University of Pennsylvania Press, 1988).

7. Chenu, *Toward Understanding St. Thomas*, 128.

8. On the role of commentary in religious traditions from a comparative perspective, see Paul J. Griffiths, *Religious Reading: The Place of Reading in the Practice of Religion* (New York/Oxford: Oxford University Press, 1999). On medieval forms of commentary, see A. J. Minnis and A. B. Scott, *Medieval Literary Theory and Criticism c. 1100–c. 1375: The Commentary Tradition* (Oxford: Clarendon Press, 1991).

9. On medieval techniques of memorization and the general role of memory in

medieval culture, see Mary Carruthers, *The Book of Memory: A Study of Memory in Medieval Culture* (Cambridge: Cambridge University Press, 1990); and Janet Coleman, *Ancient and Medieval Memories: Studies in the Reconstruction of the Past* (Cambridge: Cambridge University Press, 1992).

10. Thomas Aquinas, *In I De Caelo*, lect. 22, no.228: Studium philosophiae non est ad hoc quod sciatur quid homines senserint, sed qualiter se habeat veritas rerum.

11. Alan of Lille, *De fide catholica* 1.30 (PL 210:333A): Auctoritas cereum habet nasum, id est, in diversum potest flecti sensum.

12. One example given above concerns the identification of the *caritas* in the soul with the Holy Spirit; see the discussion in chapter 5, p. 89.

13. See the discussion of the role of inner intention in determining the morality of actions, cited in chapter 6, p. 155.

14. R. J. Henle, S.J., *Saint Thomas and Platonism: A Study of the "Plato" and "Platonici" Texts in the Writings of Saint Thomas* (The Hague: Martinus Nijhoff, 1956), especially 290–308 and 420–22.

15. For example, Eckhart's use of both Maimonides and Thomas Aquinas with regard to the treatise *De nominibus dei* in the *Commentary on Exodus* (see chapter 5, pp. 95–97) is close to what Henle would call the *positio-auctoritas* model. The Dominican's disagreement with Gonsalvo of Spain and other Franciscans on the priority of intellect and will would be an example of analyzing and rejecting a *via-positio*.

16. There is considerable variation, however, in the degree to which Eckhart cites sources in the Prr. For example, in DW 1 there are sermons such as Pr. 12 that feature no direct reference to authorities, while others, such as Pr. 8, have many (two from Augustine, one from Gregory, and eleven ascribed to *ein meister*).

17. There were many variants on this, some with more specification: *die meister sprechent gemeinliche* (DW 1:88.8–9); *die besten meister sprechent* (DW 1:122.5); *die heidnischen meister sprechent* (DW 1:211.7); *unser natiurlichen meister* (DW 1:288.3–4); etc.

18. This appears to be the case with the reference to *ein meister* in Pr. 52 and Jostes no. 82 (see chapter 6, p. 145), but there are other examples where the doctrine ascribed to *ein meister* is so close to Eckhart's own that it is difficult to think who else may have put it in this way. E.g., in DW 1, see, e.g., Prr. 17; 21; and 22 (DW 1:287.2 ff., 360.1–361.5 and 361.10–363.8; 379.10 ff.). Eckhart's self-referencing deserves a separate study.

19. This text, dealing with the effects of sin in the soul, is in the forthcoming Pr. 105 in DW 4: Unt daz widerspriche ich, meister Eckehart, zemâle und spriche alsô (= Pfeiffer XV, 71.30–31).

20. They are inflated because the indices in DW and LW often list multiple places in an author (especially Augustine and Aquinas) where one particular doctrine or teaching is being discussed. For example, in In Sap. n.71 (LW 2:400.6) Eckhart says "Thomas etiam hanc materiam [de providentia] plene prosequitur p.I q.22 et in aliis locis multis." The Index to LW 2 lists not only the reference to STh 1a, q.22, but seven other places (multis aliis locis) where the Angelic Doctor discusses providence (STh 1a, qq. 103 and 104; *Summa contra Gentiles* 3.64, 65, and 71–76; *De veritate* q.5; and *De potentia* q.5).

21. The tabulation for the frequency of Eckhart's explicit references by name to non-Christian authorities gives the LW figures first and the DW figures in parentheses in boldface.

Aristotle: 247 (**7 in Pr. 15 + 10 as "ein meister"**)
Maimonides: 120 (**0**)

Avicenna: 66 (1 + 13 as "ein meister")
Liber de causis: 64 (**10 citations as "ein meister" in 7 Prr.**)
Seneca: 50 (**3 + 3 as "ein meister"**)
Cicero: 34 (**1 + 1 as "ein meister"**)
Averroes: 24 (**0**)
Macrobius: 23 (**3 as "ein meister"**)
Liber XXIV Philosophorum: 22 (**5 as "heidnisch meister"**)
Avencebrol (Ibn Gabirol): 17 (**0**)
Plato: 15 (**4**)
Horace: 15 (**0**)
Proclus: 12 (**0**)

22. Aquinas's relation to Platonism and Aristotelianism remains a subject of investigation. Although Henle's *St. Thomas and Platonism* showed that Thomas could distinguish between the philosophy of the two greatest ancient thinkers, and clearly preferred Aristotle, the significance of the Platonic element in Thomas's thought is still in contention. Important recent work has underlined the role of the Neoplatonic element in his thought, especially as filtered through Pseudo-Dionysius and Proclus, two "authoritative" texts on which he wrote commentaries. See, e.g., Edward Booth, *Aristotelian Aporetic Ontology in Islamic and Christian Thinkers* (Cambridge: Cambridge University Press, 1983); W. J. Hankey, *God in Himself: Aquinas' Doctrine of God as expounded in the "Summa Theologiae"* (Oxford: Oxford University Press, 1987); and Fran O'Rourke, *Pseudo-Dionysius and the Metaphysics of Aquinas* (Leiden: Brill, 1992).

23. In Eccli. n.20 (LW 2:248.1–2): . . . in divinis "quodlibet est in quolibet" et maximum in minimo, et sic fructus in flore. The *principium Anaxagorae* can also be found in Proclus, *Elementatio theologica,* prop. 103d, and the *Liber de causis* prop. XII (ed. Pattin, 73–74). For some of Eckhart's citations, see In Ex. n.16 (LW 2:22); In Sap. nn.134, 271 (LW 2:473, 601); In Ioh. n.320 (LW 3:269); SS. XXVII, XXX, and XLIV (LW 4:251, 275, and 366).

24. The Indices to the LW list the following appearances of Plato by name: LW 1:187.3, 204.10, 208.9 (citing *Timaeus* 31B), 273.8 (citing *Tim.* 28A), 509.8, 520.12, 534.9, 538.1, and 694.10; LW 2:429.1, and 593.6; LW 3:45.5 (quoting *Tim.* 28A), 217.7 (quoting *Tim.* 29E), 219.1, and 556.4 (again quoting *Tim.* 29E). From this list it appears that Eckhart had read the *Timaeus* in Chalcidius's partial Latin version, but probably did not have access to other Platonic texts, relying on summaries found in other authorities.

25. Eckhart names Plato in Prr. 28, 36a, 36b, and 57 (DW 2:67.1, 192.6, 202.6, and 602.6). In addition, in BgT 1, Eckhart summarizes a passage in the name of Socrates: Ein heidenischer meister, Socrates, sprichet, daz tugende machent unmügelîchiu dinc mügelîch und ouch lîht und süeze (DW 5:59.12–13). This quotation is based on Plato, *Republic* 617E; it would have been available to Eckhart through its citation in Chalcidius's *Commentarius in Timaeum* CLIV (*Timaeus a Calcidio translatus comentarioque instructus,* ed. J. H. Waszink [London-Leiden: Warburg Institute and Brill, 1962]), 189.4–5).

26. There are a few treatments of Eckhart's relation to Aristotle that repay reading, such as Philip Merlan, "Aristoteles, Averroes und die beiden Eckharts," in *Autour d'Aristote: Recueil d'Études de Philosophie ancienne et médiévale offert à Monseigneur A. Mansion* (Louvain: Publications Universitaires, 1955), 543–66; and Bernhard Welte, "Meister Eckhart als Aristoteliker," *Philosophisches Jahrbuch* 69 (1961): 64–74. The

major Aristotelian works cited by Eckhart are: (1) *De anima* (71 citatons in LW 1–3); (2) *Metaphysica* (50 citations); (3) *Ethica Nichomachaea* (38 citations); (4) *Physica* (32 citations). He quotes less frequently from a large range of other texts.

27. For some aspects of the use of Aristotle, see the discussions found in chapters 4, 5, and 6. For example: (1) the distinction of active and passive intellect (chapter 4, pp. 66–67); (2) the two modes of unknowing (chapter 5, p. 99); (3) the appeal to *actio/passio* analysis (chapter 5, pp. 104–5); (4) the formlessness of the intellect (chapter 6, p. 134); (5) the theory of vision (chapter 6, p. 149); etc.

28. The Aristotelian discussion of Pr. 15 can be found in DW 1:249–51. Eckhart summarizes *De anima* 1, and *Metaphysics* 12.8.

29. Pr. 15 (DW 1:252.7–253.2): <*Das leste ende*> des wesens ist das vinsterniss oder das vnbekantniss der verborgenen gothait, dem dis lieht schinet, vnd dis vinsterniss enbegraiff das nit [cf. John1:5] (my trans.).

30. See Pr. 20a and 20b (DW 1:335.5–336.5, and 349.10–350.3); Prr. 36a and 36B (DW 2:191.12–193.3, and 202.4–9). For comments on these texts, see Largier 1:927, 930–31, 992–93. Eckhart links Plato and Augustine thus: Sant Augustînus sprichet und spichet ouch Plâtô, ein heidenischer meister, daz diu sêle in ir hât natiurlîche alle kunst . . . (202.6–7).

31. For a comparison of these two forms of Neoplatonism and their influence in the Middle Ages, see Josef Koch, "Augustinische und dionysischer Neuplatonismus im Mittelalter," in *Platonismus in der Philosophie des Mittelalters*, ed. Werner Beierwaltes (Darmstadt: Wissenschaftliche Buchhandlung, 1969), 317–42.

32. See, e.g., the use of Macrobius in Eckhart's commentary on the One of Wisdom 7:27 discussed in chapter 5, p. 94. Macrobius is cited as "ein meister" three times in the MHG sermons.

33. This is especially the case with regard to how to relate Eckhart's view of the *negatio negationis* with that found in Proclus. See chapter 5, pp. 92–93.

34. For an edition, see *Proclus: Elementatio theologica translata a Guillelmo de Moerbecca*, ed. H. Boese (Louvain: Peeters, 1987). Eckhart's references to the *Elementatio theologica* include: In Gen.I n.114 (LW 1:269); In Gen.II n.15 (LW 1:485); In Ex. n.101 (LW 2:103); In Sap. nn.39, 151, 293 (LW 2:360, 488, 629). A text in In Ioh. n.396 (LW 3:337.12–14) links Proclus and the author of the *Liber de causis*, a sign that Eckhart, probably following Aquinas, recognized the affinity of the texts, but the difference of authorship.

35. For editions of these texts, see *Procli Diadochi Tria Opuscula (De Providentia, Libertate, Malo)*, ed. H. Boese (Berlin: Walter De Gruyter, 1960); and *Proclus. Commentaire sur le Parménide de Platon: Traduction de Guillaume de Moerbeke*, ed. Carlos Steel, 2 vols. (Leuven: Leuven University Press; Leiden: Brill, 1982, 1985).

36. The standard edition is Adriaan Pattin, *Le LIBER DE CAUSIS. Édition établie à l'aide de 90 manuscrits avec introduction et notes* (Leuven: Uitgave van "Tijdschrift voor Filosopfie," n.d.). For a translation and study, see *The Book of Causes [Liber de Causis]*, translated from the Latin with an introduction by Dennis J. Brand (Milwaukee: Marquette University Press, 1984). In addition, see *St. Thomas Aquinas: Commentary on the Book of Causes*, translated by Vincent A. Guagliardo, Charles R. Hess, and Richard Taylor (Washington: Catholic University Press, 1996), ix–xxxv, containing an excellent bibliography.

37. Commentaries on the *Liber de causis* were written not only by Aquinas, but also by Roger Bacon, Albert the Great, Siger of Brabant, Giles of Rome, and Henry of Ghent.

38. Two important studies of the influence of the *Liber de causis* on Eckhart are Werner Beierwaltes, "*Primum est dives per se:* Meister Eckhart und der Liber de Causis," in *On Proclus and His Influence in Medieval Philosophy,* ed. E. P. Bos and P. A. Meijer (Leiden: Brill, 1992), 141–69; and Ruh, *Geschichte* 3:19–32. Eckhart's favorite axiom from the *Liber de causis* was prop. 21: Primum est dives per seipsum et non est dives maius (ed. Pattin, 92). He cites this at least thirty times in his Latin writings. In addition, there is an important discussion of the axiom in Pr. 80 (DW 3:382–88) in which Eckhart explores five reasons why "got [ist] rîche in im selber und in allen dingen," invoking "bischof Albreht" three times by name to help explain this central aspect of his metaphysics.

39. Numerous aspects of Eckhart's Procleanism, for which the *Liber de causis* is the primary channel, have been touched on in the previous chapters. See, for example: (1) deep, or indistinct, union (chapter 3, p. 47, and chapter 6, p. 148); (2) the concept of *causa essentialis* (chapter 5, pp. 101–2); (3) dialectical thinking (chapter 5, pp. 92–95); (4) the One and the *negatio negationis* (chapter 5, idem); (5) *esse* as the first of created things (chapter 5, pp. 97–98); (6) the *unum animae* (chapter 5, p. 113); and (7) the *reditio completa* of intellectual being upon itself (chapter 5, p. 73).

40. On the role of Proclus in Eckhart's time, see Ruedi Imbach, "Le (Néo-)Platonisme médiévale: Proclus latin et l'école dominicain allemande," *Revue de théologie et philosophie* 110 (1978): 427–48; Loris Sturlese, "Il dibattito sul Proclo latino nel medioevo fra l'Università di Parigi et lo Studium di Colonia," in *Proclus et son influence: Actes du Colloque de Neuchâtel,* ed. G. Boss and G. Seel (Zurich: Éditions du Grand Midi, 1987), 263–85; idem, "Proclo ed Ermete in Germania da Alberto Magno a Bertoldo di Moosburg," in *Von Meister Dietrich zu Meister Eckhart,* ed. Kurt Flasch (Hamburg: Meiner, 1984), 22–33. See also Alain de Libera *La mystique rhénane d'Albert le Grand à Maître Eckhart* (Paris: Éditions du Seuil, 1994), 25–33. For a wider view of Proclus's role in the history of philosophy, see Paul Oskar Kristeller, "Proclus as a Reader of Plato and Plotinus, and his Influence in the Middle Ages and the Renaissance," in *Proclus: Lecteur et interprète des anciens* (Paris: CNRS, 1987), 191–211.

41. The study of this work has been recently enhanced by the first critical edition, *Liber Viginti Quattuor Philosophorum,* ed. Françoise Hudry, Corpus Christianorum Continuatio Mediaevalis 143A (Turnhout: Brepols, 1997). See also the discussion of the role of the work in the thirteenth century in Ruh, *Geschichte* 3:33–44.

42. For a list and discussion, see Ruh, *Geschichte* 3:38–44. Among the propositions most often cited by Eckhart are: No. I: Deus est monas monadem gignens, in se unum reflectens ardorem (see, e.g., In Ex. n.16 [LW 2:22]; In Ioh. n.164 [LW 3:135]); No. II: Deus est sphaera infinita cuius centrum est ubique, circumferentia nusquam (see, e.g., In Ex. n. 91 [LW 2:94–95]; In Eccli. n.20 [LW 2:248]; In Ioh. n.604 [LW 3:527]; SS. XLV n.458, and LV n.546 [LW 4:379–80, 55]); and No. XXIII: Deus est qui sola ignorantia mente cognoscitur (see, e.g., Pr. 3 [DW 1:50]; Pr. 71 [DW 3:224]; and Pr. 97 [DW 4:227]). On the history of the famous definition of God as the *sphaera infinita,* see Dietrich Mahnke, *Unendliche Sphäre und Allmittelpunkt. Beiträge zur Genealogie der mathematischen Mystik* (Halle: Niemeyer, 1937), who discusses Eckhart on pp. 144–58; and Karsten Harries, "The Infinite Sphere: Comments on the History of a Metaphor," *Journal of the History of Philosophy* 13 (1975): 5–15.

43. Pr. 9 (DW 1:142–43).

44. On the role of Gabirol in scholasticism, see Bernard McGinn, "Ibn Gabirol: The Sage among the Schoolmen," in *Neoplatonism and Jewish Thought,* ed. Lenn E. Goodman (Albany: SUNY Press, 1992), 77–109.

45. The extensive literature on the relation between Maimonides and Eckhart is listed in the notes to the discussion above in chapter 2, p. 25, and chapter 5, pp. 95–96.

46. For some possible references to Maimonides among the anonymous *meister* in Eckhart's preaching, see DW 1:143; DW 2:121, 181, 588; DW 3:170, 217, 379, 441. Eckhart's public may not have been ready to hear an express mention of a Jewish authority.

47. The Indices to LW 1–3 show what should be obvious: Eckhart could use Maimonides extensively in exegeting texts of the Old Testament (thirty-five citations in LW 1, and no fewer than eighty in LW 2), but rarely turned to him in explaining the Gospel of John in LW 3 (five citations).

48. E.g., Eckhart's notion of God as the *illocalis locus* (chapter 5, p. 80 note 56), or his use of Maimonides in discussing creation (chapter 5, p. 100), or his citing of the Jewish philosopher on the intellective nature of humanity (chapter 6. p. 151).

49. The only study is Fernand Brunner, "Maître Eckhart et Avicébron," in *Lectionum Varietates: Hommage à Paul Vignaux (1904–1987)* (Paris: Vrin, 1991), 133–52.

50. In Ex. n.58 (LW 2:64.12–65.4): In uno autem nulla prorsus cadit nec cadere potest differentia, sed omnis>differentia sub uno< est, ut dicitur De fonte vitae l.V. >Hoc enim vere unum est, in quo nullus est numerus<, ut ait Boethius. Et Rabbi Moyses, ut supra dictum est, dicit quod deus est unus >omnibus modis et secundum omnem rationem<, ita ut in ipso non sit invenire aliquam >multitudinem in intellectu vel extra intellectum<. The references are *De fonte vitae* 5.23; Boethius, *De trinitate* 2; and Maimonides, *Dux neutrorum* 1.51. Eckhart also joins Gabirol to Maimonides in In Ex. n.281 (LW 2:225–26).

51. There are some remarks on Avicenna's influence on Eckhart in Loris Sturlese, "Zu Predigt 17," in *Lectura Eckhardi*, 90–96. For a brief sketch of the influence of Avicenna's view of emanation on German thinkers of the time, see A. de Libera, *La mystique rhénane*, 46–53.

52. For a discussion, see chapter 5, p. 76.

53. Pr. 16b (DW 1:275), citing Avicenna, *De anima* 4.2. Eckhart quotes the same passage In Ioh. n.262 (LW 3:217).

54. Pr. 18 (DW 1:300.3–301.2): Ez sprichet gar ein hôher meister, daz der oberste engel der geiste sô nâhe sî dem êrsten ûzbruche . . . , daz er habe geschaffen alle dise werlt und dar zuo alle die engel, di under im sint. Hie liget guotiu lêre ane, . . . (trans. Walshe). (The teaching is based in Avicenna's *Metaphysica* 9.4). Some manuscripts add a disclaimer to qualify Eckhart's praise of this teaching, but B. Hasebrink in his study of this sermon in "GRENZVERSCHIEBUNG: Zu Kongruenz und Differenz von Latein und Deutsche bei Meister Eckhart," *Zeitschrift für deutsches Altertum und deutsche Literatur* 121 (1992): 386–92, denies the authenticity of the comment.

55. For Aquinas's attack on Avicenna, see STh 1a, q.47, a.1. Eckhart accepts Thomas's view, e.g., In Gen.I n. 21 (LW 1:202); In Sap. n.36 (LW 2:356–57); and Pr. 8 (DW 1:130–31). Hasebrink believes that Eckhart changed his mind in Pr. 18, but others are not convinced (see, e.g., Largier, 1:831–32 and 917–18).

56. Pr. 17 (DW 1:281–93). Eckhart also has a long quotation of the base passage from *Metaphysica* 9.7 in S. LV nn.550–51 (LW 4:460–62). See the discussions of the sermon by Hasebrink, "GRENZVERSCHIEBUNG," 92–98, who identifies five citations; and also Sturlese, "Zu Predigt 17," in *Lectura Eckhardi*, 75–96. Both authors stress the deeply Avicennan cast of this homily. For another significant appeal to Avicenna, see the use of his *Metaphysica* 8.6 in S. XLIX.3. n. 511 (LW 4:426).

57. As in the case of the non-Christian authorities, the following list gives the

number of explicit references to identifiable texts by name, beginning with LW 1–3 and followed by the DW numbers in bold.

Augustine: 709 (**93**)
Thomas Aquinas: 122 (**2**)
Boethius: 70 (**4**)
Chrysostom: 45 (29 to the Ps.-Chrysostom) (**0**)
Gregory: 40 (**11**)
Jerome: 31 (**2**)
Bernard of Clairvaux: 26 (**11**)
Origen: 24 (a number of these to Ps.-Origen) (**4**)
Dionysius: 22 (**16**)
John Damascene: 21 (**1**)
Ambrose: 12 (**1**)
Hugh of Saint Victor: 7 (**0**)
Anselm: 6 (**0**)
Bede: 5 (**0**)
Isidore of Seville: 5 (**0**)
Peter Lombard: 5 (**0**)
Albert the Great: 4 (**7**)

58. See Pr. 90 (DW 4:65.127); and the forthcoming Pr. 104 (= Pfeiffer III, 18.21).

59. In Pr. 90 (DW 4:58.33–35) a position of Peter Lombard's is praised as follows: "Diz sprichet ein hôher meister von den künsten."

60. There are some five direct citations of Albert that have been identified in the MHG sermons (see DW 2:465, 488, 507; DW 3:387 (three times); DW 4:56). In addition, a number of unidentified texts are also ascribed to Albert. In referring to contemporaries, Eckhart generally followed the pattern of anonymity. For example, in his account of his debate with the Franciscan Master Gonsalvo of Spain in Pr. 9, he mentions him only as *ein meister in einer andern schuole* (DW 1:152.10–11).

61. For more detail, see Bernard McGinn, "The Spiritual Heritage of Origen in the West. Aspects of Origen's Influence in the Middle Ages" (forthcoming).

62. This tally of thirty-seven explicit mentions is higher than that given in note 57 above because it represents an independent survey of all Eckhart's works. The numbers also include the appeals to the Pseudo-Origenian homily on Mary Magdalene that was one of Eckhart's favorites (fifteen times).

63. BgT 1 (DW 5:113.1–4): Von disem innern edeln menschen, dâ gotes sâme und gotes bilde îngedrücket und îngesaejet ist, wie der sâme und daz bilde götlîcher natûre und götlîches wesens, gotes sun, erchîne und man sîn gewar werde und ouch etwenne verborgen werde, sprichet der grôze meister Origenes ein glîchnisse … (trans. Walshe). The "seed" texts that Eckhart often cited were Origen's *Homilia in Exodum* 8.6, *Homilia in Psalmum XXXVI* 4, and *Homilia in Genesim* 10–13. Another favorite passage was *Homilia in Jeremiam* 9.4. On the connection between Eckhart's view of the mysticism of birthing and Origen, see Rahner, "Die Gottesgeburt," especially 81–87. The essay by Katharina Comoth, "Hegemonikon: Meister Eckharts Rückbegriff auf Origenes," in *Origeniana Tertia*, ed. Lothar Lies (Innsbrück/Vienna: Tyrolia, 1987), 265–69, is not helpful. See the comments in chapter 6, p. 141 on Eckhart and Origen on the birth of the Word in the soul, as well as Origen's use of the motif of the soul as virgin wife discussed in chapter 6, p. 139.

64. Chrysostom's John commentary is used sixteen times in Eckhart's In Ioh.; the

other twenty-nine references to *Chrysostomus* in LW 1–3 are to the *Opus imperfectum in Matthaeum,* a work whose origins are still in dispute. It appears to be a fifth- or sixth-century production, possibly of Arian tendencies.

65. Many works on Eckhart have something to say about his use of Augustine, but there are few explicit studies. Among those that take up particular themes, see, e.g., Otto Karrer, "Das Gotteserlebnis bei Augustinus und Meister Eckhart," in *Das Gotteserlebnis,* ed. Otto Karrer and Ludwig Köhler (Zurich: Schweizer-Spiegel Verlag, 1934), 20–54; Burkhard Mojsisch, "Der Begriff der Liebe bei Augustin und Meister Eckhart," in *Philosophie: Anregungen für die Unterrichtspraxis, Heft 12, Freundschaft und Liebe,* ed. Jürgen Hengelbrock (Frankfurt, 1984), 19–27; and Anne Marie Vannier, "Saint Augustin et Eckhart: Sur le problème de la création," *Augustinus* 39 (1994): 551–61.

66. On the influence of Augustine's *Confessiones,* see Pierre Courcelle, *Les Confessions de Saint Augustin dans la tradition littéraire: Antécédents et Postérité* (Paris: Études Augustiniennes, 1963), who discusses Eckhart on pp. 316–19.

67. In LW 1–3, for example, we find Eckhart referencing the *Confessiones* under Augustine's name 198 times. The relevant figures for other often-cited works are *De Trinitate* (111 citations), *De vera religione* (41 citations), *Quaestiones in Heptateucham* (38 citations), *De civitate dei* (21 citations). Somewhat surprising, given Eckhart's concern for Genesis, is the relatively modest use of the *De genesi ad litteram* with only 15 direct notices. An understandable variation is created by the 52 references to Augustine's *Tractatus in Iohannem* in Eckhart's In Ioh.

68. In LW 1–3 the *De libero arbitrio* is cited under Augustine's name nineteen times.

69. See chapter 5, p. 103.

70. See Prr. 20a and 20b; and 36a and 36b, discussed above (DW 1:335–36, 349–50; DW 2:191–92, and 204).

71. E.g., chapter 5, pp. 107–9.

72. The *Consolatio philosophiae* was one of the most read books in the medieval schools. Like many others, Eckhart often cites lines from the famous cosmological poem "O qui perpetua," which is metrum 9 in book 3 (nineteen citations of the seventy in LW 1–3). For a study of the influence of this work, see Pierre Courcelle, *La Consolation de Philosophie dans la tradition littéraire: Antécédents et posterité de Boèce* (Paris: Vrin, 1967).

73. For a brief account of Dionysian thought and mysticism, see Bernard McGinn, *The Foundations of Mysticism: Origins to the Fifth Century* (New York: Crossroad, 1991), 157–82, and the literature cited there. For a commentary on the *corpus dionysiacum* and a brief survey of its influence, see Paul Rorem, *Pseudo-Dionysius: A Commentary on the Texts and an Introduction to Their Influence* (New York/Oxford: Oxford University Press, 1993). A recent summary of the role of Dionysius in medieval thought is Édouard Jeauneau, "Denys l'Aréopagite: Promoteur du Néoplatonisme en Occident," in *Néoplatonisme et Philosophie Médiévale,* ed. Linos G. Benakis, Société Internationale pour l'Étude de la Philosophie Médiévale (Turnhout: Brepols, 1997), 1–23.

74. This form of Dionysianism is aptly termed "affective" in the sense that Gallus sees ecstatic love as the power that penetrates beyond the Dionysian cloud of unknowing to attain God. Such a reading of Dionysius was to be found in many later medieval mystics, such as Bonaventure, Hugh of Balma, and the author of the Middle English treatise *The Cloud of Unknowing.* For Gallus, see McGinn, *Flowering of Mysticism,* 78–87.

75. The most recent helpful overview is in A. de Libera, *La mystique rhénane,* chap. 2.

76. Kurt Ruh, "Dionysius Areopagita im deutschen Predigtwerk Meister Eckhart," *Perspektiven der Philosophie: Neues Jahrbuch* 13 (1987): 207–23; idem, *Geschichte* 3:280–90.

77. Some of these comparisons have been touched on above. For example, in chapter 3, p. 48 on negative anthropology, and in chapter 5, p. 92 on dialectical Neo-platonism, and chapter 6 on mystical birthing (p. 141) and the desert of God (p. 143). A number of studies have compared Eriugena and Eckhart. See especially Hans Liebe-schütz, "Mittelalterliche Platonismus bei Johannes Eriugena und Meister Eckhart," *Archiv für Kulturgeschichte* 56 (1974): 241–69; and Alois M. Haas, "Eriugena und die Mystik," in *Eriugena Redivivus: Zur Wirkungsgeschichte seines Denkens im Mittelalter und im Übergang zur Neuzeit,* ed. Werner Beierwaltes (Heidelberg: Carl Winter, 1987), 254–78.

78. Eckhart never, to the best of my knowledge, refers to Eriugena by name, and the parallels to Eriugenean texts adduced by the editors of LW and DW remain mostly rather distant—interesting for comparison, but scarcely evident sources.

79. Kurt Ruh has shown that Eriugena is cited in some MHG works from Eckhart's circle ("Johannes Scotus Eriugena Deutsch," *Zeitschrift für deutsches Altertum und deutsche Literatur* 99 [1988]: 24–31), especially the Latin commentary on the "Granum sinapis." Eckhart certainly knew Eriugena's translation of Dionysius, and parts of the Irishman's masterpiece, the *Periphyseon,* had been absorbed into the Paris university glossed version of the *corpus dionysiacum,* a text that would have been accessible to Eckhart. In addition, he could have been acquainted with the *Clavis Physicae,* a twelfth-century precis of the *Periphyseon* put together by Honorius Augustodunensis and cited by a number of thirteenth-century scholastics. The only direct citations of Eriugena thus far identified, however, are a few places in Eckhart's In Ioh. that quote or echo Eri-ugena's *Homilia,* a well-known text that circulated under the name of Origen, made its way into the *Glosa ordinaria* and was also employed by Thomas Aquinas (see, e.g., In Ioh. nn.65, 111 [LW 3:54 and 96]). For recent attempts to survey the possible connec-tions between the two thinkers, see Ruh, *Geschichte* 1:176–83; and Werner Beierwaltes, *Eriugena: Grundzüge seines Denkens* (Frankfurt: Klostermann, 1994), 263–65.

80. On Bernard's role in Eckhart's thought, see McGinn, "St. Bernard and Meister Eckhart"; and Georg Steer, "Bernhard von Clairvaux als theologische Authorität für Meister Eckhart, Johannes Tauler und Heinrich Seuse," 249–59 on Eckhart. Steer rightly names Bernard as "einer der prominentesten Gesprächspartner" of Eckhart, Tauler, and Suso (p. 259).

81. On the relation between Anselm and Eckhart, see Bardo Weiss, "Der Einfluss Anselms von Canterbury auf Meister Eckhart," *Analecta Anselmiana* 4 (1975), Vol. 2:209–21.

82. Obviously, a considerable literature exists on the relation of Aquinas and Eck-hart. The most detailed account is that of Ruedi Imbach, *DEUS EST INTELLIGERE,* often cited in the foregoing chapters. Another survey is that of Heribert Fischer, "Thomas von Aquin und Meister Eckhart," *Theologie und Philosophie* 49 (1974): 213–35.

83. A. de Libera, *La mystique rhénane,* 11.

84. To mention a few of those considered above: (1) the understanding of the rela-tion between faith and reason (chapter 2, p. 22); (2) the *processio Verbi* in the Trinity (chapter 4, p. 56 note 17); (3) the trinitarian structure of reality (chapter 5, p. 76); (4) the doctrine of grace (chapter 6, pp. 128–29); (5) the understanding of action and

contemplation (chapter 6, pp. 157–58); and (6) the constitution of *beatitudo* (chapter 4, pp. 61–62).

85. See Loris Sturlese, "Tauler im Kontext: Die philosophischen Voraussetzungen des 'Seelengrundes' in der Lehre des deutschen Neuplatonikers Berthold von Moosburg," *Beiträge zur Geschichte der deutschen Sprache und Literatur* 109 (1987): 390–426.

86. On this difference, see chapter 4, p. 16; see also the remarks on Albert and Dietrich in chapter 1, pp. 2–3. Considerable literature has been devoted to the relations between Dietrich and Eckhart in recent years, especially by Kurt Flasch, Burkhard Mojsisch, Loris Sturlese, Alain de Libera, and Niklaus Largier.

87. For treatments, see chapter 1, pp. 9–10; chapter 3, pp. 39–40; chapter 4, p. 62; and chapter 5, passim, and the literature cited at these locations. For an early consideration of the influence of the female mystics, such as Beatrice of Nazareth and Hadewijch, on Eckhart, see Emilie Zum Brunn, "Une source méconnu de l'ontologie Eckhartiene," in *Métaphysique, Histoire de la philosophie: Recueil d'études offert à Fernand Brunner* (Neuchâtel: A la Baconnière, 1981), 111–17.

88. See the discussions in chapter 1, pp. 9–10; chapter 4, p. 62; and chapter 5, e.g., p. 74; and chapter 6, e.g., pp. 136, 139, 144, 148, 154.

89. For some possible links between Eckhart and Mechthild, see above, chapter 1, pp. 9–10; chapter 4, p. 63; and chapter 6, pp. 139, 150. On Eckhart and Mechthild, see Oliver Davies, *Meister Eckhart: Mystical Theologian* (London: SPCK, 1991), 59–65; and Frank Tobin, "Mechthild of Magdeburg and Meister Eckhart: Points of Comparison," in *Meister Eckhart and the Beguine Mystics: Hadewijch of Brabant, Mechthild of Magdeburg, and Marguerite Porete,* ed. Bernard McGinn (New York: Continuum, 1994), 44–61.

90. See the remarks on the use of the language of ground and the mutual abyss motif, e.g., chapter 3, pp. 40, 44; chapter 4, p. 62; and chapter 6, p. 150. On the relation between Hadewijch and Eckhart, see Saskia Murk Jansen, "Hadewijch and Eckhart: Amor intellegere est," in *Meister Eckhart and the Beguine Mystics,* ed. McGinn, 17–30. In addition, some of the poems ascribed to Hadewijch, especially Mengeldichten 25–29, are deeply influenced by Eckhart's apophaticism and appear to be the product of a Dutch (female?) follower of the Dominican. See Paul A. Dietrich, "The Wilderness of God in Hadewijch II and Meister Eckhart," in *Meister Eckhart and the Beguine Mystics,* ed. McGinn, 31–43.

Bibliography

Abendländische Mystik im Mittelalter. Symposion Kloster Engelberg 1984, ed. Kurt Ruh. Stuttgart: Metaler, 1986.

Aertsen, J. A. "Ontology and Henology in Medieval Philosophy (Thomas Aquinas, Meister Eckhart and Berthold of Moosburg)." In *On Proclus and His Influence in Medieval Philosophy,* ed. E. P. Bos and P. A. Meijer, 120–40. Leiden: Brill, 1992.

Albert, Karl. "Meister Eckhart über das Schweigen" In *Festschrift für Lauri Seppänen zum 60. Geburtstag,* 301–9. Tampere: Universität Tampere, 1984.

———. "Die philosophische Grundgedanke Meister Eckharts." *Tijdschrift voor Philosophie* 27 (1965): 321 n. 5.

Almond, Ian. "How *Not* to Deconstruct a Dominican: Derrida on God and 'Hypertruth.'" *Journal of the American Academy of Religion* 68 (2000): 338–40.

Ancelet-Hustache, Jeanne. *Master Eckhart and the Rhineland Mystics.* New York: Harper, 1957. French original, Paris, 1956.

Appel, Heinrich. "Die Synteresis in der mittelalterlichen Mystik." *Zeitschrift für Kirchengeschichte* 13 (1982): 535–44.

Auerbach, Erich. *Literary Language & Its Public in Late Latin Antiquity and the Middle Ages.* Princeton: Princeton University Press, 1965.

Bach, Josef. *Meister Eckhart: Der Vater der deutschen Speculation.* Vienna: Braumüller, 1864.

Barbet, Jeanne, ed. *Thomas Gallus: Commentaires du Cantique des Cantiques.* Paris: Vrin, 1967.

Bechstein, Reinhold, and Peter Ganz, eds. *Gottfried von Strassburg, Tristan.* 2 vols. Wiesbaden: Brockhaus, 1978.

Beierwaltes, Werner. *Eriugena: Grundzüge seines Denkens.* Frankfurt: Klostermann, 1994.

———. *Platonismus und Idealismus.* Frankfurt: Klostermann, 1972.

———. "Primum est dives per se: Meister Eckhart und der 'Liber de causis.'" In *On Proclus and his Influence in Medieval Philosophy,* ed. E. P. Bos and P. A. Meijer, 141–69. Leiden: Brill, 1992.

———. "Unity and Trinity East and West." In *Eriugena East and West,* ed. Bernard McGinn and Willemien Otten, 209–31. Notre Dame, Ind.: University of Notre Dame Press, 1995.

Bernhart, Joseph. *Die philosophische Mystik des Mittelalters von ihren antiken Ursprüngen bis zur Renaissance.* Munich: Reinhard, 1922.

Bindschedler, Maria, ed. *Der lateinische Kommentar zum Granum Sinapis.* Basel: Schwabe, 1949.

Blakeney, Raymond Bernard. *Meister Eckhart: A Modern Translation.* New York: Harper & Row, 1941.

Blumenberg, Hans. "Ausblick auf eine Theorie der Unbegrifflichkeit." In *Theorie der Metapher,* ed. Anselm Haverkamp, 438–54. Darmstadt: Wissenschaftliche Buchgesellschaft, 1983.

———. "Beobachtungen an Metaphern," *Archiv für Begriffsgeschichte* 15 (1971): 161–214.

———. "Paradigmen zu einer Metaphorologie." *Archiv für Begriffsgeschichte* 6 (1960): 7–142.

Boese, H., ed. *Procli Diadochi Tria Opuscula (De Providentia, Libertate, Malo).* Berlin: Walter De Gruyter, 1960.

———, ed. *Proclus: Elementatio theologica translata a Guillelmo de Moerbecca.* Louvain: Peeters, 1987.

Booth, Edward. *Aristotelian Aporetic Ontology in Islamic and Christian Thinkers.* Cambridge: Cambridge University Press, 1983.

Brand, Dennis J., trans. *The Book of Causes [Liber de Causis],* translated from the Latin with an introduction by Dennis J. Brand. Milwaukee: Marquette University Press, 1984.

Brunner, Fernand. "L'analogie chez Maître Eckhart." *Freiburger Zeitschrift für Philosophie und Theologie* 16 (1969): 333–49.

———. "Maître Eckhart et Avicébron" In *Lectionum Varietates: Hommage à Paul Vignaux (1904–1987),* 133–52. Paris: Vrin, 1991.

———. "Maître Eckhart et le mysticisme speculatif." *Revue de théologie et de philosophie* 3 (1970): 1–11.

Buning, Marius. "Negativity Then and Now: An Exploration of Meister Eckhart, Angelus Silesius and Jacques Derrida." *Eckhart Review* (spring 1995): 19–35.

Burrell, David. *Knowing the Unknown God: Ibn Sina, Maimonides, Aquinas.* Notre Dame, Ind.: University of Notre Dame Press, 1986.

Caputo, John. "Fundamental Themes of Eckhart's Mysticism." *The Thomist* 42 (1978): 197–225.

———. *The Mystical Element in Heidegger's Thought.* Athens, Oh.: Ohio University Press, 1978.

———. "Mysticism and Transgression: Derrida and Meister Eckhart." In *Derrida and Deconstruction,* ed. Hugh J. Silverman, 24–39. London: Routledge, 1989.

———. "The Nothingness of the Intellect in Meister Eckhart's 'Parisian Questions,'" *The Thomist* 39 (1975): 85–115.

Carruthers, Mary. *The Book of Memory: A Study of Memory in Medieval Culture.* Cambridge: Cambridge University Press, 1990.

Charles-Saget, Annick. "Non-être et Néant chez Maître Eckhart." In *Voici Maître Eckhart,* ed. Emilie Zum Brunn, 301–18. Paris: Jérôme Millon, 1994.

Chenu, M.-D. *La théologie au douzième siècle.* Paris: Vrin, 1957.

———. *Toward Understanding St. Thomas.* Chicago: Regnery, 1964.

Clark, James M. and John V. Skinner. *Treatises and Sermons of Meister Eckhart.* New York: Harper & Brothers, 1958.

Cognet, Louis. *Introduction aux mystiques rhéno-flamands.* Paris: Desclée, 1968.

Coleman, Janet. *Ancient and Medieval Memories: Studies in the Reconstruction of the Past.* Cambridge: Cambridge University Press, 1992.

Colledge, Edmund, and J .C. Marler. "'Poverty of Will': Ruusbroec, Eckhart and the Mirror of Simple Souls." In *Jan van Ruusbroec: The Sources, Content, and Sequels of His Mysticism,* ed. Paul Mommaers and N. de Paepe, 14–47. Leuven: Leuven University Press, 1984.

Comoth, Katharina. "Hegemonikon: Meister Eckharts Rückbegriff auf Origenes." In *Origeniana Tertia,* ed. Lothar Lies, 265–69. Innsbrück/Vienna: Tyrolia, 1987.

Constable, Giles. *Three Studies in Medieval Religious and Social Thought.* Cambridge: Cambridge University Press, 1995.

Courcelle, Pierre. *Les Confessions de Saint Augustin dans la tradition littéraire: Antécédents et Postérité.* Paris: Études Augustiniennes, 1963.

———. *La Consolation de Philosophie dans la tradition littéraire: Antécédents et posterité de Boèce.* Paris: Vrin, 1967.

Cousins, Ewert. "The Humanity and Passion of Christ." In *Christian Spirituality, II, High Middle Ages and Reformation,* ed. Jill Raitt in collaboration with Bernard McGinn and John Meyendorff, 375–91. New York: Crossroad, 1987.

Davies, Oliver. *Meister Eckhart: Mystical Theologian.* London: SPCK, 1991.

———. "Why were Eckhart's propositions condemned?" *New Blackfriars* 71 (1990): 433–45.

de Gandillac, Maurice. "La 'dialectique' du Maître Eckhart." In *La mystique rhénane,* 59–94. Paris: Presses Universitaires de France, 1963.

Delacroix, Henry. *Essai sur le mysticisme spéculatif en Allemagne au quatorzième siècle.* Paris: Alcan, 1900.

de Libera, Alain. *Albert le Grand et la philosophie.* Paris: Vrin, 1990.

———. "À propos de quelques théories logiques de Maître Eckhart: Existe-t-il une tradition médiévale de la logique néo-platonicienne?" *Revue de théologie et de philosophie* 113 (1981): 1–24.

———. "L'être et le bien: Exode 3,14 dans la théologie rhénane." In *Celui qui est: Interprétations juives et chrétiennes d'Exode 3.14,* ed. Alain de Libera and Emilie Zum Brunn. Paris: Cerf, 1986.

———. *Maître Eckhart: Le grain de sènève.* Paris: Arfuyen, 1996.

———. *La mystique rhénane d'Albert le Grand à Maître Eckhart.* Paris: Éditions du Seuil, 1994.

———. "On Some Philosophical Aspects of Meister Eckhart's Teaching." *Freiburger Zeitschrift für Philosophie und Theologie* 45 (1998): 150–68.

———. *Le problème de l'être chez Maître Eckhart: Logique et métaphysique de l'analogie.* Geneva: Cahiers de la Revue de théologie et de philosophie, 1980.

———. "Les 'raisons d'Eckhart.'" In *Maître Eckhart à Paris: Une critique médiévale de l'ontothéologie. Les Questions parisiennes no. 1 et no. 2,* 109–40. Paris: Presses Universitaires de France, 1984.

———. "L'Un ou la Trinité." *Revue des sciences religieuses* 70 (1996): 31–47.

Degenhardt, Ingeborg. *Studien zum Wandel des Eckhartbildes.* Leiden: Brill, 1967.

Denifle, Heinrich Seuse. "Meister Eckeharts lateinische Schriften und die Grundanschauungen seiner Lehre." *Archiv für Literatur und Kirchengeschichte des Mittelalters* 2 (1886).

Deutsche Mystik im abendländischen Zusammenhang. Neue erschlossene Texte, neue methodische Ansätze, neue theoretische Konzepte, ed. Walter Haug and Wolfram Schneider-Lastin. Tübingen: Niemeyer, 2000.

Dietrich, Paul A. "The Wilderness of God in Hadewijch II and Meister Eckhart." In *Meister Eckhart and the Beguine Mystics: Hadewijch of Brabant, Mechthild of Magdeburg, and Marguerite Porete,* ed. Bernard McGinn, 31–43. New York: Continuum, 1994.

Dietsche, Bernward. "Der Seelengrund nach den deutschen und lateinischen Predigten." In *Meister Eckhart der Prediger: Festschrift zum Eckhart-Gedenkjahr,* ed. Udo M. Nix and Raphael Öchslin, 200–258. Freiburg: Herder, 1960.

Dodds, E. J., ed. *Proclus: The Elements of Theology.* 2nd ed. Oxford: Clarendon Press, 1963.

Duclow, Donald F. "Hermeneutics and Meister Eckhart." *Philosophy Today* 28 (1984): 36–43.

———. "The Hungers of Hadewijch and Eckhart." *Journal of Religion* 80 (2000): 421–41.

———. "Meister Eckhart on the Book of Wisdom: Commentary and Sermons." *Traditio* 43 (1987): 215–35.

———. "'My Suffering is God': Meister Eckhart's *Book of Divine Consolation.*" *Theological Studies* 44 (1983): 570–86.

———. "'Whose Image is This?' in Eckhart's *Sermones.*" *Mystics Quarterly* 15 (1989): 29–40.

Eckardus Theutonicus, homo doctus et sanctus: Nachweise und Berichte zum Prozess gegen Meister Eckhart, ed. Heinrich Stirnimann and Ruedi Imbach. Freiburg, Switzerland: Universitätsverlag, 1992.

Egerding, Michael. *Die Metaphorik der spätmittelalterlichen Mystik.* 2 vols. Paderborn: Schöningh, 1997.

Fauser, Winfried, ed. *Alberti Magni Opera Omnia.* Monasterii Westfalorum: Aschendorff, 1993.

Fischer, Heribert. "Fond de l'Ame. I, Chez Maitre Eckhart." In DS 5:650–61.

———. "Grundgedanken der deutschen Predigten." In *Meister Eckhart der Prediger: Festschrift zum Eckhart-Gedenkjahr,* ed. Udo M. Nix and Raphael Öchslin, 25–72. Freiburg: Herder, 1960.

———. *Meister Eckhart: Einführung in sein philosophisches Denken.* Munich: Karl Alber, 1974.

———. "Thomas von Aquin und Meister Eckhart." *Theologie und Philosophie* 49 (1974): 213–35.

———. "Zur Frage nach der Mystik in den Werken Meister Eckharts." In *La mystique rhénane,* 109–32. Paris: Presses Universitaires de France, 1963.

Fishbane, Michael. *The Kiss of God: Spiritual and Mystical Death in Judaism.* Seattle/London: University of Washington Press, 1994.

Flasch, Kurt. "Die Intention Meister Eckharts." In *Sprache und Begriff: Festschrift für Bruno Liebrucks,* ed. Heinz Röttges, 292–318. Meisenheim am Glan: Hain, 1974.

———. "Meister Eckhart: Versuch, ihn aus dem mystischen Strom zu retten." In *Gnosis und Mystik in der Geschichte der Philosophie,* ed. Peter Koslowski, 94–110. Darmstadt: Wissenschaftliche Buchgesellschaft, 1988.

———. "Procedere ut imago: Das Hervorgehen des Intellekts aus seinem göttlichen Grund bei Meister Dietrich, Meister Eckhart und Berthold von Moosburg." In *Abendländische Mystik im Mittelalter,* ed. Kurt Ruh, 125–34. Stuttgart: Metzler, 1986.

Forman, Robert K. C. *Meister Eckhart: Mystic as Theologian.* Rockport: Element Books, 1991.

Gnädinger, Louise. "Der Abgrund ruft dem Abgrund: Taulers Predigt Beati oculi (V 45)." In *Das "Einig Ein": Studien zur Theorie und Sprache der deutschen Mystik,* ed. Alois M. Haas and Heinrich Stirnimann, 167–207. Freiburg, Switzerland: Universitätsverlag, 1980.

————. *Johannes Tauler: Lebenswelt und mystische Lehre.* Munich: C. H. Beck, 1993.

Goris, Wouter. *Einheit als Prinzip und Ziel: Versuch über die Einheitsmetaphysik des "Opus tripartitum" Meister Eckharts.* Leiden: Brill, 1997.

Grabmann, Martin. "Die Lehre des hl. Thomas von Aquin von der *scintilla animae* in ihre Bedeutung für die deutsche Mystik des Predigerordens." *Jahrbuch für Philosophie und spekulativen Theologie* 14 (1900): 413–27.

Greith, Carl. *Die deutsche Mystik im Prediger-Orden (von 1250–1350).* Freiburg-im-Breisgau: Herder, 1861.

Griffiths, Paul J. *Religious Reading: The Place of Reading in the Practice of Religion.* New York/Oxford: Oxford University Press, 1999.

Guagliardo, Vincent, Charles R. Hess, and Richard Taylor. *St. Thomas Aquinas: Commentary on the Book of Causes.* Washington: Catholic University Press, 1996.

Haas, Alois M. "Die Aktualität Meister Eckhart: Ein Klassiker der Mystik (ca. 1260–1328)." In *Gottes Nähe: Religiöse Erfahrung in Mystik und Offenbarung. Festschrift zum 65. Geburtstag von Josef Sudbruck SJ,* ed. Paul Imhoff S.J., 79–94. Würzburg: Echter, 1990.

————. "Aktualität und Normativität Meister Eckharts." In *Eckhardus Theutonicus, homo doctus et sanctus: Nachweise und Berichte zum Prozess gegen Meister Eckhart,* ed. Heinrich Stirnimann and Ruedi Imbach, 203–68. Freiburg, Switzerland: Universitätsverlag, 1992.

————. "Die Beurteilung der vita contemplativa und vita activa in der Dominikanermystik des 14. Jahrhunderts." In *Gottleiden-Gottlieben. Zur volkssprachlichen Mystik im Mittelalter,* 97–108. Frankfort: Insel, 1989.

————. "Deutsche Mystik." In *Geschichte der deutschen Literatur, III/2, Die deutsche Literatur im späten Mittelalter 1250–1370,* ed. Ingeborg Glier, 234–305. Munich: C. H. Beck, 1987.

————. "Die deutsche Mystik. 5.1, Das Verhältnis von Sprache und Erfahrung." In *Sermo Mysticus: Studien zu Theologie und Sprache der deutschen Mystik,* 136–67. Freiburg, Switzerland: Universitätsverlag, 1979.

————. "Eriugena und die Mystik." In *Eriugena Redivivus: Zur Wirkungsgeschichte seines Denkens im Mittelalter und im Übergang zur Neuzeit,* ed. Werner Beierwaltes, 254–78. Heidelberg: Carl Winter, 1987.

————. *Geistliches Mittelalter.* Freiburg, Switzerland: Universitätsverlag, 1984.

————. "Granum sinapis—An den Grenzen der Sprache." In *Sermo Mysticus: Studien zu Theologie und Sprache der deutschen Mystik,* 301–29. Freiburg, Switzerland: Universitätsverlag, 1979.

————. "Jesus Christus—Inbegriff des Heils und verwirkliche Transzendenz im Geist der deutschen Mystik." In *Epiphanie des Heils. Zur Heilsgegenwart in indischer und christlicher Religion,* 193–216. Vienna: Institut für Indologie der Universität Wien, 1983.

————. "Meister Eckhart: Mystische Bildlehre." In *Sermo Mysticus: Studien zu Theologie und Sprache der deutschen Mystik,* 209–37. Freiburg, Switzerland: Universitätsverlag, 1979.

———. *Meister Eckhart als normative Gestalt geistlichen Lebens.* 2nd ed. Freiburg: Johannes, 1995.

———. "Meister Eckharts Auffassung von Zeit und Ewigkeit." In *Geistliches Mittelalter,* [339–55]. Freiburg, Switzerland: Universitätsverlag, 1984.

———. "Meister Eckharts geistliches Predigtprogramm." In *Geistliches Mittelalter,* [317–37]. Freiburg, Switzerland: Universitätsverlag, 1984.

———. "Meister Eckhart und die deutsche Sprache." In *Geistliches Mittelalter.* [215–37]. Freiburg, Switzerland: Universitätsverlag, 1984.

———. "MORS MYSTICA: Ein mystologisches Motiv." In *Sermo Mysticus: Studien zu Theologie und Sprache der deutschen Mystik,* 392–480. Freiburg, Switzerland: Universitätsverlag, 1979.

———. "Mystische Erfahrung und Sprache." In *Sermo Mysticus: Studien zu Theologie und Sprache der deutschen Mystik,* 18–36. Freiburg, Switzerland: Universitätsverlag, 1979.

———. "Das mystische Paradox." In *Das Paradox: Eine Herausforderung des abendländische Denkens,* ed. Paul Geyer and Roland Hagenbüchle, 273–89. Tübingen: Stauffenberg, 1992.

———. *Nim Din Selbes War: Studien zur Lehre von der Selbsterkenntnis bei Meister Eckhart, Johannes Tauler und Heinrich Seuse.* Freiburg, Switzerland: Universtätsverlag, 1971.

———. "The Nothingness of God and its Explosive Metaphors." *The Eckhart Review* no. 8 (1999): 6–17.

———. "'. . . DAS PERSÖNLICHE UND EIGENE VERLEUGNEN': Mystische *vernichtigkeit und verworfwenheit sein selbs* im Geiste Meister Eckharts." In *INDIVIDUALITÄT: Poetik und Hermeneutik XIII,* ed. Manfred Frank and Anselm Haverkamp, 106–22. Munich: Fink, 1988.

———. "Schools of Late Medieval Mysticism." In *Christian Spirituality, II: High Middle Ages and Reformation,* ed. Jill Raitt. New York: Crossroad, 1987.

———. "Seinsspekulation und Geschöpflichkeit in der Mystik Meister Eckharts." In *Sein und Nichts in der abendländischen Mystik,* ed. Walter Strolz, 33–58. Freiburg: Herder, 1984.

———. "'Trage Leiden geduldiglich': Die Einstellung der deutschen Mystik zum Leiden." *Zeitwende* 57, no. 3 (1986): 154–75.

Hankey, W. J. *God in Himself: Aquinas' Doctrine of God as expounded in the "Summa Theologiae."* Oxford: Oxford University Press, 1987.

Hanratty, Gerald. "The Origin and Development of Mystical Atheism." *Neue Zeitschrift für Systematische Theologie* 30 (1988): 1–17.

Harries, Karsten. "The Infinite Sphere: Comments on the History of a Metaphor." *Journal of the History of Philosophy* 13 (1975): 5–15.

Hasebrink, Burkhard. *Formen inizitativer Rede bei Meister Eckhart: Untersuchungen zur literarische Konzeption der deutschen Predigt.* Tübingen: Niemeyer, 1992.

———. "GRENZVERSCHIEBUNG: Zu Kongruenz und Differenz von Latein und Deutsche bei Meister Eckhart." In *Zeitschrift für deutsches Altertum und deutsche Literatur* 121 (1992): 369–98.

———. "Studies on the Redaction and Use of the *Paradisus anime intelligentis.*" In *De l'homélie au sermon: Histoire de la prédication médiévale,* ed. Jacqueline Hamesse and Xavier Hermand, 144–58. Louvain-la-neuve: Université Catholique, 1993.

Haucke, Rainer. *Trinität und Denken: Die Unterscheidung der Einheit von Gott und Mensch bei Eckhart.* Frankfurt: Peter Lang, 1986.

Haug, Walter. "Das Wort und die Sprache bei Meister Eckhart." In *Zur deutschen Literatur und Sprache des 14. Jahrhunderts: Dubliner Colloquium 1981*, ed. Walter Haug, Timothy R. Jackson, Johannes Janota, 25–44. Heidelberg: Carl Winter, 1983.

Heffner, Blake R. "Meister Eckhart and a Millennium with Mary and Martha." In *Biblical Hermeneutics in Historical Perspective*, ed. Mark S. Burrows and Paul Rorem, 117–30. Grand Rapids: Eerdmans, 1991.

Henkel, Niklaus, and Nigel F. Palmer, eds. *Latein und Volkssprache im deutschen Mittelalter 1100–1500*. Tübingen: Niemeyer, 1992.

Henle, R. J., S.J. *Saint Thomas and Platonism: A Study of the "Plato" and "Platonici" Texts in the Writings of Saint Thomas*. The Hague: Martinus Nijhoff, 1956.

Hof, Hans. *Scintilla animae: Eine Studie zu einem Grundbegriff in Meister Eckharts Philosophie*. Lund: Gleerup, 1952.

Hollywood, Amy. *The Soul as Virgin Wife. Mechthild of Magdeburg, Marguerite Porete, and Meister Eckhart*. Notre Dame: University of Notre Dame Press, 1995.

———. "Preaching as Social Practice in Meister Eckhart." In *Mysticism and Social Transformation*, ed. Janet K. Ruffing, 76–90. Syracuse: Syracuse University Press, 2001.

Hudry, Françoise, ed. *Liber Viginti Quattuor Philosophorum*. Corpus Christianorum Continuatio Mediaevalis 143A. Turnholt: Brepols, 1997.

Imbach, Ruedi. *Deus est Intelligere: Das Verhältnis von Sein und Denken in seiner Bedeutung für das Gottesverständnis bei Thomas von Aquin und in den Pariser Quaestionen Meister Eckharts*. Freiburg, Switzerland: Universitätsverlag, 1976.

———. "Le (Néo-)Platonisme médiévale: Proclus latin et l'école dominicain allemande." *Revue de théologie et philosophie* 110 (1978): 427–48.

———. "Ut ait Rabbi Moses: Maimonidische Philosopheme bei Thomas von Aquin und Meister Eckhart." *Collectanea Franciscana* 60 (1990): 99–116.

Iohn, Friedrich. *Die Predigt Meister Eckharts*. Heidelberg: Carl Winter, 1993.

Jansen, Saskia Murk. "Hadewijch and Eckhart: Amor intelligere est." In *Meister Eckhart and the Beguine Mystics: Hadewijch of Brabant, Mechthild of Magdeburg, and Marguerite Porete*, ed. Bernard McGinn, 17–30. New York: Continuum, 1994.

Jeauneau, Édouard. "Denys l'Aréopagite: Promoteur du Néoplatonisme en Occident." In *Néoplatonisme et Philosophie Médievale*, ed. Linos G. Benakis, 1–23. Société Internationale pour l'Étude de la Philosophie Médiévale. Turnholt: Brepols, 1997.

———, ed. *Jean Scot: Commentaire sur l'évangile de Jean*. SC 180. Paris: Cerf, 1972.

Jostes, Franz. *Meister Eckhart und seine Jünger: Ungedruckte Texte zur Geschichte der deutschen Mystik*. Freiburg, Switzerland: Universitätsbuchhandlung, 1895.

Kampmann, Irmgard. *"Ihr sollt der Sohn selber sein": Eine fundamentaltheologische Studie zur Soteriologie Meister Eckharts*. Frankfurt: Peter Lang, 1996.

Karrer, Otto. "Das Gotteserlebnis bei Augustinus und Meister Eckhart." In *Das Gotteserlebnis*, ed. Otto Karrer and Ludwig Köhler, 20–54. Zurich: Schweizer-Spiegel Verlag, 1934.

———. *Meister Eckehart: Das System seiner religiösen Lehre und Lebensweisheit*. Munich: Josef Müller, 1926.

Kelley, C. F. *Meister Eckhart on Divine Knowledge*. New Haven: Yale University Press, 1977.

Kertz, Karl G., S.J. "Meister Eckhart's Teaching on the Birth of the Divine Word in the Soul." *Traditio* 15 (1959): 339–63.

Kieckhefer, Richard. "Meister Eckhart's Conception of Union with God." *Harvard Theological Review* 71 (1978): 203–25.

Köbele, Susanne. *Bilder der unbegriffenen Wahrheit: Zur Struktur mystischer Rede im Spannungsfeld von Latein und Volkssprache.* Tübingen/Basel: Francke, 1993.

———. *"BÎWORT SÎN:* 'Absolute' Grammatik bei Meister Eckhart." *Zeitschrift für deutsche Philologie* 113 (1994): 190–206.

———. "Predigt 16b: 'Quasi vas auri solidum.'" In *Lectura Eckhardi,* 43–74.

———. *"PRIMO ASPECTU MONSTRUOSA:* Schriftauslegung bei Meister Eckhart." *Zeitschrift für deutsches Altertum und deutsche Literatur* 122 (1993): 62–81.

Koch, Josef. "Augustinische und dionysischer Neuplatonismus im Mittelalter." In *Platonismus in der Philosophie des Mittelalters,* ed. Werner Beierwaltes, 317–42. Darmstadt: Wissenschaftliche Buchhandlung, 1969.

———. "Kritische Studien zum Leben Meister Eckharts." *Archivum Fratrum Praedicatorum* 29 (1959): 1–51; 30 (1960): 1–52.

———. "Meister Eckhart und die jüdische Religionsphilosophie des Mittelalters." *Jahresbericht der Schleschischen Gesellschaft, Philosophisch-pyschologische Sektion* 101 (1928): 134–48.

———. "Sinn und Struktur der Schriftauslegungen." In *Meister Eckhart der Prediger: Festschrift zum Eckhart-Gedenkjahr,* ed. Udo M. Nix and Raphael Öchslin, 73–103. Freiburg: Herder, 1960.

———. "Zur Analogielehre Meister Eckharts." In *Mélanges offerts à Etienne Gilson,* 327–50. Paris: Vrin, 1959.

Kremer, Klaus. "Das Seelenfunklein bei Meister Eckhart." *Trierer theologische Zeitschrift* 97 (1988): 8–38.

Kristeller, Paul Oskar. "Proclus as a Reader of Plato and Plotinus, and his Influence in the Middle Ages and the Renaissance." In *Proclus: Lecteur et interprète des anciens,* 191–211. Paris: CNRS, 1987.

Kunisch, Herman. *Das Wort "Grund" in der Sprache der deutschen Mystik des 14. und 15. Jahrhunderts.* Osnabrück: Pagenkämper, 1929.

Lane, Belden C. *The Solace of Fierce Landscapes: Exploring Desert and Mountain Spirituality.* New York/Oxford: Oxford University Press, 1998.

Langer, Otto. "Meister Eckharts Lehre vom Seelengrund." In *Grundfragen christliche Mystik,* ed. Margot Schmidt and Dieter R. Bauer, 173–91. Stuttgart/Bad Cannstatt: frommann-holzboog, 1987.

———. *Mystische Erfahrung und spirituelle Theologie: Zu Meister Eckharts Auseinandersetzung mit der Frauenfrömmigkeit seiner Zeit.* Munich/Zurich: Artemis, 1987.

Lanzetta, Beverly. "Three Categories of Nothingness in Meister Eckhart." *Journal of Religion* 72 (1992): 248–68.

Largier, Niklaus. *Bibliographie zu Meister Eckhart.* Freiburg, Switzerland: Universitätsverlag, 1989.

———. *"Figurata Locutio:* Philosophie und Hermeneutik bei Eckhart von Hochheim und Heinrich Seuse." In *Meister Eckhart: Lebensstationen—Redesituationen,* ed. Klaus Jacobi, 303–32. Berlin: Walter de Gruyter, 1997.

———. "Intellekttheorie, Hermeneutik und Allegorie: Subjekt und Subjektivität bei Meister Eckhart." In *Geschichte und Vorgeschichte der modernen Subjektivität,* ed. Reto Luzius Fetz, Roland Hagenbüchle, and Peter Schulz, 460–86. Berlin/New York: Walter de Gruyter, 1998.

———. *"Intellectus in deum ascensus":* Intellekttheoretische Auseinandersetzungen in Texten der deutschen Mystik." *Deutsche Vierteljahrsschrift für Literaturwissenschaft und Geistesgeschichte* 69 (1995): 423–71.

————. "Meister Eckhart: Perspektiven der Forschung, 1980–1993," *Zeitschrift für deutsche Philologie* 114 (1995): 29–98.

————. "Negativität, Möglichkeit, Freiheit. Zur Differenz zwischen der Philosophie Dietrichs von Freiberg und Eckharts von Hochheim." In *Dietrich von Freiberg: Neue Perspektiven seiner Philosophie, Theologie und Naturwissenschaften,* ed. Karl-Herman Kandler, Burkhard Mojsisch, Franz-Bernard Stamkötter, 149–68. Amsterdam: B. R. Gruner, 1998.

————. "Penser la finitude: Création, détachment et les limites de la philosophie dans la pensée de maître Eckhart." *Revue des sciences religieuses* 71 (1997): 458–73.

————. "Repräsentation und Negativität: Meister Eckharts Kritik als Dekonstruktion." In *Contemplata aliis tradere: Studien zum Verhältnis von Literatur und Spiritualität,* ed. C. Brinker, U. Herzog, et al., 371–90. Frankfurt: Lang, 1995.

————. "Recent Work on Meister Eckhart: Positions, Problems, New Perspectives, 1990–1997." *Recherches de Théologie et Philosophie médiévales* 65 (1998): 147–67.

————. *Zeit, Zeitlichkeit, Ewigkeit: Ein Aufriss des Zeitproblems bei Dietrich von Freiburg and Meister Eckhart.* Frankfurt: Peter Lang, 1989.

Laurent, M.-H. "Autour de procès de Maître Eckhart." *Divus Thomas,* ser. III, 13 (1936): 331–48, 430–47.

Leclercq, Jean, et al., eds. *S. Bernardi Opera.* 8 vols. Rome: Editiones Cistercienses, 1957–77.

Lerner, Robert E. *The Heresy of the Free Spirit.* 2nd ed. Notre Dame, Ind.: University of Notre Dame Press, 1997.

————. "New Evidence for the Condemnation of Meister Eckhart." *Speculum* 72 (1997): 347–66.

Liebeschütz, Hans. "Meister Eckhart und Moses Maimonides." *Archiv für Kulturgeschichte* 54 (1972): 64–96.

————. "Mittelalterliche Platonismus bei Johannes Eriugena und Meister Eckhart." *Archiv für Kulturgeschichte* 56 (1974): 241–69.

Löser, Freimut. "'*Oratio est cum deo confabulatio*': Meister Eckharts Auffassung vom Beten und seine Gebetspraxis." In *Deutsche Mystik im abendländischen Zusammenhang,* ed. Walter Haug and Wolfram Schneider-Lastin, 283–316.

Lossky, Vladimir. *Théologie négative et connaissance de Dieu chez Maître Eckhart.* Paris: Vrin, 1960.

Louth, Andrew. *The Wilderness of God.* Nashville: Abingdon, 1991.

Magistri Petri Lombardi Sententiae in IV Libris Distinctae. 3rd ed. Grottaferrata: Editiones Collegii S. Bonaventurae ad Claras Aquas, 1971.

Mahnke, Dietrich. *Unendliche Sphäre und Allmittelpunkt: Beiträge zur Genealogie der mathematischen Mystik.* Halle: Niemeyer, 1937.

Maître Eckhart à Paris: Une critique médiévale de l'ontothéologie. Les Questions parisiennes no. 1 et no. 2. Paris: Presses Universitaires de France, 1984.

Manstetten, Reiner. *Esse est Deus: Meister Eckharts christologische Versöhnung von Philosophie und Religion und ihre Ursprünge in der Tradition des Abendländes.* Munich: Karl Alber, 1993.

Marguerite Porete. *Le Mirouer des simples ames.* Edited by Romana Guarnieri and Paul Verdeyen. Turnholt: Brepols, 1986.

Maurer, Armand. *Master Eckhart: Parisian Questions and Prologues.* Toronto: PIMS, 1974.

McGinn, Bernard. "The Abyss of Love." In *The Joy of Learning and the Love of God: Studies in Honor of Jean Leclercq,* ed. E. Rozanne Elder, 95–120. Kalamazoo: Cistercian Publications, 1995.

———. "Asceticism and Mysticism in Late Antiquity and the Middle Ages." In *Asceticism,* ed. Vincent L. Wimbush and Richard Valantasis, 58–74. New York: Oxford, 1995.

———. "Do Christian Platonists Really Believe in Creation?" In *God and Creation: An Ecumenical Symposium,* ed. David B. Burrell and Bernard McGinn, 197–223. Notre Dame, Ind.: University of Notre Dame Press, 1990.

———. "Does the Trinity Add Up? Transcendental Mathematics and Trinitarian Speculation in the Twelfth and Thirteenth Centuries" (forthcoming).

———. "Eckhart's Condemnation Reconsidered." *The Thomist* 44 (1980): 390–414.

———. *The Flowering of Mysticism: Men and Women in the New Mysticism (1200–1350).* Volume 3 of *The Presence of God: A History of Western Christian Mysticism.* New York: Crossroad, 1998.

———. *The Foundations of Mysticism: Origins to the Fifth Century.* Volume 1 of *The Presence of God: A History of Western Christian Mysticism.* New York: Crossroad, 1991.

———. "The God beyond God: Theology and Mysticism in the Thought of Meister Eckhart." *Journal of Religion* 61 (1981): 1–19.

———. *The Growth of Mysticism: Gregory the Great to the Twelfth Century.* Volume 2 of *The Presence of God: A History of Western Christian Mysticism.* New York: Crossroad, 1994.

———. "The Human Person as Image of God, II, Western Christianity." In *Christian Spirituality, I, Origins to the Fifth Century,* ed. Jean Leclercq, Bernard McGinn, John Meyendorff, 312–30. New York: Crossroad, 1985.

———. "Ibn Gabirol: The Sage among the Schoolmen." In *Neoplatonism and Jewish Thought,* ed. Lenn E. Goodman, 77–109. Albany: SUNY Press, 1992.

———. "Introduction, 2, On Speaking about God." In *Teacher and Preacher,* 15–30.

———. "The Language of Love in Jewish and Christian Mysticism." In *Mysticism and Language,* ed. Steven T. Katz, 202–35. New York: Oxford University Press, 1992.

———. "Love, Knowledge and *Unio mystica* in the Western Christian Tradition." In *Mystical Union in Judaism, Christianity, and Islam: An Ecumenical Dialogue,* ed. Moshe Idel and Bernard McGinn, 59–86. New York: Continuum, 1996.

———. "Meister Eckhart." In *Medieval Philosophers: Dictionary of Literary Biography, Volume 115,* ed. Jeremiah Hackett, 150–68. Detroit/London: Bruccoli Clark, 1992.

———. "Meister Eckhart on God as Absolute Unity." In *Neoplatonism and Christian Thought,* ed. Dominic O'Meara, 128–39. Albany: SUNY Press, 1982.

———. "Meister Eckhart: An Introduction." In *An Introduction to the Medieval Mystics of Europe,* ed. Paul Szarmach, 237–57. Albany: SUNY Press, 1984.

———. "Ocean and Desert as Symbols of Mystical Absorption in the Christian Tradition." *Journal of Religion* 74 (1994): 155–81.

———. "The Originality of Eriugena's Spiritual Exegesis." In *Iohannes Scottus Eriugena: The Bible and Hermeneutics,* ed. Gerd Van Riel, Carlos Steel, and James McEvoy, 55–80. Leuven: Leuven University Press, 1996.

———. "A Prolegomenon to the Role of the Trinity in Meister Eckhart's Mysticism." *Eckhart Review* (spring 1997): 51–61.

———. "*Quo vadis?* Reflections on the Current Study of Mysticism." *Christian Spirituality Bulletin* (spring 1998): 13–21.

———. "*SAPIENTIA JUDAEORUM:* The Role of Jewish Philosophers in Some Scholastic Thinkers." In *Continuity and Change. The Harvest of Late Medieval and Reformation History. Essays presented to Heiko A. Oberman on his 70th Birthday,* ed. Robert F. Bast and Andrew C. Gow, 206–28. Leiden Brill, 2000.

———. "Sermo IV." In *Lectura Eckhardi,* 289–316.

———. "St. Bernard and Meister Eckhart." *Cîteaux* 31 (1980): 373–86.

———. "Suffering, emptiness and annihilation in three beguine mystics." In *Homo Medietas: Aufsätze zu Religiosität, Literatur und Denkformen des Menschen vom Mittelalter bis in die Neuzeit. Festschrift für Alois Maria Haas zum 65. Geburtstag,* ed. Claudia Brinker-von der Heyde and Niklaus Largier, 162–69. Frankfurt: Peter Lang, 1999.

———. "2. Theological Summary." In *Meister Eckhart: The Essential Sermons, Commentaries, Treatises, and Defense,* 24–61. Translation and introduction by Edmund Colledge, O.S.A., and Bernard McGinn. New York: Paulist Press, 1981.

———. "*Vere tu es Deus absconditus:* The Hidden God in Luther and Some Mystics." (forthcoming).

———, ed. *Meister Eckhart and the Beguine Mystics: Hadewijch of Brabant, Mechthild of Magdeburg, and Marguerite Porete.* New York: Continuum, 1994.

Meister Eckhart: Lebensstationen—Redesituationen, ed. Klaus Jacobi. Berlin: Walter de Gruyter, 1997.

Meister Eckhart: Selected Writings. Selected and translated by Oliver Davies. London: Penguin, 1994.

Merlan, Philip. "Aristoteles, Averroes und die beiden Eckharts." In *Autour d'Aristote: Recueil d'Études de Philosophie ancienne et médiévale offert à Monseigneur A. Mansion,* 543–66. Louvain: Publications Universitaires, 1955.

Merle, Hélène. "*DEITAS:* Quelques aspects de la signification de ce mot d'Augustin à Maître Eckhart." In *Von Meister Dietrich zu Meister Eckhart,* ed. Kurt Flasch, 12–21. Hamburg: Felix Meiner, 1984.

Mieth, Dietmar. *Christus—Das Soziale im Menschen.* Düsseldorf: Patmos, 1972.

———. *Die Einheit von Vita Activa und Vita Passiva in den deutschen Predigten und Traktaten Meister Eckharts und bei Johannes Tauler.* Regensburg: Pustet, 1969.

———. "Gottesschau und Gottesgeburt: Zwei Typen Christlicher Gotteserfahrung in der Tradition." *Freiburger Zeitschrift für Theologie und Philosophie* 27 (1980): 204–23.

———. "Die theologische transposition der Tugendethik bei Meister Eckhart." In *Abendländische Mystik im Mittelalter,* ed. Kurt Ruh, 63–79. Stuttgart: J. B. Metzler, 1986.

Miethke, Jürgen. "Der Prozess gegen Meister Eckhart im Rahmen der spätmittelalter Lehrzuchtverfahren gegen Dominikanertheologen." In *Meister Eckhart: Lebensstationen—Redesituationen,* ed. Klaus Jacobi, 353–75. Berlin: Walter de Gruyter, 1997.

Milem, Bruce. "Meister Eckhart and the Image: Sermon 16b." *Eckhart Review* (spring 1999): 47–59.

Minnis, A. J. *Medieval Theory of Authorship.* 2nd ed. Philadelphia: University of Pennsylvania Press, 1988.

———, and A. B. Scott. *Medieval Literary Theory and Criticism c. 1100–c. 1375: The Commentary Tradition.* Oxford: Clarendon Press, 1991.

Mojsisch, Burkhard. "Der Begriff der Liebe bei Augustin und Meister Eckhart." In

Philosophie: Anregungen für die Unterrichtspraxis, Heft 12, Freundschaft und Liebe, ed. Jürgen Hengelbrock, 19–27. Frankfurt, 1984.

———. "'Causa essentialis' bei Dietrich von Freiburg und Meister Eckhart." In *Von Meister Eckhart zu Meister Dietrich*, ed. Kurt Flasch, 106–14. Hamburg: Meiner, 1984.

———. "'Ce moi': La conception du moi de Maître Eckhart." *Revue des sciences religieuses* 70 (1996): 27–28.

———. "'Dynamik' der Vernunft bei Dietrich von Freiberg und Meister Eckhart." In *Abendländische Mystik im Mittelalter*, ed. Kurt Ruh, 116–44.

———. *Meister Eckhart: Analogie, Univozität und Einheit*. Hamburg: Felix Meiner, 1983.

———. "*Nichts* und *Negation*: Meister Eckhart und Nikolaus von Kues." In *Historia philosophiae medii aevi: Studien zur Geschichte der Philosophie des Mittelalters*, ed. Burkhard Mojsisch, 2:675–93. Amsterdam: G. R. Grüner, 1991.

Mojsisch, Burkhard, et al., eds. *Dietrich von Freiberg: Opera Omnia*. Hamburg: Felix Meiner, 1977–.

Morard, Meinrad. "Ist, istic, istikeit bei Meister Eckhart." *Freiburger Zeitschrift für Philosophie und Theologie* 3 (1956): 169–86.

Morrow, Glenn R. and John M. Dillon. *Proclus' Commentary on Plato's "Parmenides."* Princeton: Princeton University Press, 1987.

Murk-Jansen, Saskia. "Hadewijch and Eckhart: Amor intelligere est." In *Meister Eckhart and the Beguine Mystics: Hadewijch of Brabant, Mechthild of Magdeburg, and Marguerite Porete*, ed. Bernard McGinn, 17–30. New York: Continuum, 1994.

La mystique rhénane. Paris: Presses Universitaires de France, 1963.

Nuchelmans, Gabriel. *Secundum/tertium adiacens: Vicissitudes of a logical distinction*. Amsterdam: Koninklijke Nederlandse Akademie, 1992.

Oechslin, R.-L. "Eckhart et la mystique trinitaire." *Lumière et vie* 30 (1956): 99–120.

———. "Der Eine und Dreieinige in den deutschen Predigten." In *Meister Eckhart der Prediger: Festschrift zum Eckhart-Gedenkjahr*, ed. Udo M. Nix and Raphael Öchslin, 149–66. Freiburg: Herder, 1960.

O'Rourke, Fran. *Pseudo-Dionysius and the Metaphysics of Aquinas*. Leiden: Brill, 1992.

Patschovsky, Alexander. "Strassburger Beginenvervolgerung im 14. Jahrhundert." *Deutsches Archiv für Erforschung des Mittelalters* 30 (1974): 56–198.

Pattin, Adriaan, ed. *Le LIBER DE CAUSIS: Édition établie à l'aide de 90 manuscrits avec introduction et notes*. Leuven: Uitgave van "Tijdschrift voor Filosofie," n.d.

Pelster, Franz. "Eine Gutachten aus dem Eckehart-Prozess in Avignon." In *Aus der Geisteswelt des Mittelalters: Festgabe Martin Grabmann*, 1099–1124. Münster: Aschendorff, 1935.

Poems of Gerard Manley Hopkins. 3rd ed. London: Oxford University Press, 1948.

Preger, Wilhelm. *Geschichte der deutschen Mystik im Mittelalter: Nach den Quellen untersucht und dargestellt*. 3 vols. Leipzig: Dörffling & Franke, 1874–93.

Quint, Josef. *Meister Eckehart: Deutsche Predigten und Traktate*. Munich: Carl Hanser, 1963.

———. "Mystik und Sprache: Ihr Verhältnis zueinander, insbesondere in der spekulativen Mystik Meister Eckeharts." In *Altdeutsche und altniederländische Mystik*, ed. Kurt Ruh, 113–51. Wege der Forschung 23. Darmstadt: Wissenschaftliche Buchhandlung, 1964.

Rahner, Hugo. "Die Gottesgeburt: Die Lehre der Kirchenväter von der Geburt Christi aus den Herzen der Kirche und der Gläubigen." In *Symbole der Kirche: Die Ekklesiologie der Väter*, 7–41. Salzburg: Müller, 1964.

Reichert, Benedict Maria, ed. *Monumenta Ordinis Praedicatorum Historica, Tomus IV,* *Acta Capitulorum Generalium,* vol. II. Rome: Propaganda Fidei, 1899.

Reiter, Peter. *Der Seele Grund. Meister Eckhart und die Tradition der Seelenlehre.* Würzburg: Königshausen & Neumann, 1993.

Renna, Thomas. "Angels and Spirituality: The Augustinian Tradition to Eckhardt." *Augustinian Studies* 16 (1985): 29–37.

Reynolds, Lyndon P. "*Bullitio* and the God beyond God: Meister Eckhart's Trinitarian Theology." *New Blackfriars* 70 (1989): 169–81, 235–44.

Reypens, Léonce. "Ame (structure)." In DS 1:433–69.

Reypens, Léonce, and Jan van Mierlo, eds. *Beatrijs van Nazareth: Seven Manieren van Minne.* Leuven: S.V. de Vlaamsche Boekenhalle, 1926.

Rorem, Paul. "Procession and Return in Thomas Aquinas and His Predecessors." *Princeton Seminary Bulletin* 13 (1992): 147–63.

———. *Pseudo-Dionysius: A Commentary on the Texts and an Introduction to Their Influence.* New York/Oxford: Oxford University Press, 1993.

Ruh, Kurt. "Dionysius Areopagita im deutschen Predigtwerk Meister Eckharts, Perspektiven der Philosophie," *Neues Jahrbuch* 13 (1987): 207–23.

———. "Johannes Scotus Eriugena Deutsch," *Zeitschrift für deutsches Altertum und deutsche Literatur* 99 (1988): 24–31.

———. "Kapitel XXXVI: Meister Eckhart." In Kurt Ruh, *Geschichte der abendländische Mystik.* Vol. 3, *Die Mystik des deutschen Predigerordens und ihre Grundlegung durch die Hochscholastik,* 216–353, Munich: C. H. Beck, 1996.

———. *Geschichte der abendländische Mystik.* Vol. 2, *Frauenmystik und Franziskanische Mystik der Frühzeit.* Munich: C. H. Beck, 1993.

———. *Meister Eckhart: Theologe. Prediger. Mystiker.* Munich: C. H. Beck, 1985.

———. "Das mystische Schweigen und die mystische Rede." In *Festschrift für Ingo Reiffenstein zum 60. Geburtstag,* 463–72. Göppingen: Kümmerle, 1988.

———. "Neuplatonische Quellen Meister Eckhart." In *Contemplata aliis tradere: Studien zum Verhältnis von Literatur und Spiritualität,* ed. Claudia Brinker, Urs Herzog, Niklaus Largier, and Paul Michel, 317–52. Frankfurt: Peter Lang, 1995.

———. "Paradisus animae intelligentis" ("Paradis der fornunftigen sele"). In VL 7:298–303.

———. "Textkritik zum Mystikerlied 'Granum sinapis.'" In *Kleine Schriften,* vol. 2, *Scholastik und Mystik im Spätmittelalter,* ed. Volker Mertens, 77–93. Berlin/New York: Walter de Gruyter, 1984.

———. "Die trinitarische Spekulation in deutscher Mystik." In *Kleine Schriften,* vol. 2, *Scholastik und Mystik im Spätmittelalter,* ed. Volker Mertens, 14–45. Berlin/New York: Walter de Gruyter, 1984.

Schaller, Toni. "Die Meister-Eckhart Forschung von der Jahrhundertwende bis zum Gegenwart." *Freiburger Zeitschrift für Philosophie und Theologie* 15 (1968): 262–316, 403–26.

———. "Zur Eckhart-Deutung der letzten 30 Jahre." *Freiburger Zeitschrift für Philosophie und Theologie* 16 (1969): 22–39.

Scheepsma, Wybren. "Hadewijch und die *Limburgse sermoenen:* Überlegung zu Datierung. Identität und Authentizität." In *Deutsche Mystik im abendländischen Zusammenhang,* ed. Walter Haug and Wolfram Schneider-Lastin, 683–702. Tübingen: Niemeyer, 2000.

Schmoldt, Benno. *Die deutsche Begriffssprache Meister Eckharts: Studien zur philosophischen terminologie des Mittelhochdeutschen.* Heidelberg: Quelle & Meyer, 1954.

Schneider, Richard. "The Functional Christology of Meister Eckhart." *Recherches de théologie ancienne et médiévale* 35 (1968): 291–332.

Schulze-Maizier, Friedrich. *Meister Eckharts deutsche Predigten und Traktate*. Leipzig: Insel Verlag, 1932.

Schürmann, Reiner. *Meister Eckhart Mystic and Philosopher*. Bloomington: Indiana University Press, 1978.

Schwartz, Yossef. "'*Ecce est locus apud me*': Maimonides und Eckharts Raumvorstellung als Begriff des Göttlichen." In *Raum und Raumvorstellungen im Mittelalter*, ed. Jan A. Aertsen and Andreas Speer, 348–64. Berlin/New York: Walter de Gruyter, 1998.

———. "Metaphysiche oder theologische Hermeneutik? Meister Eckhart in den Spuren des Maimonides und des Thomas von Aquin" (forthcoming).

Sells, Michael A. *Mystical Languages of Unsaying*. Chicago: University of Chicago Press, 1994.

Senner, Walter. "Meister Eckhart in Köln." In *Meister Eckhart: Lebensstationen—Redesituationen*, ed. Klaus Jacobi, 207–37. Berlin: Walter de Gruyter, 1997.

Solignac, Aimé. "NOUS et MENS." In DS 11:459–60.

———. "Synderesis." In DS 14:1407–12.

Speer, Andreas, and Wouter Goris. "Das Meister-Eckhart-Archiv am Thomas-Institut der Universität zu Köln: Die Kontinuität der Forschungsaufgaben." *Bulletin de philosophie médiévale* 37 (1995): 149–74.

Stachel, Günter. "Streit um Meister Eckhart: Spekulativer Theologe, beinahe Häretischer Scholastiker oder grosser Mystiker?" *Zeitschrift für Katholische Theologie* 111 (1989): 57–65.

Stadler, Hermann, ed. *Albertus Magnus: De animalibus libri XXVI*, Beiträge zur Geschichte der Philosophie des Mittelalters 16. Münster: Aschendorff, 1920.

Steel, Carlos, ed. *Proclus: Commentaire sur le Parménide de Platon. Traduction de Guillaume de Moerbeke*. 2 vols. Leuven: Leuven University Press; Leiden: Brill, 1982–85.

Steer, Georg. "Bernhard von Clairvaux als theologische Authorität für Meister Eckhart, Johannes Tauler und Heinrich Seuse." In *Bernhard von Clairvaux: Rezeption und Wirkung im mittelalter und in der Neuzeit*, ed. Kaspar Elm, 249–59. Wiesbaden: Harrassowitz, 1994.

———. "Meister Eckharts Predigtzyklus *von der êwigen geburt*: Mutmassungen über die Zeit seiner Entstehung." In *Deutsche Mystik im abendländischen Zusammenhang: Neue erschlossene Texte, neue methodische Ansätze, neue theoretische Konzepte*, ed. Walter Haug and Wolfram Schneider-Lastin, 253–81. Tübingen: Niemeyer, 2000.

———. "Predigt 101: 'Dum medium silentium tenerent omnia.'" In *Lectura Eckhardi*, 247–88.

———. *Scholastische Gnadenlehre in mittelhochdeutschen Sprache*. Munich: Beck, 1961.

———. "Zur Authentizität der deutschen Predigten Meister Eckharts." In *Eckhardus Theutonicus, homo doctus et sanctus: Nachweise und Berichte zum Prozess gegen Meister Eckhart*, ed. Heinrich Stirnimann and Ruedi Imbach, 127–68. Freiburg, Switzerland: Universitätsverlag, 1992.

Strauch, Philip, ed. *Paradisus anime intelligentis (Paradis der fornunftigen sele): Aus der Oxforder Hs. Cod. Laud. Misc. 479 nach E. Sievers Abschrift*. Deutsche Texte des Mittelalters 30. Berlin, 1919.

Sturlese, Loris. "Il dibattito sul Proclo latino nel medioevo fra l'Università di Parigi e lo Studium di Colonia." In *Proclus et son influence: Actes du Colloque de Neuchâtel*, ed. G. Boss and G. Seel, 263–85. Zurich: Éditions du Grand Midi, 1987.

———. "Meister Eckhart: Ein Porträt." In *Eichstätter Hochschulreden* 90. Regensburg: Pustet, 1993.

———. "Meister Eckhart in der Bibliotheca Amploniana: Neues zur Datierung des 'Opus tripartitum.'" In *Der Bibliotheca Amploniana: Ihre Bedeutung im Spannungsfeld von Aristotelismus, Nominalismus und Humanismus,* ed. Andreas Speer, 434–46. Miscellanea Mediaevalia 23. Berlin/New York: Walter de Gruyter, 1995.

———. "Mysticism and Theology in Meister Eckhart's Theory of the Image." *Eckhart Review* (March 1993): 18–31.

———. "Un nuovo manoscritto delle opere latine di Eckhart e il suo significato per la ricostruzione del testo e della storia del Opus tripartitum." *Freiburger Zeitschrift für Philosophie und Theologie* 32 (1985): 145–54.

———. "A Portrait of Meister Eckhart." *Eckhart Review* (spring 1996): 7–12.

———. "Predigt 17: 'Qui odit animam suam.'" In *Lectura Eckhardi,* 75–96.

———. "Proclo ed Ermete in Germania da Alberto Magno a Bertoldo di Moosburg." In *Von Meister Dietrich zu Meister Eckhart,* ed. Kurt Flasch, 22–33. Hamburg: Meiner, 1984.

———. "Tauler im Kontext: Die philosophischen Voraussetzungen des 'Seelengrundes' in der Lehre des deutschen Neoplatonikers Berthold von Moosburg." *Beiträge zur Geschichte der deutschen Sprache und Literatur* 109 (1987): 390–426.

Sturlese, Loris, et al., eds. *Berthold, Expositio super Elementationem theologicam Procli.* Hamburg: Felix Meiner, 1984–.

Tarrant, Jacqueline. "The Clementine Decrees on the Beguines: Conciliar and Papal Versions." *Archivum Historiae Pontificiae* 12 (1974): 300–307.

Theisen, Joachim. *Predigt und Gottesdienst: Liturgische Strukturen in den Predigten Meister Eckharts.* Frankfurt: Peter Lang, 1990.

Tobin, Frank. "Creativity and Interpreting Scripture: Meister Eckhart in Practice." *Monatshefte* 74 (1982): 410–18.

———. "Eckhart's Mystical Use of Language: The Contexts of *eigenschaft.*" *Seminar* 8 (1972): 160–68.

———. "Mechthild of Magdeburg and Meister Eckhart: Points of Comparison." In *Meister Eckhart and the Beguine Mystics: Hadewijch of Brabant, Mechthild of Magdeburg, and Marguerite Porete,* ed. Bernard McGinn, 44–61. New York: Continuum, 1994.

———. *Meister Eckhart: Thought and Language.* Philadelphia: University of Pennsylvania Press, 1986.

———. "Meister Eckhart and the Angels" In *In hôhem prîse: A Festschrift in Honor of Ernst S. Dick,* ed. Winder McConnell, 379–93. Göppingen: Kümmerle Verlag, 1989.

Trottmann, Christian. *La vision béatifique: Des disputes scolastiques à sa définition per Benoît XII.* Rome: École Française de Rome, 1995.

Trusen, Winfried. "Meister Eckhart vor seinen Richtern und Zensoren." In *Meister Eckhart: Lebensstationen—Redesituationen,* ed. Klaus Jacobi, 335–52. Berlin: Walter de Gruyter, 1997.

———. *Der Prozess gegen Meister Eckhart: Vorgeschichte, Verlauf und Folgen.* Paderborn: Pustet, 1988.

Turner, Denys. *The Darkness of God: Negativity in Christian Mysticism.* Cambridge: Cambridge University Press, 1995.

Ueda, Shizuteru. *Die Gottesgeburt in der Seele und der Durchbruch zur Gott: Die mystische Anthropologie Meister Eckharts und ihre Konfrontation mit der Mystik der Zen-Buddhismus.* Gütersloh: Mohn, 1965.

van den Brandt, Ria. "Die Eckhart-Predigten der Sammlung *PARADISUS ANIME INTELLIGENTIS* näher betrachtet." In *Albertus Magnus und der Albertismus: Deutsche philosophische Kultur des Mittelalters*, ed. Maarten J. F. M. Hoenen and Alain de Libera, 173–87. Leiden: Brill, 1995.

Van Mierlo, Joseph. *Hadewijch: Brieven*. 2 vols. Antwerp: N.V. Standaard, 1947.

Vannier, Anne-Marie. "Déconstruction de l'individualité ou assomption de la personne chez Eckhart?" In *Individuum und Individualität im Mittelalter*, ed. Jan. A. Aertsen and Andreas Speer, 622–41. Berlin: Walter de Gruyter, 1996.

————. "Eckhart à Strasbourg (1313–1323/24)." In *Dominicains et Dominicaines en Alsace XIIIe–XXe S.*, ed. Jean-Luc Eichenlaub, 197–208. Colmar: Éditions d'Alsace, 1996.

————. "L'homme noble, figure de l'ouevre d'Eckhart à Strasbourg." *Revue des sciences religieuses* 70 (1996): 73–89.

————. "Saint Augustin et Eckhart: Sur le problème de la création." *Augustinus* 39 (1994): 551–61.

Vannini, Marco. "*Praedica Verbum*: La *generazione* della parola dal silenzio in Meister Eckhart" In *Il Silenzio e La Parola da Eckhart a Jabès*, ed. Massimo Baldini and Silvano Zucal, 17–31. Trent: Morcelliana, 1987.

Van Steenberghen, Fernand. *La philosophie au XIIIe siècle*. Louvain/Paris: Publications Universitaires, 1966.

Voici Maître Eckhart. Textes et études réunis par Emilie Zum Brunn. Paris: Jérôme Millon, 1994.

von Ivanka, Endré. "Apex mentis: Wanderung und Wandlung eines stoischen Terminus." *Zeitschrift für katholischen Theologien* 72 (1950): 129–76.

Wackernagel, Wolfgang. *YMAGINE DENUDARI: Éthique de l'image et métaphysique de l'abstraction chez Maître Eckhart*. Paris: Vrin, 1991.

Waldschütz, Erwin. *Denken und Erfahren des Grundes: Zur philosophischen Deutung Meister Eckharts*. Vienna/Freiburg/Basel: Herder, 1989.

————. "Probleme philosophische Mystik am Beispiel Meister Eckharts." In *Probleme philosophischer Mystik: Festschrift für Karl Albert zum siebigsten Geburtstag*, ed. Elenor Jain and Reinhard Margreiter, 71–92. Sankt Augustin: Academia Verlag, 1991.

Waszink, J. H., ed. *Timaeus a Calcidio translatus comentarioque instructus*. London: Warburg Institute; Leiden: Brill, 1962.

Weber, Édouard. "Eckhart et l'ontothéologisme: Histoire et conditions d'une rupture." In *Maître Eckhart à Paris: Une critique médiévale de l'ontothéologie. Les Questions parisiennes no. 1 et no. 2*, 13–83. Paris: Presses Universitaires de France, 1984.

————. "Eléments néoplatoniciens en théologie mystique au XIIIième siècle." In *Abendländische Mystik im Mittelalter: Symposium Kloster Engelberg*, ed. Kurt Ruh, 196–207. Stuttgart: Metzler, 1986.

————. "Maître Eckhart et la grande tradition théologique," in *Eckardus Theutonicus, homo doctus et sanctus*, 97–125.

————. "La théologie de la grâce chez Maître Eckhart." *Revue des sciences religieuses* 70 (1996): 48–72.

Weiss, Bardo. "Der Einfluss Anselms von Canterbury auf Meister Eckhart." *Analecta Anselmiana* 4 (1975): Vol. 2:209–21.

————. *Die Heilsgeschichte bei Meister Eckhart*. Mainz: Matthias Grünewald Verlag, 1965.

Weiss, Konrad. "Meister Eckharts biblische Hermeneutik." In *La mystique rhénane*, 95–108. Paris: Presses Universitaires de France, 1963.

———. "Meister Eckharts philosophische und theologische Autoritäten." *Studia Theologica* 21 (1967): 13–19.

Welte, Bernhard. *Meister Eckhart: Gedanken zu seinem Gedanken.* Freiburg: Herder, 1979.

———. "Meister Eckhart als Aristoteliker." *Philosophisches Jahrbuch* 69 (1961): 64–74.

Wilms, Hieronymus. "Das Seelenfünklein in der deutschen Mystik." *Zeitschrift für Aszese und Mystik* 12 (1937): 157–66.

Winkler, Eberhard. *Exegetische Methoden bei Meister Eckhart.* Tübingen: Mohr, 1965.

Wippel, John F. "The Condemnations of 1270 and 1277 at Paris." *Journal of Medieval and Renaissance Studies* 7 (1977): 169–201.

Wolfson, Harry A. "St. Thomas on the Divine Attributes." In *Studies in the History of Philosophy and Religion,* ed. Isadore Twersky and George H. Williams. 2 vols. Cambridge, Mass.: Harvard University Press, 1973, 1977.

Wyser, Paul. "Taulers Terminologie vom Seelengrund." In *Altdeutsche und altniederländische Mystik,* ed. Kurt Ruh, 324–52. Wege der Forschung 23. Darmstadt: Wissenschaftliche Buchhandlung, 1964.

Zum Brunn, Émilie. "Dieu n'est pas être." In *Maître Eckhart à Paris: Une critique médiévale de l'ontothéologie. Les Questions parisiennes no. 1 et no. 2.* Paris: Presses Universitaires de France, 1984.

———. "Une source méconnu de l'ontologie Eckhartiene." In *Métaphysique, Histoire de la philosophie: Recueil d'études offert à Fernand Brunner,* 111–17. Neuchâtel: A la Baconnière, 1981.

Zum Brunn, Émilie, and Alain de Libera. *Métaphysique du Verbe et théologie négative.* Paris: Beauchesne, 1984.

Index